The World's RAREST MOVIE POSTERS

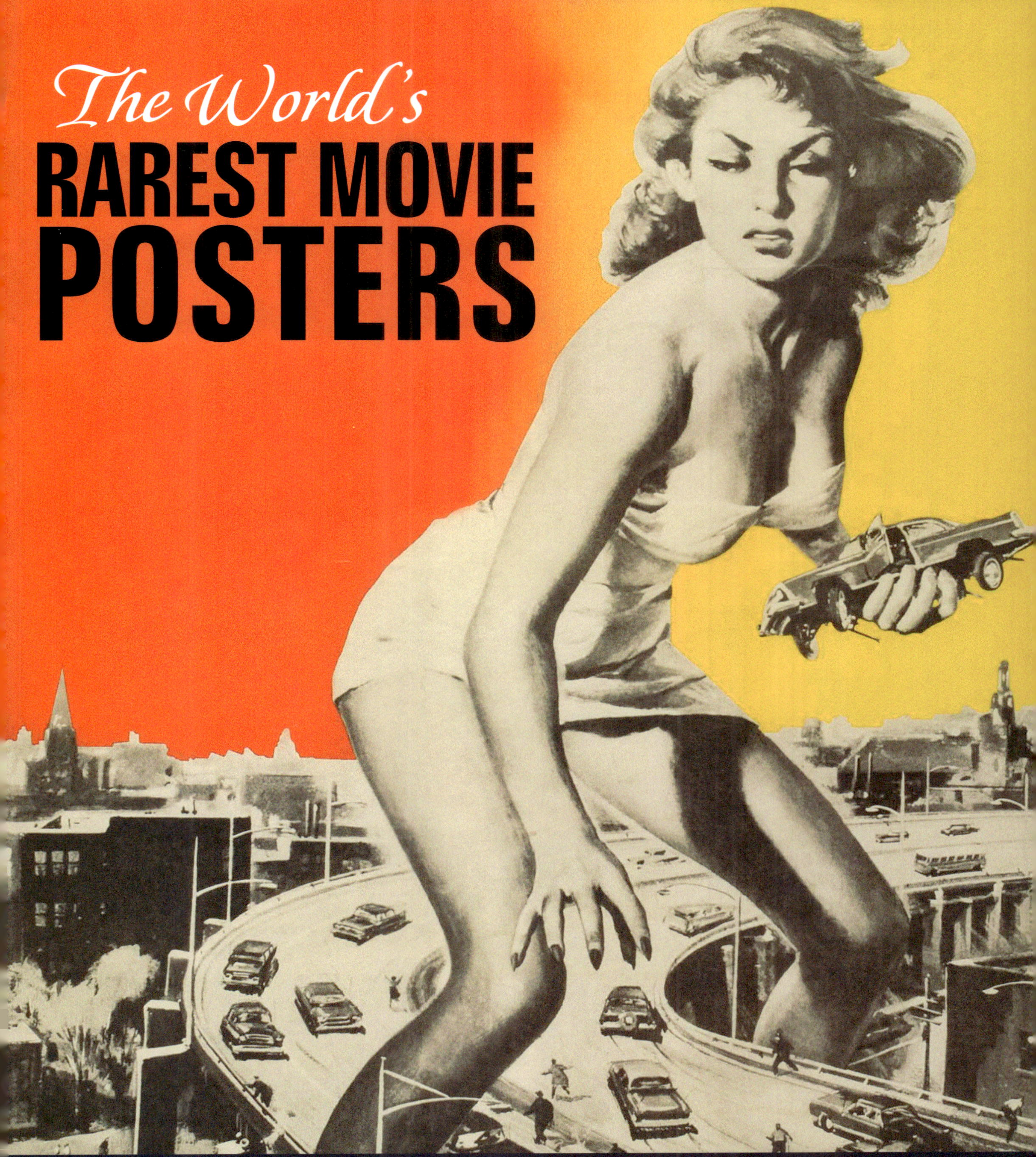

Schiffer Publishing Ltd
80 Lower Valley Road, Atglen, PA 19310

TODD SPOOR

SPECIAL THANKS

To my Wife, Laura, for allowing our house to be overrun with posters! To Todd Feiertag, for spending countless hours on the phone discussing posters. To Grey Smith, of Heritage Galleries, for supplying what seemed like an endless amount of images.

Library of Congress Control Number: 2010923805

Designed by John P. Cheek
Cover design by Bruce Waters

Type set in Modern No. 20/Zurich BT

ISBN: 978-0-7643-3498-6

Printed in China

Schiffer Books are available at special discounts for bulk purchases for sales promotions or premiums. Special editions, including personalized covers, corporate imprints, and excerpts can be created in large quantities for special needs. For more information contact the publisher:

Published by Schiffer Publishing Ltd.
4880 Lower Valley Road
Atglen, PA 19310
Phone: (610) 593-1777; Fax: (610) 593-2002
E-mail: Info@schifferbooks.com

For the largest selection of fine reference books on this and related subjects, please visit our web site at
www.schifferbooks.com
We are always looking for people to write books on new and related subjects. If you have an idea for a book please contact us at the above address.

This book may be purchased from the publisher.
Include $5.00 for shipping.
Please try your bookstore first.
You may write for a free catalog.

In Europe, Schiffer books are distributed by
Bushwood Books
6 Marksbury Ave.
Kew Gardens
Surrey TW9 4JF England
Phone: 44 (0) 20 8392 8585; Fax: 44 (0) 20 8392 9876
E-mail: info@bushwoodbooks.co.uk
Website: www.bushwoodbooks.co.uk

CONTENTS

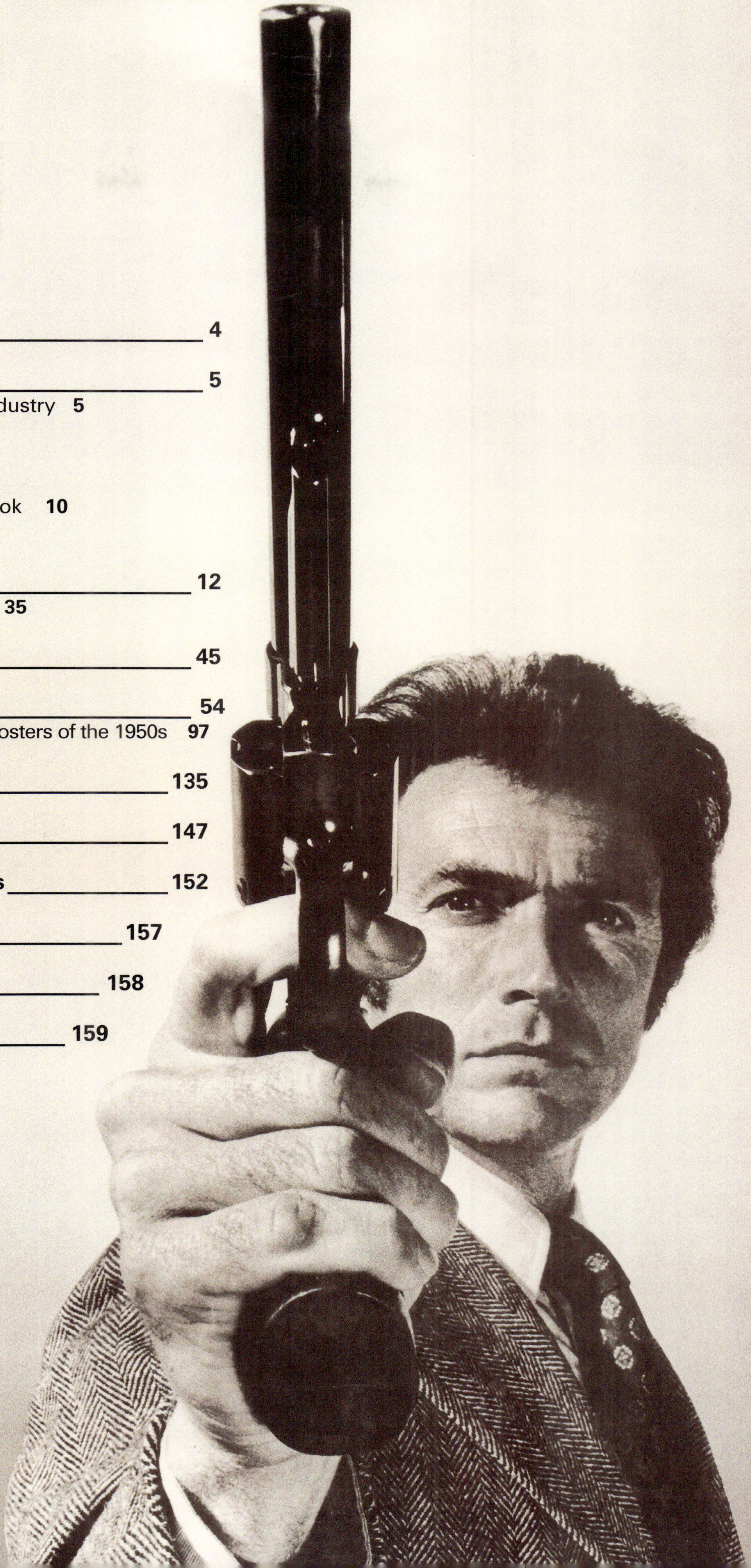

FOREWORD

Poster collecting has been a fascination for me for over thirty years and continues to enthrall me to this day. The allure of finding a rare and beautifully illustrated movie poster from a classic film's original release is, "the stuff that dreams are made of."

The French were the most prescient as to the cultural value of posters as they were saving and giving exhibitions of their posters as far back as the late 19th century, and it is to them that the full color printing of posters is attributed. Chéret, Mucha, and Toulouse-Lautrec were the artists whose works graced these beautiful pieces of paper art. By the early 20th century, lithographers were using the litho bed to produce the one sheet (27" x 41") posters not only for product advertising, but also for theatrical advertising, and the brand new medium of motion pictures! It took another fifty to sixty years for the movie poster to build a collectors' following in the United States.

Though the one sheet has remained the most popular of the collectible sizes for movie posters over the last forty years, there are various sizes that were printed in far fewer numbers and with completely different graphics. These formats were ordered by theater owners in small quantities and, when the theaters finished showing the films the posters promoted, they were either destroyed, as they were too cumbersome to store, or the backsides of the hard-stock poster was used as sign board for another coming feature film. They were also given to the nearby grocery stores or local grade schools for use as either signs or for art projects. In other words, they were disposed of!

Admirably, Todd Spoor has taken it upon himself to collect and protect some of these scarce format movie posters for a number of years and has amassed a collection and information concerning these posters that will be invaluable to all poster collectors in years to come. My hat is off to him!

Grey Smith
Director of Vintage Movie Poster Auctions
Heritage Auction Galleries
Dallas, Texas

INTRODUCTION

I first became involved in movie posters in 1998, while attending San Diego's Comic Convention. I was searching for some original art when I stumbled across a comic dealer selling a bunch of folded, one sheet movie posters. I dug through the box and found some titles I liked, movies such as *Alien, The Blues Brothers,* and *Caddy Shack*. I bought them for $10 each and brought them home. Being curious about my purchase and knowing nothing about posters, I checked Ebay to see if what I had purchased had any value. I was stunned to find that each of these posters were selling for well over $100. A year later I purchased a one sheet of *Attack of the 50ft. Women.* I paid $2,500 and sold it on Ebay seven days later for $5,500. I was hooked... not only could I collect posters for the movies that I grew up loving, but, I could make money doing it too.

THE MOVIE POSTER COLLECTING INDUSTRY

Today, scarce and top quality movie posters are selling at an all time high. Heritage Auction Galleries, in Dallas, Texas, is leading the way with three major auction events every year. Each sale generates over 2 million dollars in revenue. Bruce Hershenson's "eMoviePoster.com," based in Missouri, sells thousands of posters each week through the internet, all with a "no reserve" $1.00 starting price. His sales generated over 3 million dollars in 2008 and 2009 and he has been in business for over 20 years.

"One sheet" movie posters, which measure 27" x 41", have dominated the movie poster collecting industry since auction houses first started recognizing their rarity in the early 1990s. Movie posters rose even further in value and garnished national attention when a one sheet from the 1932 classic Universal horror film, *The Mummy,* sold for an astonishing $453,500 at Todd Feiertag's single owner sale at Sotheby's in 1995. More recently, Heritage's November, 2009, auction saw another one of Todd Feiertag's rare posters, entitled *The Black Cat,* from 1934, sell for $334,600. This seems to indicate that movie posters are not just a passing fad enjoyed by a small group of film enthusiasts, but have become a viable investment item as precious and valuable as major works of art.

THE "ONE SHEET"

"One sheet" posters were printed in large quantities to be used inside theatre lobbies or in showcases in front of the theatre. They were printed on light paper stock, folded into a tight rectangle, and, until 1940, leased to the theaters by the studios. From 1940 until the early 1980s, the National Screen Service (NSS) then took over production and distribution of movie posters. During that period, each poster was given a NSS number which indicated the year and number of its release within that year. For example, the NSS number, 57/133 would mean it was issued in 1957 and it was the 133rd film released in 1957.

Many of the posters from the early part of the 20th century ended up in paper drives in World War II or were discarded or destroyed after their use, as they were seen as disposable products. In the 1950s and 1960s, the enforcement of fire codes throughout the country led many theaters to destroy their stock of the older material. However, many theaters that escaped the notice of the Fire Marshal, or that would simply went out of business, had stock rooms full of hundreds, or even thousands, of old posters. Over time they made their way into auction houses and then into the hands of savvy collectors. Today, thousands of posters appear on Ebay and other auctions sites every week, however, posters from the 1920s, 1930s, 1940s, and even 1950s are far less common than later posters and usually much more expensive depending on the title and condition.

30x40s & 40x60s

"30x40s and 40x60s, are the rarest of the rare..."
—Todd Feiertag

Theater owners were shipped a "pressbook" prior to the premier of each film's release. The pressbook contained different items intended to help promote and advertise the film's opening and subsequent run at the theater. Each pressbook offered various sizes of posters that were available to lease. These included: "lobby cards" that measured 11" x 14"; "window cards" that measure 14" x 22"; "half sheets" that measure 22" x 28"; "inserts" that measure 14" x 36"; "one sheets" that measure 27" x 41"; "three sheets" that measure 41" x 81"; "six sheets" that measure 81" x 81"; and giant, billboard-sized "twenty-four sheets" that measure 104" x 232."

Very rarely, if ever, did these pressbooks show pictures of the 30"x 40" or the 40"x 60" size posters. In many pressbooks they were not even listed as being available for lease, and theater owners usually wouldn't order what they couldn't see.

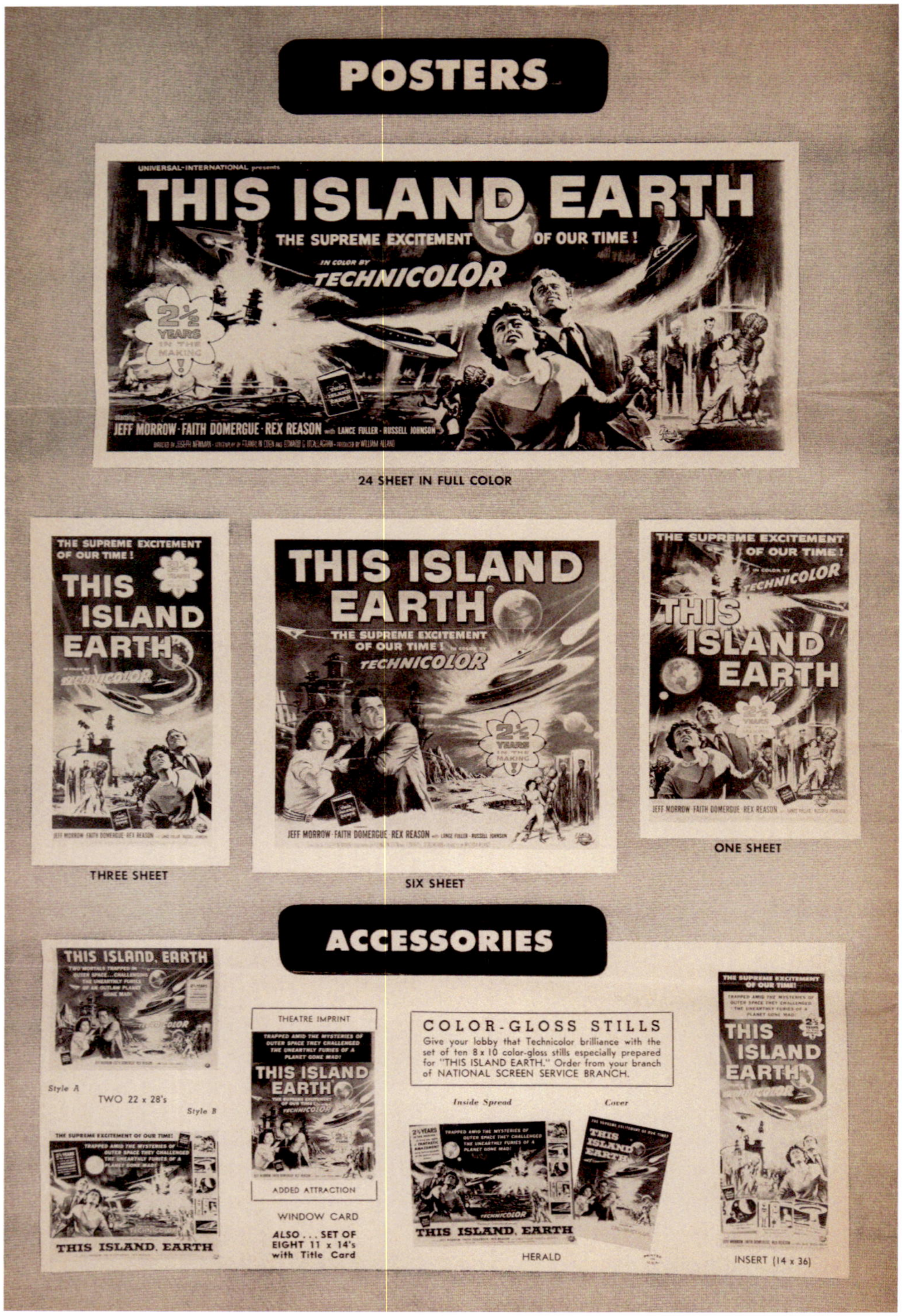

This Island Earth Pressbook not only has no picture of the 30x40 or 40x60 poster; there is no mention of them even being offered for lease.

Why are 30x40s and 40x60s so rare?

30" x 40" and 40" x 60" poster sizes were almost always printed on heavy card stock, though some studios did produce a photo gelatin paper stock version during the late 1930s and early 1940s. These larger size posters would cost theater owners between 20-150% more to lease. It is quite possible that for many movie titles these posters were never printed because there were too few orders for them. If the posters were ordered and printed, sometimes less than a few dozen made it to the theaters and even fewer were ever returned to the National Screen Service. This is why, for certain films, there are few if any surviving examples today. In 2007, Heritage Auction Galleries offered an extremely rare, never before seen 40"x 60" for the 1937 film *Snow White and the Seven Dwarfs*. It sold for an amazing $65,725, more than any other poster from that film. Today, it remains one of only two known to exist.

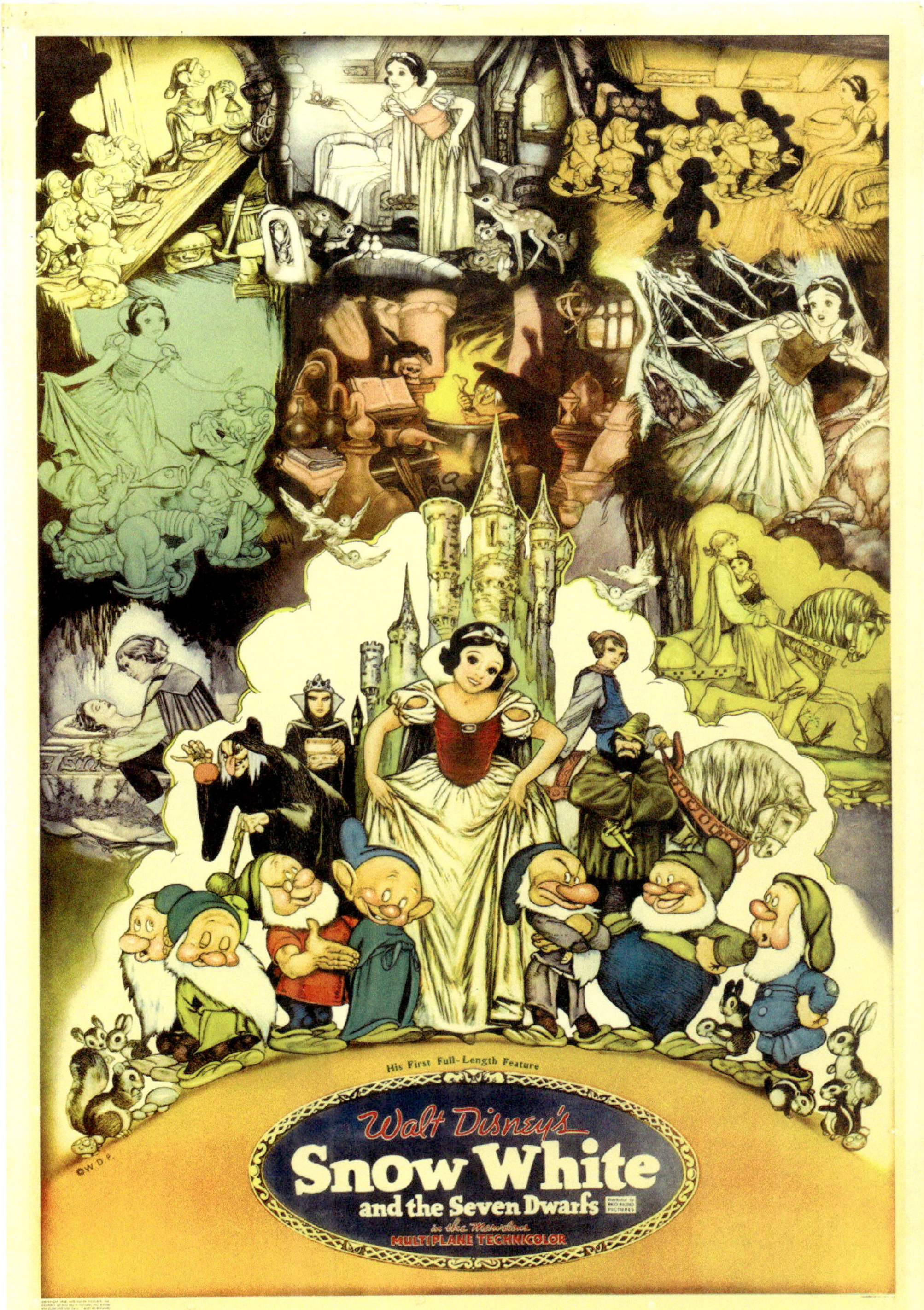

The "Unique" image of the 30x40 and 40x60

For some movies, studios produced two unique versions or "styles" of each 30x40 and 40x60 poster. Each style had a different image, which, quite often, differed from the one sheet poster. Each style was usually designated with an "A" or a "B," or a "Y" and "Z" before the NSS number. These posters were very often silkscreened, which made for some exceptionally vibrant colors. They were also printed on heavy card stock and were shipped "rolled" to the theaters. Because of their larger size and more durable material, they were displayed in the theater lobbies or outdoors at drive-in movie theaters. Since they were often used outside, the elements usually ravaged them and the theater owners would eventually throw them away instead of returning them to the Nation Screen Service.

As I collected posters of my favorite movies, I was drawn to this larger format. I loved the giant sizes, vibrant colors and unique images that often differed from that of the one sheet. I found, however, that very few dealers had these large size posters. It seemed that movie poster dealers and store owners shunned these posters for the simple fact that they were hard to find than the folded one sheets and even harder to store. Because of this, I was usually able to get them for slightly more than the one sheet, even though they were hundreds of times more rare.

A perfect example of this scarcity is with the 40x60 for *This Island Earth*–Style Y, which is not shown or listed in the pressbook. There are at least 35 of the one sheet posters known to exist today, which typically sell for just over $1,000. In contrast, there are only 4 known copies of the 40x60 poster, the last one being purchased in 2006 for $12,500.

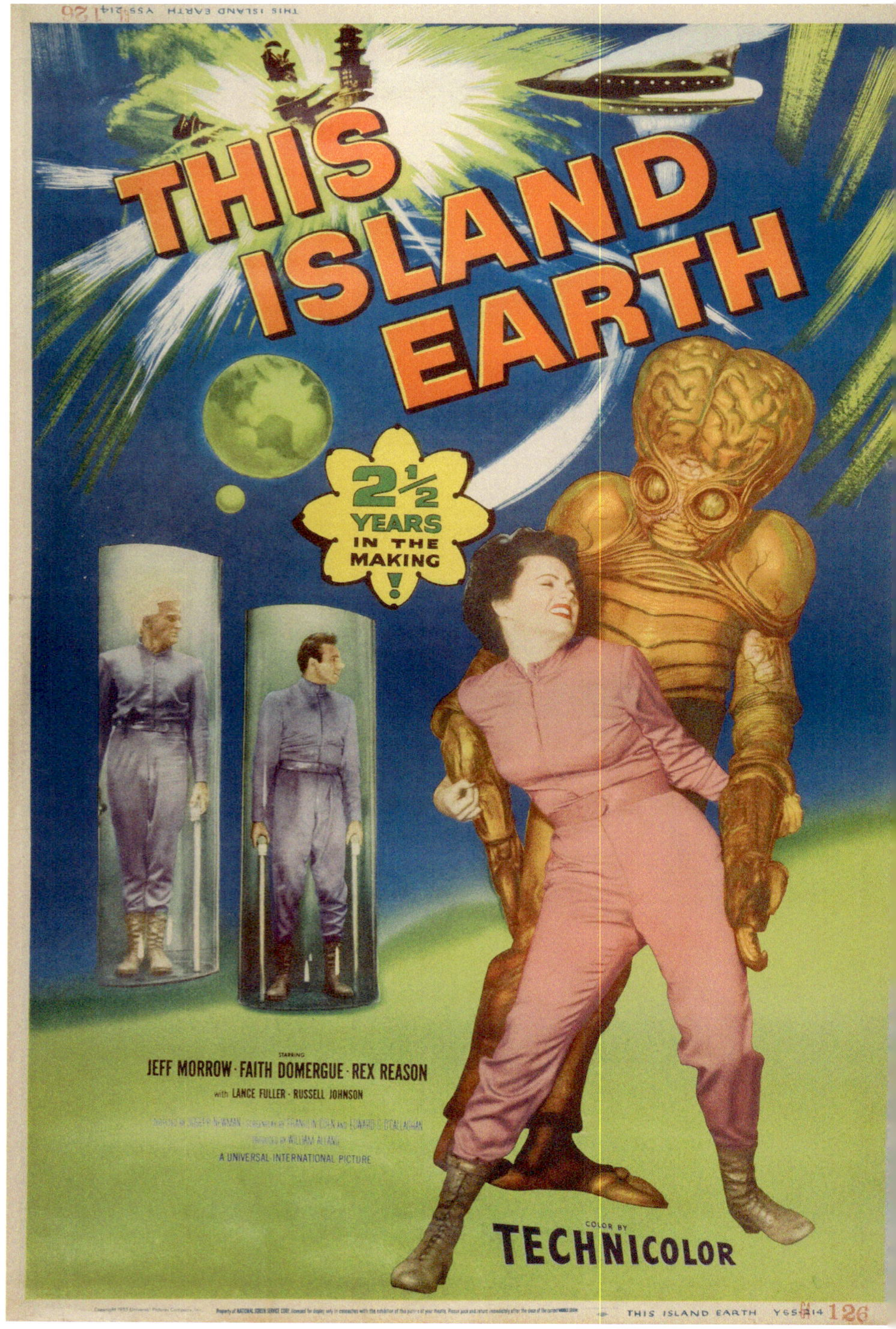

Escaping Detection...

As you peruse the pages of this book, you will sometimes notice that many 30x40s and 40x60s sell for less than the corresponding one sheet even though there may only be a few known copies to exist. After discussing this with Bruce Hershenson of eMoviePoster.com, he believes that these rare sized posters are simply, "not on people's radar." This does seem to be changing, however.

Take for instance, the one sheet for *Breakfast at Tiffany's*. As I researched old catalogs and sales data, I noticed that this poster had been at auction 67 times since 1989 and that doesn't include Ebay sales. Since the image is highly collectable and the poster was in demand, the sale price increased from $275, in 1989, to $10,800 by the year 2000. That's a staggering 3,800%. Now, however, the market has become somewhat saturated and the poster has consistently decreased in value year after year to its current average selling price of around $3,500 in 2009. That's a 150% reduction from its all time high price in 2000. On the contrary, there are only 8 known 30x40s, and for the 40x60s there are only 2 Style Y and 3 known Style Z known to exist. These posters are still escalating in price and, from an investment standpoint, should continue to do so because they are truly "rare."

Collectors of 30x40s and 40x60s are beginning to see that their rarity can be a driving force in determining price. A perfect example is the poster for the 1956 film *Bus Stop* with Marilyn Monroe. More than 75 one sheets from the film still exist today and typically sell for $300 to $600 at auction houses and on Ebay. However, only 2 copies of the 40x60–Style Z are known, and a 40x60–Style Y is not known to exist at all. The Style Z in "very fine" condition was last sold at Christie's in 2008 for $3,133. This is over 500% more that the one sheet selling prices.

National Screen Service Number

All 30x40s and 40x60s after 1940 have an NSS number printed on them. On 30x40s the NSS number is printed on the side of the poster, while on 40x60s it is printed on the top and bottom. One sheets, inserts and half sheets all have the NSS number printed on the bottom of the poster only.

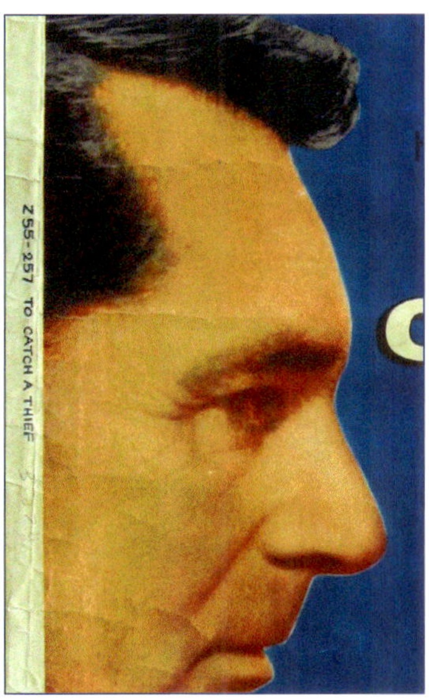

30x40, NSS printed on each side of the poster.

The Misnomer...

40x60s have been sometimes referred to as a "two sheets." This, however, is a complete misnomer. No reference to a 40x60 poster as a "two sheet" or "2 sheet" has been found in any pressbook. Bruce Hershenson has stated that, "In an effort to save money and for a very short time in the 1950's, some studios that produced "B" movie westerns and exploitation films did print a lightweight paper poster in two (one sheet) sized sections that when put together sided by side measured 41"x 54." However, this is not the heavy stock paper of the true 40x60.

The erroneous "2 sheet" term may have taken root in December, 1996, when Sotheby's, in an apparent effort to explain the 40x60, dubbed it a "2 sheet." Christie's followed suit in a December, 1997, auction, also referring to the 40x60 as a "2 sheet." The following year, however, after realizing this error, Christie's quietly began to once again refer to it by its proper name. Sotheby's, though, has continued to incorrectly use the term "2 sheet" in all of their subsequent auctions.

INVESTING IN MOVIE POSTERS

In researching this book, I painstakingly went through over 120 auction catalogs from 1989 to the 2009, recording every time a listed poster was offered at auction and the price it brought. I was amazed by how much certain posters have increased in value over the years. Although the cosmic rise of some posters has tapered off in 2009 due to the current economic climate, I maintain that a rare poster will always increase in value over the long term.

For example, the poster for the 1957 film *Invasion of the Saucer-men* has appeared at auction

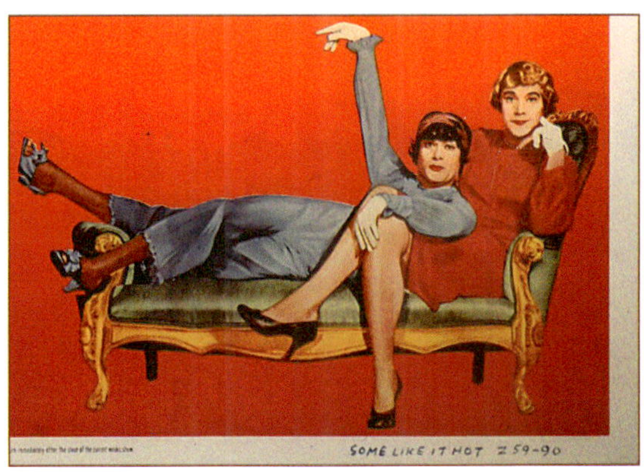

40x60, NSS number printed on the top and bottom of the poster.

33 times since 1989. This poster, bearing the images of "giant cabbage headed aliens," abducting a scantily clad woman is perhaps the iconic image from the 1950s B-movie genre. This poster appears on Ebay at least 2-4 times per year and at major auction houses at least once a year, usually topping the price paid from the previous sale. From an investment stand point, if you had purchased this poster in fine condition from Sotheby's Auction House in December, 1993, you would have paid $1,093. In July, 2009, that same title sold at Heritage for $5,377. That's an increase of over 500%. On the contrary, during that same 15 year period, if your money was invested in the stock market your $1,093 would be worth approximately $2,576 today, a 135% increase. Still not a bad return, but movie posters, especially ones that are in high demand and rare or aesthetically pleasing, will continue to increase in value and collectibility well into the future. In contrast to stocks and bonds, which are readily available, there is a finite number of posters for the astute collector's investment.

Condition

Condition in posters varies tremendously, and there is a corresponding variation in price. Collectors are paying top dollar for one sheets that have had little restoration (*Very Fine* condition – VF) to no restoration what so ever (*Near Mint* – NM).

Usually, there are many copies of one sheets around from which to choose, so the discerning collector can afford to be selective. 30x40s and 40x60s, on the other hand, turn up far less often, sometimes once every five to ten years, so condition, though it still matters, is far less of a priority.

Restoration

Restoration is very typical for most movie posters. One sheet posters, because they were shipped folded, are often linen-backed, a process that applies archival linen to the back of the poster. "Touch ups" are usually performed on the fold lines and any separation that has occurred by folding and unfolding the poster. This restoration gives the posters a beautiful "new look," allowing it to be displayed and framed properly.

Since 30x40s and 40x60s were shipped rolled and not folded, they usually do not need restoration. Minor creasing and edge "bumping" are usually tolerated by most collectors. However, when restoration is performed, these heavy stock posters, along with inserts and half sheets, are "paper-backed." Paper backing is the application of archival paper to the back of the poster, adding to its rigidity and allowing for any restoration work to be conducted. Linen-backing is also sometimes used, but slight "cracking" and "spider veins" can occur because the linen is too flexible for the heavy stock paper once restoration has been performed. Lightweight paper posters such as one sheets, three sheets and six sheets work much better on linen.

ADDITIONAL NOTES ABOUT THIS BOOK

As I stated earlier, the number of times each poster has shown up at auction or in private sales is based on research and due diligence. Many posters were showing up at auctions so frequently I quit counting after seventy-five times and for these posters I simply put a current average selling price instead of the last 5 auction results.

For most one sheets, I also listed the first time the poster ever came to auction, the selling price, and the number of times it has sold since. I did not and could not include Ebay sales unless the poster was from a verified auction house. It is quite possible that a poster sold at Christie's in 1999 was later sold at Heritage in 2003 to capitalize on a sudden increase in market value. There is simply no way to track each unique poster at this time. Therefore, I am in no way saying that the number of times a poster has been at auction is an exact indication as to how many are known to exist, but it can be a very good indicator of its rarity. Most movie poster experts do agree though, that the number of one sheet posters that are actually in the hands of collectors and are shown in this book could be closer to double that of what has shown up at auctions since 1989.

Since there are far fewer 30x40s and 40x60s, it is much easier to track each individual poster. I have given a "known to exist" *estimate* for these posters. This estimate, however, should always be viewed with caution because one never knows what sales go on between dealers and clients or with "Buy it Now" Ebay sales. Nor will we ever know when the next discovery might be made in some decrepit theater, a dusty attic, or the walls of some remodeled house. Movie posters have the unusual habit of turning up in the weirdest places.

Silk screened 30x40s and 40x60s posters were produced by every major studio throughout the 1930s, yet they are virtually non-existent today. At a time when one sheets were being leased to theater owners for just $.10 each, 30x40s and 40x60s were being leased for the outlandish amount of $1.50 each, and this was during the depression! Theater owners who were trying to be economical could often get fifteen one sheets for the price of one 40x60.

Therefore, only the very largest theaters ever order these magnificent posters. Today, they remain the most elusive and most beautiful of all known posters to have been printed during any time period.

Meloy Brothers

From 1935 to 1936, Meloy Brothers Theatre Supply in Shelbyville, Indiana, produced 40x60 displays intended for outside exhibitions. They were created by using original photo negatives supplied to them by the studios and the posters featured hand painted lettering and highlights. They were mounted on board and produced in very limited numbers. Meloy Brothers produced many different styles or versions for the same film, however, they did not differentiate between these posters by giving them any identifiable mark, therefore, I also did not try to give them an individual "Style" identifier.

Choosing these Posters...

The 30x40s and 40x60s I chose to be represented in this book had to have at least one of the following criteria:

- There had to be less than 10 known copies to exist.
- The image had to be different from the one sheet image.
- They had to sell for around a $1,000 or more.

For instance, I did not list any *Star Wars,* spaghetti westerns, or Beatles 30x40s and 40x60s, and only one Bond film made the cut even though they are highly collectible and can often sell for double that of the price of the corresponding one sheet. There certainly are, however, more than 10 known copies for each of those titles and the art work is almost always the same as the one sheet. I have over 150 more 30x40s and 40x60s from the 1960s to the 1980s in my own collection that are very rare and I would have loved to show images of, but unfortunately they too suffer the same limitations as the aforementioned material.

SO, WHY COLLECT?

Whether it's a love for a particular movie, the art of the poster, or strictly for investment purposes, a large number of people have a passion for collecting movie posters. History has shown that when something is so rare that it only turns up at auction only once or twice every several years, it will not only retain its value, but continue to appreciate. Plus, unlike stocks or bonds, you can hang a movie poster on the wall and look at it every day as a piece of art and cinematic history.

I hope you fall in love with these rare posters as much as I have...

Poster Grading Terms

Mint (M): A poster that has never been used or displayed. The poster may show some minor signs of age. It should have no pin holes or tears and vibrant colors.

Near Mint (NM): A very lightly used poster with fresh vibrant colors. In folded posters, it may show the most minimal wear at the folds. The poster should have no holes, no tears, and no paper loss.

Very Fine (VF): A poster with bright colors and a clean overall appearance. It may have general signs of wear with slight fold separation and fold wear. It may have a few pinholes and/or minor tears.

Fine (FN): A poster with good color and is very presentable. It may have tears into the image area, slight paper loss and minor stains. It may have pin holes, fold separation and splitting. May have had or is need of minor restoration.

Very Good (VG): A poster that is brittle due to age and may have paper loss and/or staining. It may have tears into the image area, writing on the back that has bled through to the front. It may have very light fading to its colors, pin holes and/or tape and tape stains. May have had or is in need of medium restoration.

Good (GD): An average poster which may have tears, paper loss and general wear. It may have tears into the image area. I may have some color fading, tape and/or tape stains and multiple pin holes within the image area. May have had or is in need of medium restoration.

Fair (FR): Poster may have faded colors, brittle paper, and show signs of heavy use including multiple pin holes, tape, tape stains, paper loss, multiple tears into the image and stains in the image. It may have had small sections of paper missing or had its borders trimmed. May have had or is in need medium restoration.

Poor (PR): A poster that has been heavily used and badly damaged. May have large sections of paper missing, stains and tears in the images area and serious fading. May have had major restoration or is in dire need of major restoration.

Note: DNS means "Did Not Sell"

MOVIE POSTERS OF THE 1930s

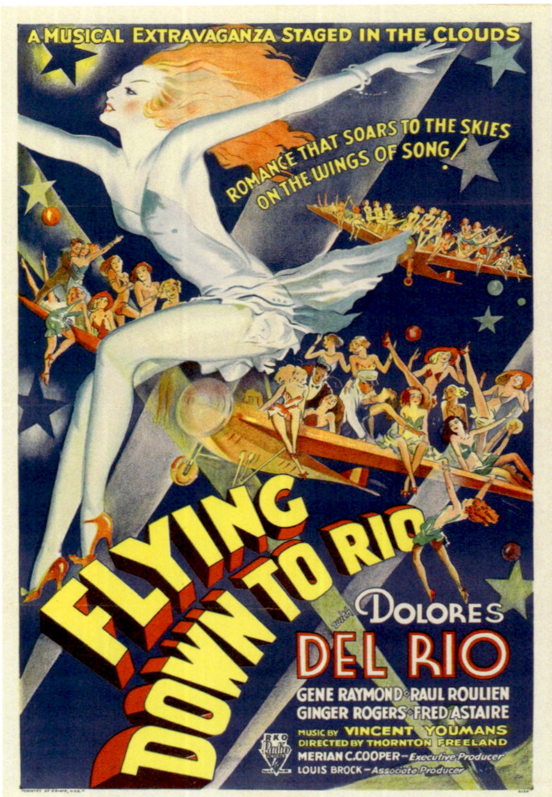

Courtesy of Heritage

Flying Down to Rio	1933	27x41	
Heritage	$239,000	VF/NM	11/08
Private	$50,000	VG	10/97
Christie's	$82,800	NM	12/96
Sotheby's	$23,000	VF	12/96

Highest price realized:

Heritage	$239,000	VF/NM	11/08

- This poster has appeared at auction 5 times since 1989.
- There is no *Flying Down to Rio* 30x40 known to exist.

Flying Down To Rio	1933	40x60	
Heritage	$26,290	FN/VF	07/08

- There is 1 known to exist

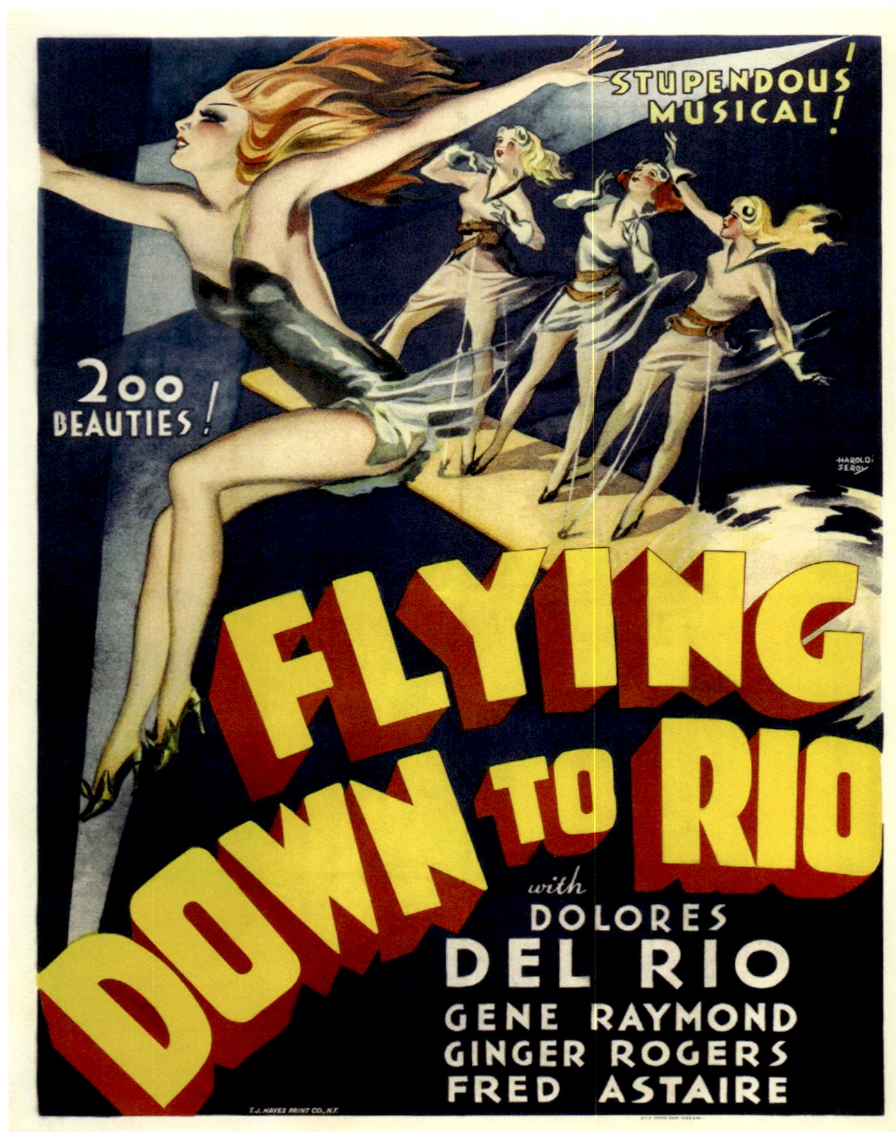

Courtesy of Heritage

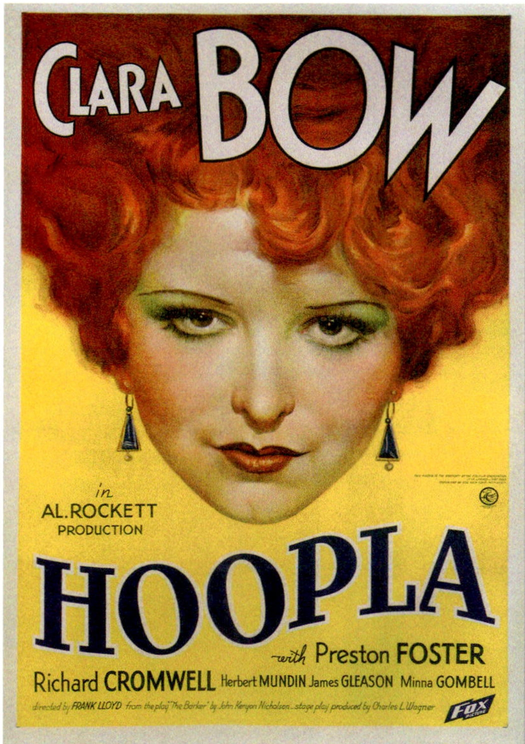

Courtesy of Hershenson/Allen archive

Hoopla 1933 27x41
Christie's $8,151 VF 12/02

- This poster has appeared at auction 1 time since 1989.
- There is no *Hoopla* 30x40 known to exist.

Hoopla 1933 40x60
Heritage $5,975 FN/VF 07/08

There is 1 known to exist.

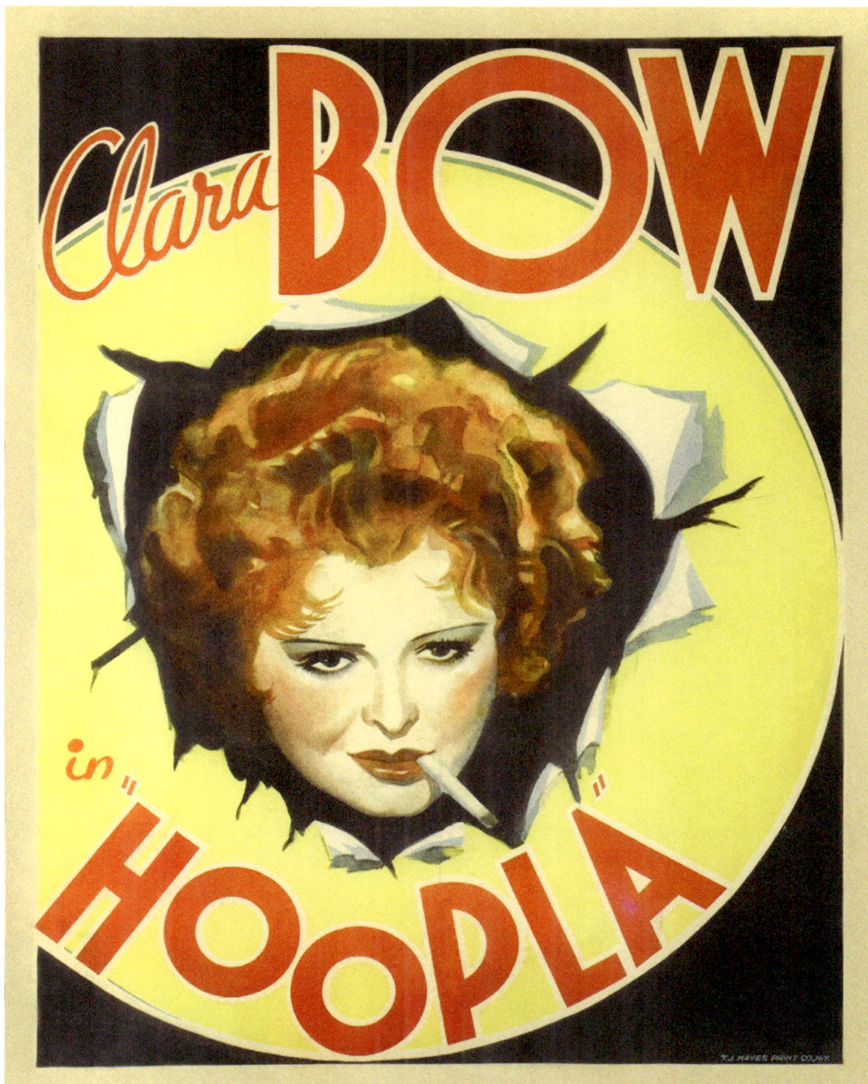

Courtesy of Heritage

Design for Living 1933 40x60
Heritage $4,780 FN/VF 07/08

- There is 1 known to exist.
- There was no image available for *Design for Living* 27x41.
- There is no *Design for Living* 30x40 known to exist.

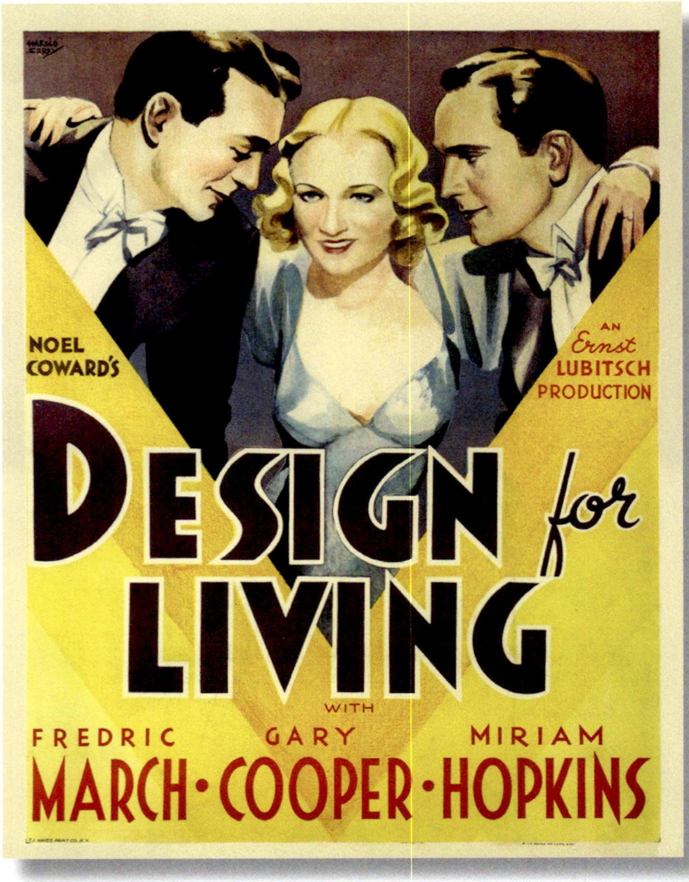

Courtesy of Heritage

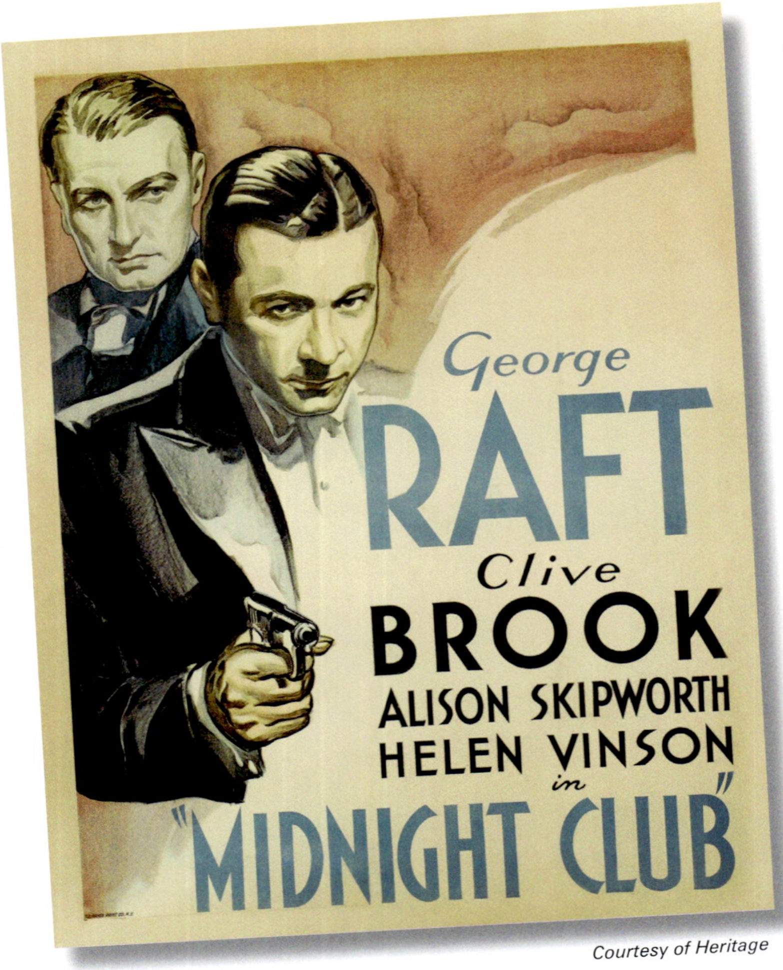

Courtesy of Heritage

Midnight Club 1933 40x60
Heritage $4,780 FN/VF 07/08

- There is 1 known to exist.
- There was no image available for *Midnight Club* 27x41.
- There is no *Midnight Club* 30x40 known to exist.

Courtesy of Christie's

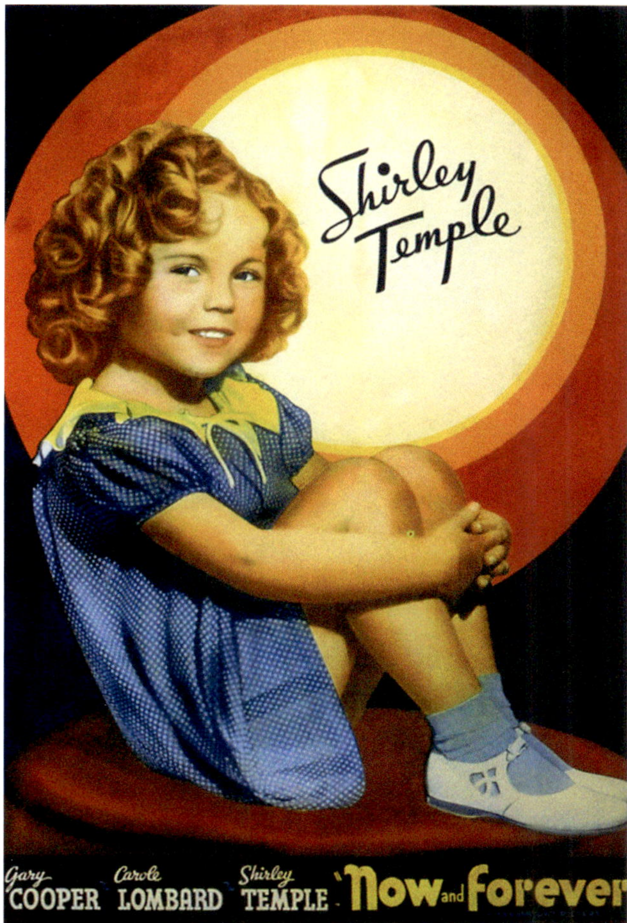

Now and Forever 1934 40x60
Christie's $3,220 VF- 12/93
Estimate: $6,500 - $8,500

• There is 1 known to exist.

Courtesy of Christie's

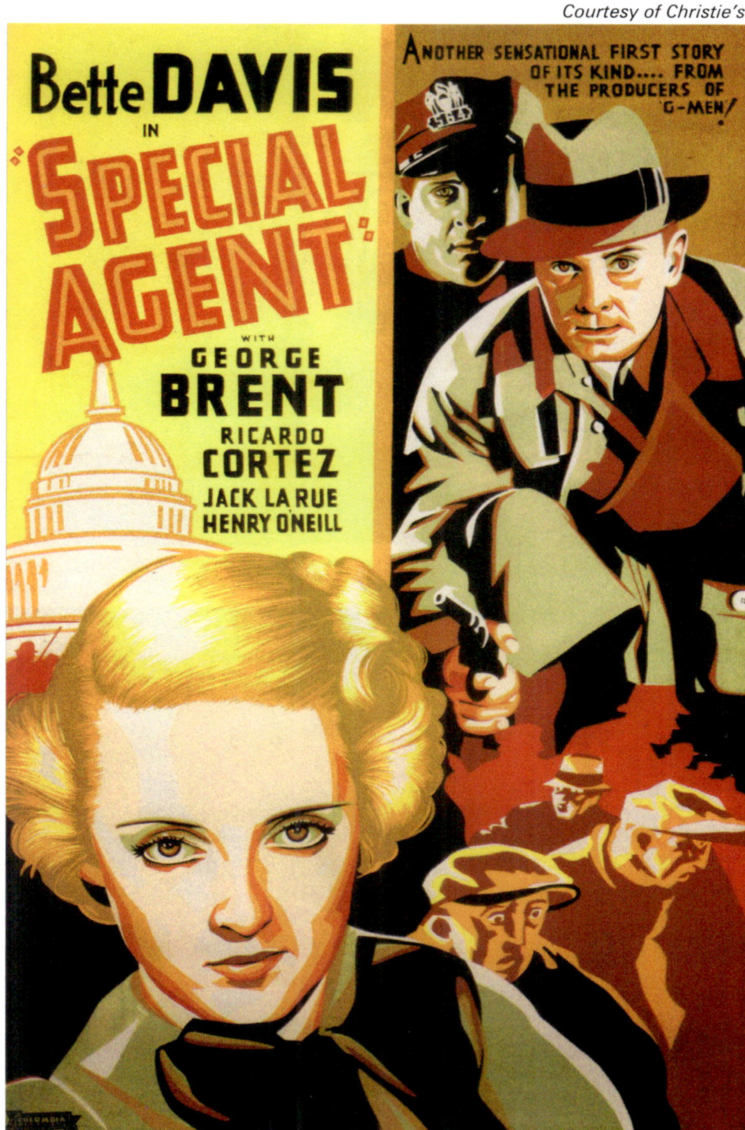

Special Agent 1935 40x60
Christie's $1,380 VF 12/96
Estimate: $5,000 - $7,500

• There is 1 known to exist.
• There was no image available for *Special Agent* 27x41.
• There is no *Special Agent* 30x40 known to exist.

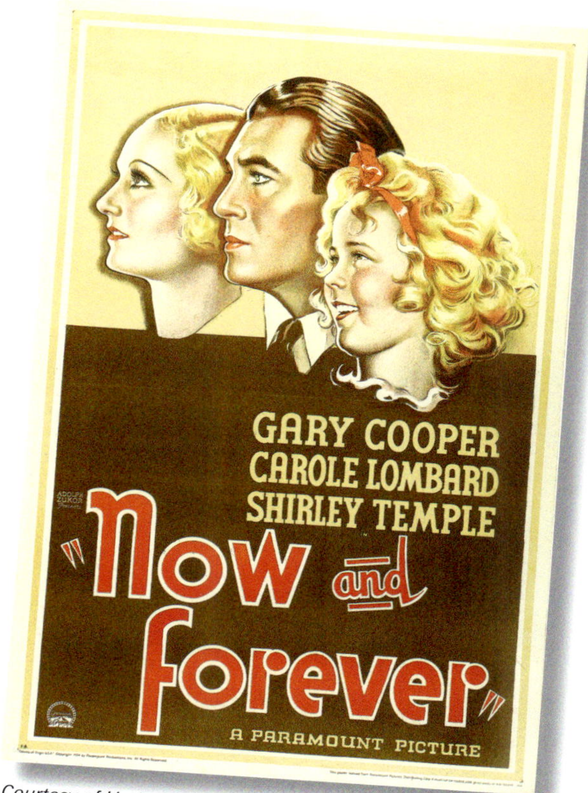

Courtesy of Heritage

Now and Forever 1934 27x41
Heritage $2,070 VF+ 07/06
Bonhams & Butterfields $2,938 NM 12/05

• This poster has appeared at auction 3 times since 1989.
• There is no *Now and Forever* 30x40 known to exist.

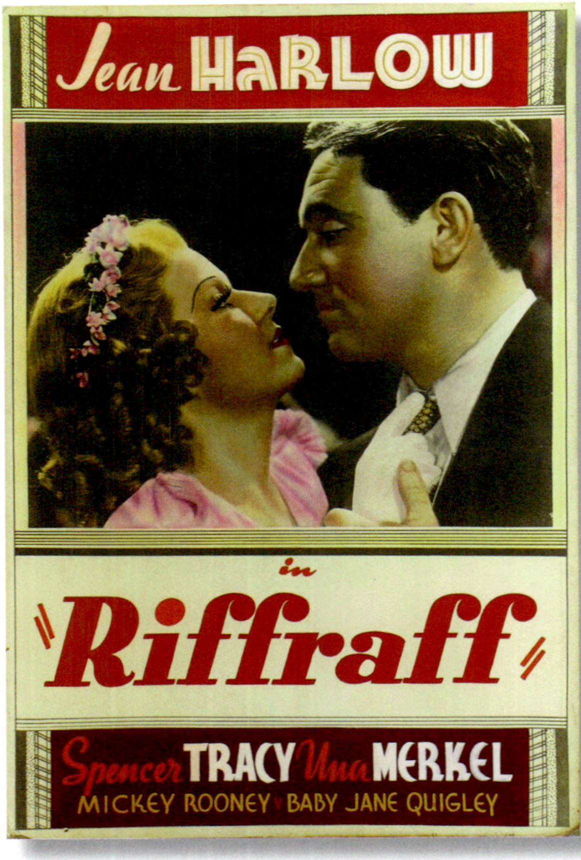

Courtesy of Hershenson/Allen Archive

Riffraff – Meloy Brothers	1935	40x60	
eMoviePoster	$787	VF	02/08

• There is 1 known to exist.

Riffraff – Meloy Brothers	1935	40x60	
eMoviePoster	$1,625	VF	04/08

• There is 1 known to exist.

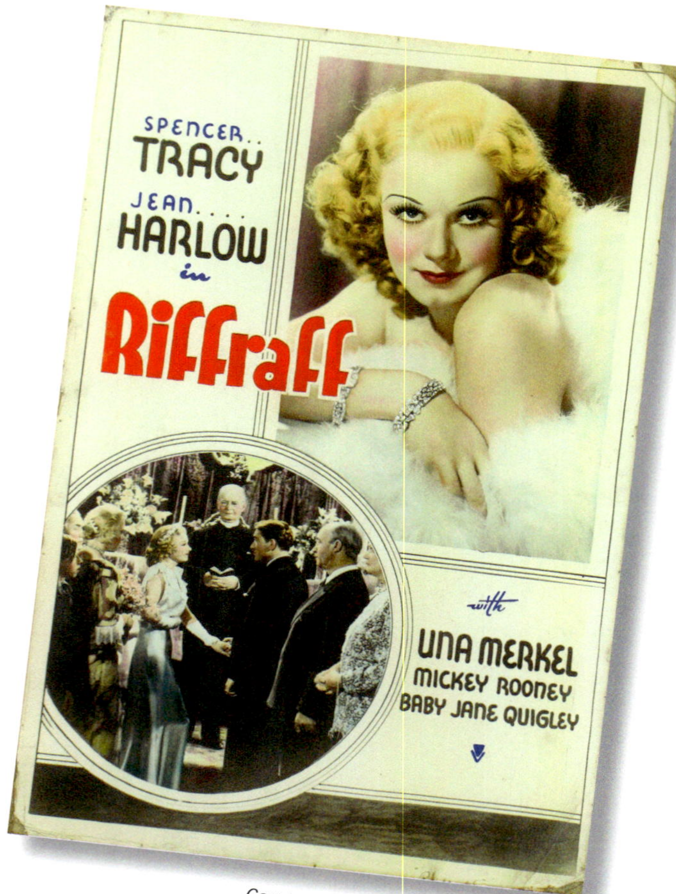

Courtesy of Hershenson/Allen Archive

Courtesy of Heritage

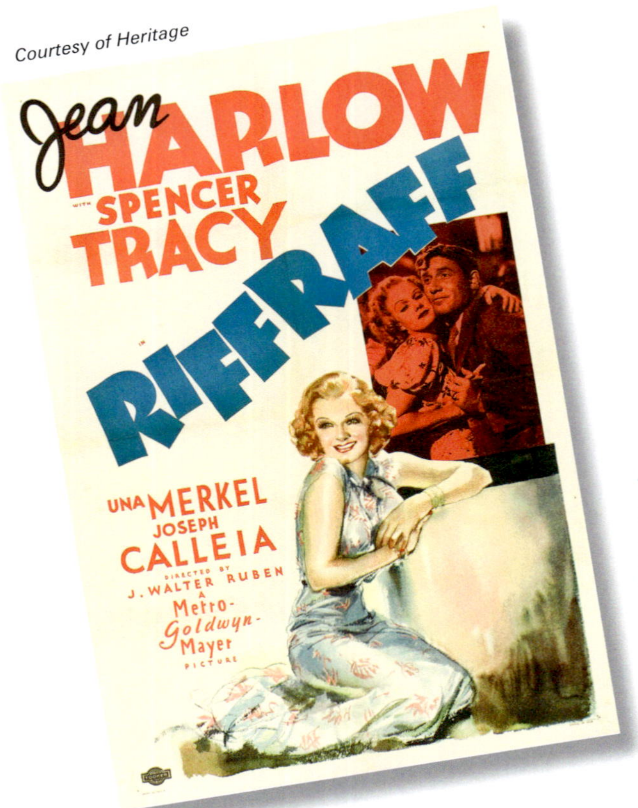

Riffraff — Style C	1935	27x41	
Heritage	$1,792	VF	07/09
Vintage Poster Art	$977	VF	05/97
Butterfield & Butterfield	$1,000	NM	11/96
Camden House	$1,000	FN	03/90

• This poster has appeared at auction 4 times since 1989.
• There is no *Riffraff* 30x40 known to exist.

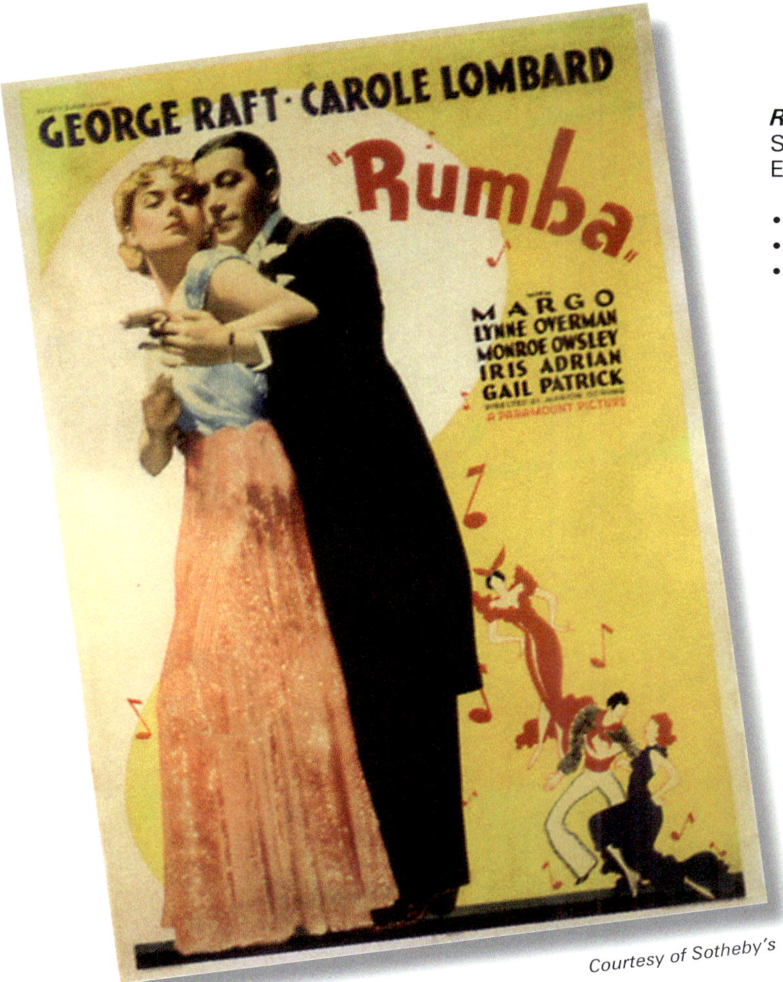

Courtesy of Sotheby's

Rumba 1935 40x60
Sotheby's DNS VF 12/94
Estimate: $4,000 - $6,000

- There is 1 known to exist.
- There was no image available for *Rumba* 27x41.
- There is no *Rumba* 30x40 known to exist.

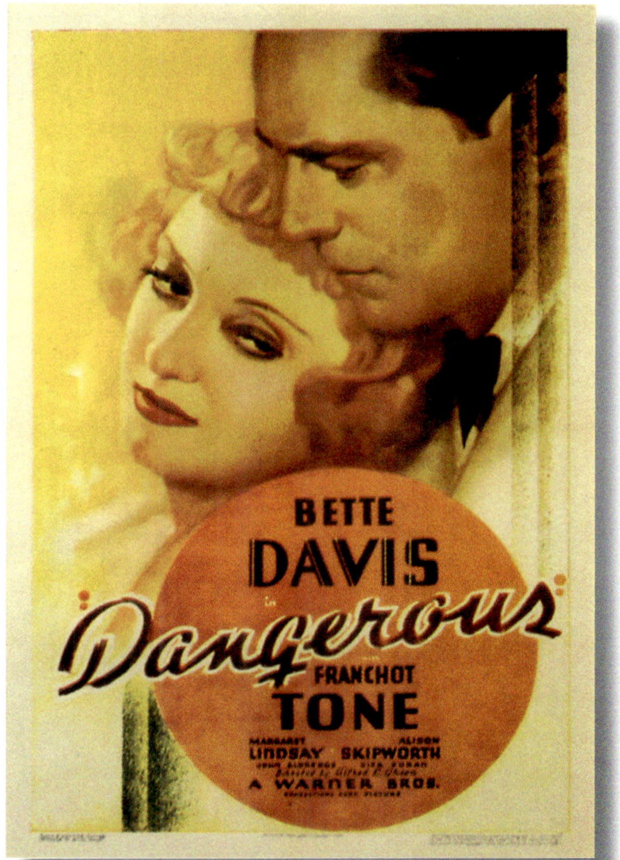

Courtesy of Sotheby's

Dangerous 1935 27x41
Sotheby's $8,625 VF 12/99

- This poster has appeared at auction 1 time since 1989.

Courtesy of Hershenson/Allen Archive

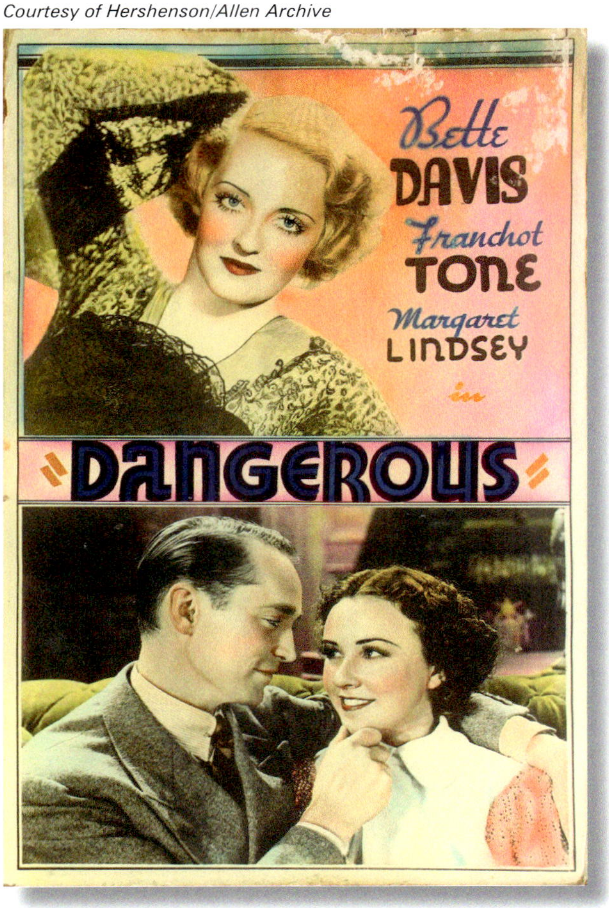

Dangerous – Meloy Brothers 1935 40X60
eMoviePoster $1,125 GD 02/08

- There is 1 known to exist.

Courtesy of Christie's

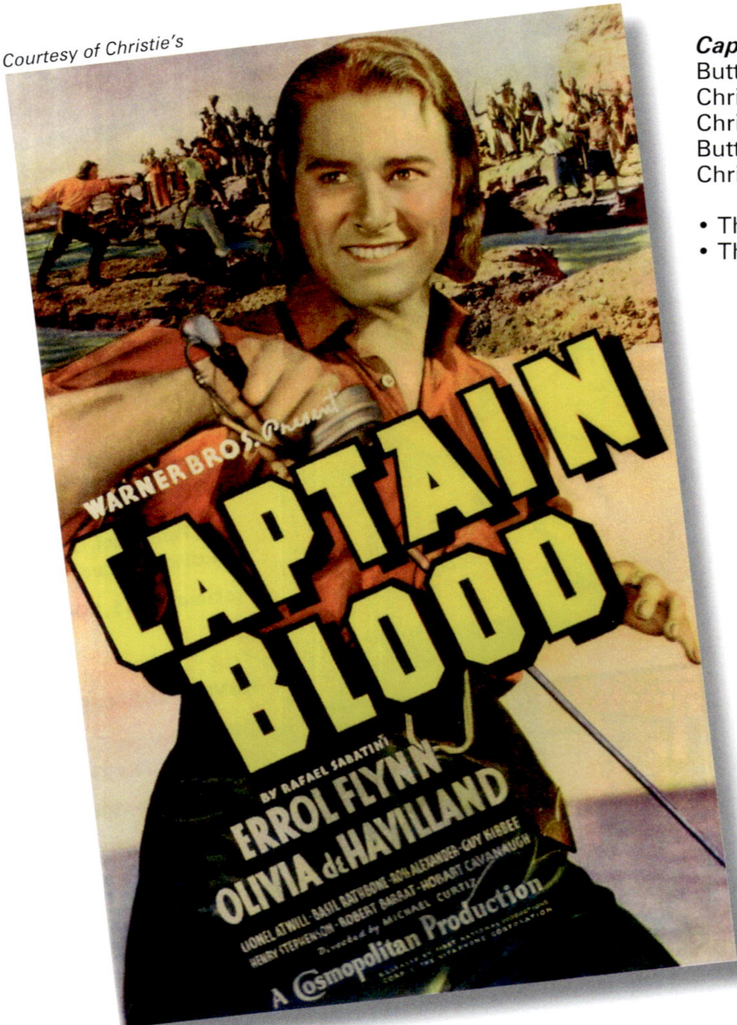

Captain Blood 1935 27x41

Butterfield & Butterfield	$7,000	VF	11/02
Christie's	$9,400	VF	11/01
Christie's	$4,600	FN	12/96
Butterfield & Butterfield	$9,775	VF	10/94
Christie's	$6,820	FN	12/92

- This poster has appeared at auction 5 times since 1989.
- There is no *Captain Blood* 30x40 known to exist.

Captain Blood – Meloy Brothers 1935 40x60

eMoviePoster	$3,138	VG	12/08

- There is 1 known to exist.

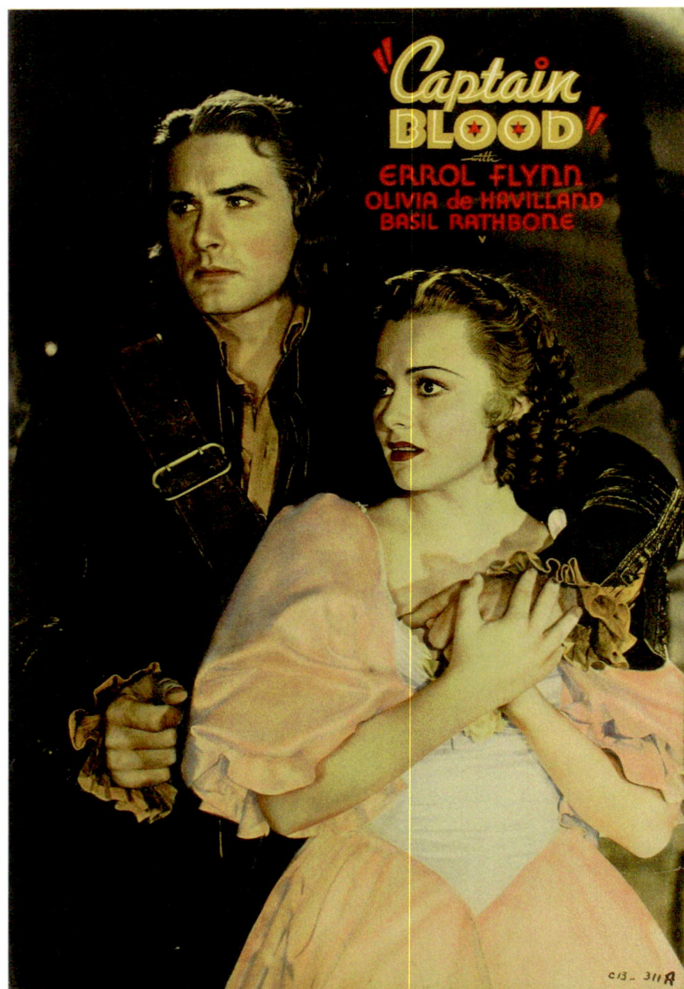

Courtesy of Hershenson/Allen Archive

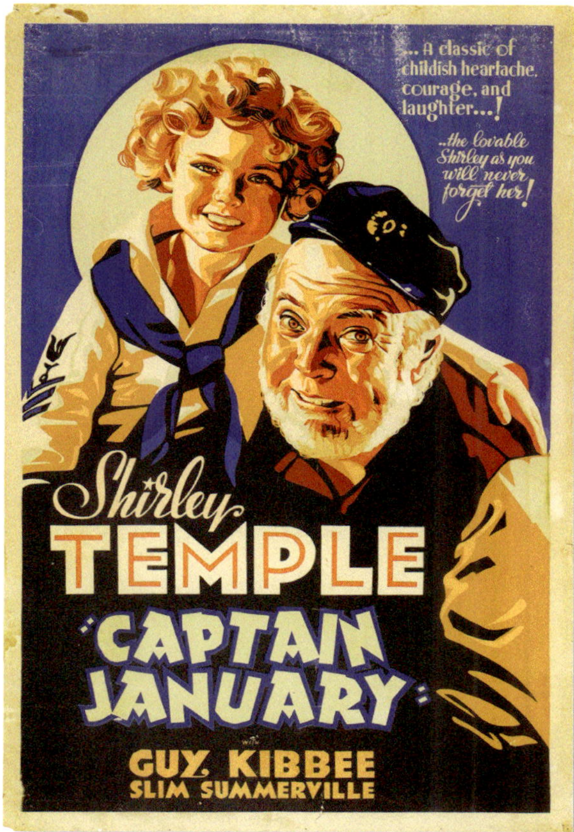

Courtesy of Hershenson/Allen Archive

Captain January 1936 40x60

eMoviePoster	$626	GD	12/08
Private	$1,500	VF	05/97

• There are 2 known to exist.

Captain January – Meloy Brothers 1936 40x60

eMoviePoster	$1,071	GD	02/08

• There is 1 known to exist.

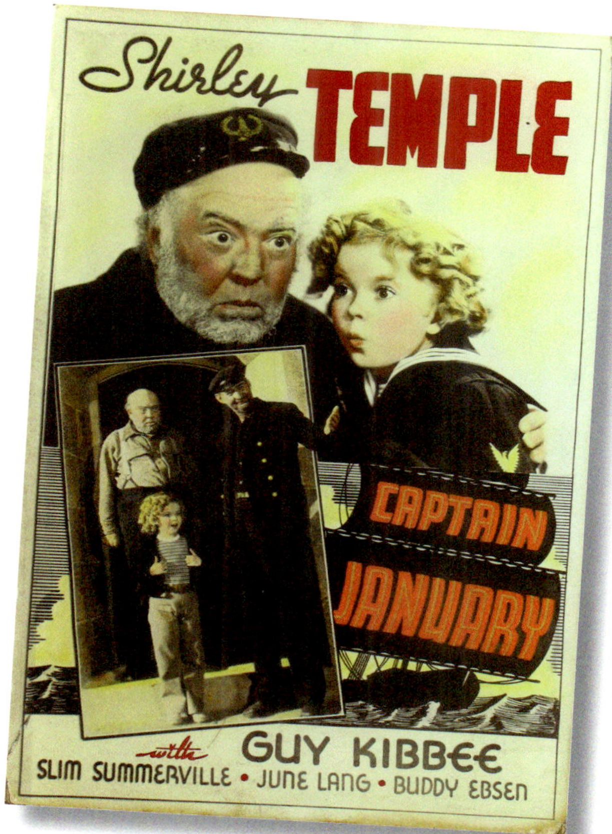

Courtesy of Hershenson/Allen Archive

Courtesy of Heritage

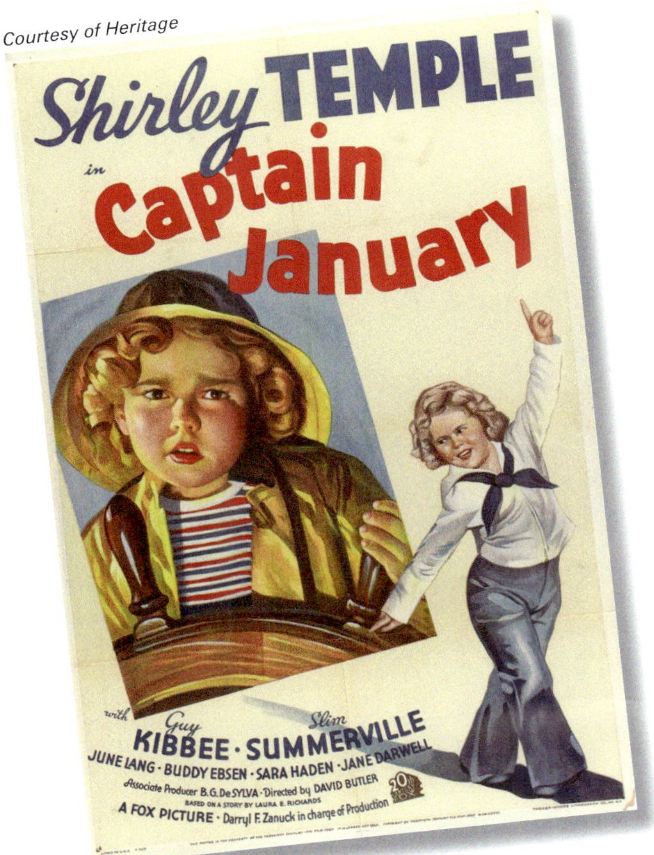

Captain January—Style A 1936 27x41

Heritage	$1,092	VG	03/06
Butterfield & Butterfield	$1,035	VF	05/96
Butterfield & Butterfield	$1,265	VF	02/96
Christie's	$2,200	FN	12/91

• This poster has appeared at auction 4 times since 1989.
• There is no *Captain January* 30x40 known to exist.

Captain January – Meloy Brothers 1936 40x60
Camden House $500 VG 06/95

• There is 1 known to exist.

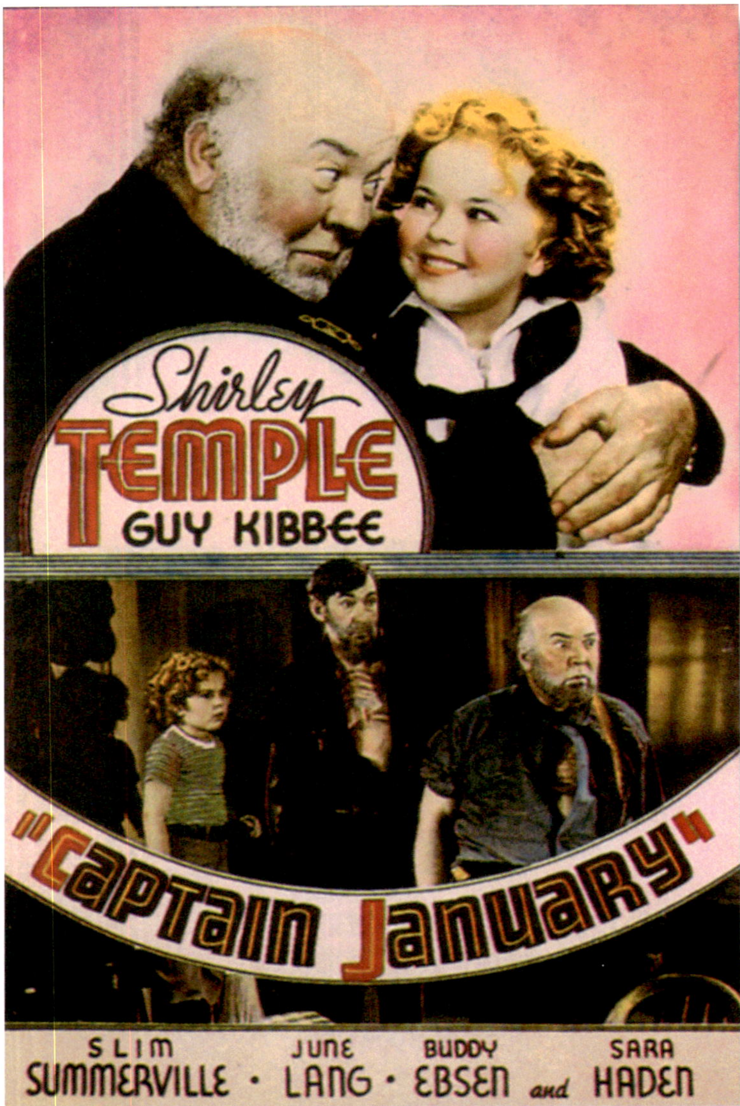

Courtesy of Camden House

Courtesy of Heritage

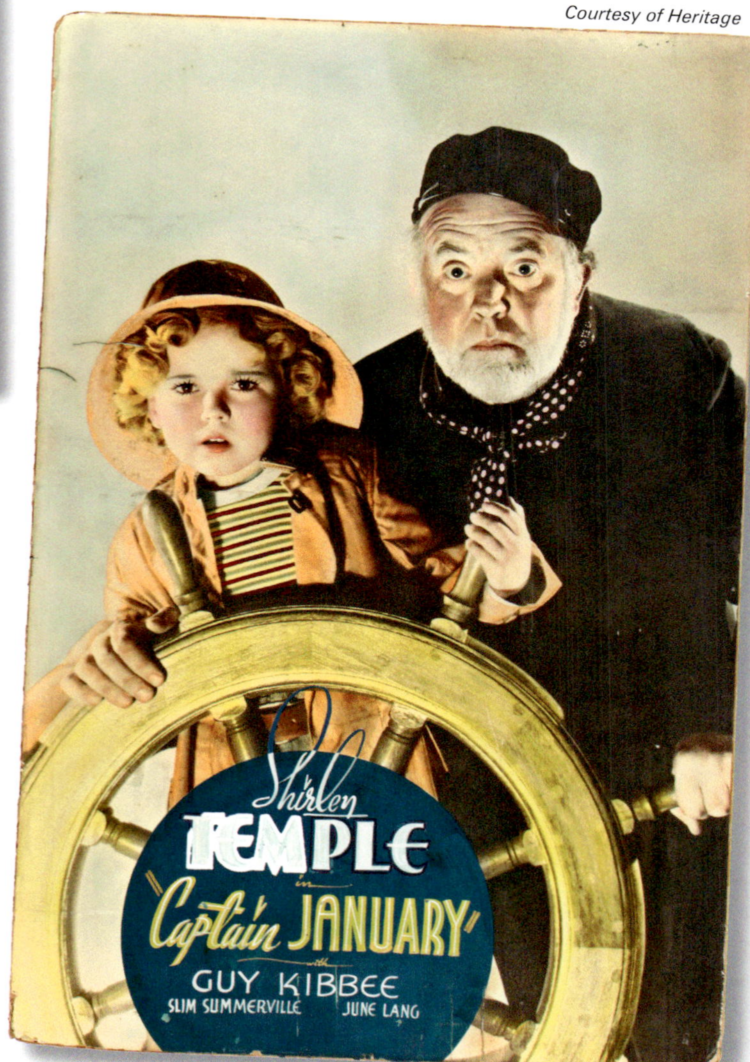

Captain January – Meloy Brothers 1936 40x60
Heritage $776 VG/FN 02/08

• There is 1 known to exist.

Courtesy of Sotheby's

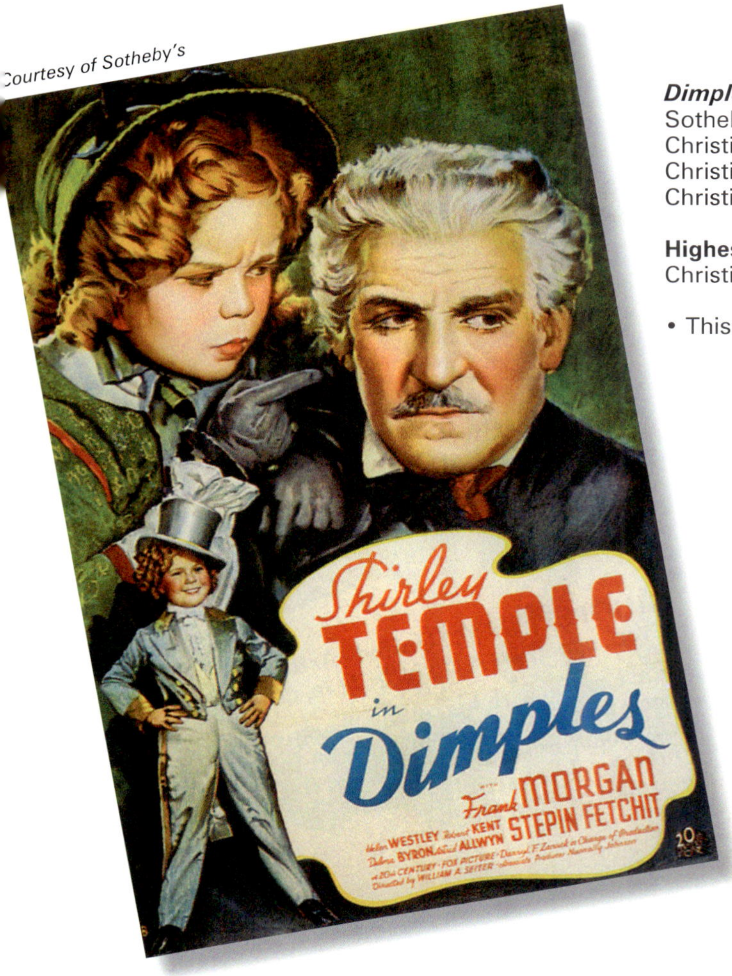

Dimples — Style B 1936 27x41

Auction House	Price	Condition	Date
Sotheby's	$1,840	NM	03/97
Christie's	$1,955	VF	12/96
Christie's	$3,680	VF	06/95
Christie's	$3,300	VF	12/91

Highest price realized:

Auction House	Price	Condition	Date
Christie's	$3,680	VF	06/95

• This poster has appeared at auction 4 times since 1989.

Dimples 1936 30x40

Auction House	Price	Condition	Date
Heritage	$403	FN-	03/04
Heritage	$603	FN+	07/03

• There are 2 known to exist.

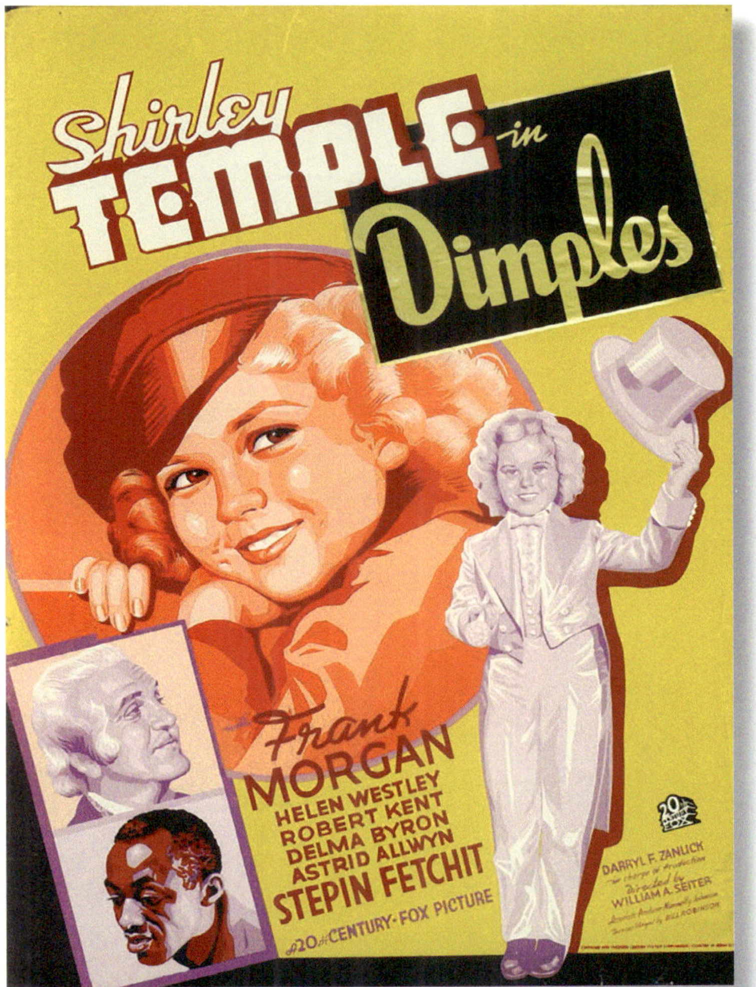

Courtesy of Heritage

Courtesy of Heritage

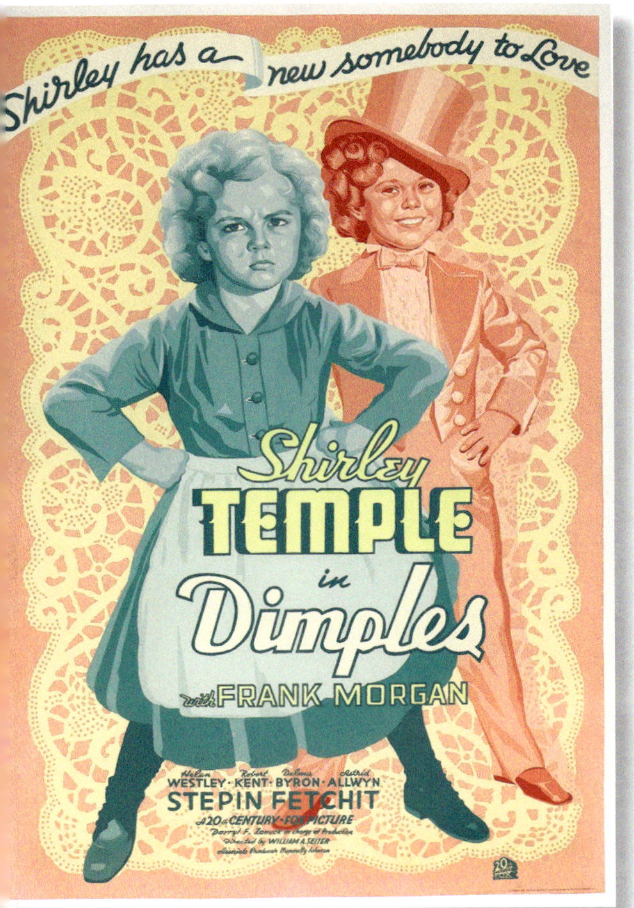

Dimples 1936 40x60

Auction House	Price	Condition	Date
Profiles in History	$1,200	VF	03/08
Heritage	$956	VF	03/07
Heritage	DNS	FN-	07/03

• There are 3 known to exist.

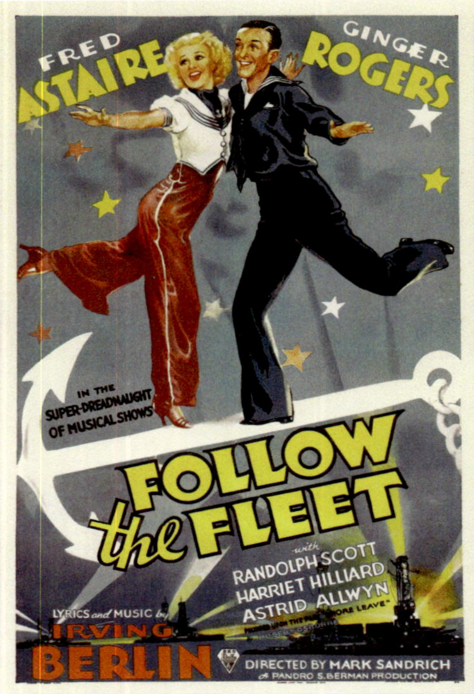

Courtesy of Heritage

Follow the Fleet	1936	27x41	
Heritage	$8,365	VG	03/07
Heritage	$3,680	VG	03/05
Butterfields	$5,875	VF	12/01
Christie's	$7,590	VG	06/93
Camden House	$2,950	VF	05/89

Highest price realized:

Heritage	$8,365	VG	03/07

Price in 1989:

Camden House	$2,950	VF	05/89

•This poster has appeared at auction 5 times since 1989.

Courtesy of Christie's

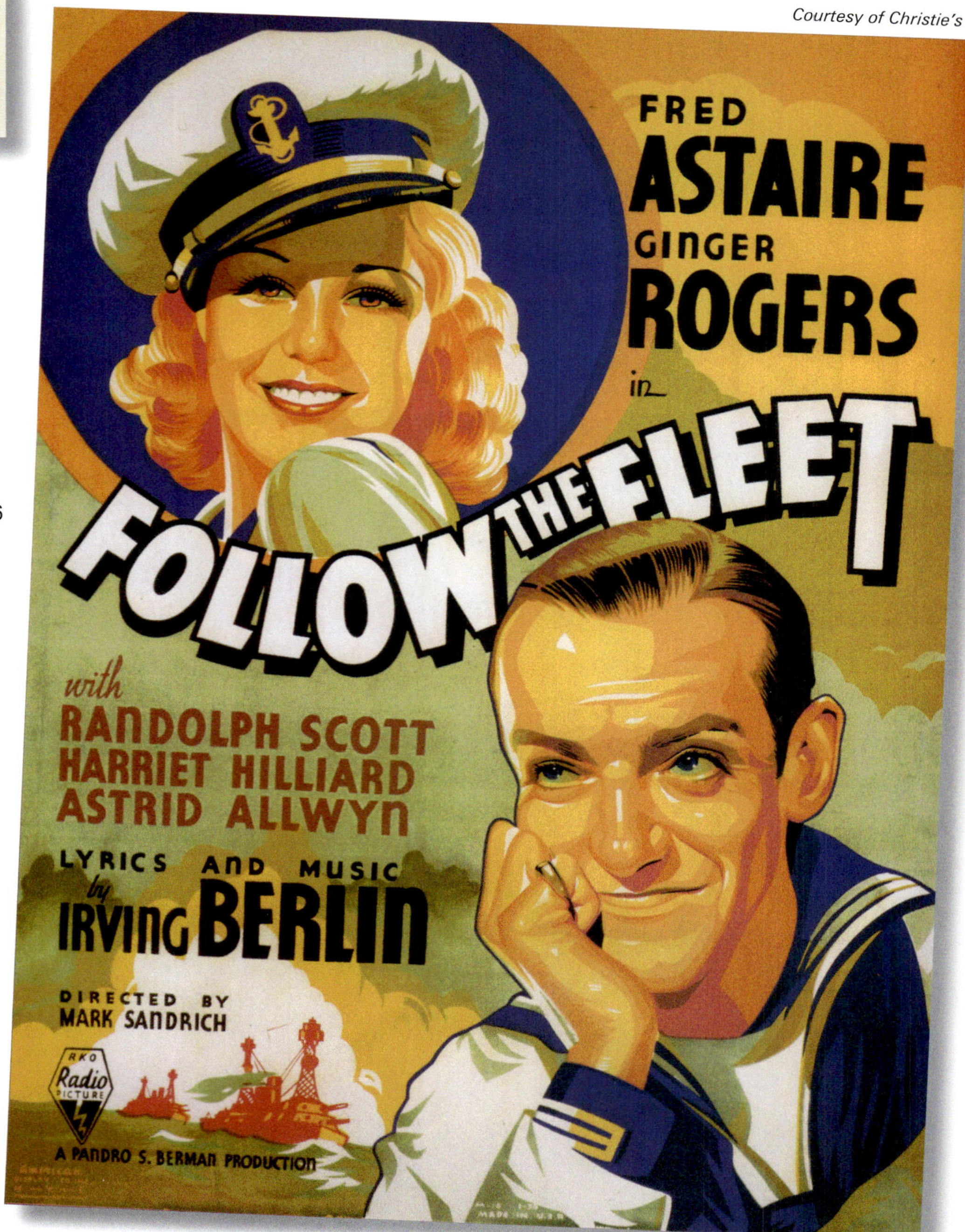

Follow the Fleet	1936	30x40	
Christie's	$17,825	FN	12/96

Estimate: $30,000 - $50,000

• There is 1 known to exist.
• There is no *Follow the Fleet* 40x60 known to exist.

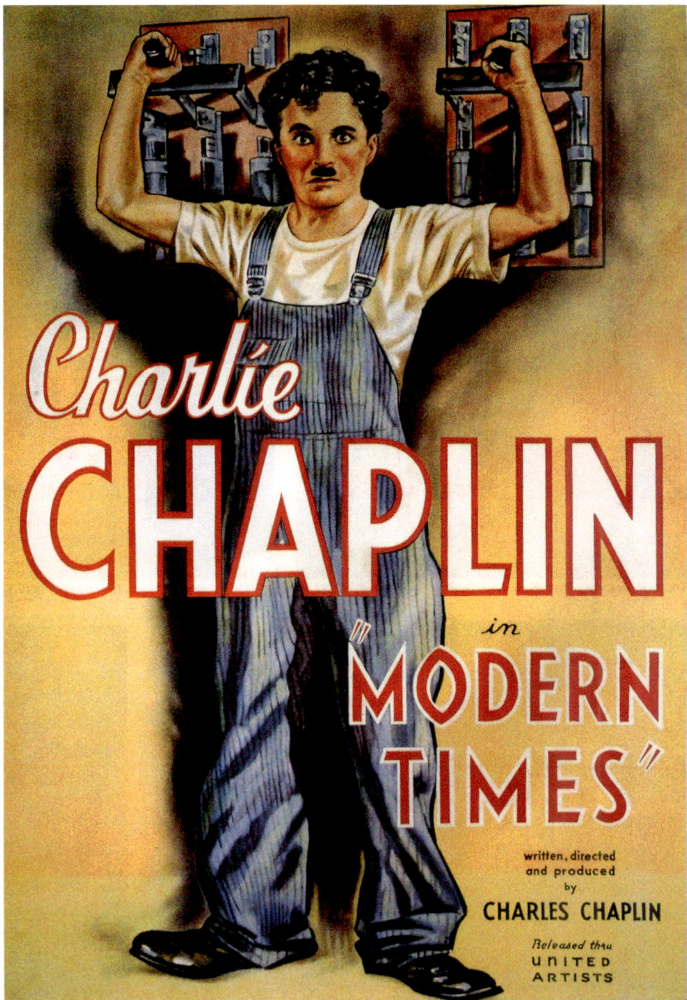

Courtesy of Christie's

Modern Times 1936 27x41

Lowery	$13,225	VG	06/00
Christie's	$16,560	FN	11/96

- This poster has appeared at auction 2 times since 1989.
- There is no *Modern Times* 30x40 known to exist.

Courtesy of Christie's

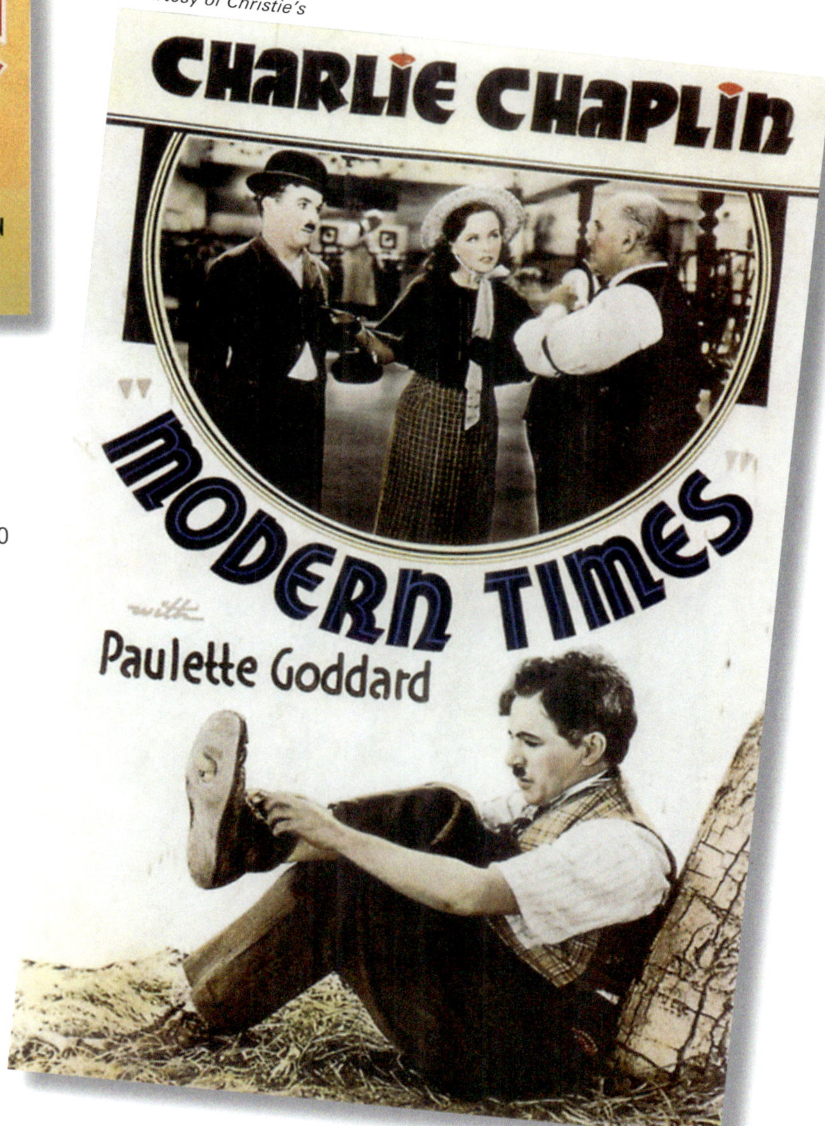

Modern Times — Meloy Brothers 1936 40x60

Christie's	$4,600	VF	12/96

Estimate: $6,500 - $9,500

- There is 1 known to exist.

Our Relations 1936 40x60
Christie's $4,830 FN 12/96
Estimate: $10,000 - $15,000

- There is 1 known to exist.
- There was no image available for *Our Relations* 27x41.
- There is no *Our Relations* 30x40 known to exist.

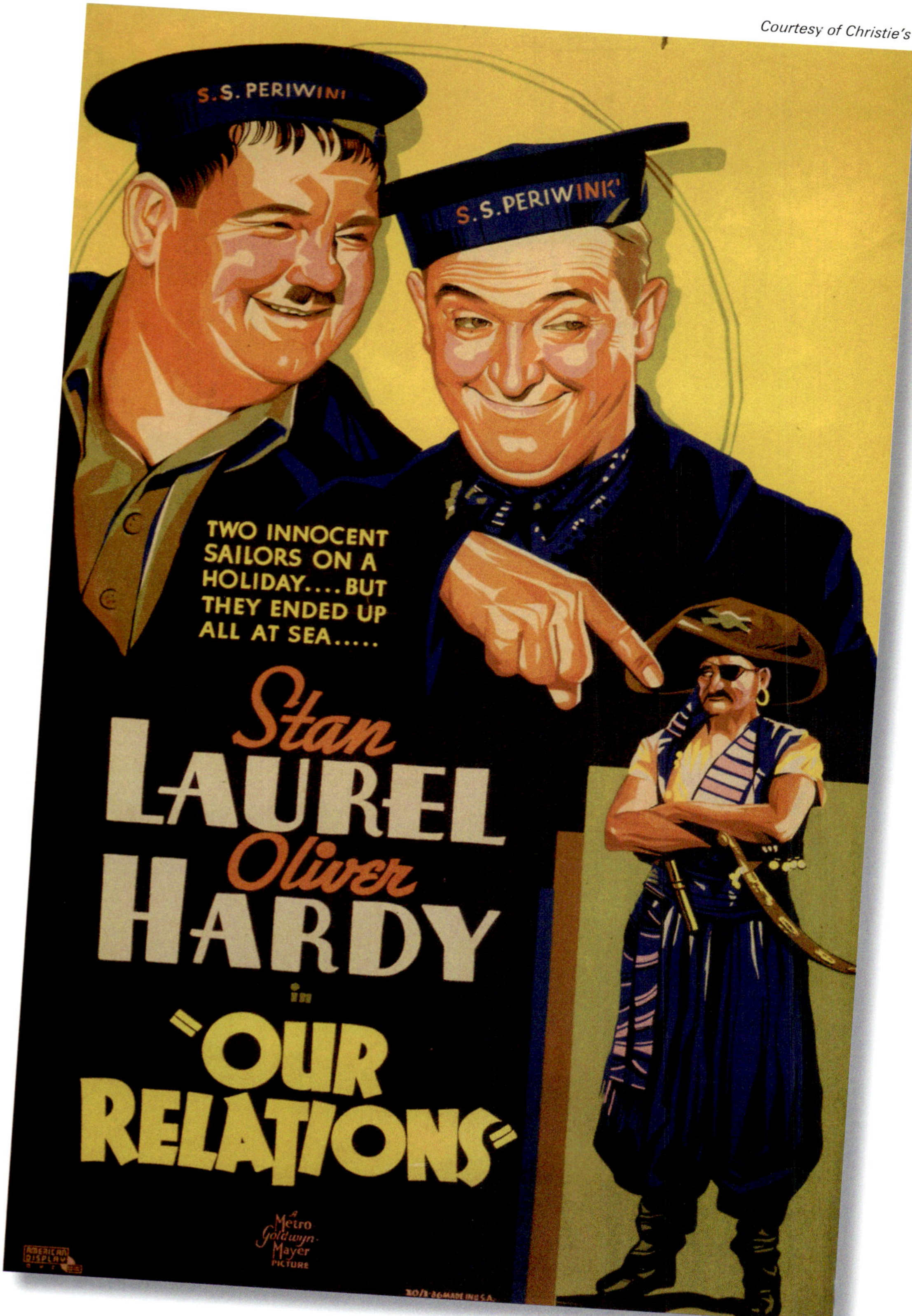

Courtesy of Christie's

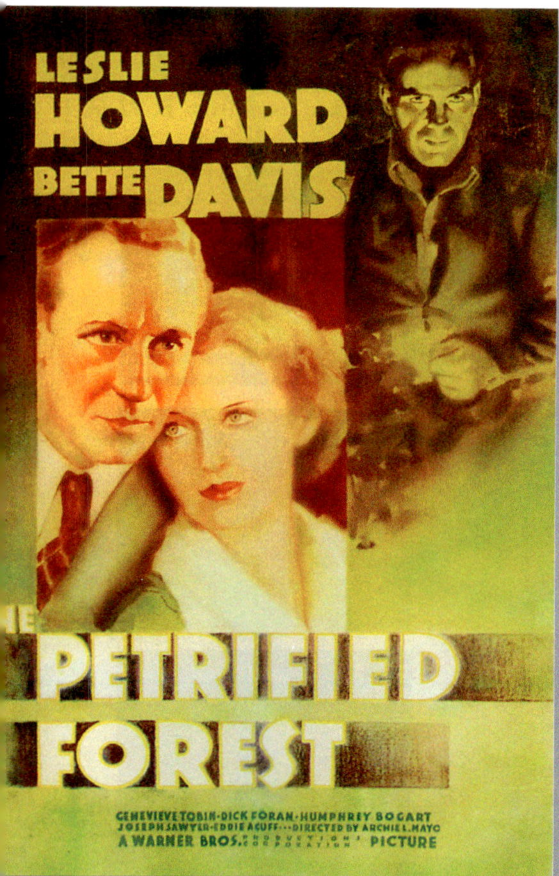

Courtesy of Sotheby's

Petrified Forest 1936 27x41

Sotheby's	$11,500	FN+	03/97
Butterfield & Butterfield	$19,500	M	05/96

- This poster has appeared at auction 2 times since 1989.
- There is no *Petrified Forest* 30x40 known to exist.

Courtesy of Hershenson/Allen Archive

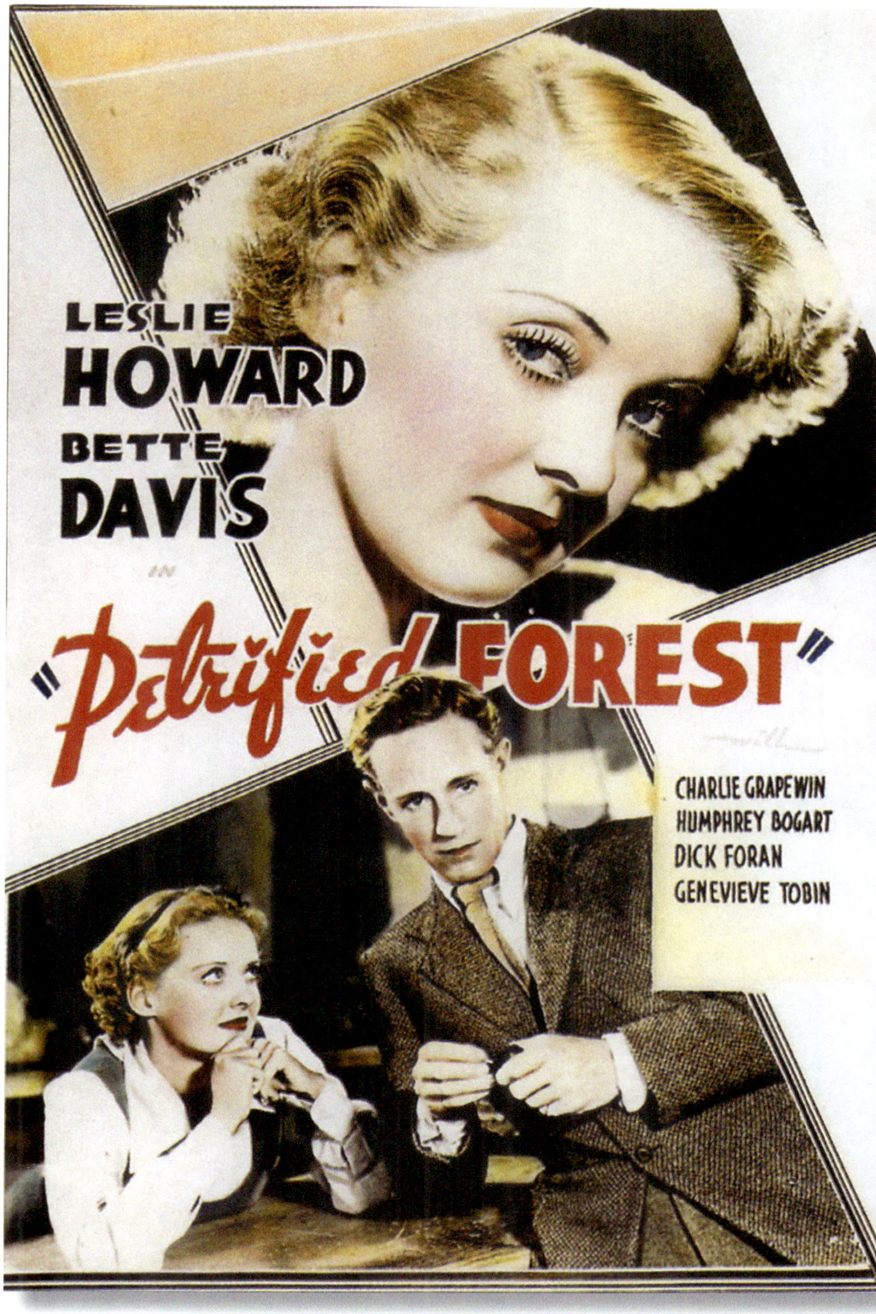

Petrified Forest—Meloy Brothers 1936 40x60

eMoviePoster	$7,900	VG	02/08*
Christie's	$8,050	VG	12/96

- There is 1 known to exist.

* This is the same poster that appeared in the Christie's Auction in 1996.

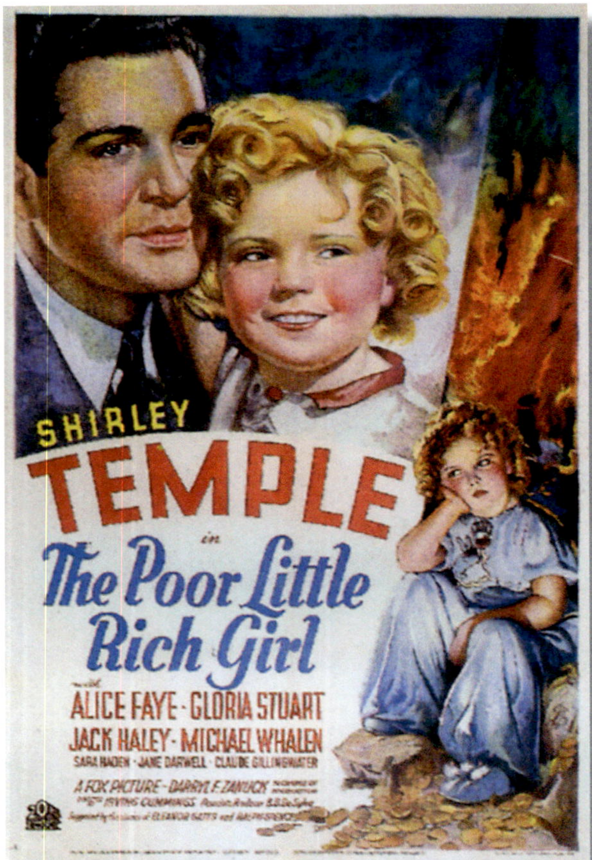

Courtesy of Butterfield & Butterfield

Poor Little Rich Girl—Style B 1936 27x41
Butterfield & Butterfield $1,092 VF 02/96

• This poster has appeared at auction 3 times since 1989.

Poor Little Rich Girl 1936 30x40
Heritage $891 VG/FN 03/04

• There is 1 known to exist.
• There is no *Poor Little Rich Girl* 40x60 known to exist.

Courtesy of Heritage

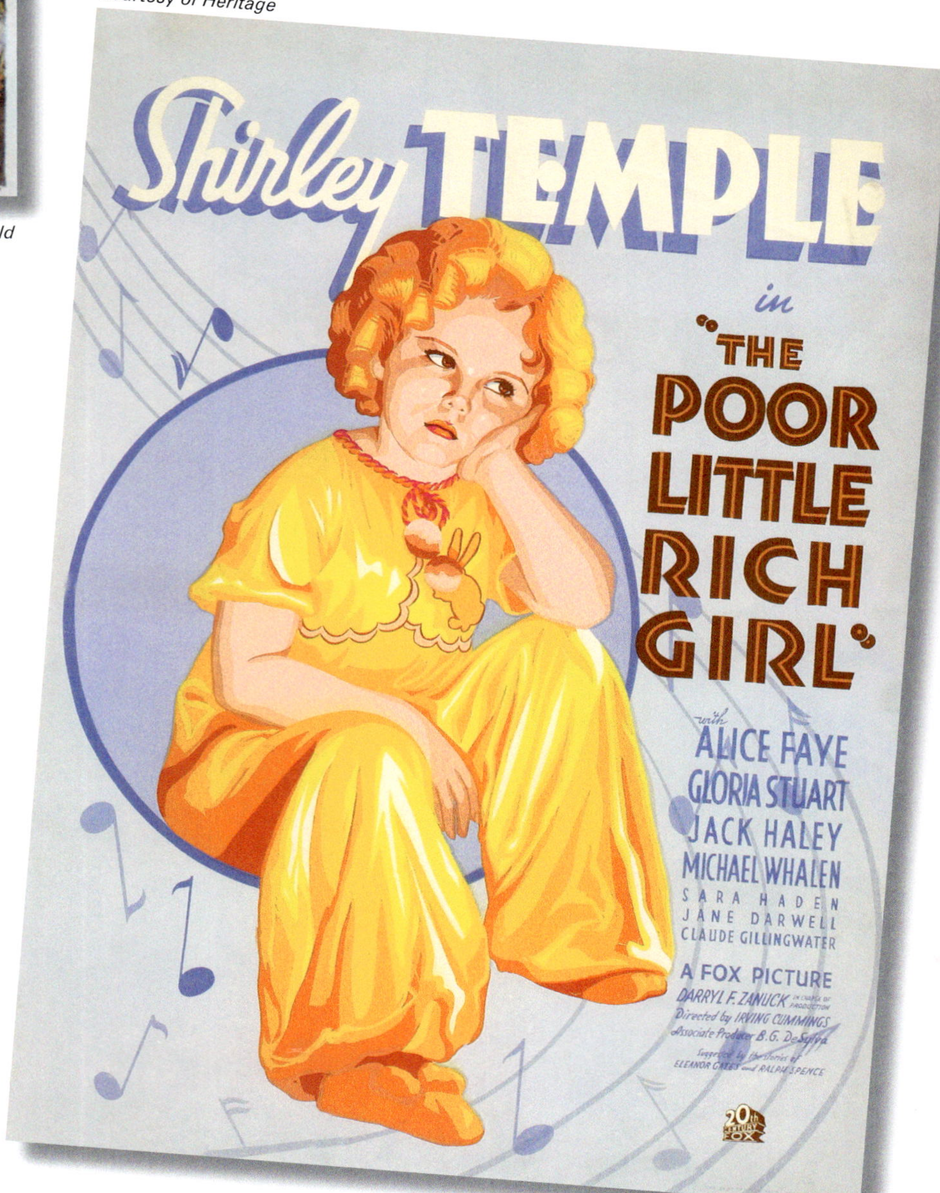

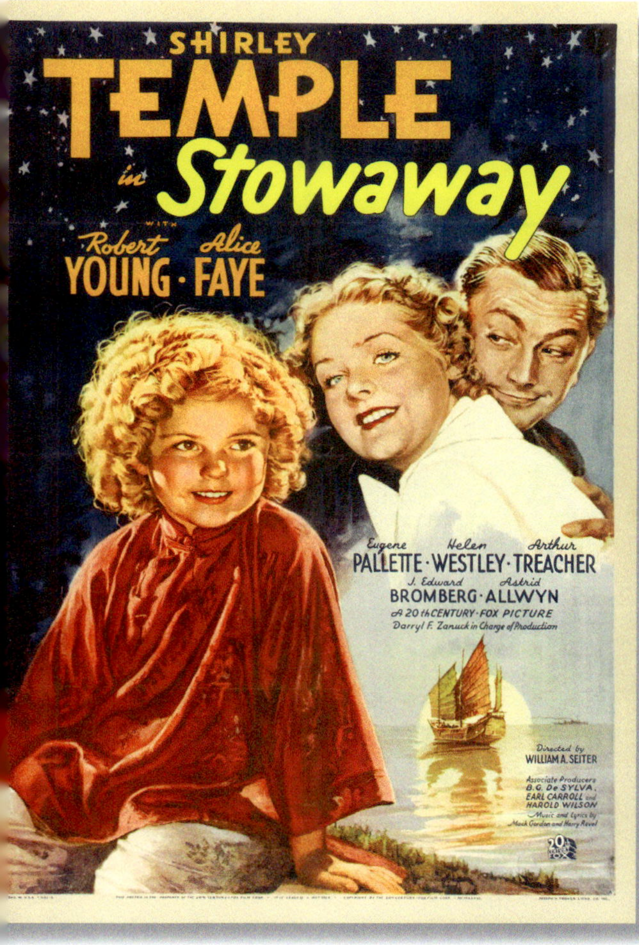

Courtesy of Heritage

Stowaway—Style A	1936	27x41	
Heritage	$2,390	VG+	07/07
Sotheby's	$1,725	NM	03/97
Butterfield & Butterfield	$1,093	FN	05/96
Christie's	$1,495	GD	12/93

Highest price realized:

Heritage	$2,390	VG+	07/07

Price in 1993:

Christie's	$1,495	GD	12/93

- This poster has appeared at auction 6 times since 1989.
- There is no *Stowaway* 30x40 known to exist.

Courtesy of Heritage

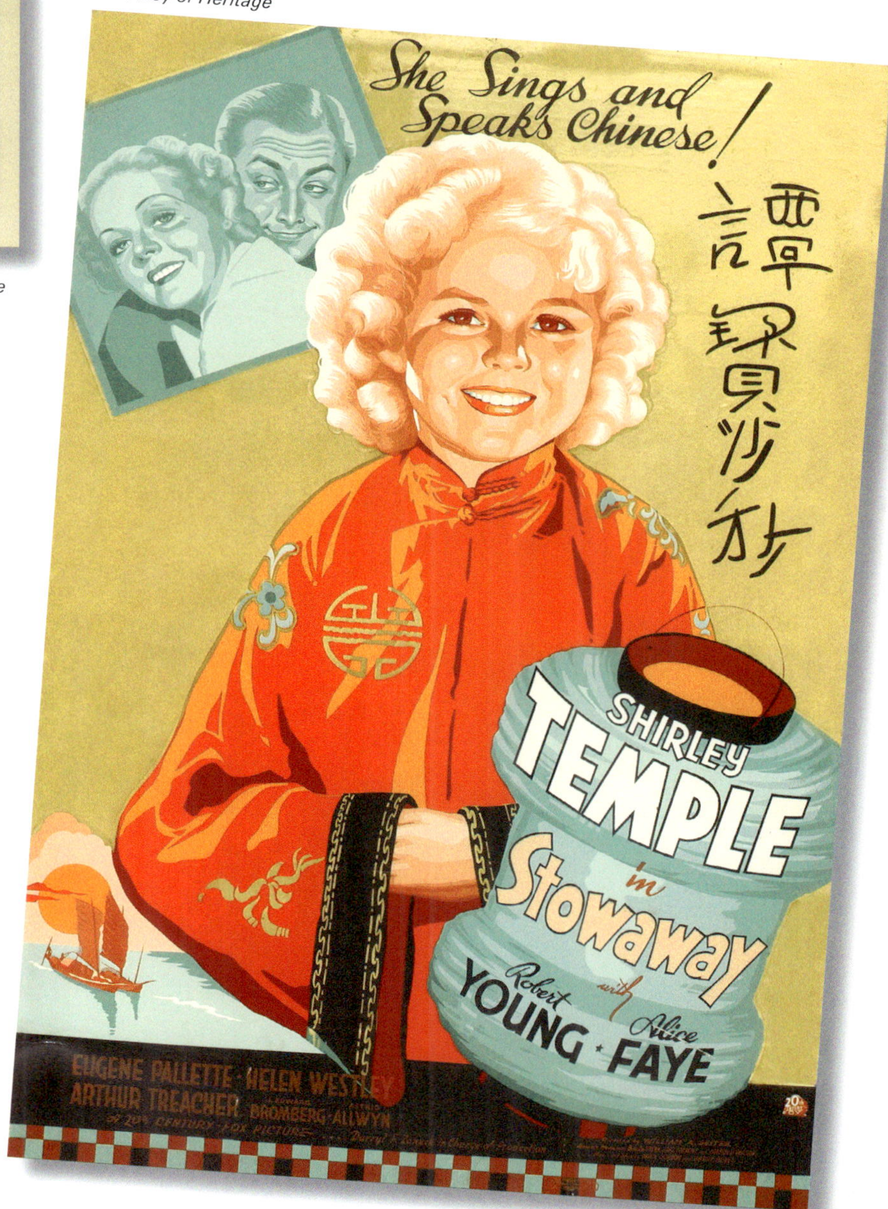

Stowaway	1936	40x60		
Heritage		$356	VF	03/04

Estimate: $1,000 - $2,000

- There is 1 known to exist.

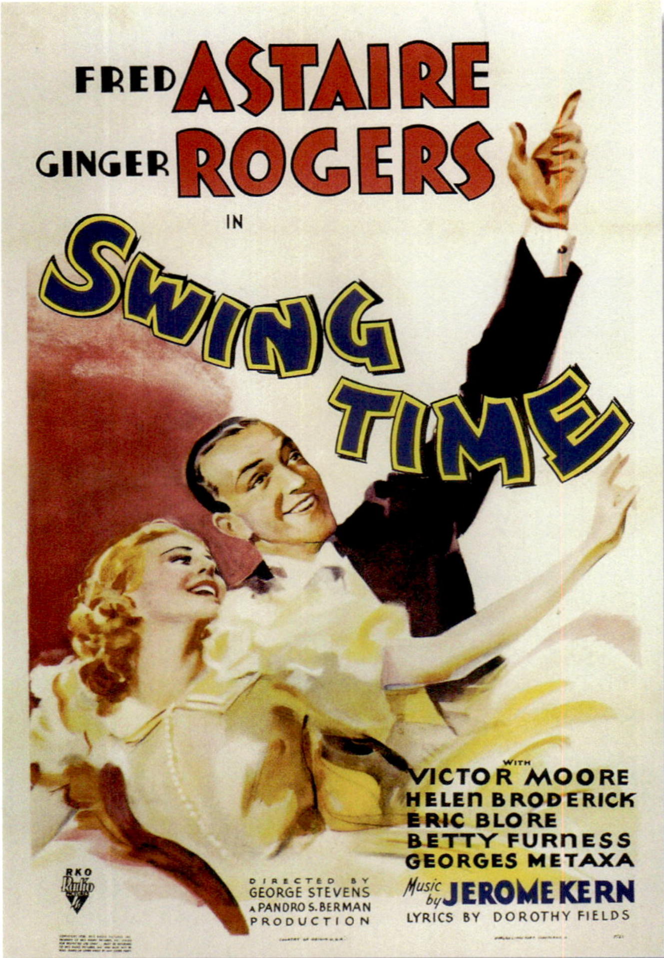

Courtesy of Sotheby's

Swing Time 1936 27x41			
Sotheby's	$4,800	VF	10/00
Sotheby's	$5,750	VF-	12/99
Lowery	$6,900	VG/FN	06/99
Sotheby's	$4,600	VG	09/98
Sotheby's	$4,888	VF	12/96

Highest price realized:

Lowery	$6,900	VG/FN	06/99

Price in 1990:

Camden House	$4,500	VF	03/90

- This poster has appeared at auction 7 times since 1989.
- There is no *Swing Time* 30x40 known to exist.

Courtesy of Heritage

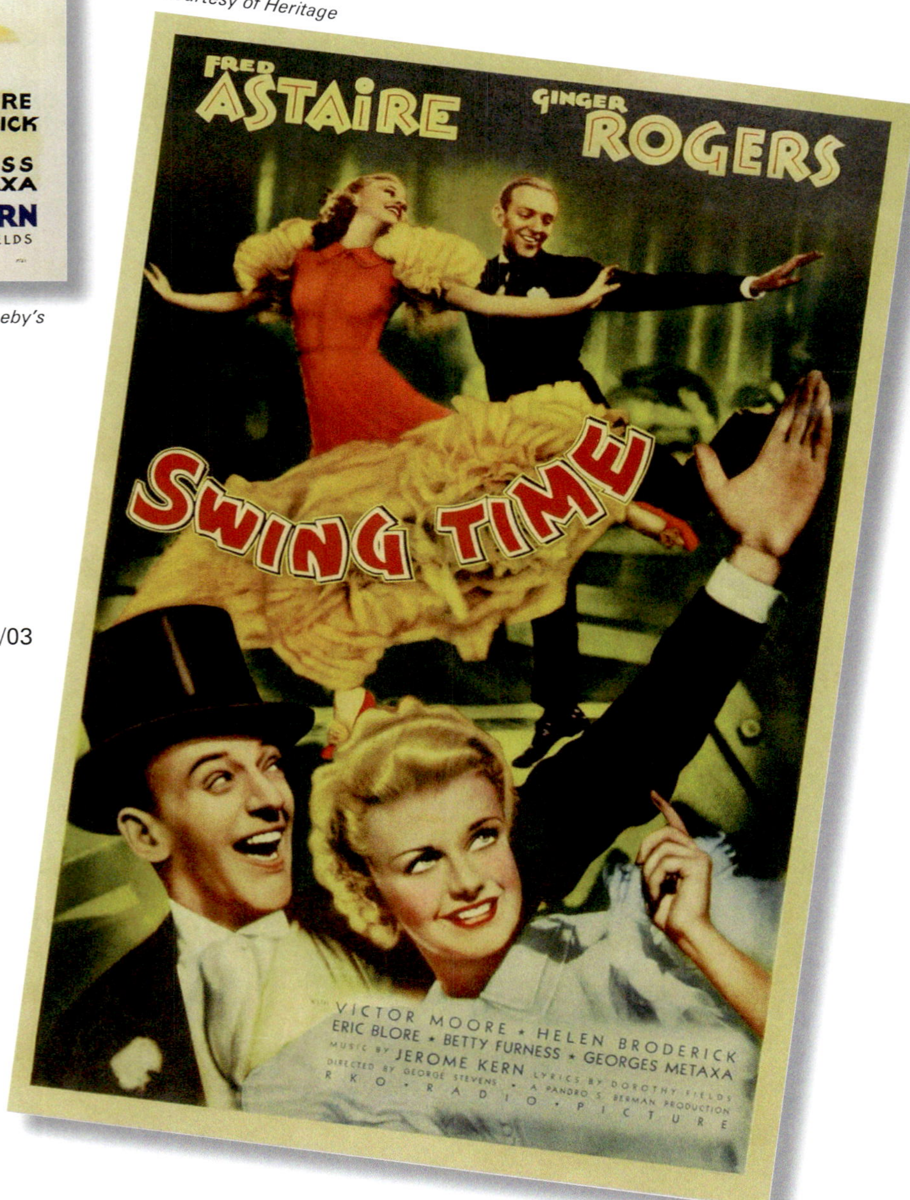

Swing Time 1936 40x60			
Heritage	$8,337	VF+	07/03

Estimate: $10,000 - $13,000

- There is 1 known to exist.

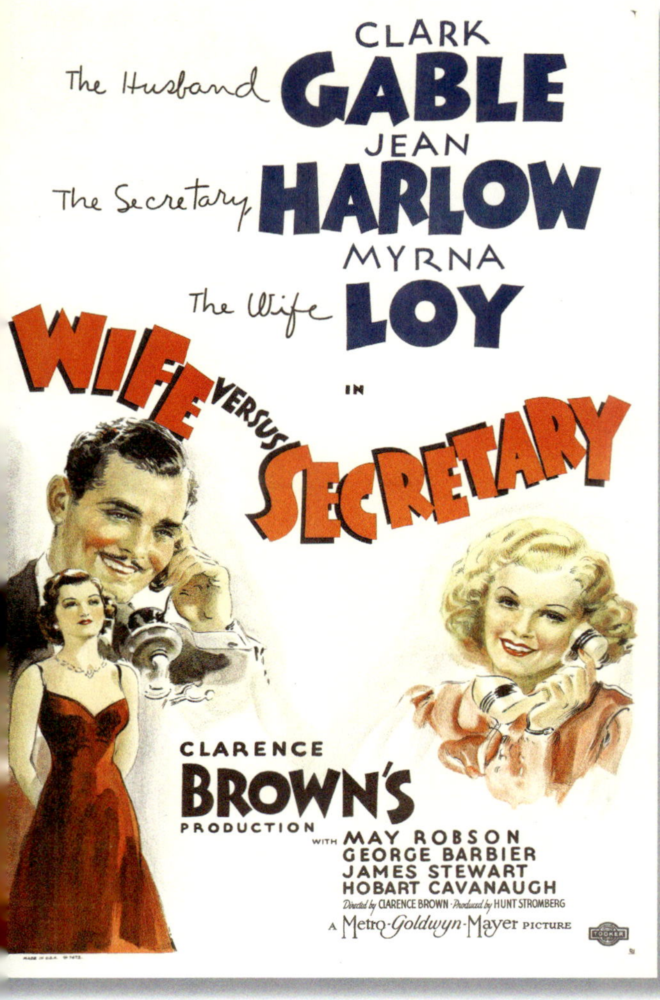

Courtesy of Heritage

Wife vs. Secretary— Style D 1936 27x41

Heritage	$1,912	FN/VF	03/09
Heritage	$2,868	FN/VF	03/07
Private	$1,700	VF	07/97
Butterfield & Butterfield	$1,100	NM	11/96

Highest price realized:

Heritage	$2,868	FN/VF	03/07

Price in 1996:

Butterfield & Butterfield	$1,100	NM	11/96

• This poster has appeared at auction 5 times since 1989.

Wife vs. Secretary—Meloy Brothers 1936 40x60

eMoviePoster	$215	GD	04/09
eMoviePoster	$405	GD/VG	12/08
eMoviePoster	$1,050	GD	08/08

• There are 3 known to exist.

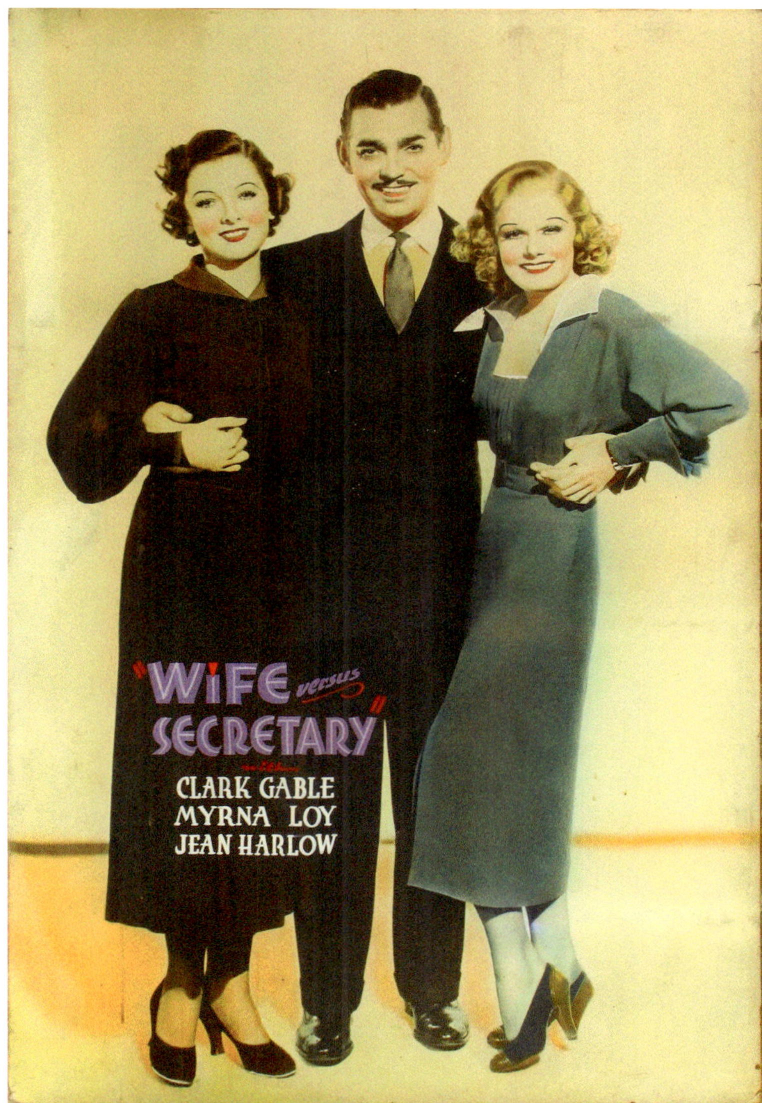

Courtesy of Hershenson/Allen Archive

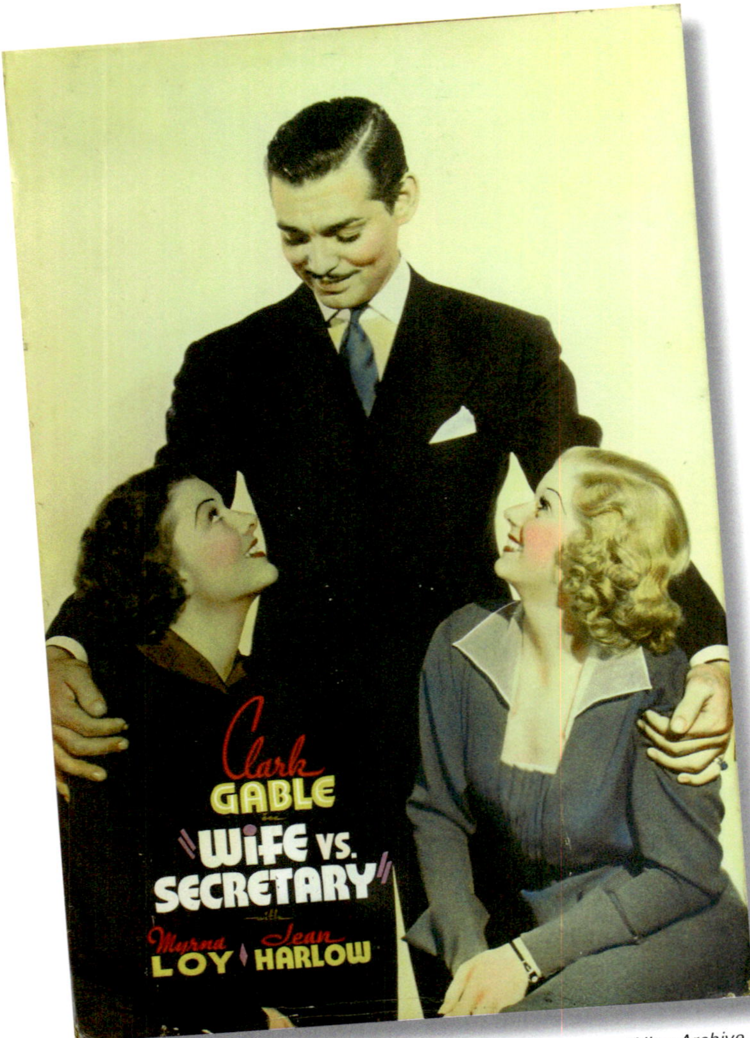

Courtesy of Hershenson/Allen Archive

Wife vs. Secretary—Meloy Brothers 1936 40x60

eMoviePoster	$1,125	GD	02/08
Camden House	$1,000	VG	06/95

- There are 2 known to exist.

Courtesy of Hershenson/Allen Archive

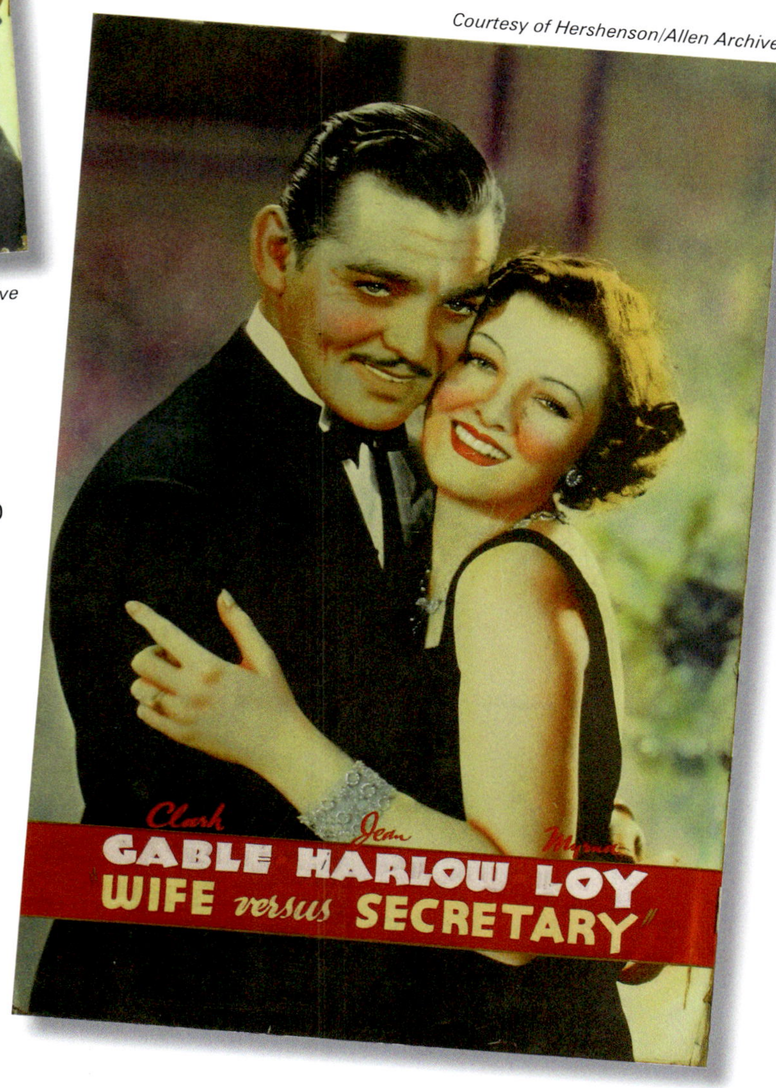

Wife vs. Secretary—Meloy Brothers 1936 40x60

eMoviePoster	$1,235	GD	02/08
Camden House	$1,000	FN	06/95

- There are 2 known to exist.

Walking Dead 1936 40x60
Heritage $8,652 FN/VF 11/04
Estimate: $14,000 - $18,000

- There is 1 known to exist.
- There was no image available for *Walking Dead* 27x41.
- There is no *Walking Dead* 30x40 known to exist.

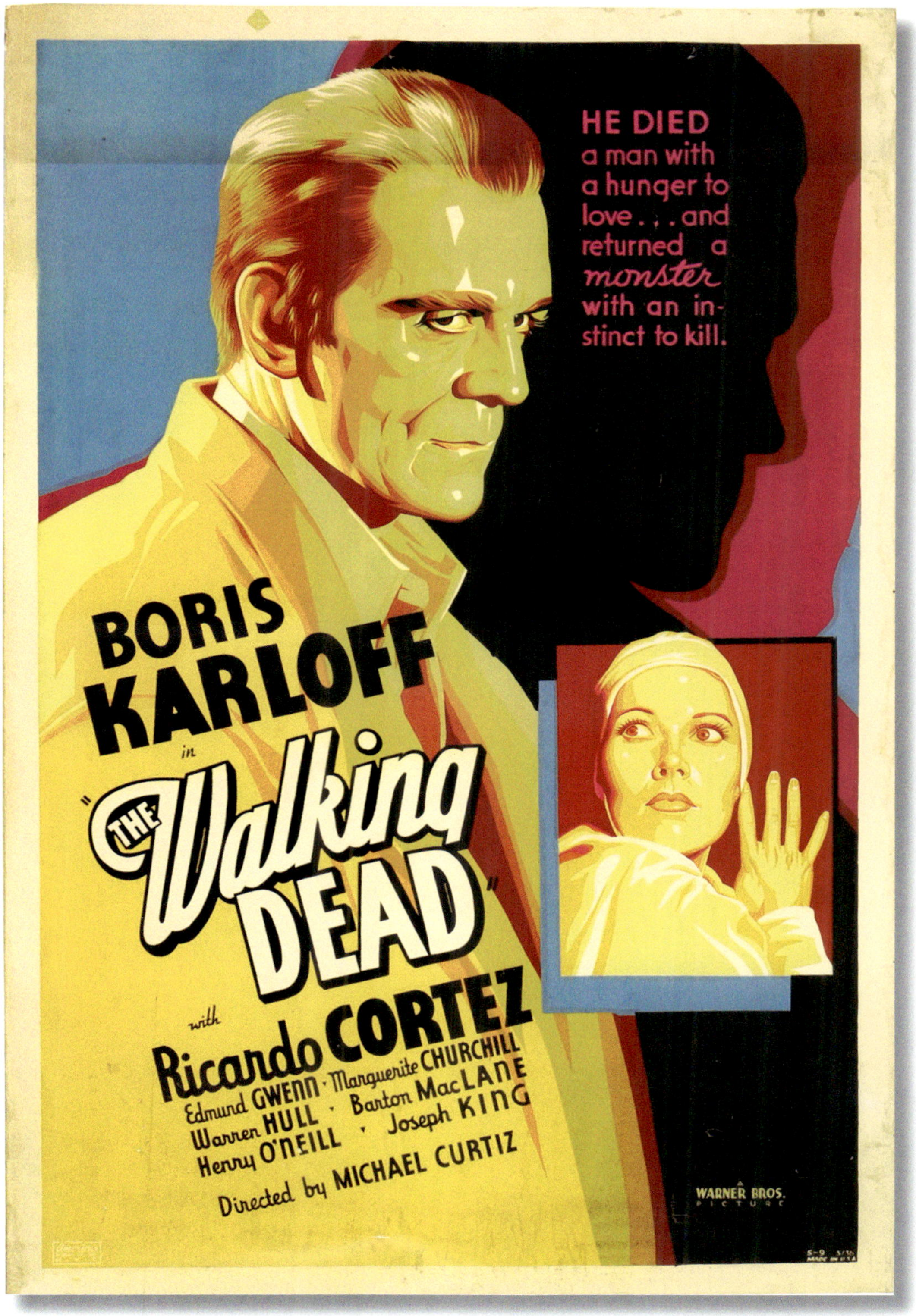

Courtesy of Heritage

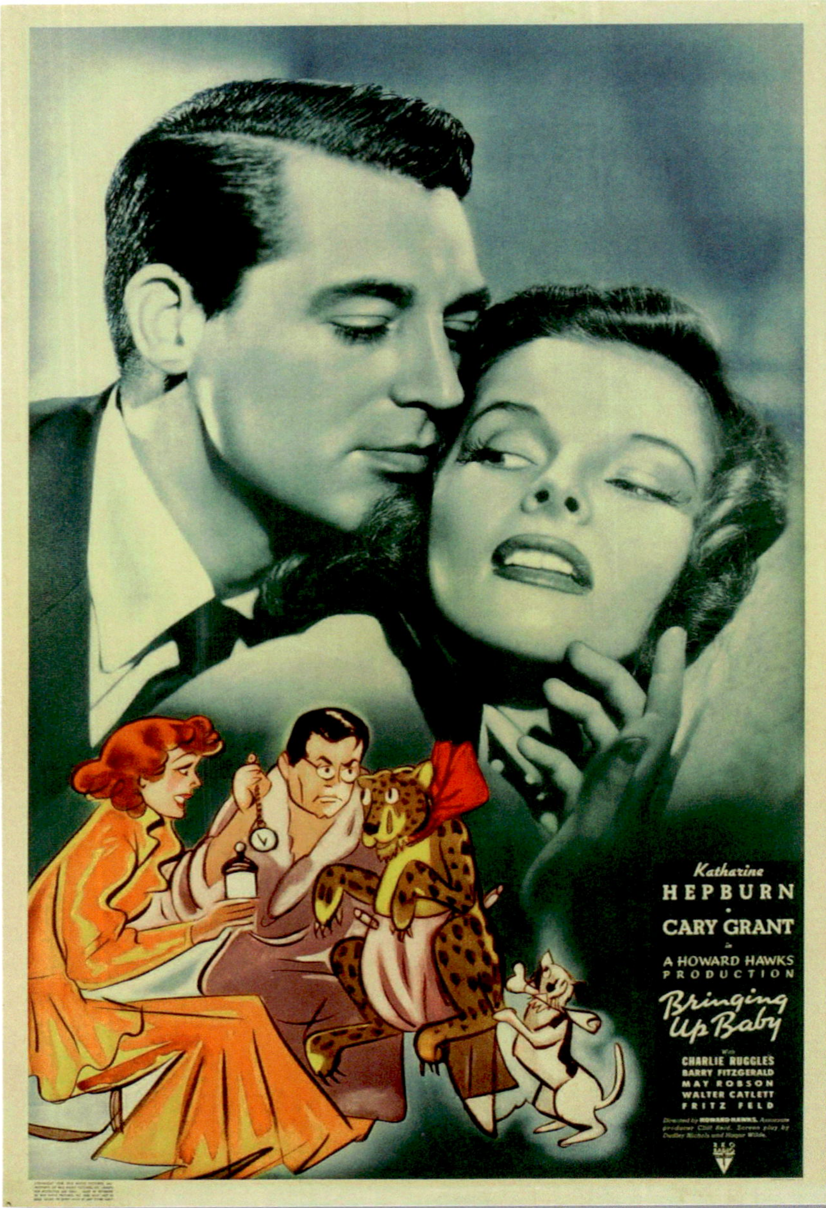

Courtesy of Heritage

Bringing up Baby 1938 40x60

Heritage	$20,700	VF+	07/03

Estimate: $25,000 - $30,000

- There is 1 known to exist.

Bringing up Baby 1938 27x41

Heritage	$9,560	VF-	07/09
Heritage	$9,560	VF	03/08
Heritage	$9,775	VF	07/04
MPA	$7,500	VF	08/01
Skinner	$2,875	VG	11/99

Highest price realized:

Heritage	$9,560	VF	03/08

Price in 1995:

Sotheby's	$2,800	FN	12/95

- This poster has appeared at auction 10 times since 1989.
- There is no *Bringing up Baby* 30x40 known to exist.

Courtesy of Heritage

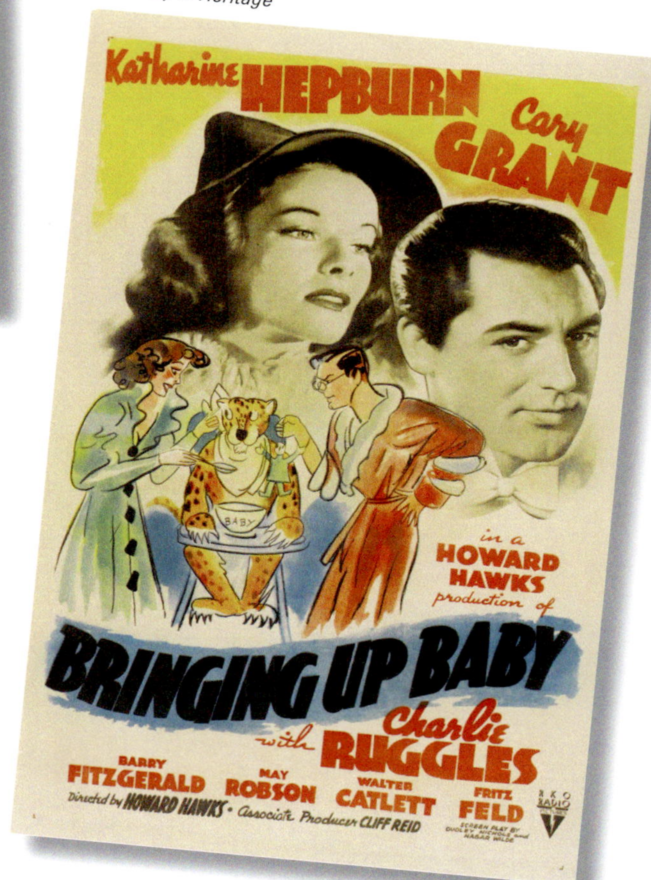

Courtesy of Heritage

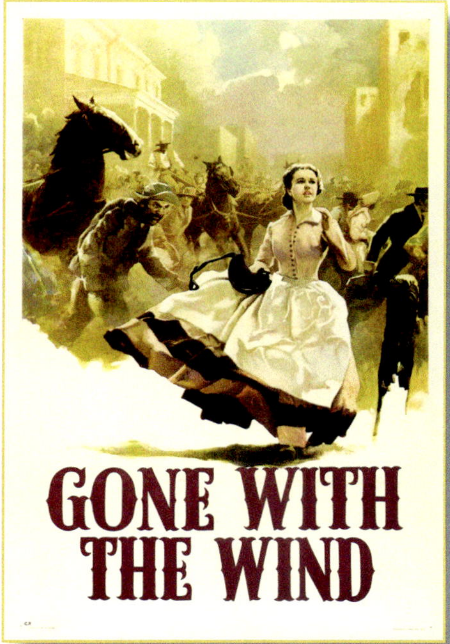

Gone With the Wind—Style CP 1939 27x41

Heritage	$20,700	VF	07/06
Heritage	$18,400	VF-	07/02
Lowery	$8,280	VF-	12/98
Christie's	$5,520	VF	12/96
Christie's	$6,992	VF	11/96

Highest price realized:

Heritage	$20,700	VF+	07/06

Price in 1995:

Christie's	$10,350	VF	12/95

• This poster has appeared at auction 7 times since 1989.

Gone With the Wind—Leading Men Style 1939 40x60

Sotheby's	$5,462	VF	04/99

Estimate: $7,500 - $9,500

• There is 1 known to exist.

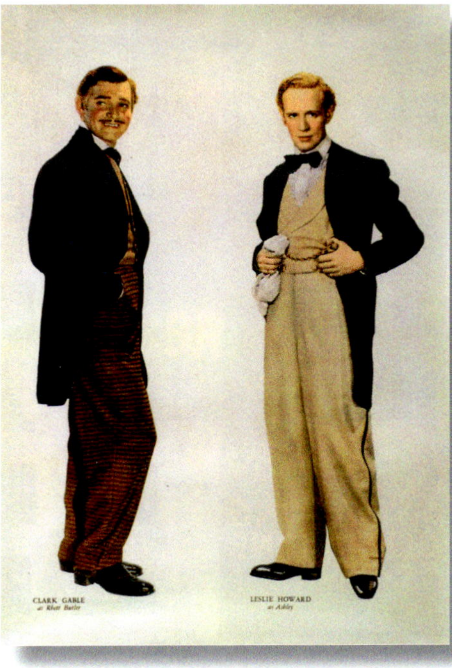

Courtesy of Sotheby's

Courtesy of Sotheby's

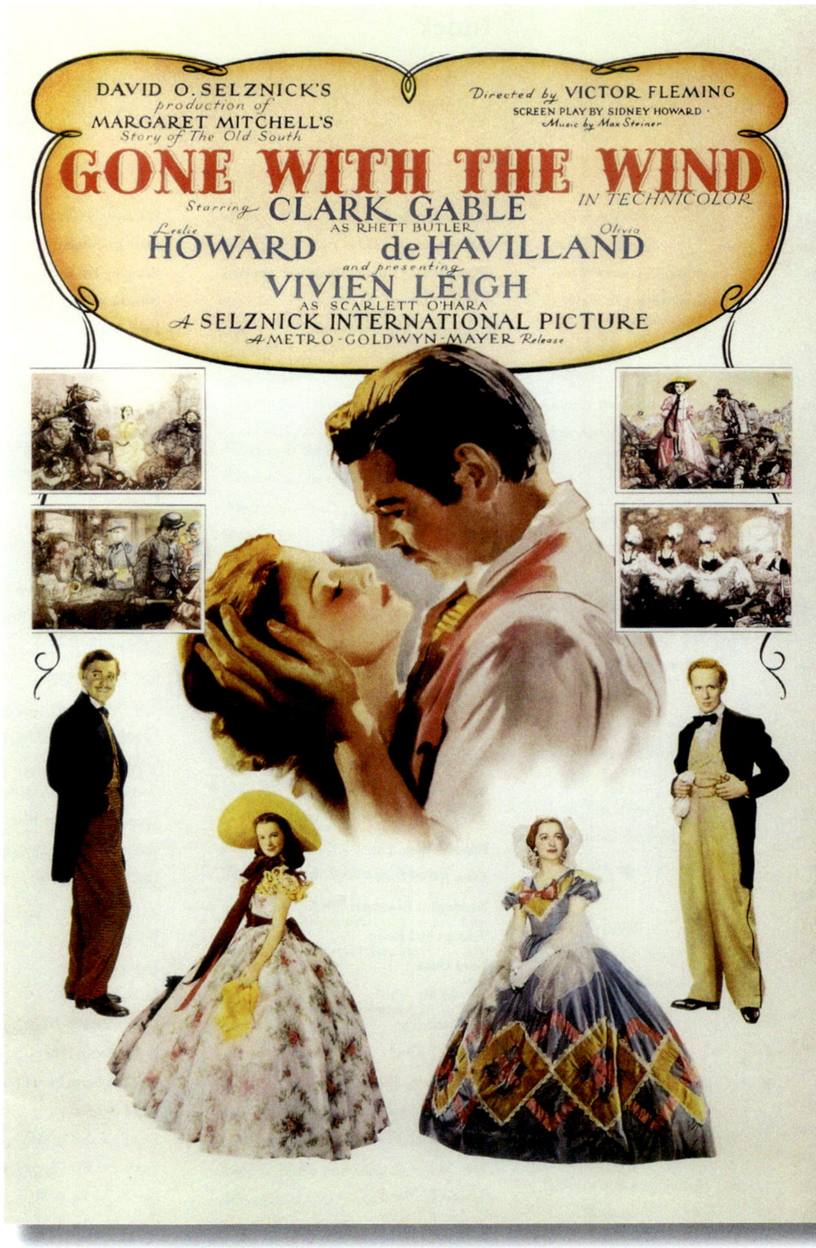

Gone With the Wind 1939 40x60 **

Sotheby's	$37,375	FN	12/99*
Sotheby's	$62,500	VF	12/94

Estimate: $50,000 - $75,000

• There is 1 known to exist.

** This is the same poster as the Sotheby's auction in 1994*
***The size of this poster actually measures 43"x 65"*

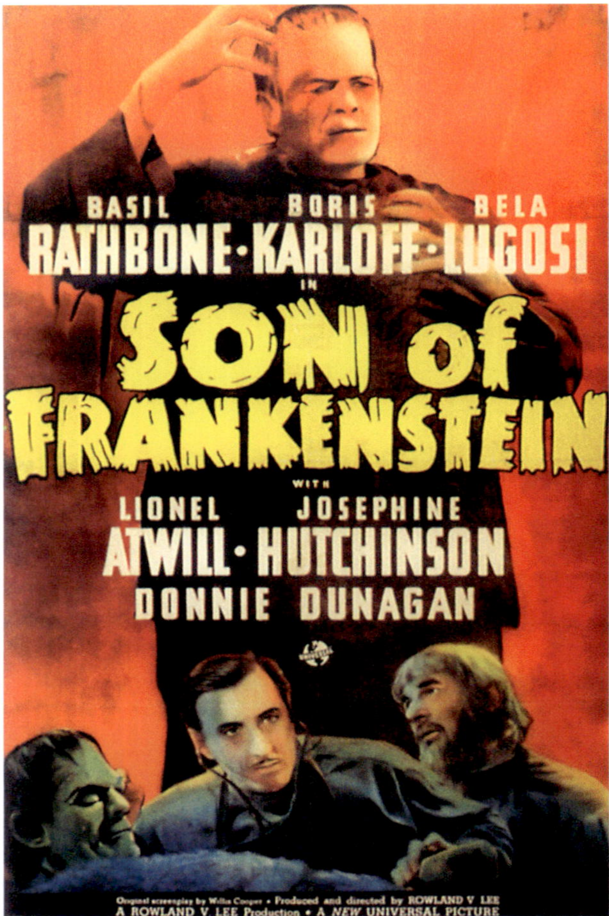

Courtesy of Ron V. Borst, Hollywood Movie Posters

Son of Frankenstein 1939 27x41
Christie's $20,125 VF 06/93
Christie's $14,300 FN+ 12/91
Estimate: $50,000 - $80,000

- This poster has appeared at auction 3 times since 1991.

Courtesy of Ron V. Borst, Hollywood Movie Posters

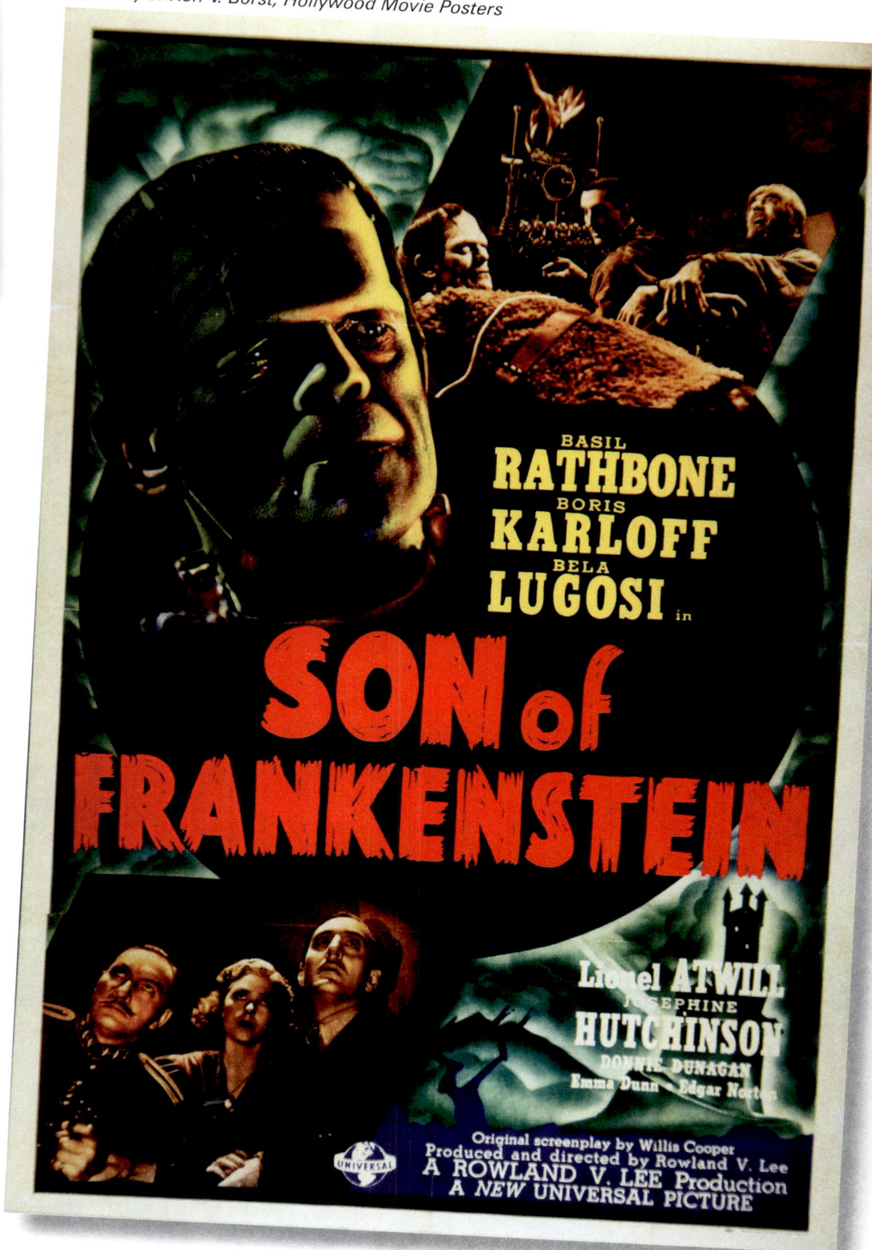

Son of Frankenstein 1939 40x60
Estimate: $150,000 - $300,000

- There is 1 known to exist.

ANIMATION FILMS OF THE 1930s

Courtesy of Christie's

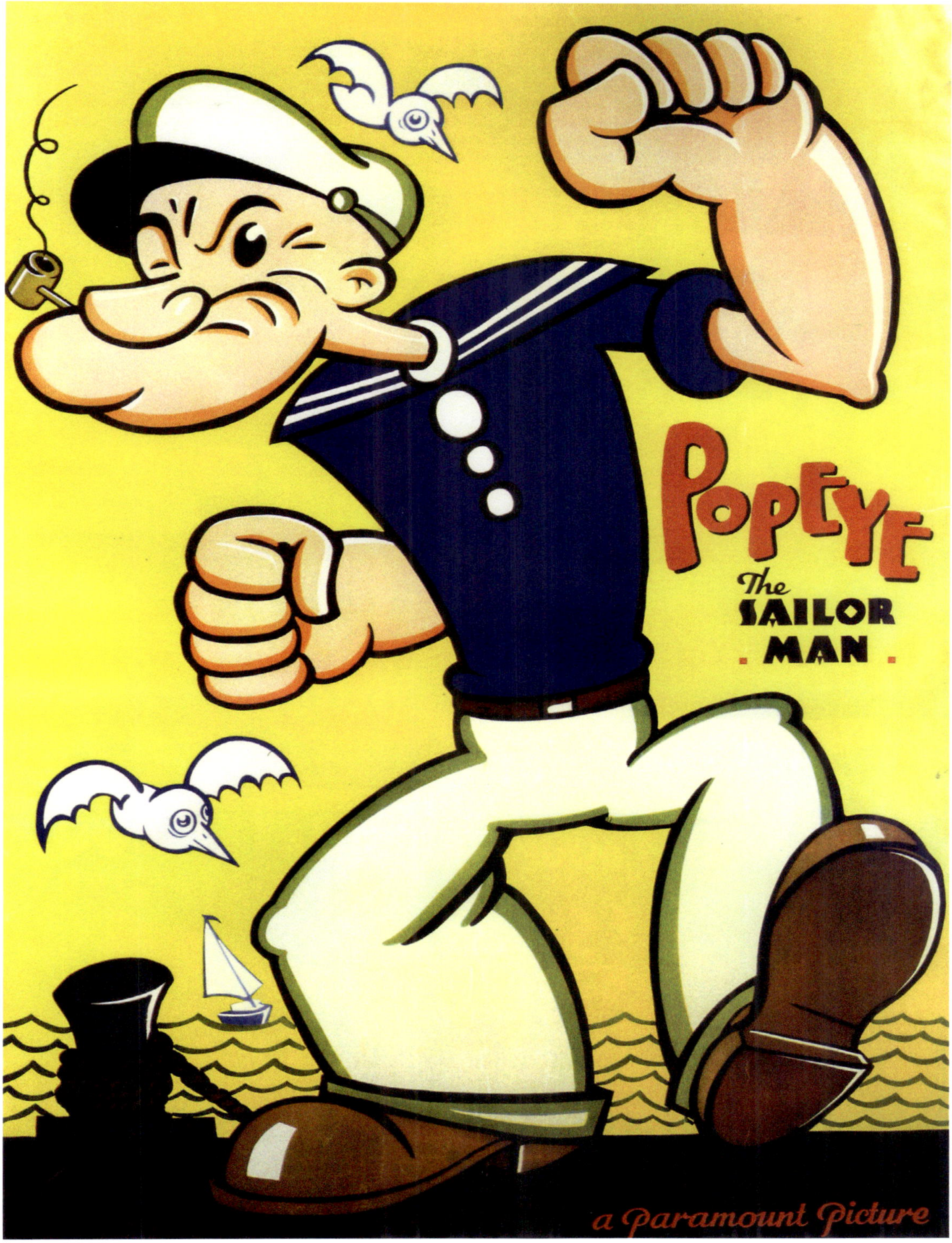

Popeye the Sailor Man 1934 40x60
Christie's $8,280 GD 12/94
Estimate: $40,000 - $55,000

• There is 1 known to exist.

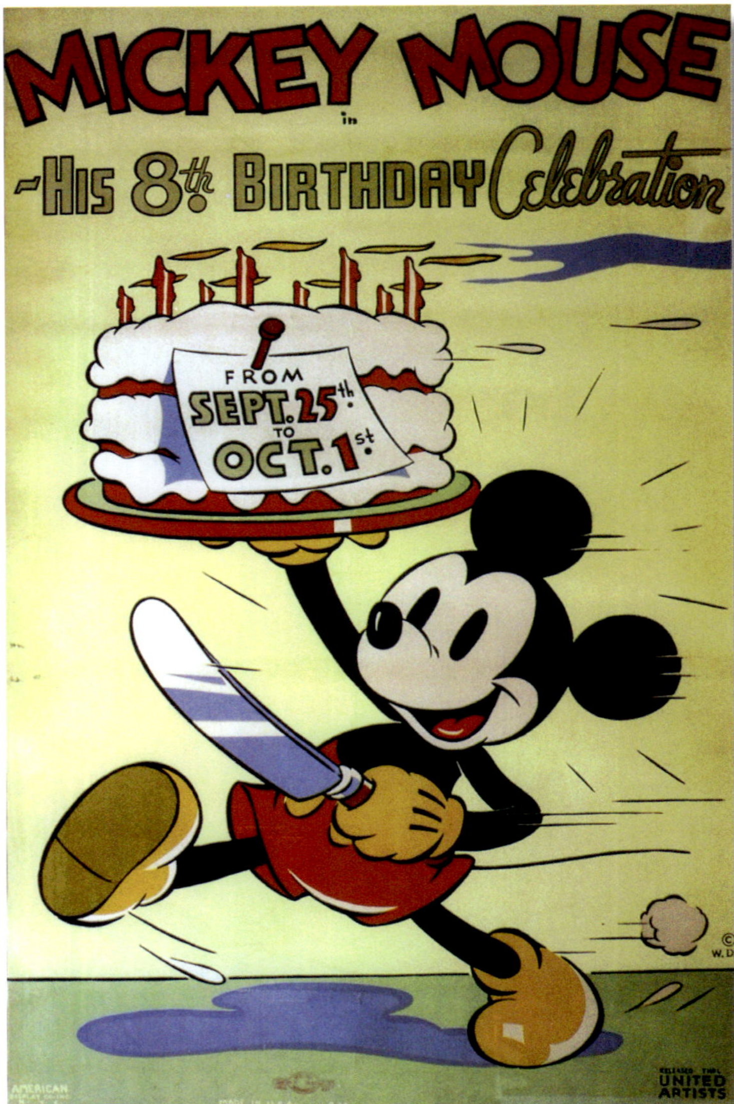

Courtesy of Hershenson/ Allen archive

Mickey Mouse 8th Birthday 1936 40x60
Estimate: $40,000 - $60,000

- There is 1 known to exist.

Mickey Mouse, Alpine Climbers 1936 40x60
Estimate: $35,000 - $55,000

- There is 1 known to exist.

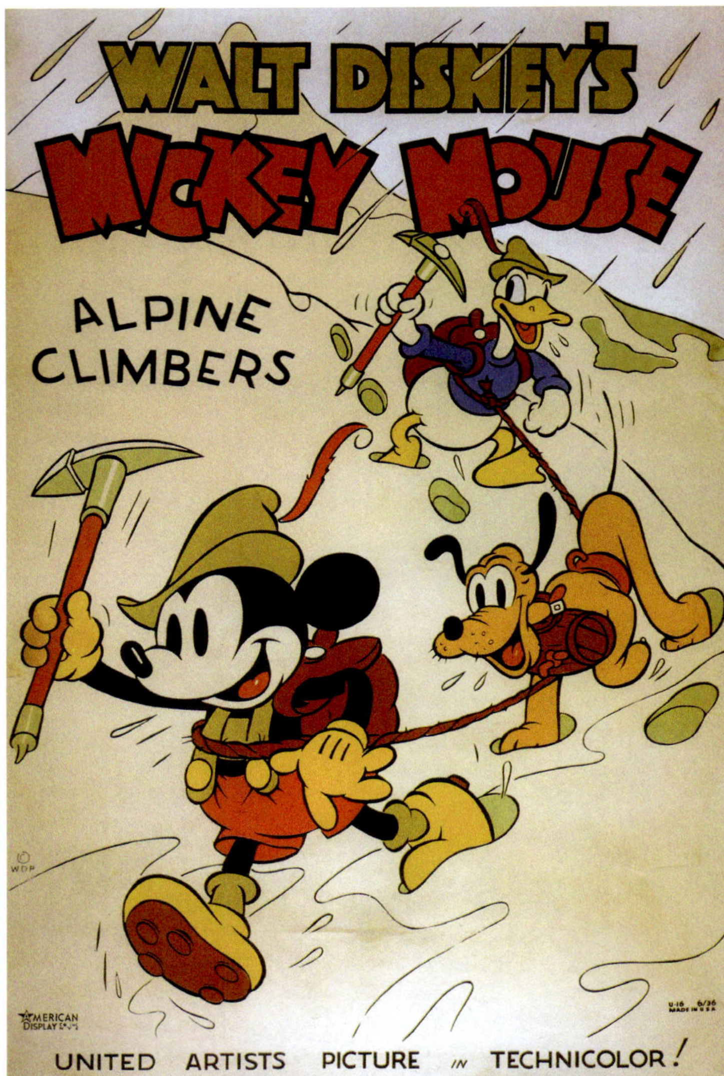

Courtesy of Hershenson / Allen archive

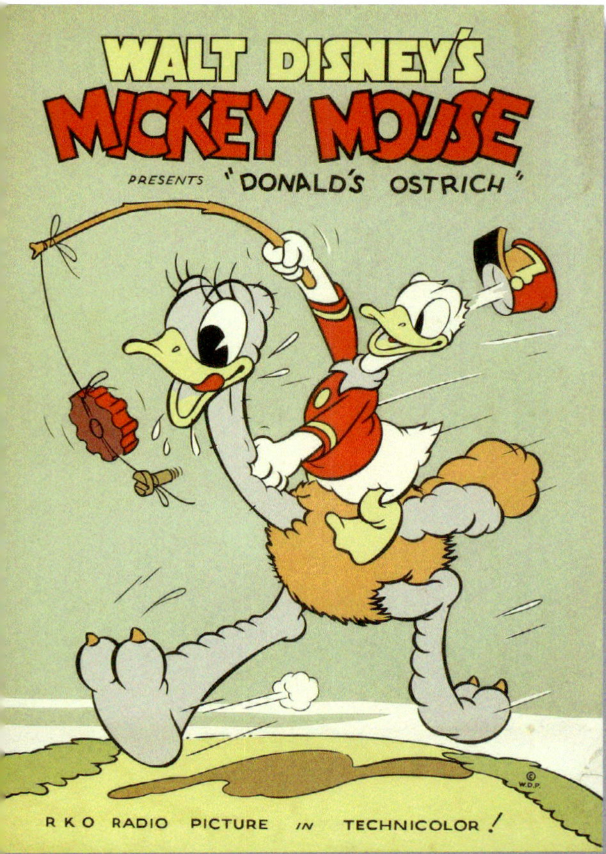

Courtesy of Heritage

Donald's Ostrich 1937 30x40
Heritage $7,475 FN 07/03
Estimate: $15,000 - $20,000

• There is 1 known to exist.

Don Donald 1937 40x60
Heritage $16,730 F/VF 11/09

• There is 1 known to exist.

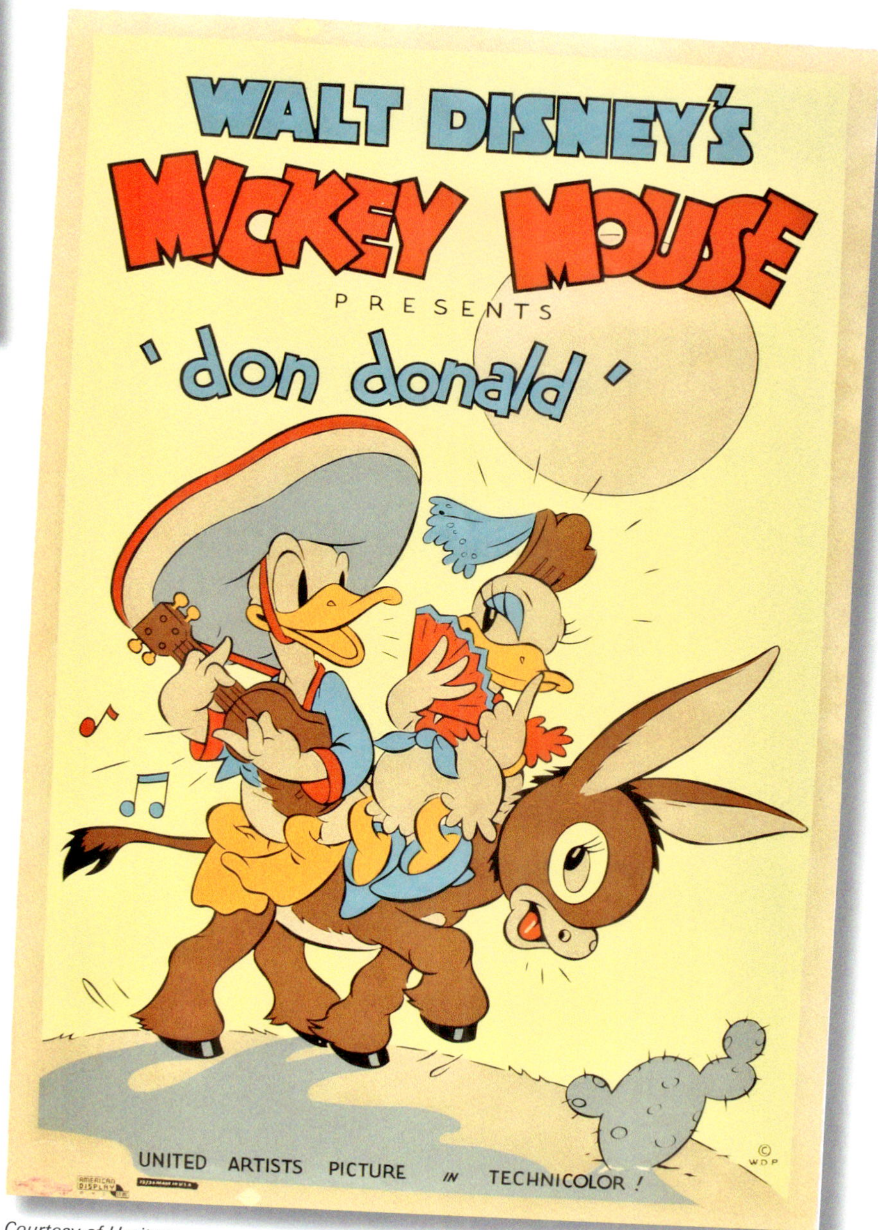

Courtesy of Heritage

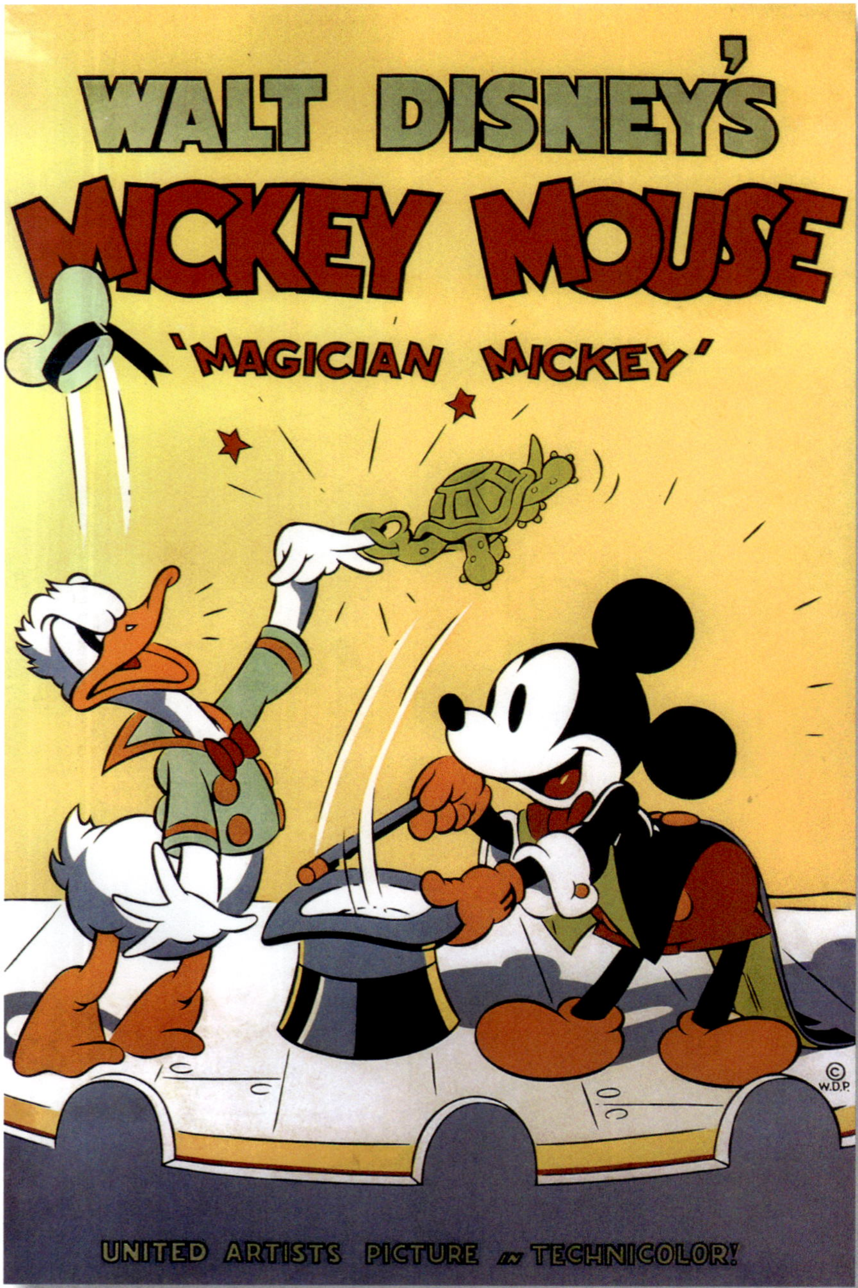

Courtesy of Hershenson/Allen archive

Magician Mickey 1937 40x60
Estimate: $35,000 - $55,000

- There is 1 known to exist.

Courtesy of Hershenson/ Allen archive

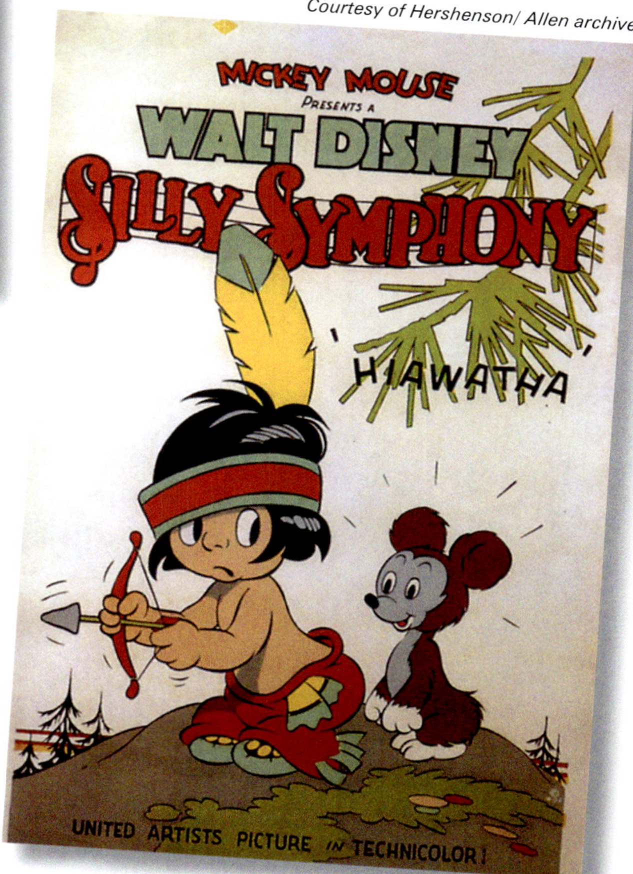

Silly Symphony, Hiawatha 1937 40x60
Estimate: $20,000 - $30,000

- There is 1 known to exist.

Mickey Mouse, Lonesome Ghosts	1937	30x40	
Heritage	$21,520	VF	07/09*
Heritage	$25,300	VF	07/06

• There is 1 known to exist.
* This is the same poster that appeared at the Heritage auction in 2006.

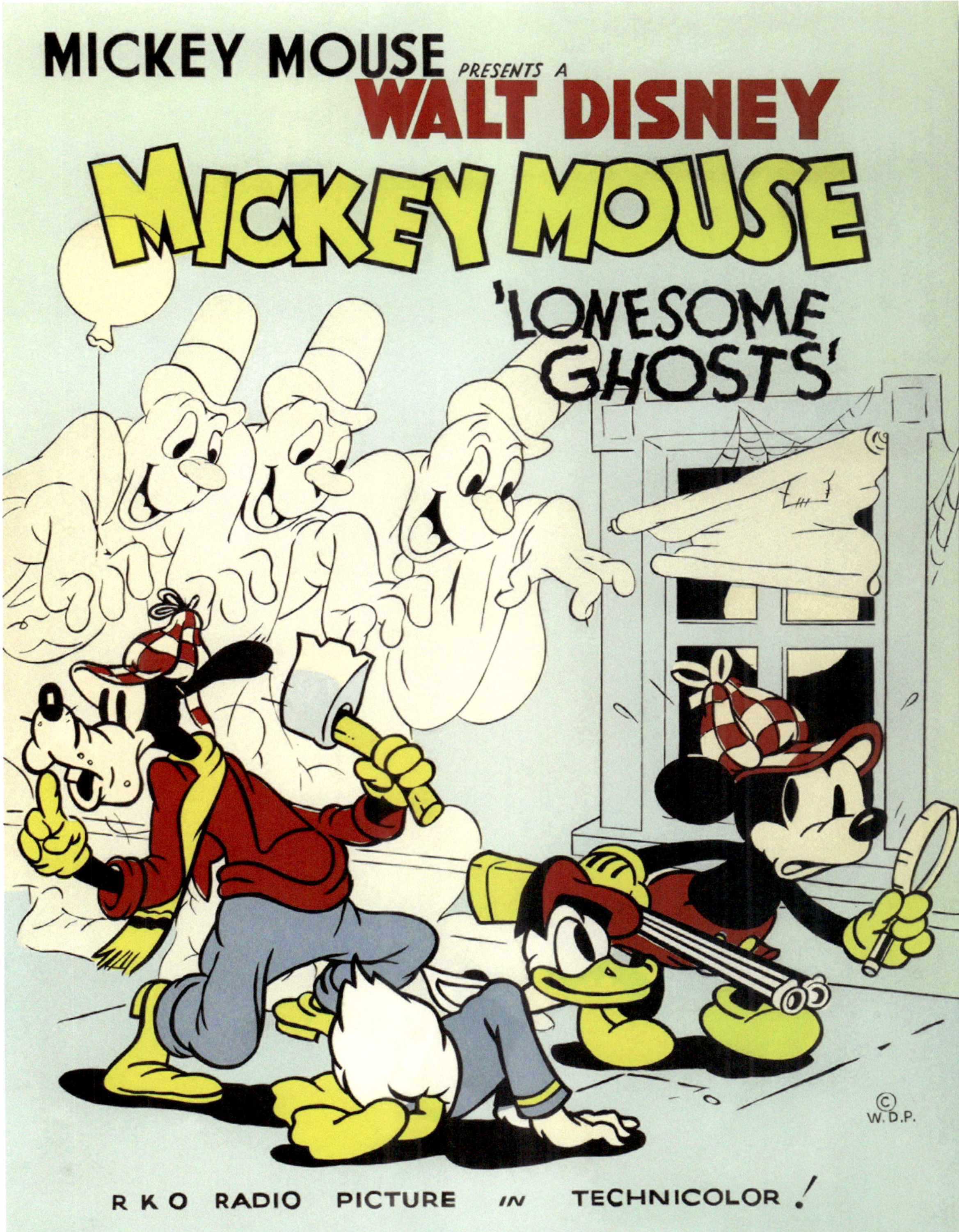

Courtesy of Heritage

Mickey Mouse, Hawaiian Holiday	1937	30x40
Heritage	$33,460	VF	03/09*
Heritage	$21,850	VF	03/04

• There is 1 known to exist.
* This is the same poster that appeared at the Heritage auction in 2004.

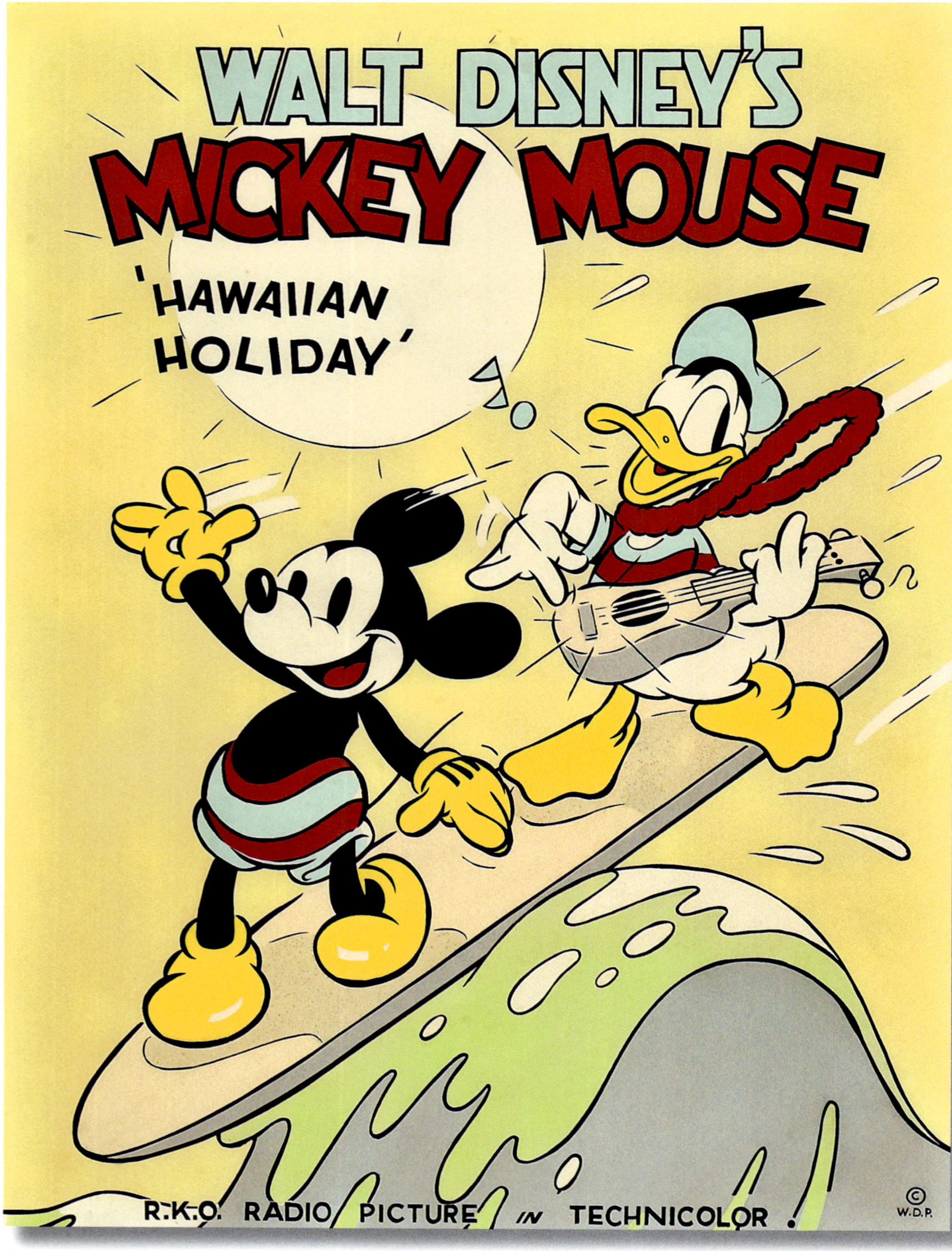

Courtesy of Heritage

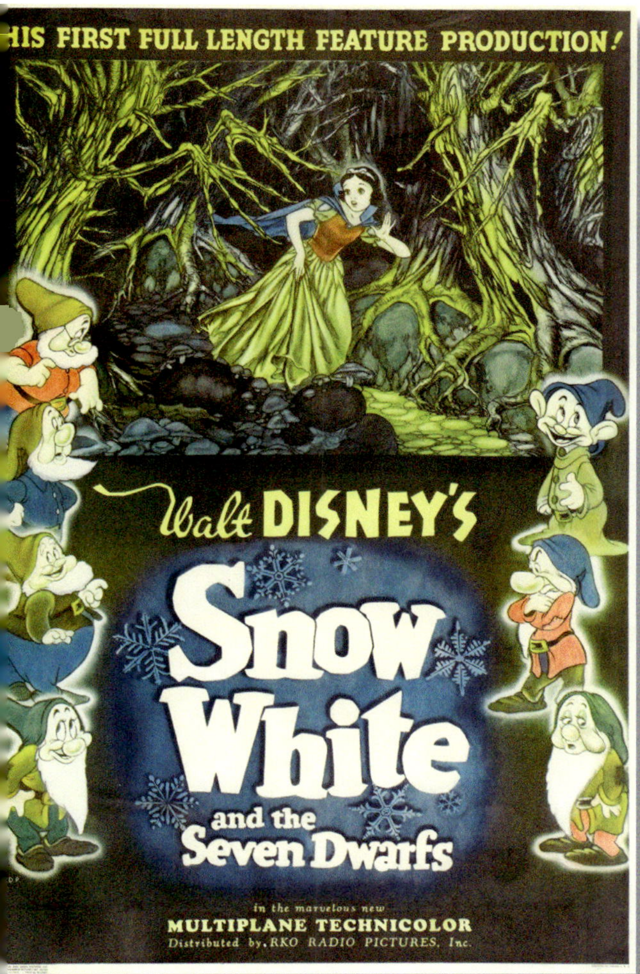

Courtesy of Heritage

Snow White—Style C	1937	27x41	
Heritage	$17,925	VG/FN	03/07
Heritage	$15,812	VG/FN	11/04
Butterfield & Butterfield	$21,850	VF	10/00
Lowery (rolled)	$32,200	VF	06/99

- This poster has appeared at auction 4 times since 1989.
- There is no *Snow White* 30x40 known to exist.

Snow White	1937	40x60	
Heritage	$65,725	VF+	11/07

- There are 2 known to exist.

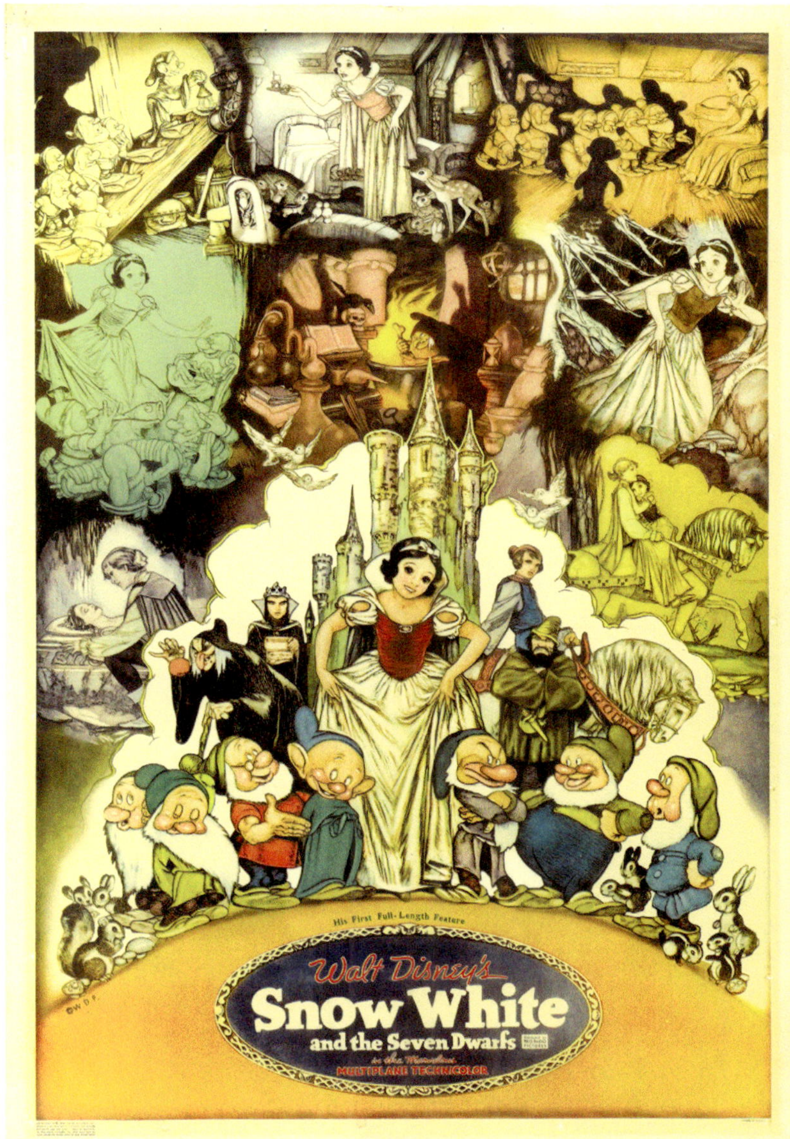

Courtesy of Heritage

Silly Symphony. Wynken, Blynken, and Nod 1938 30x40
Estimate: $15,000 - $20,000

- There is 1 known to exist.

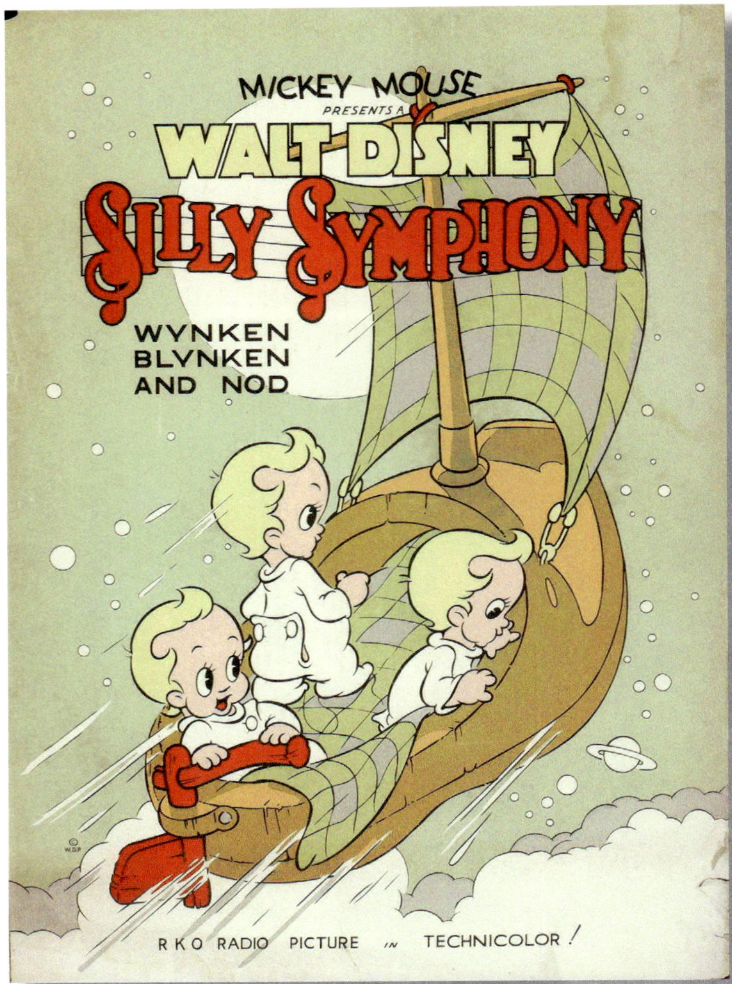

Courtesy of Heritage

Gulliver's Travel 1939 40x60
Heritage $1,840 FN 11/03
Estimate: $4,500 - $7,500

- There is 1 known to exist.

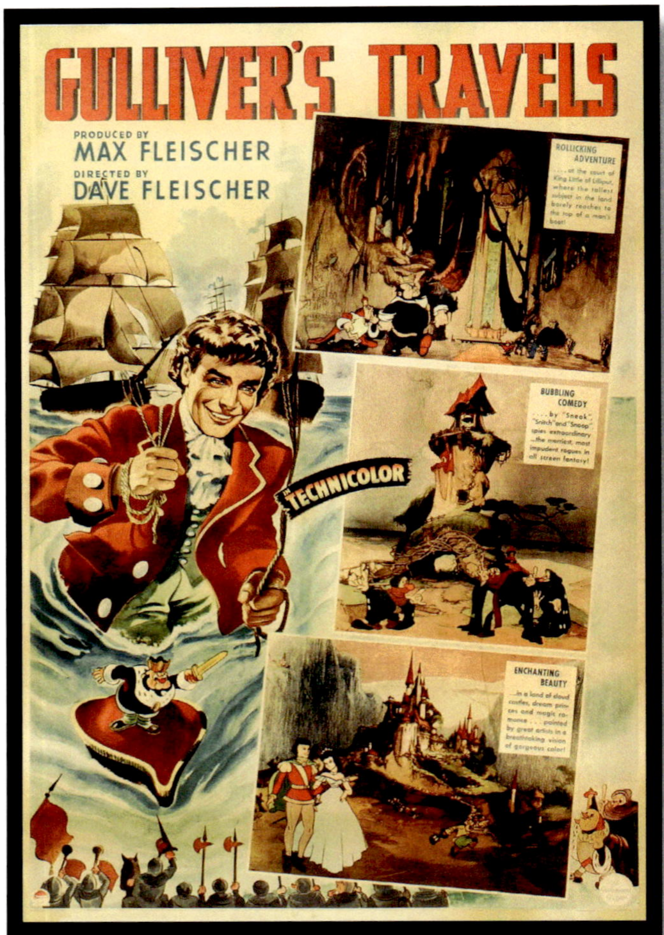

Courtesy of Heritage

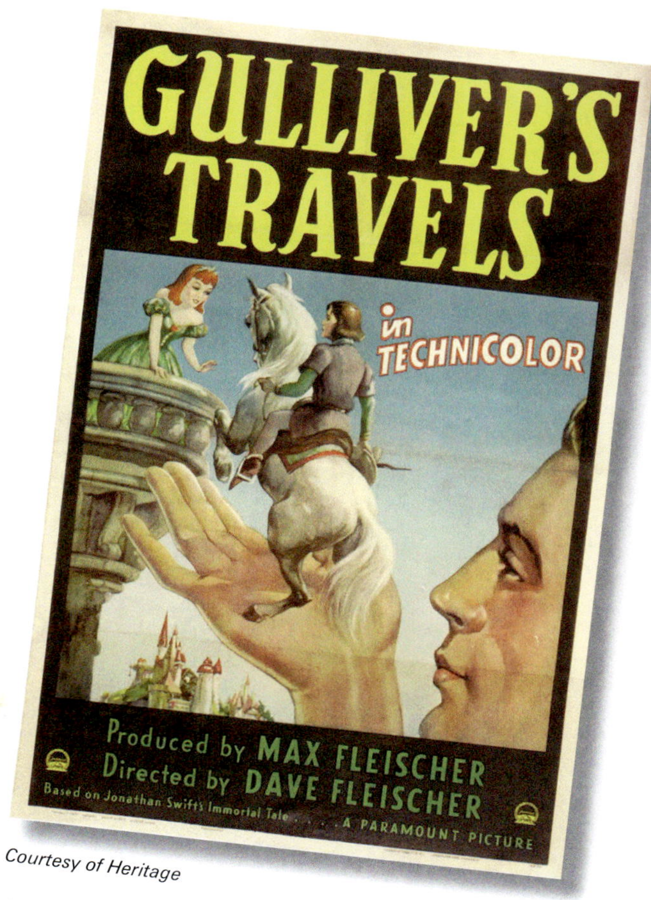

Courtesy of Heritage

Gulliver's Travels—Style B 1939 27x41

Heritage	$805	FN+	11/04
eMoviePoster	$598	VF	07/04
Christie's	DNS	VF-	09/03
Butterfield & Butterfield	$2,875	FN	11/96
Camden House	$1,600	FN	06/94

Highest price realized:

Butterfield's	$2,875	FN	11/96

Price in 1992:

Sotheby's	$1,600	GD	09/92

- This poster has appeared at auction 6 times since 1989.
- There is no *Gulliver's Travels* 30x40 known to exist.

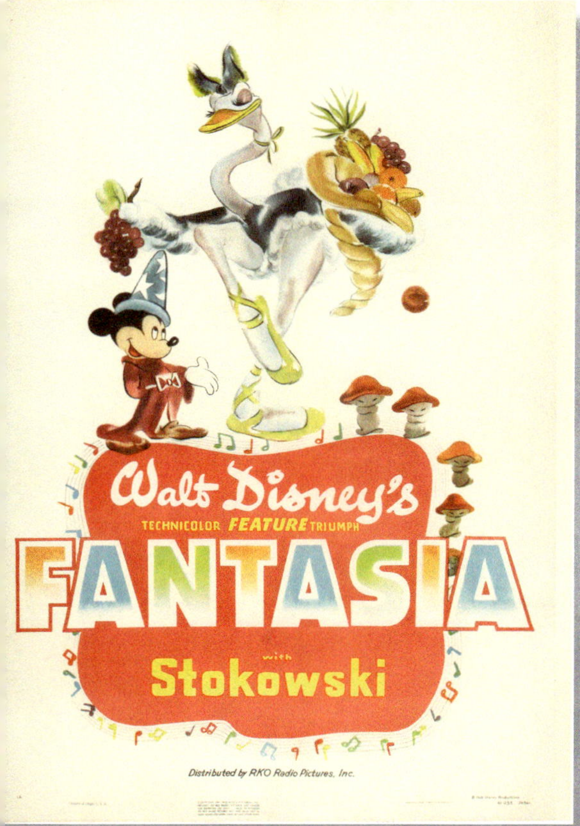

Courtesy of Heritage

Fantasia— Style A	1940	27x41	
Christie's	$5,975	VF	11/09
eMoviePoster	$1,613	VG	12/05
Heritage	$6,325	VF+	11/04
Heritage	$4,600	VF+	03/04
eMoviePoster	$3,605	VG	07/01
Highest Price:			
Christie's	$6,600	VF	12/92
Price in 1992:			
Christie's	$6,600	VF	12/92

• This poster has appeared at auction 14 times since 1989.

Courtesy of Christie's

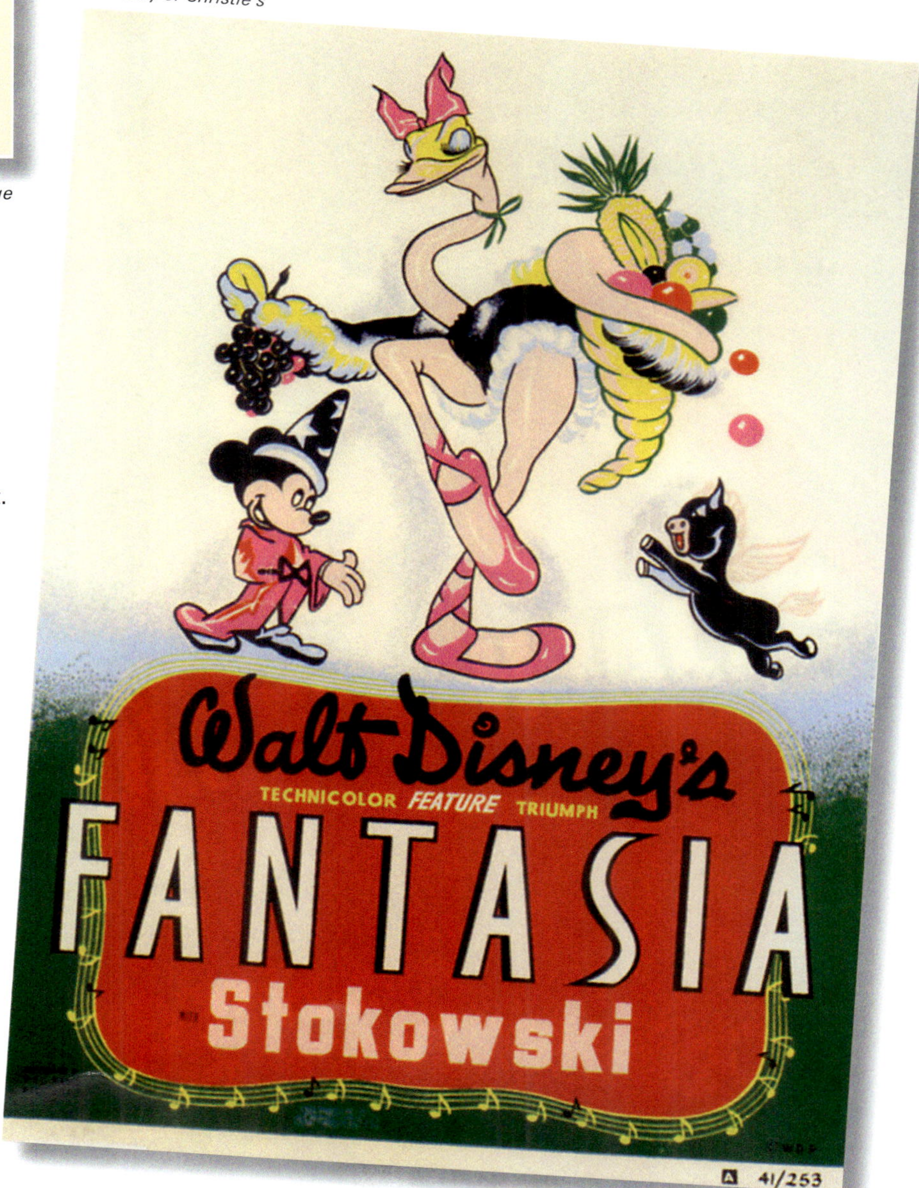

Fantasia	1940	30x40	
Lowery	$2,761	FN	12/05
Christie's	$4,833	VF	03/03

Estimate: $7,500 - $9,500

• There are 2 known to exist.
• There is no *Fantasia* 40x60 known to exist.

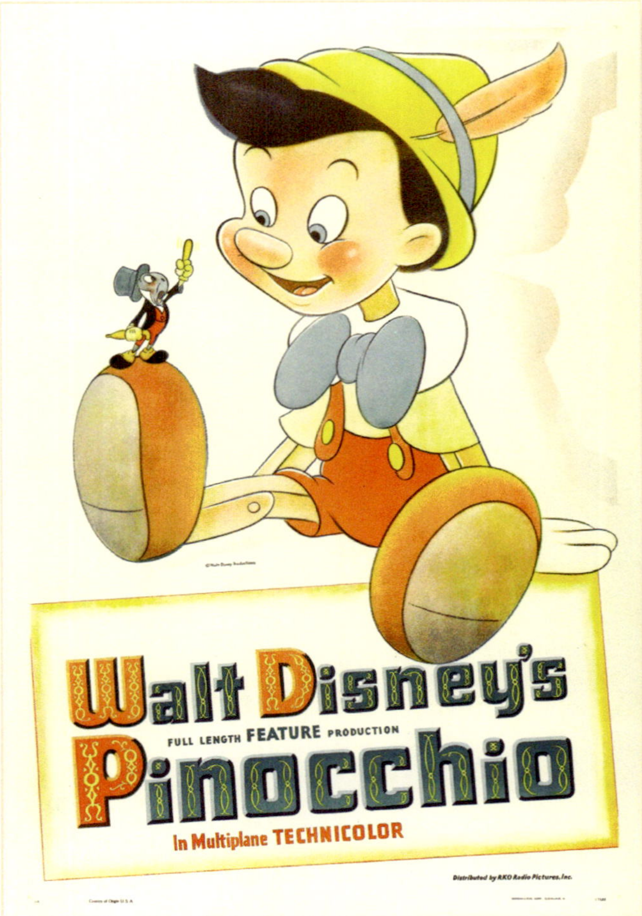

Courtesy of Heritage

Pinocchio 1940 27x41 Style A

Heritage	$5,175	VF+	07/06
Butterfield & Butterfield	$4,025	NM	10/00
Lowery	$5,290	NM	12/98
Christie's	$6,050	VF	12/92

- This poster has appeared at auction 4 times since 1989.
- There is no *Pinocchio* 30x40 known to exist.

Pinocchio—Style A 1940 40x60

Heritage	$5,377	FN+	07/09
Heritage	$7,170	FN-	11/07
Heritage	$13,145	FN-	03/07

- There are 3 known to exist.
- There is no *Pinocchio* 40x60 Style B known to exist.

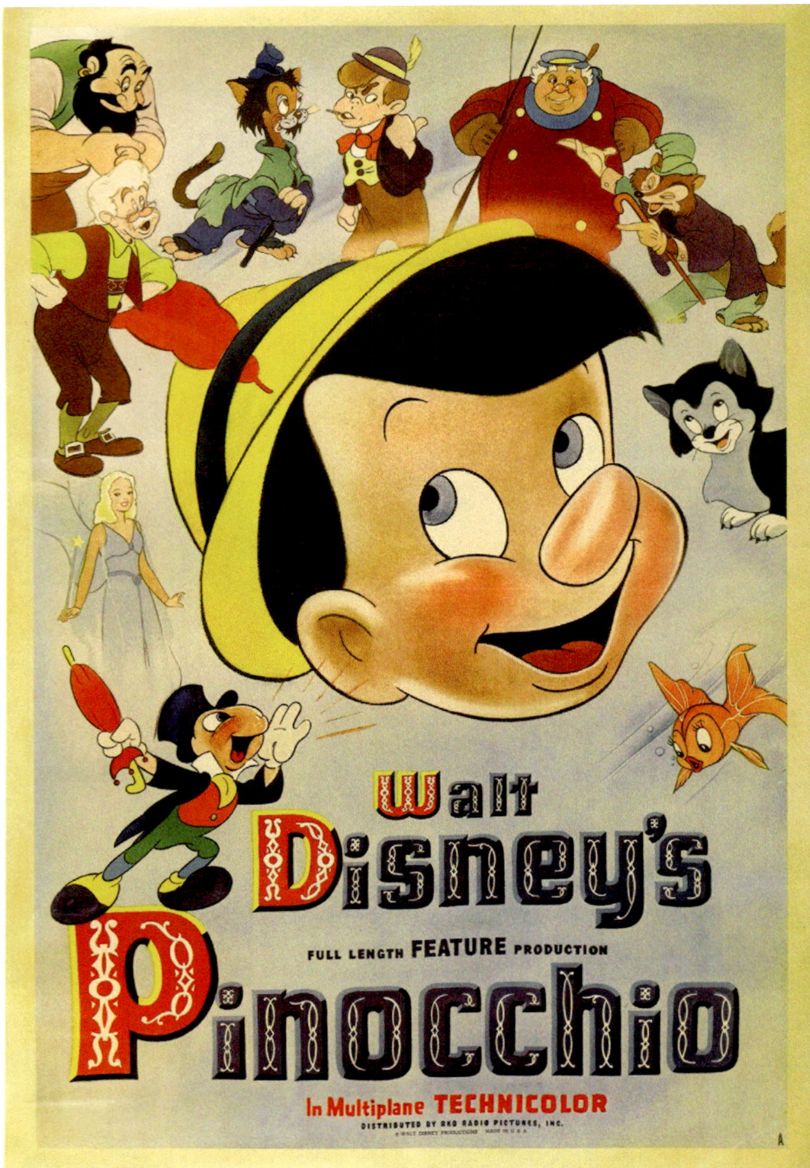

Courtesy of Heritage

MOVIE POSTERS OF THE 1940s

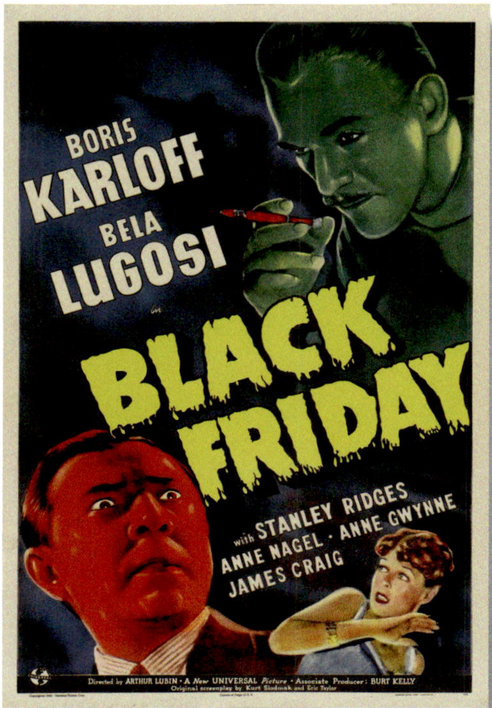

Courtesy of Heritage

Black Friday 1940 27x41			
Heritage	$5,462	NM	03/06
Heritage	$6,326	VF/NM	11/03
Christie's	$1,840	VF	03/96
Christie's	$4,830	FN	12/93
Christie's	$4,400	FN	12/92

Highest price realized:

Heritage	$6,326	VF/NM	11/03

Price in 1992:

Christie's	$4,400	FN	12/92

- This poster has appeared at auction 6 times since 1989.
- There is no *Black Friday* 30x40 known to exist.

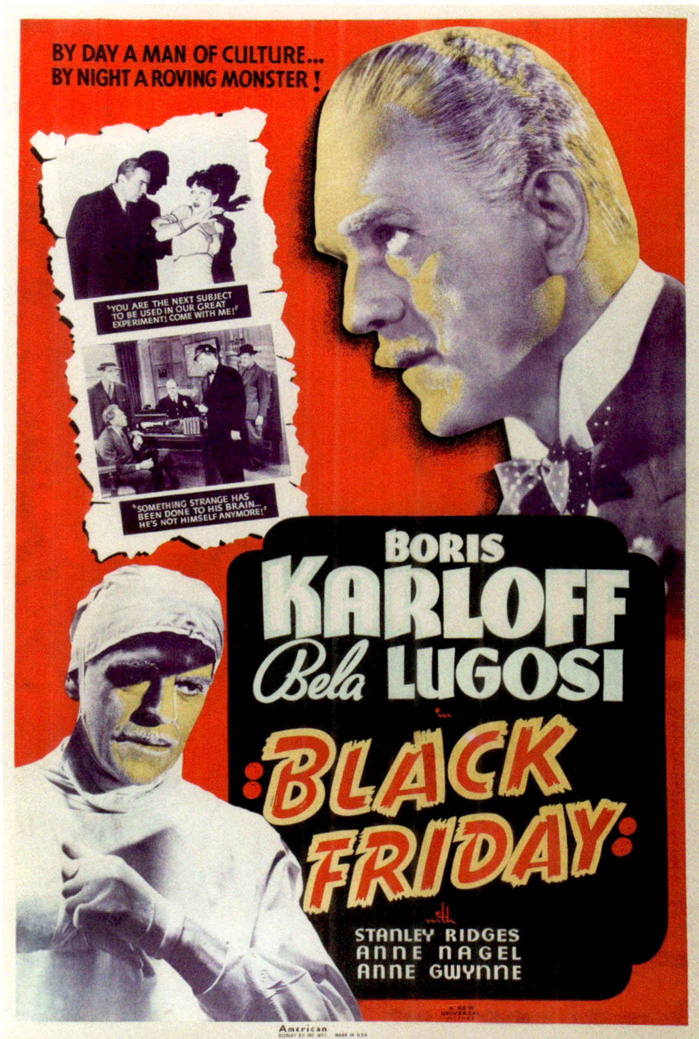

Photo by R. Aaron Raymond & Stephen Allard

Black Friday 1940 40x60			
Vintage Poster Art	$4,200	VF	05/09

- There is 1 known to exist.

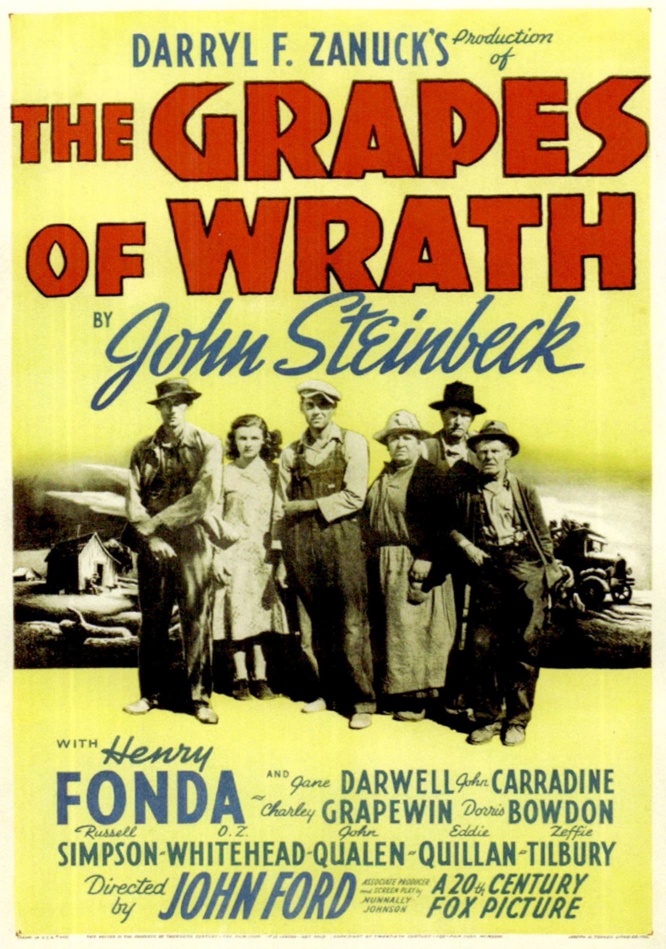

Courtesy of Heritage

Grapes of Wrath—Style B	1940	27x41	
Heritage	$10,755	FN	03/08
Private	$4,100	NM	04/01
Butterfield's	$4,600	VF	11/99
Butterfield's	$3,136	FN	05/96
Sotheby's	$4,600	FN	12/95

Highest price realized:

Heritage	$10,755	FN	03/08

Price in 1991:

Christie's	$5,280	FN	12/91

- This poster has appeared at auction 7 times since 1989.
- There is no *Grapes of Wrath* 30x40 known to exist.

Courtesy of Christie's

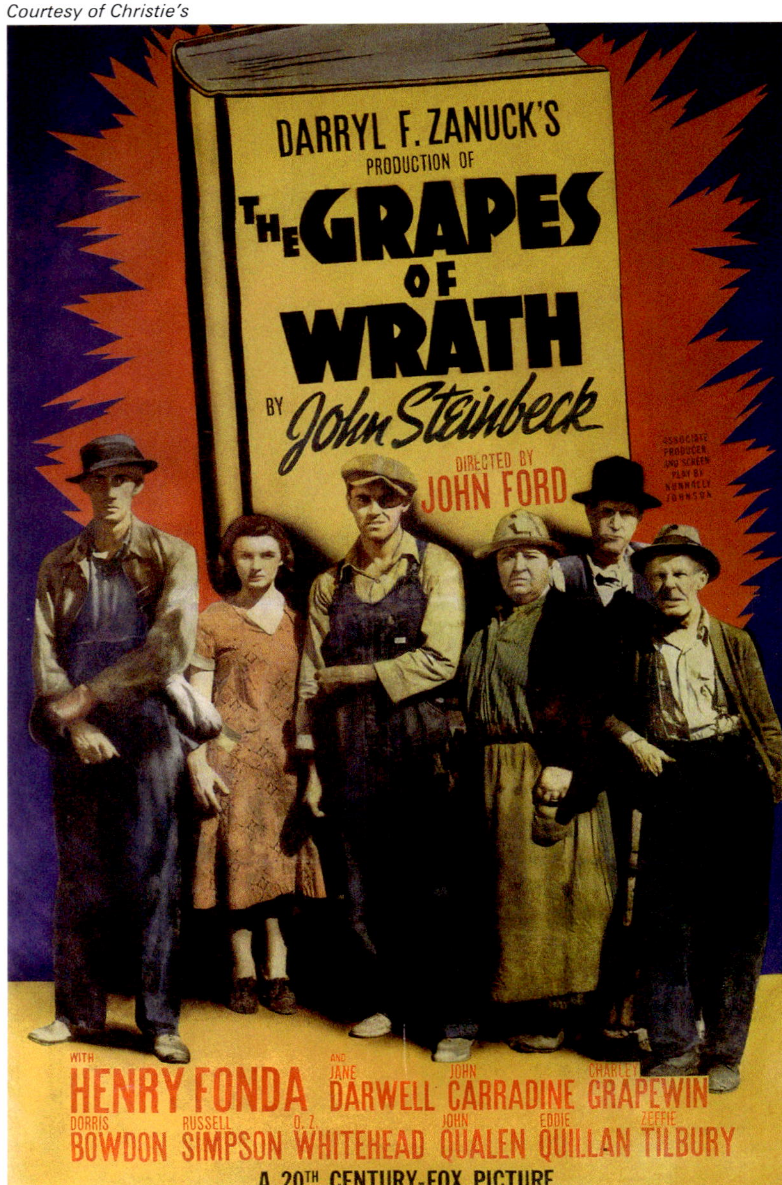

Grapes of Wrath	1940	40x60	
Christie's	$12,650	GD	12/95

Estimate: $25,000 - $35,000

- There is 1 known to exist.

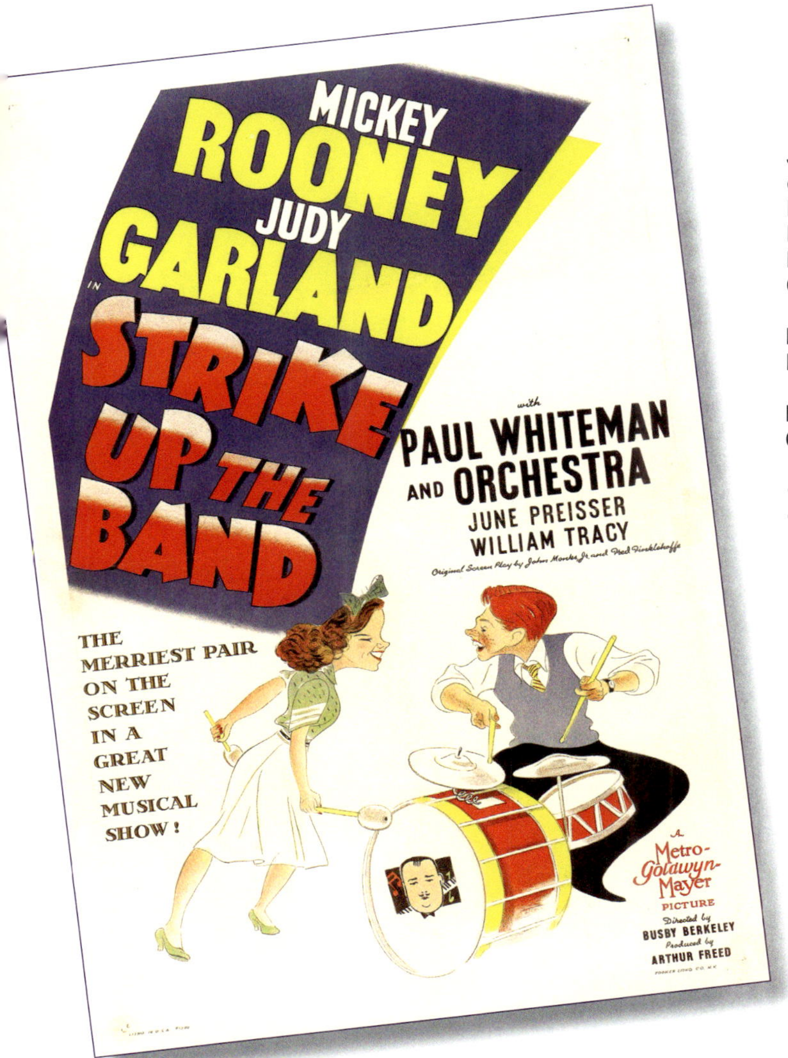

Courtesy of Heritage

Strike Up the Band	1940	27x41	
eMoviePoster	$318	VG	03/08
Heritage	$478	FN/VF	11/06
Bonhams & Butterfields	$1,293	VF	12/05
Butterfield & Butterfield	$460	VF	05/96
Camden House	$600	VF	11/94

Highest price realized:

Bonhams & Butterfields	$1,293	VF	12/05

Price in 1992:

Camden House	$200	VG	11/92

- This poster has appeared at auction 7 times since 1989.
- There is no *Strike up the Band* 30x40 known to exist.

Courtesy of Heritage

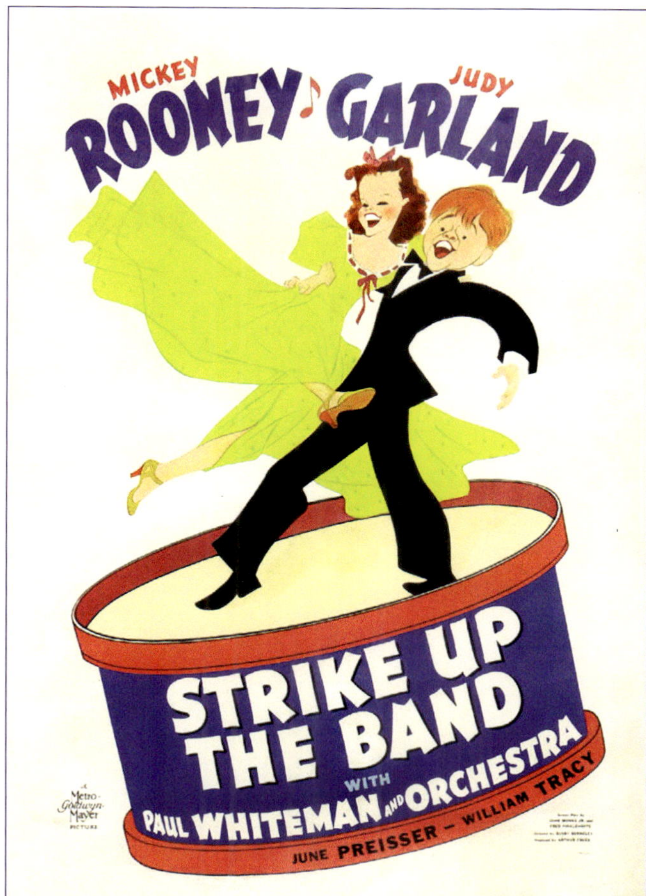

Strike Up the Band	1940	40x60	
Heritage	$1,725	FN	11/04

Estimate: $2,500 - $4,000

- There is 1 known to exist.

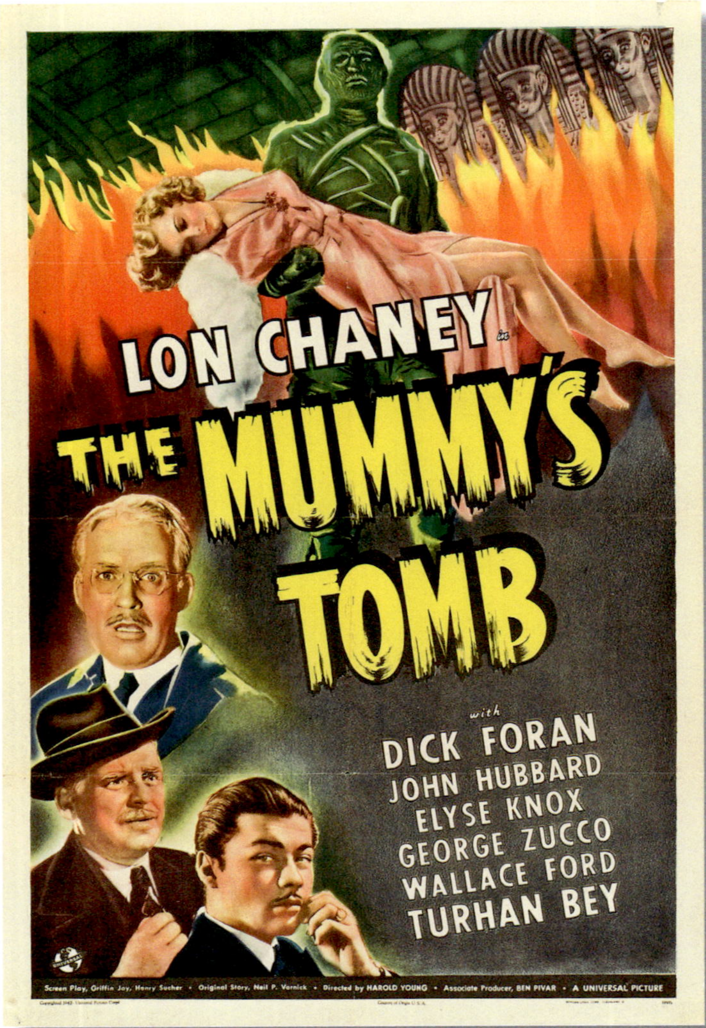

Courtesy of Heritage

Mummy's Tomb	1942	27x41	
Heritage	$8.962	VF+	03/09
Heritage	$5,290	VF+	10/02
Christie's	$4,370	FN	12/97
Christie's	$4,140	FN	12/93

- This poster has appeared at auction 5 times since 1989.
- There is no *Mummy's Tomb* 30x40 known to exist.

Mummy's Tomb	1942	40x60	
Sotheby's	DNS	VF	12/99

Estimate: $12,000 -$18,000

- There is 1 known to exist.

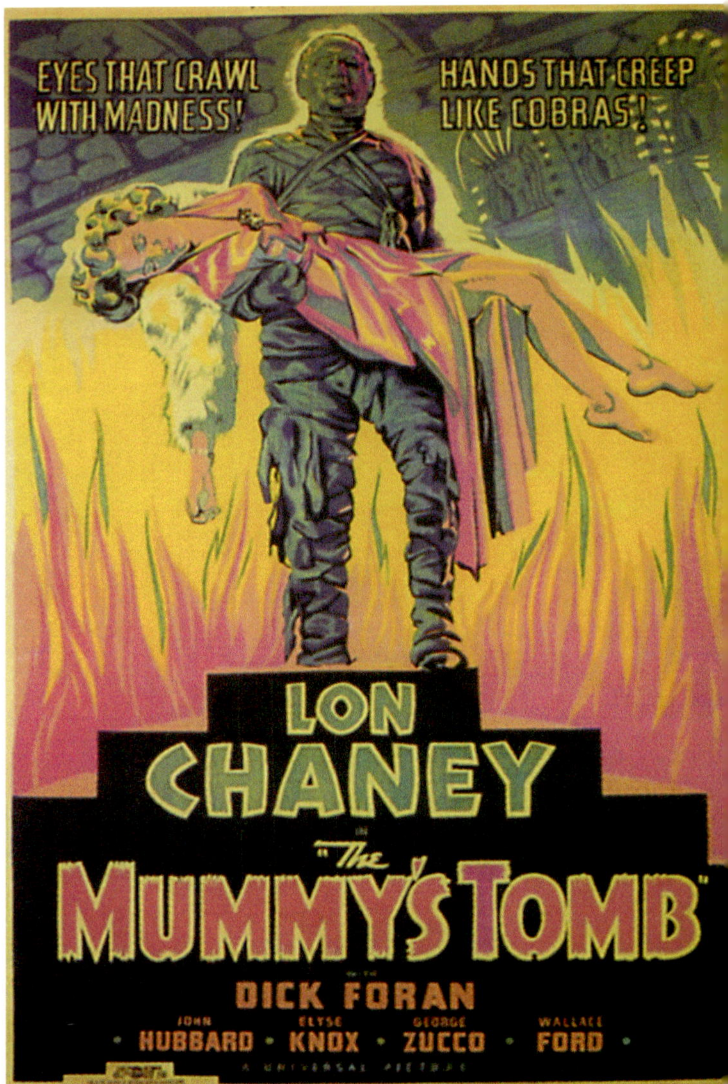

Courtesy of Sotheby's

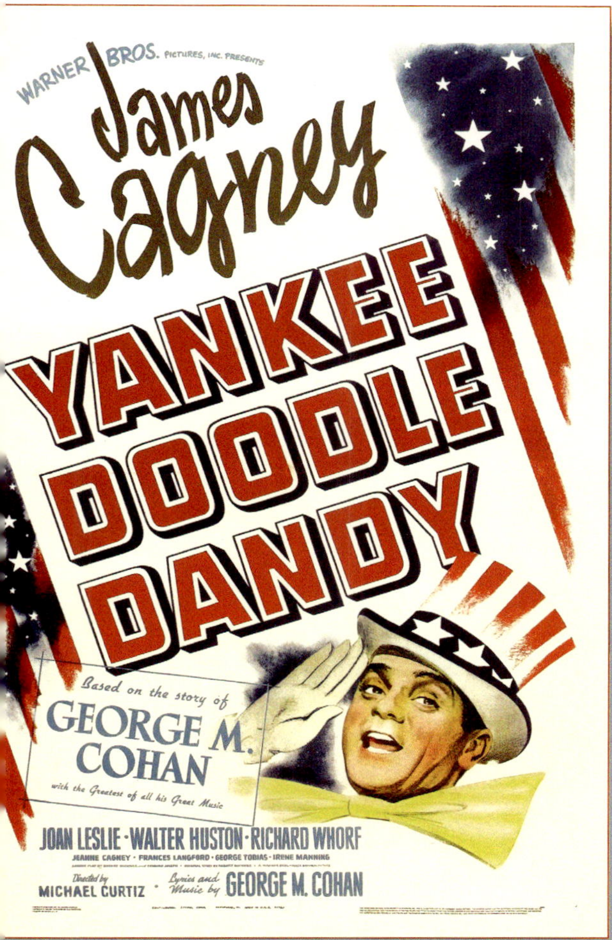

Courtesy of Heritage

Yankee Doodle Dandy 1942 27x41

eMoviePoster	$550	VF	10/09
eMoviePoster	$460	VG	12/08
eMoviePoster	$385	GD/VG	03/08
Heritage	$657	VF+	01/08
Heritage	$1,195	VG/FN	03/07

Highest price realized:

Heritage	$1,955	NM	03/05

Price in 1990:

Camden House	$450	VF	10/90

- This poster has appeared at auction 18 times since 1989.
- There is no *Yankee Doodle Dandy* 30x40 known to exist.

Photo by R. Aaron Raymond & Stephen Allard

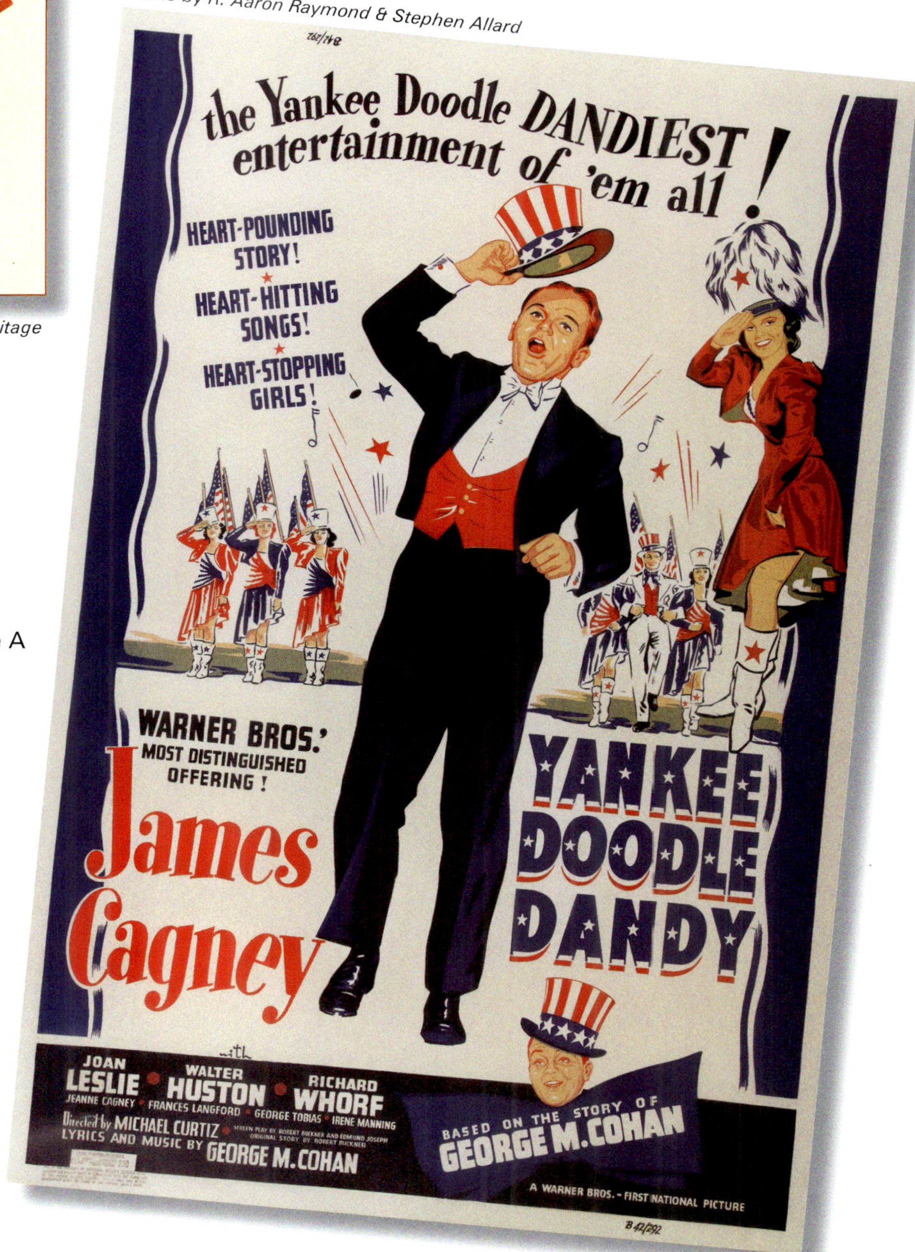

Yankee Doodle Dandy—Style B 1942 40x60
Estimate: $2,500 - $4,000

- There is 1 known to exist.
- There is no *Yankee Doodle Dandy* 40x60 Style A known to exist.

Murder My Sweet	1944	27x41	
Heritage	$3,833	VF-	11/09
Heritage	$3,585	FN-	11/08
Heritage	$7,170	VF	03/08
Heritage	$7,170	VF	07/07
Heritage	$1,782	VF	11/04

Highest price realized:
Heritage $7,170 VF 03/08

Price in 1990:
Camden House $850 FN 03/90

- This poster has appeared at auction 12 times since 1989.
- There is no *Murder My Sweet* 30x40 known to exist.

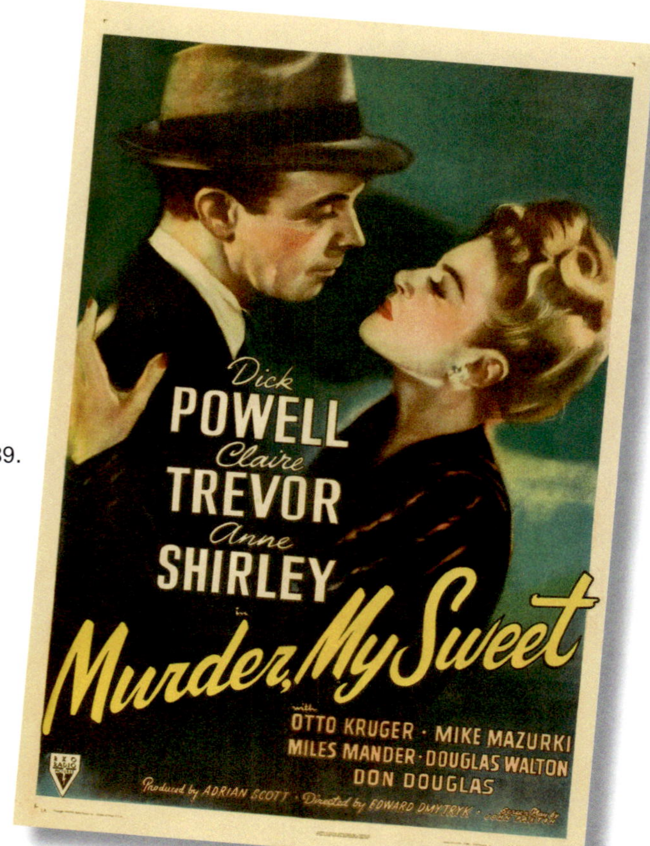

Courtesy of Heritage

Courtesy of Heritage

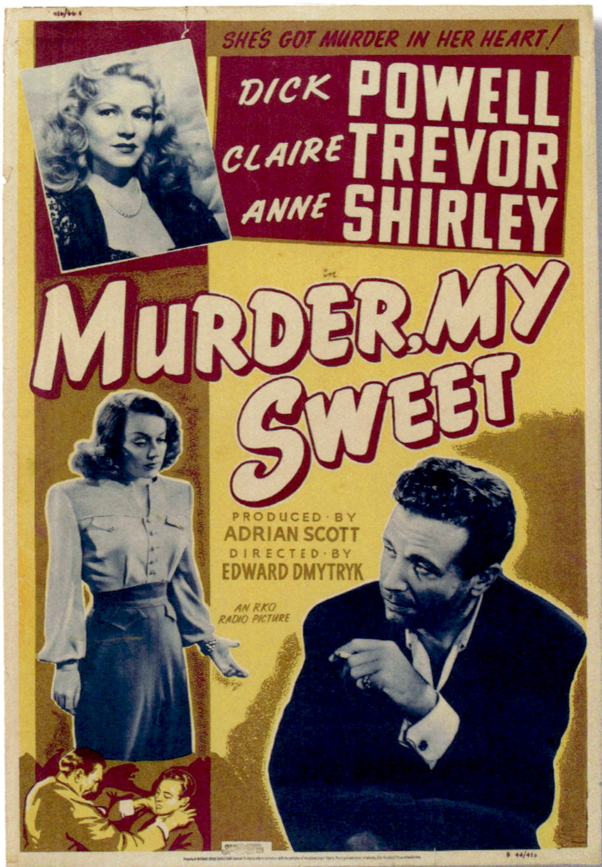

Murder My Sweet—Style B	1944	40x60	
Heritage	$836	VG/FN	12/08

- There is 1 known to exist.
- There is no *Murder My Sweet* 40x60 Style A known to exist.

Courtesy of Heritage

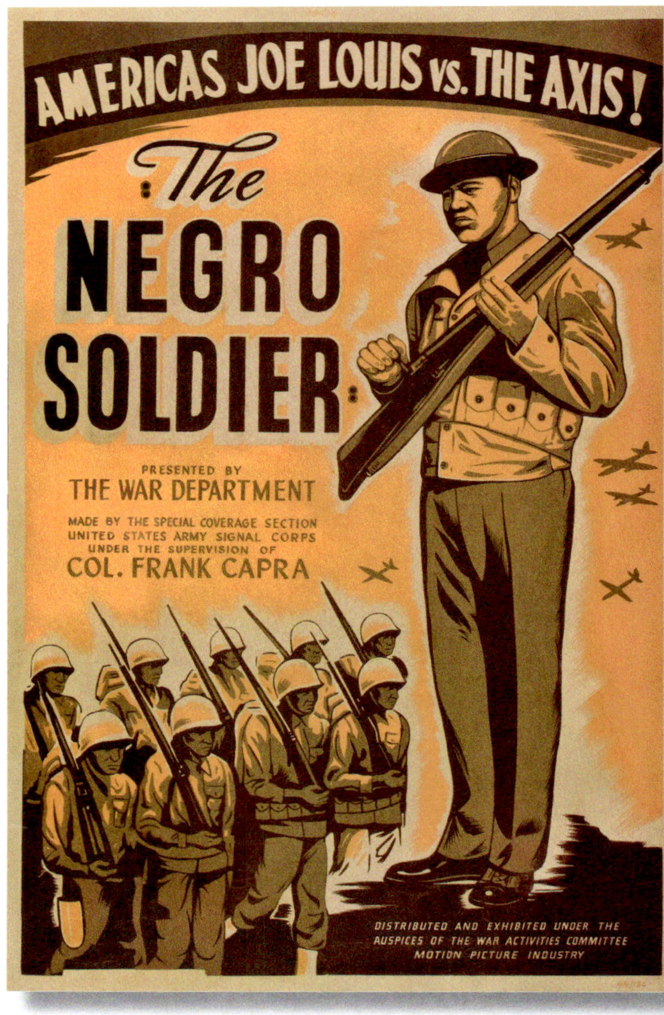

Negro Soldier	1944	40x60	
Heritage	$7,767	FN-	03/09

- There is 1 known to exist.
- There is no *Negro Soldier* 27x41 known to exist.
- There is no *Negro Soldier* 30x40 known to exist.

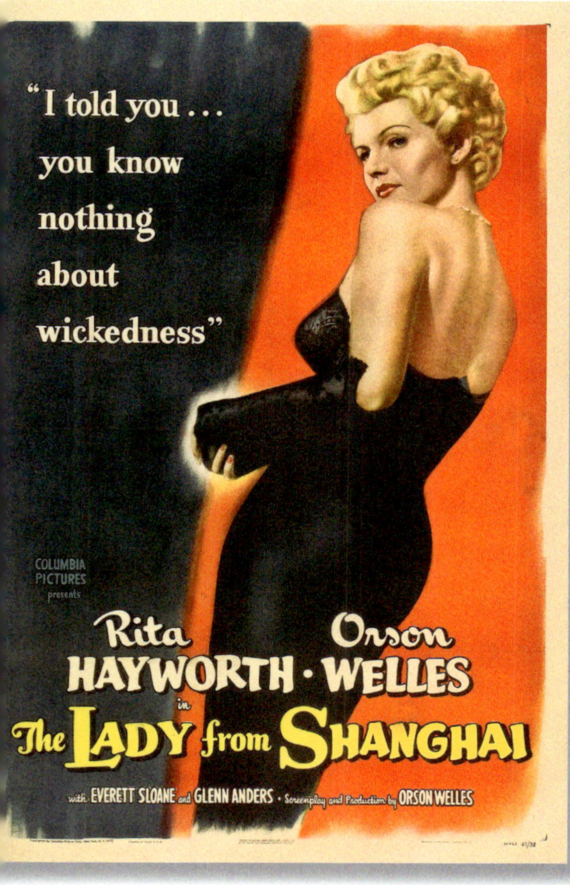

Courtesy of Heritage

Lady from Shanghai	1947	27x41	
eMoviePoster	$5,750	GD/VG	09/09
Heritage	$8,365	FN+	03/09
Heritage	$6,572	VF-	07/08
Heritage	$11,950	VF-	03/08
Christie's	$1,610	FN	12/97

Highest price realized:

Heritage	$11,950	VF-	03/08

Price in 1990:

Camden House	$1,500	NM	03/90

- This poster has appeared at auction 24 times since 1989.
- There is no *Lady from Shanghai* 30x40 known to exist.

Courtesy of Heritage

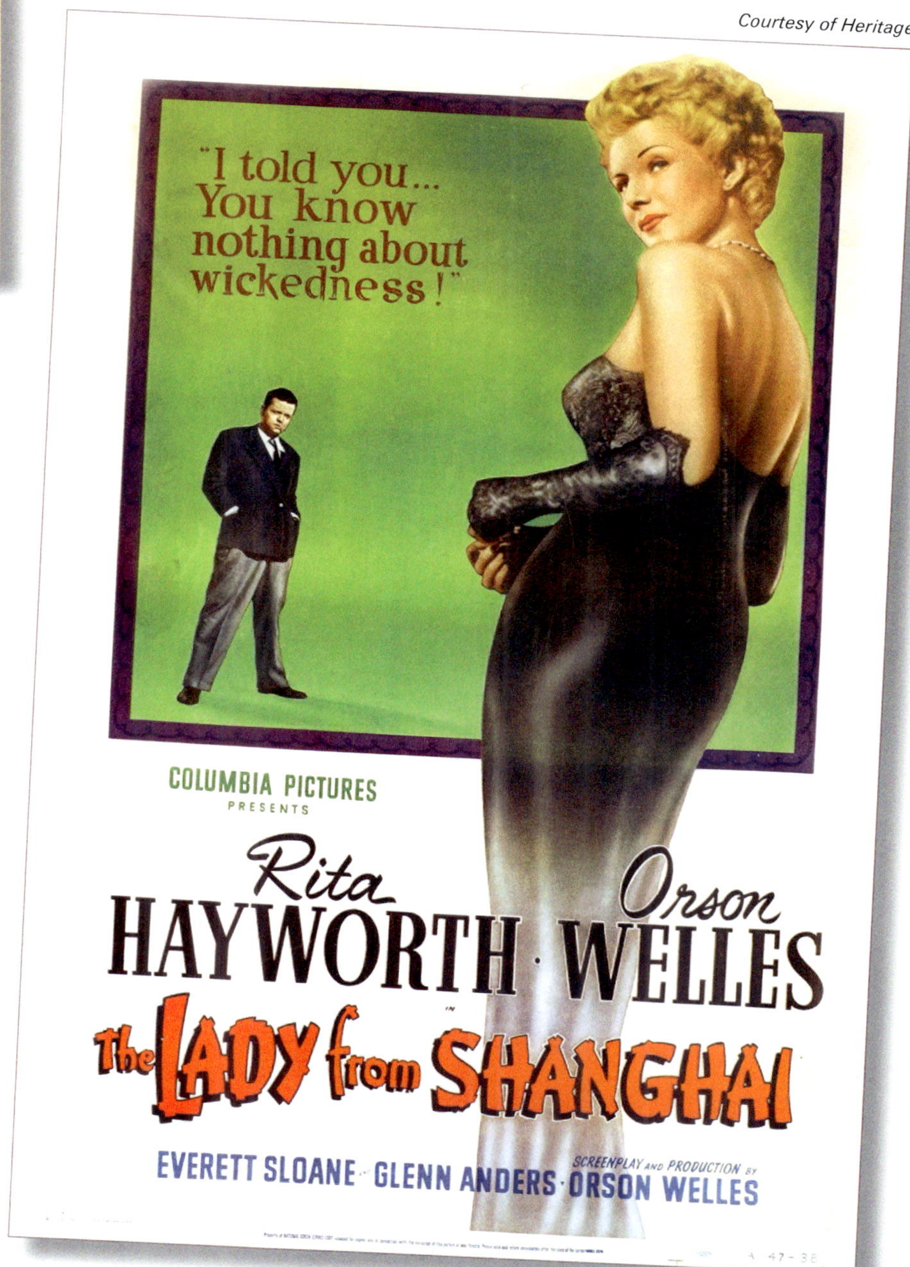

Lady from Shanghai—Style A	1947	40x60
Heritage $3,565	FN/VF	03/04

Estimate: $7,000 -$9,500

- There is 1 known to exist.
- There is no *Lady from Shanghai* 40x60 Style B known to exist.

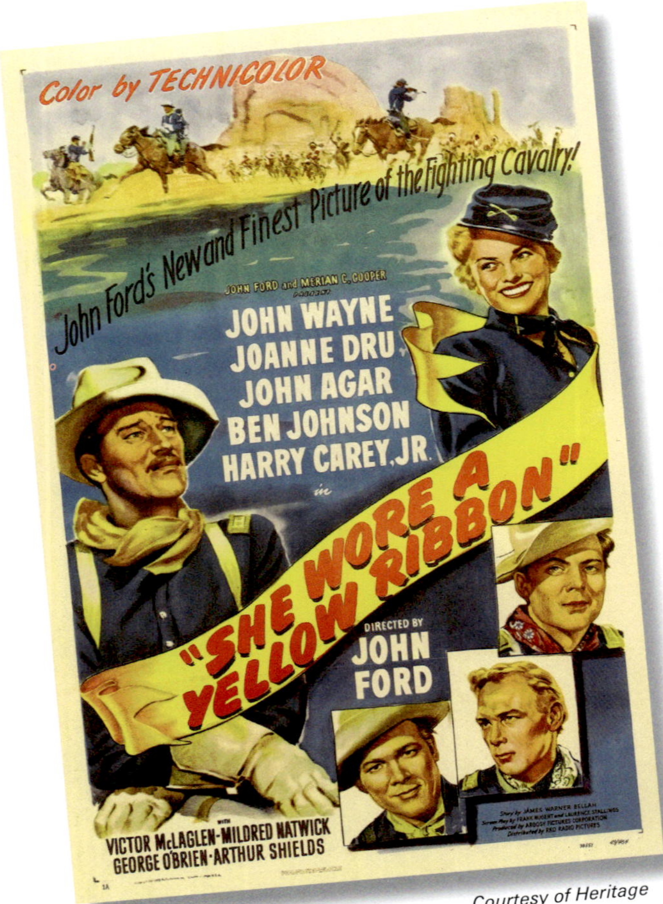

Courtesy of Heritage

She Wore a Yellow Ribbon	1949	27x41	
Heritage	$1,434	VF+	07/08
Heritage	$1,912	VF+	03/07
eMoviePoster	$811	GD/VG	07/04
Sotheby's	DNS	VF	10/00
Christie's	$937	VG	07/97

Highest Price Realized:

Christie's	$2,300	FN	06/95

Price in 1990:

Christie's	$850	VF	10/90

- This poster has appeared at auction 16 times since 1989.

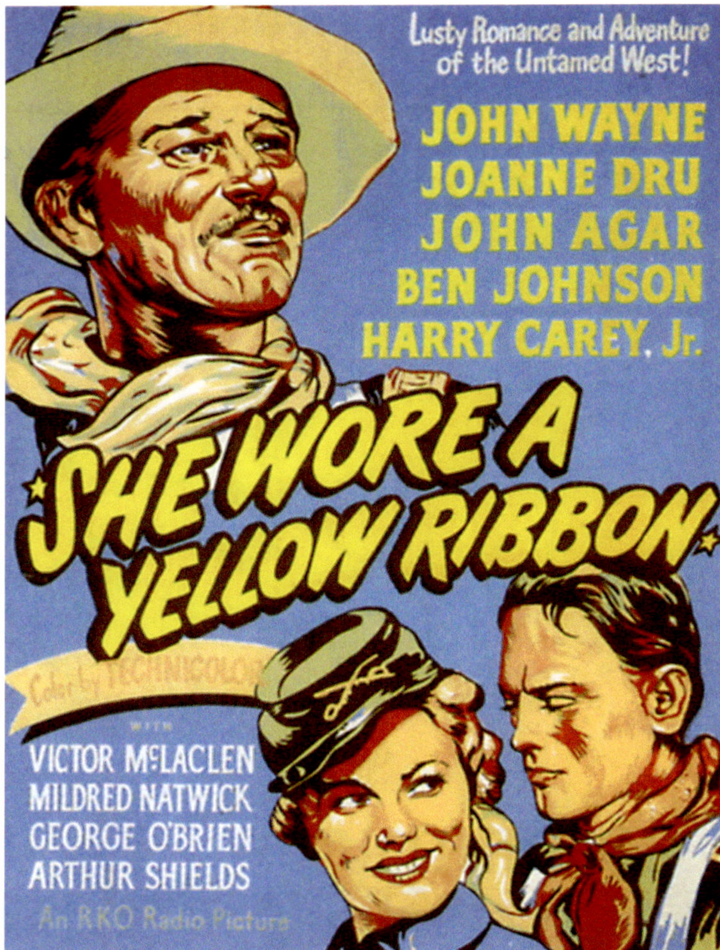

Courtesy of Christie's

She Wore a Yellow Ribbon	1949	30x40	
Vintage Poster Art	$300	FN	05/95
Christie's	$595	VF	12/93

Estimate: $2,000 - $3,000

- There are 2 known to exist.
- There is no *She Wore a Yellow Ribbon* 40x60 known to exist.

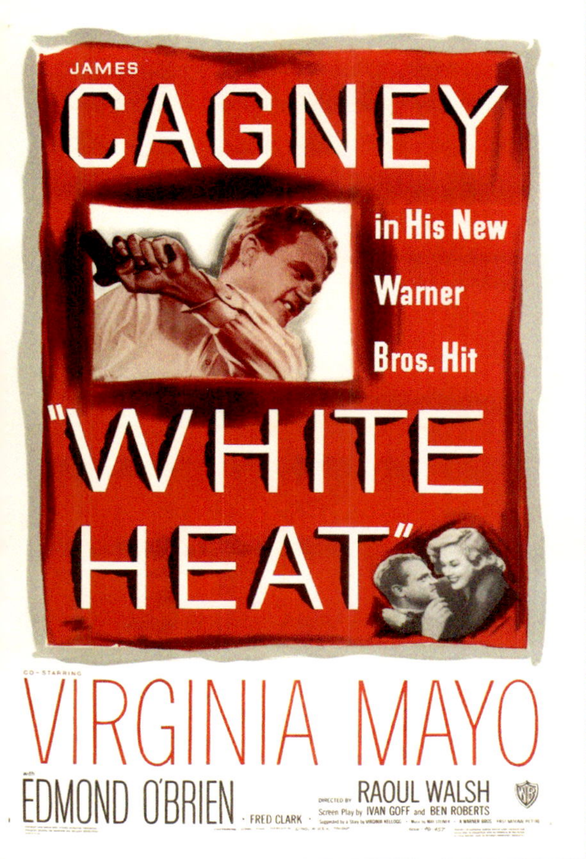

Courtesy of Heritage

White Heat 1949 27x41			
Heritage	$448	FN+	03/09
eMoviePoster	$410	G/VG	01/09
Heritage	$836	VF	03/08
Heritage	$657	VF	11/08
Heritage	$1,150	NM	07/06

Highest price realized:

Heritage	$1,150	NM	07/06

Price in 1995:

Butterfield & Butterfield	$300	VG	10/94

- This poster has appeared at auction 15 times since 1989.

Courtesy Skinner

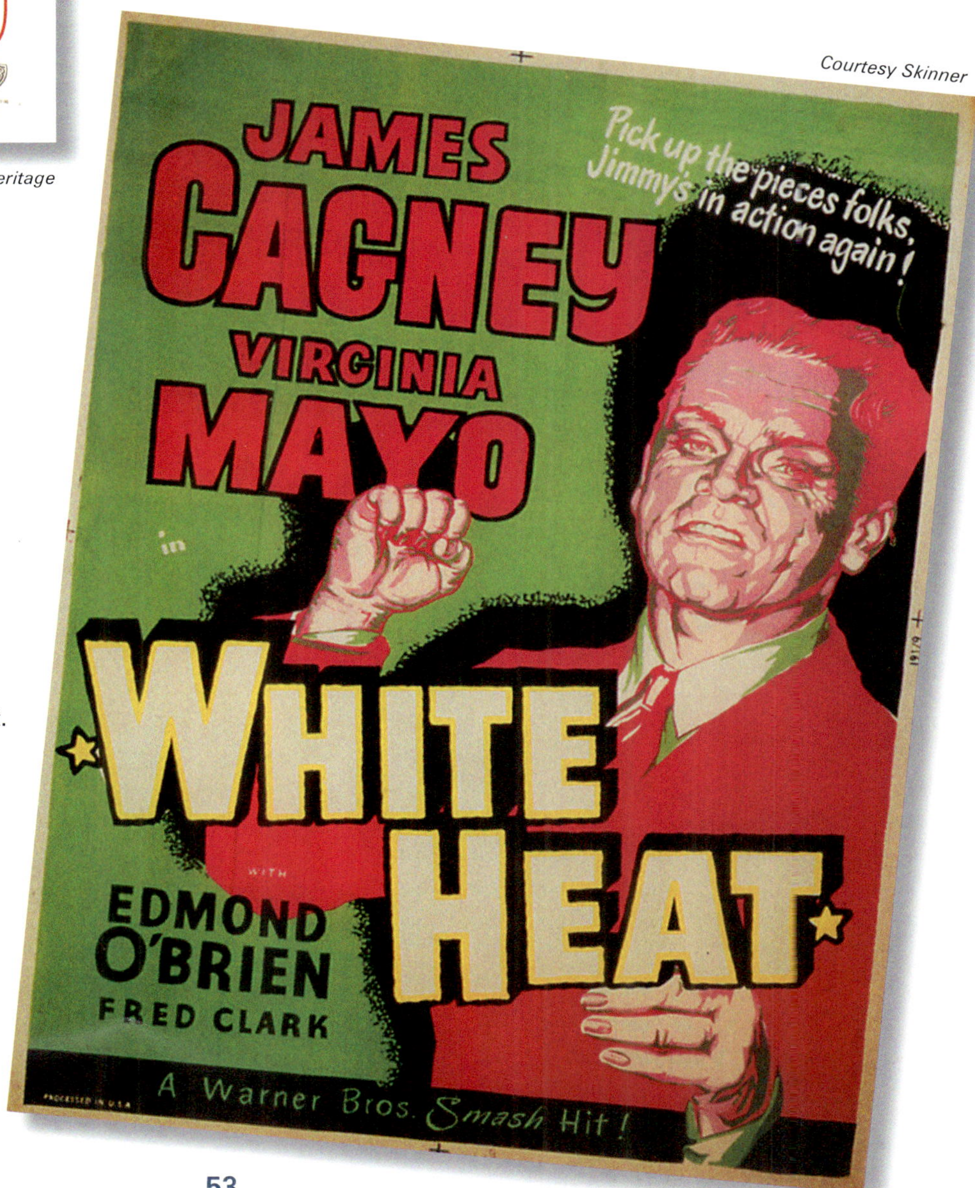

White Heat 1949 30x40			
Heritage (Faded)	$597	VF-	03/09
Skinner	DNS	VF	11/98

- There are 2 known to exist.
- There is no *White Heat* 40x60 known to exist.

MOVIE POSTERS OF THE 1950s

EVEN RARER...

Some silk-screened 30x40s from the 1950s have the unique distinction of having a black-and-white or color photo image attached to the final poster. The image was usually taken directly from a scene in the movie and was painstakingly applied to each poster by hand. These posters are almost impossible to find in very good condition.

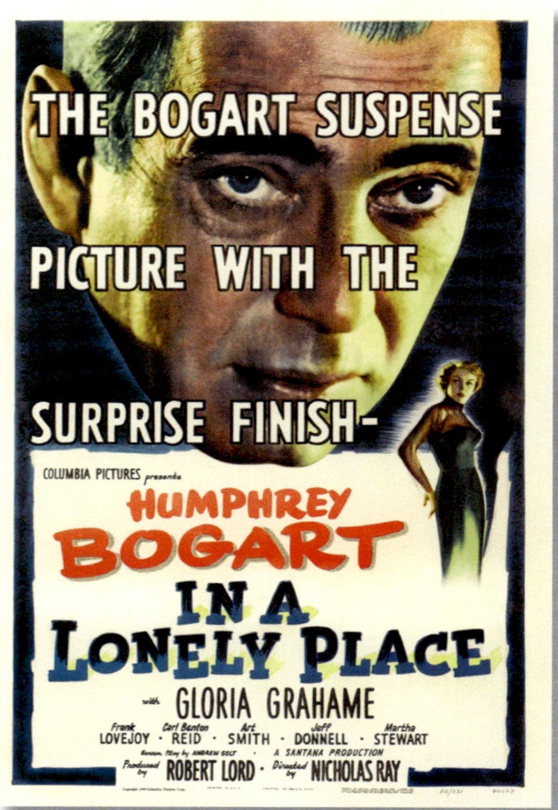

Courtesy of Heritage

In a Lonely Place	1950	30x40	
Heritage	$1,434	FN/VF	03/07
Private	$2,500	FN	09/97

- There are 2 known to exist.
- There is no *In a Lonely Place* 40x60 known to exist.

In a Lonely Place	1950	27x41	
Christie's	DNS	VF-	09/08
Heritage	$507	FN-	07/08
Heritage	$597	FN	03/08
Heritage	$657	FN	03/07
Sotheby's	DNS	VF	04/99

Highest price realized:

eMoviePoster	$2,650	VG+	05/06

• This poster has appeared at auction 11 times since 1989.

Courtesy of Heritage

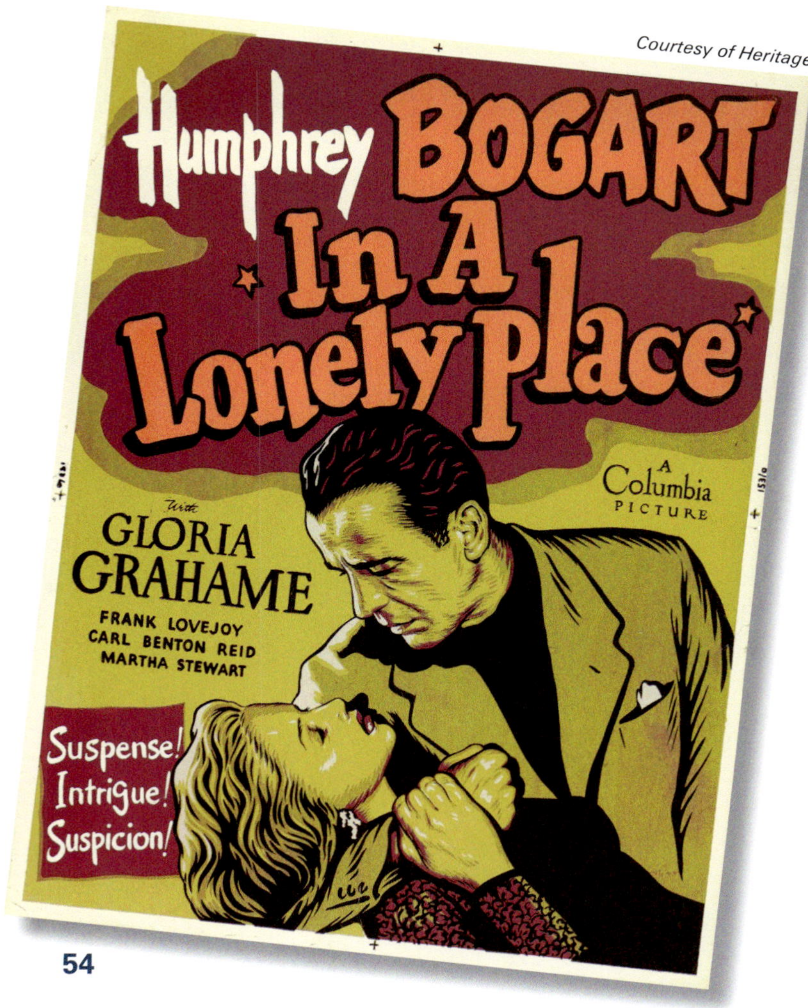

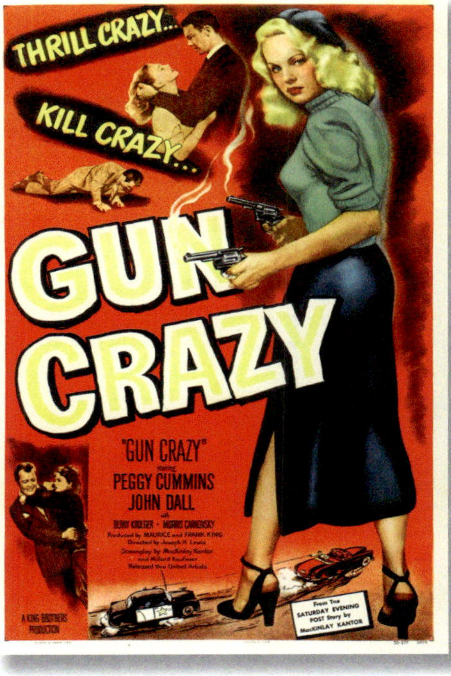

Courtesy of Heritage

Gun Crazy	1950	27x41	
Heritage	$5,975	VF	11/09
Heritage	$7,170	FN/VF	11/08
Heritage	$8,963	VF	03/08
Heritage	$4,600	VF-	11/04
Sotheby's	$3,300	VF	10/00

Highest price realized:

Heritage	$8,963	VF	03/08

Price in 1990:

Camden House	$800	VF	10/90

- This poster has appeared at auction 17 times since 1989.

Gun Crazy—Style Z	1950	30x40	
Heritage	DNS	FN/VF	03/09
Private	$350	FN	12/96*
Private	$550	VF	09/96*

- There are 3 known to exist.

* There is no way to know if the two private sales in 1996 were style "Y" or "Z," therefore, the "known to exist" estimate is most likely incorrect. There is also no way to know if either of these private sales were in the Heritage auction for 03/09.

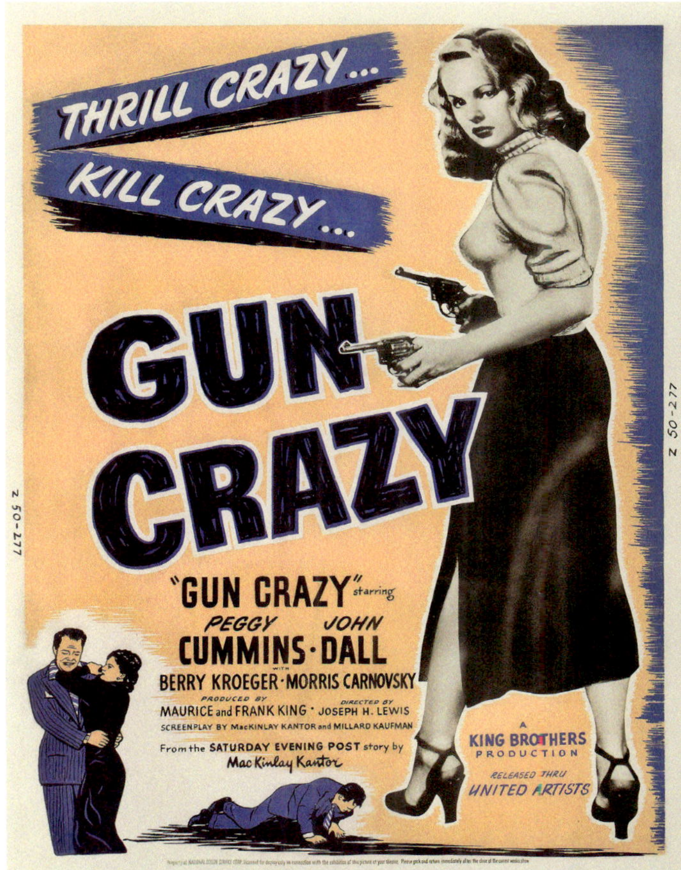

Courtesy of Heritage

Courtesy of Camden House

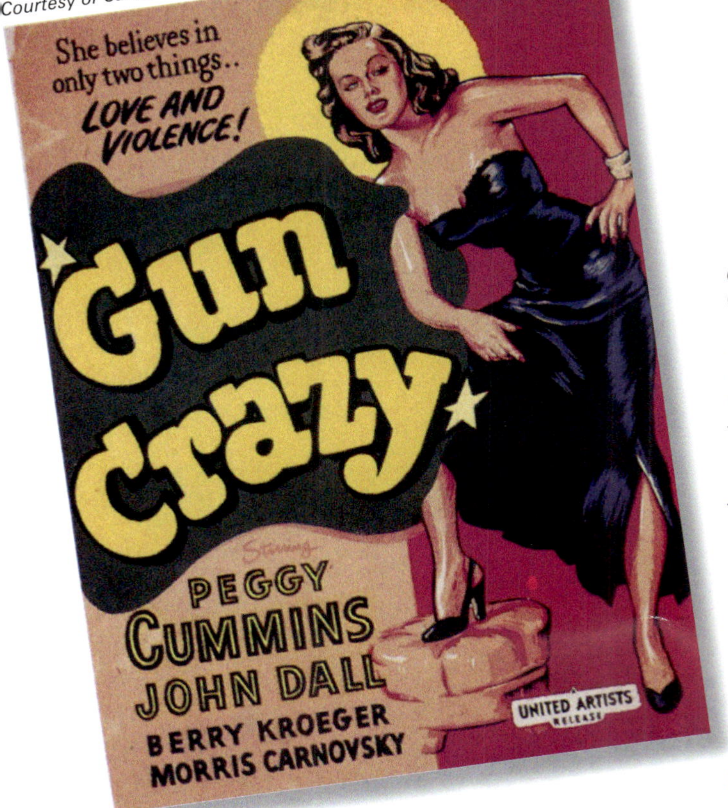

Gun Crazy—Style Y	1950	30x40	
Camden House	$600	FN	06/94*

- There is 1 known to exist.*
- There is no *Gun Crazy* 40x60 known to exist.

* There is no way to know if the two private sales in 1996 were style "Y" or "Z," therefore, the "known to exist" estimate is most likely incorrect. There is also no way to know if either of these private sales were in the Heritage auction for 03/09.

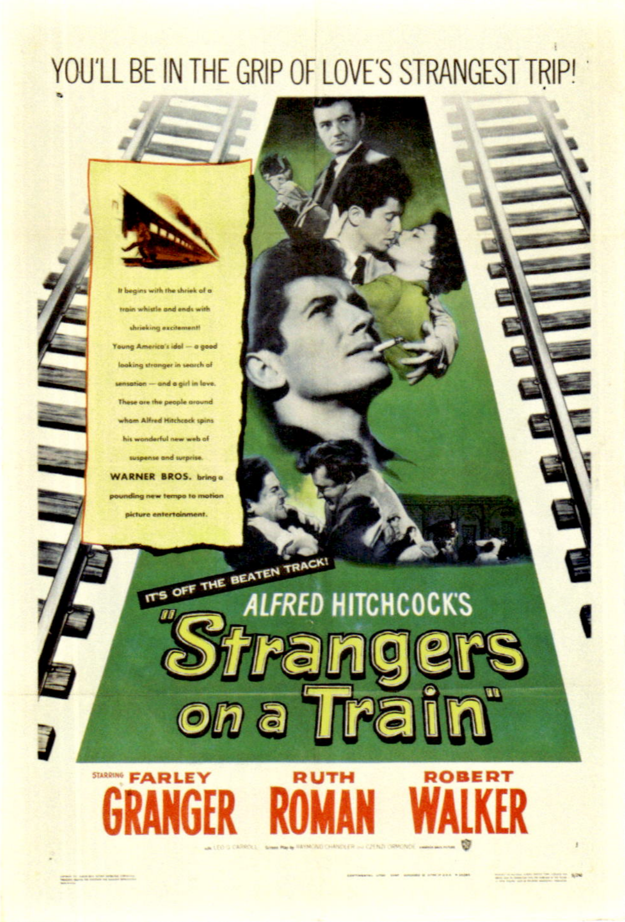

Courtesy of Heritage

Strangers on a Train	1951	27x41	
Heritage	$1,912	FN/VF	11/09
Christie's	$991	VF-	11/09
Heritage	$1,045	VF+	07/08
Heritage	$1,075	VF+	03/08
eMoviePoster	$420	GD	12/08

Highest price realized:
Heritage $ 1,912 FN/VF 11/09

Price in 1990:
Camden House $225 VF 10/90

- This poster has appeared at auction 21 times since 1989.
- There is no *Strangers on a Train* 30x40 known to exist.

Courtesy of Heritage

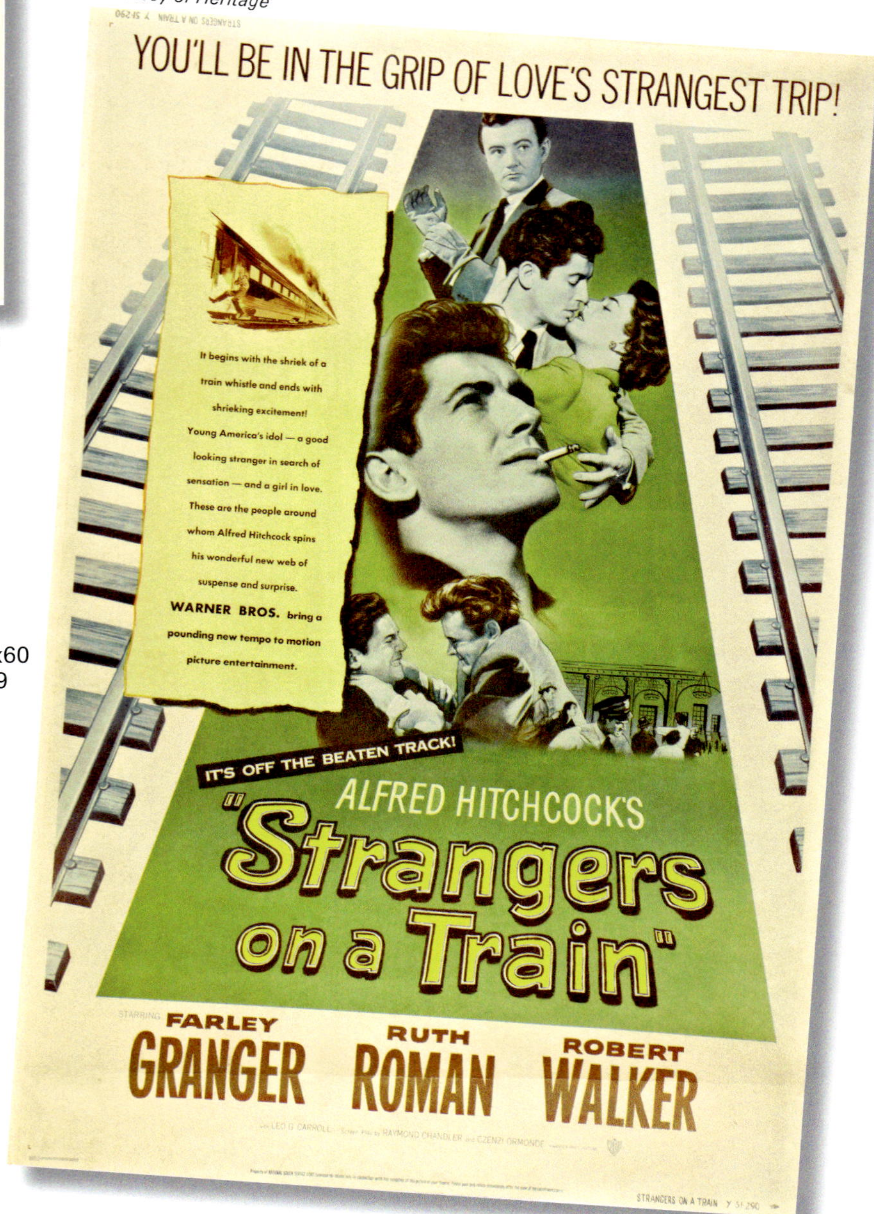

Strangers on a Train—Style Y	1951	40x60	
Heritage	$597	VF-	11/09

- There is 1 known to exist.
- There is no *Strangers on a Train* 40x60 Style Z known to exist

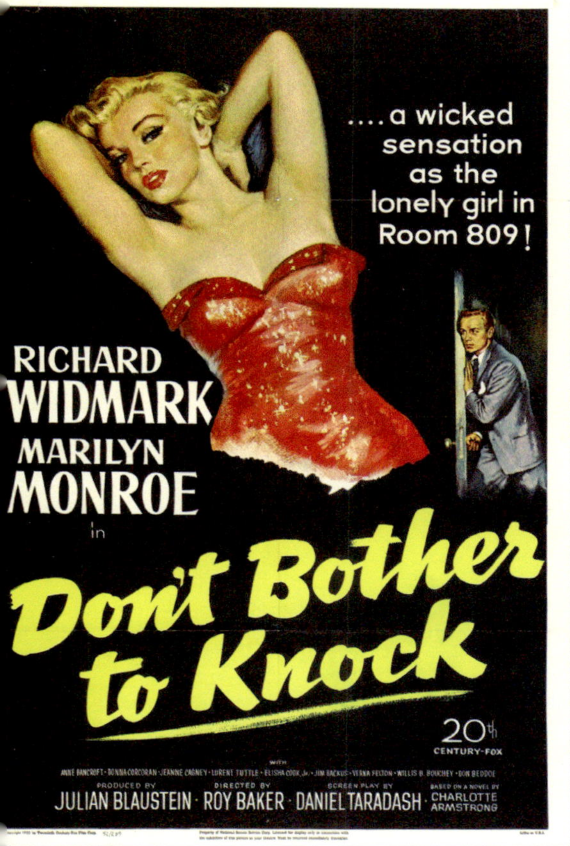

Courtesy of Heritage

Don't Bother to Knock 1952 27x41

eMoviePoster	$885	GD	11/09
eMoviePoster	$1,670	GD/VG	04/09
Heritage	$2,151	FN+	03/08
Christie's	$1,607	VF	03/08
Heritage	$1,912	F/VF	07/07

Highest price realized:
Heritage $2,151 FN+ 03/08

Price in 1990:
Camden House $450 VG 03/90

- This poster has appeared at auction 36 times since 1989.
- There is no *Don't Bother to Knock* 30x40 known to exist.

Courtesy of Christie's

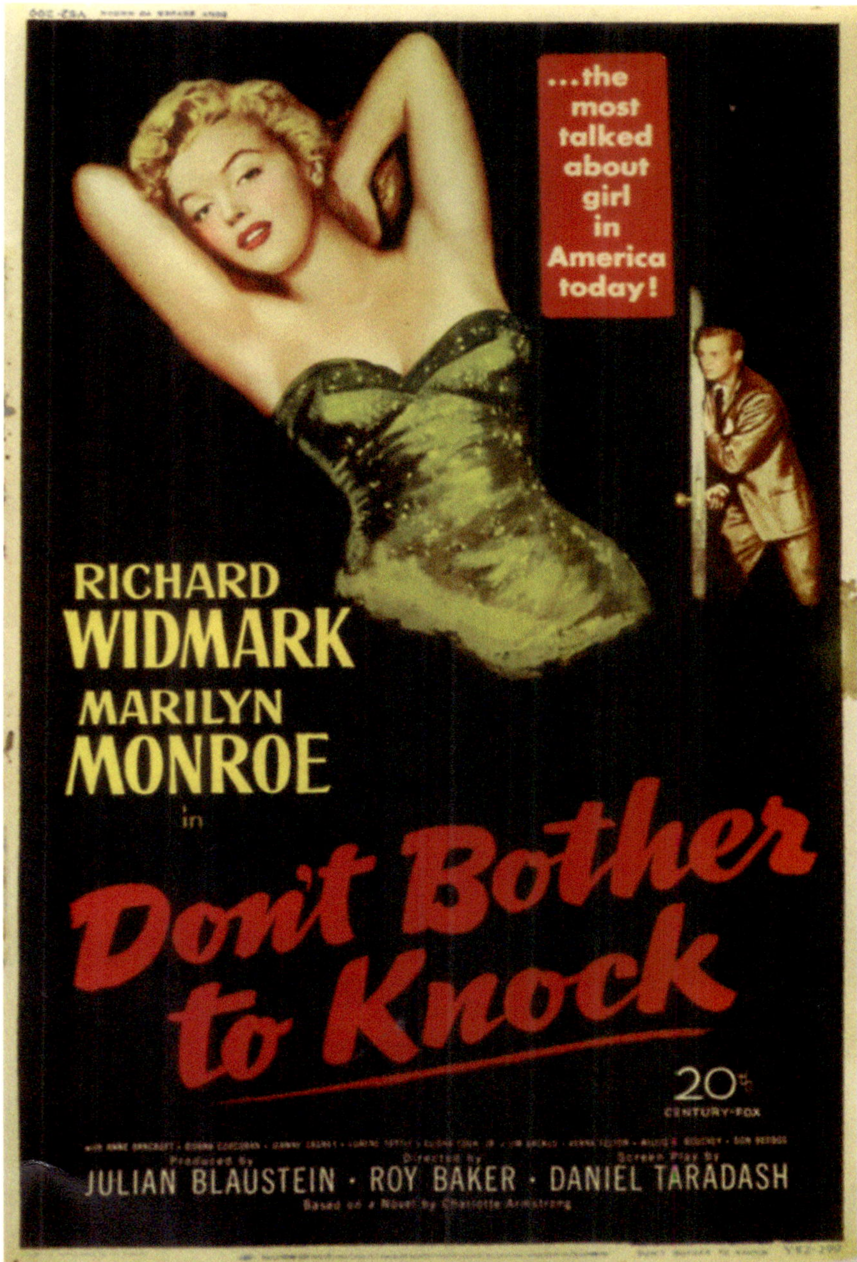

Don't Bother to Knock—Style Y 1952 40x60
Christie's $2,276 VF- 11/03
Estimate: $4,000 - $5,500

- There is 1 known to exist.
- There is no *Don't Bother to Knock* 40x60 Style Z known to exist.

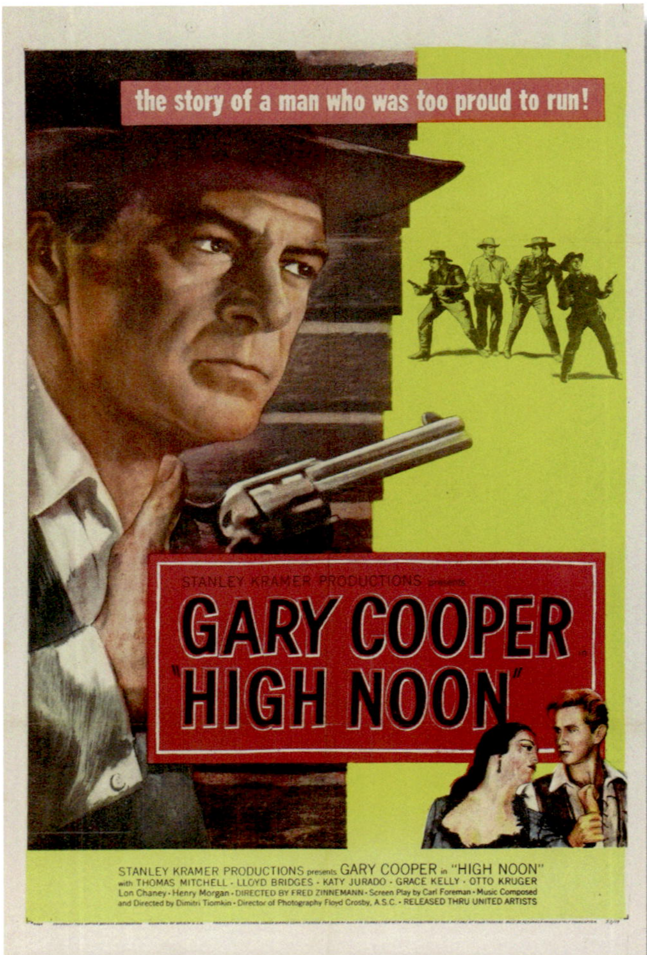

Courtesy of Heritage

High Noon 1952 27x41			
Heritage	$1,673	FN/VF	07/08
Heritage	$1,792	VF-	03/08
Heritage	$1,792	VF+	07/07
Profiles in History	$1,500	VF+	12/06
Profiles in History	$1,900	VF+	07/06

Highest price realized:

Poster City	$3,500	VF	05/01

Price in 1990:

Camden House	$325	FN	10/90

- This poster has appeared at auction 19 times since 1989.
- There is no *High Noon* 30x40 known to exist.

Courtesy of Heritage

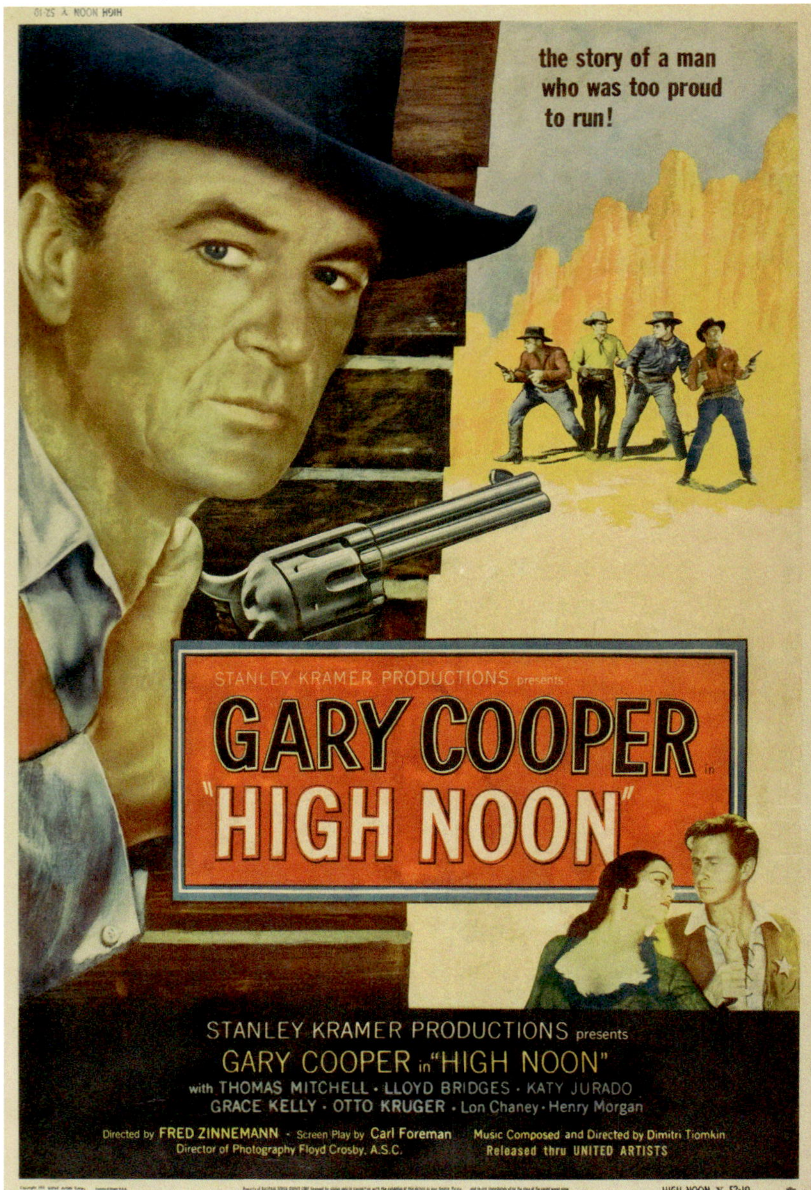

High Noon—Style Y 1952 40x60			
Heritage	$2,151	VG-	11/08
Bonhams	DNS	VF-	12/07

- There are 2 known to exist.
- There is no *High Noon* 40x60 style Z known to exist.

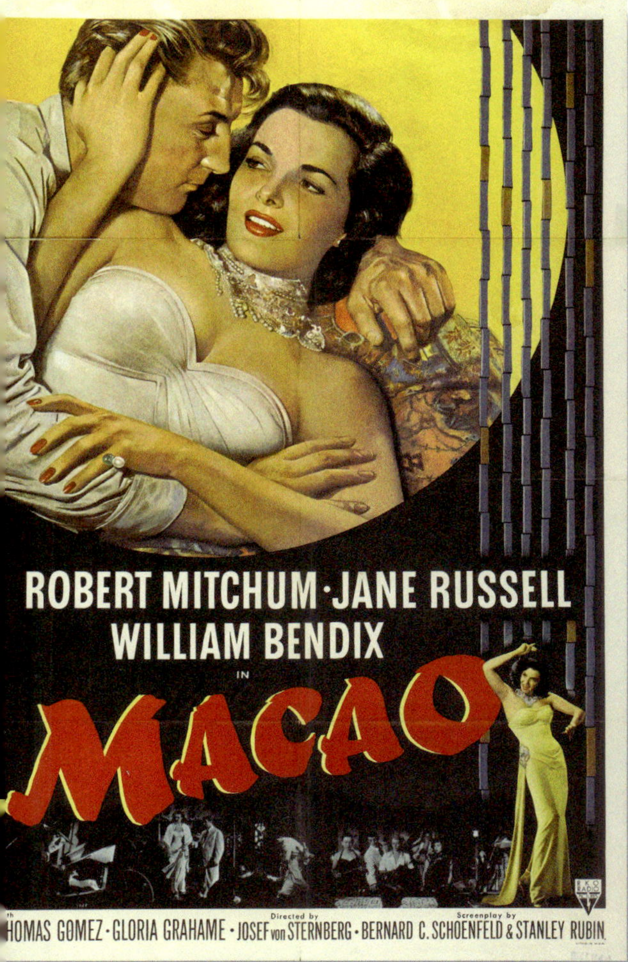

Courtesy of Heritage

Macao 1952 27x41

eMoviePoster	$460	VG	04/09
eMoviePoster	$580	VG	12/08
eMoviePoster	$343	GD	11/08
Heritage	$448	FN/VF	05/08
Heritage	$380	GD-	05/06

Highest price realized:

eMoviePoster	$ 580	VG	12/08

Price in 1996:

Christie's	$175	VF	09/96

- This poster has appeared at auction 26 times since 1989.
- There is no *Macao* 30x40 known to exist.

Courtesy of Heritage

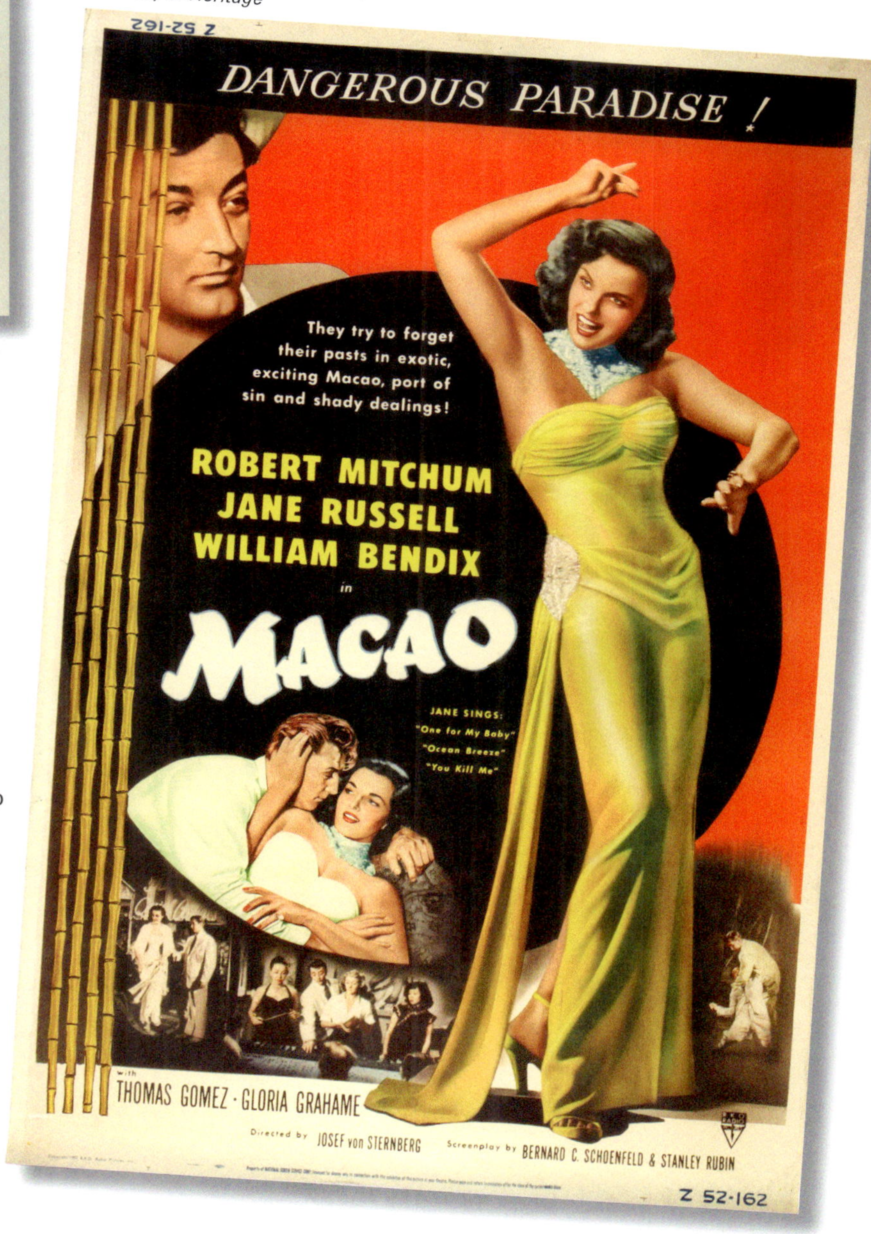

Macao—Style Z 1952 40x60

Heritage	$896	FN/VF	11/09

- There is 1 known to exist.
- There is no *Macao* 40x60 Style Y known to exist

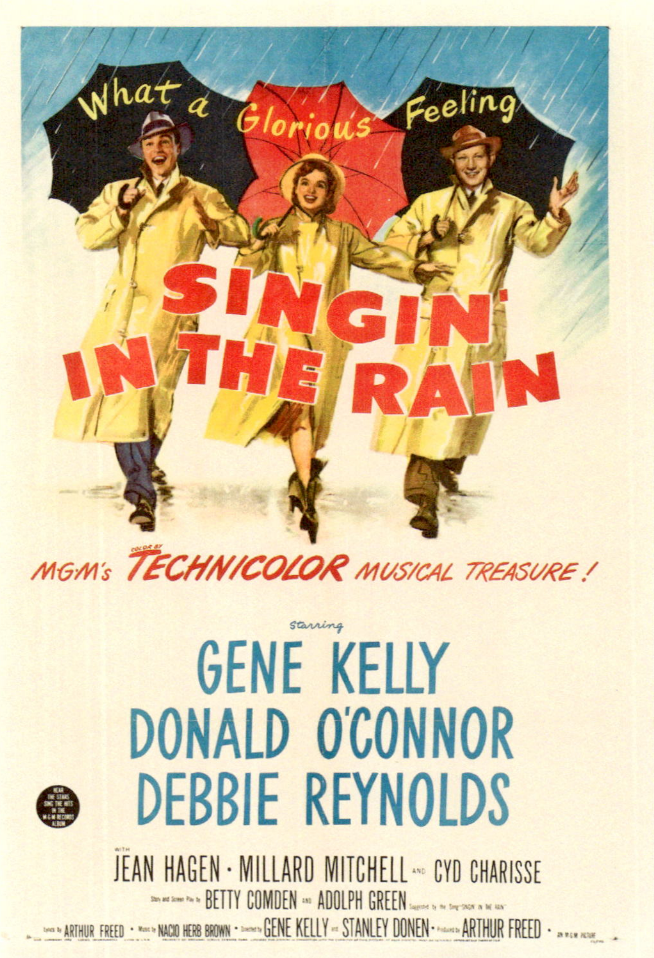

Courtesy of Heritage

Singin' In the Rain 1952 27x41

Heritage	$1,195	FN	11/09
Heritage	$1,434	VF-	03/09
Heritage	$1,912	VF-	11/08
Christie's	$2,461	VF	09/08
Heritage	$3,585	VF+	03/08

Highest price realized:

eMoviePoster (Autographed)	$3,700	VF	12/03

Price in 1991:

Camden House	$1,300	VF	11/91

- This poster has appeared at auction 36 times since 1989.
- There is no *Singin' in the Rain* 30x40 known to exist.

Courtesy of Sotheby's

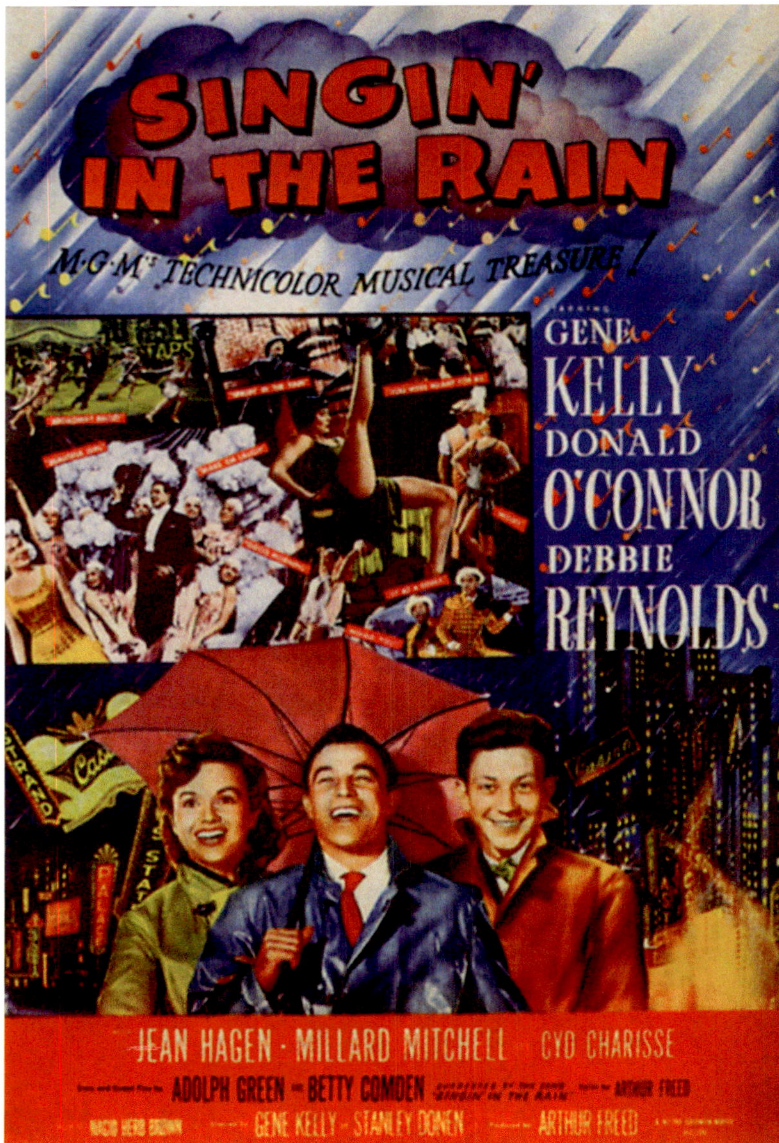

Singin' In the Rain 1952 40x60

Sotheby's	$2,875	VF	04/98

Estimate: $4,500 - $6,500

- There is 1 known to exist.

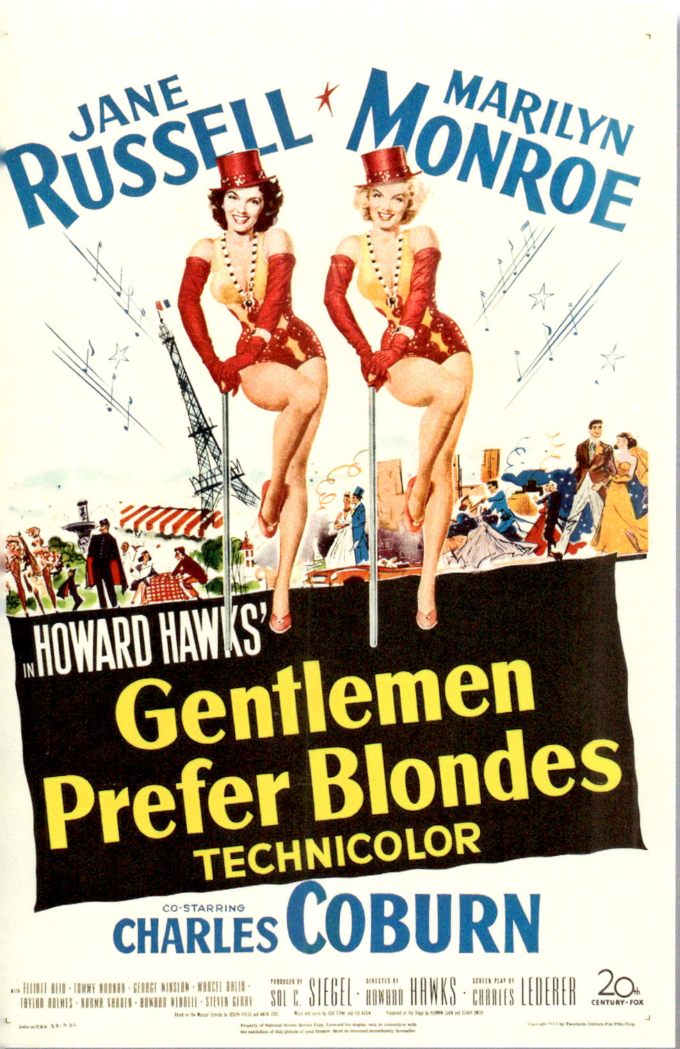

Courtesy of Heritage

Gentlemen Prefer Blondes	1953	27x41	
Heritage	$1,075	VF-	03/09
eMoviePoster	$480	FR	01/08
Heritage	$896	VF-	07/08
Profiles in History	$800	VF	07/06
Heritage	$920	VF	07/05

Highest price realized:

Sotheby's	$4,312	VF	04/99

Price in 1990:

Camden House	$400	FN	03/90

- This poster has appeared at auction 27 times since 1989.
- There is no *Gentlemen Prefer Blondes* 30x40 known to exist.

Courtesy of Heritage

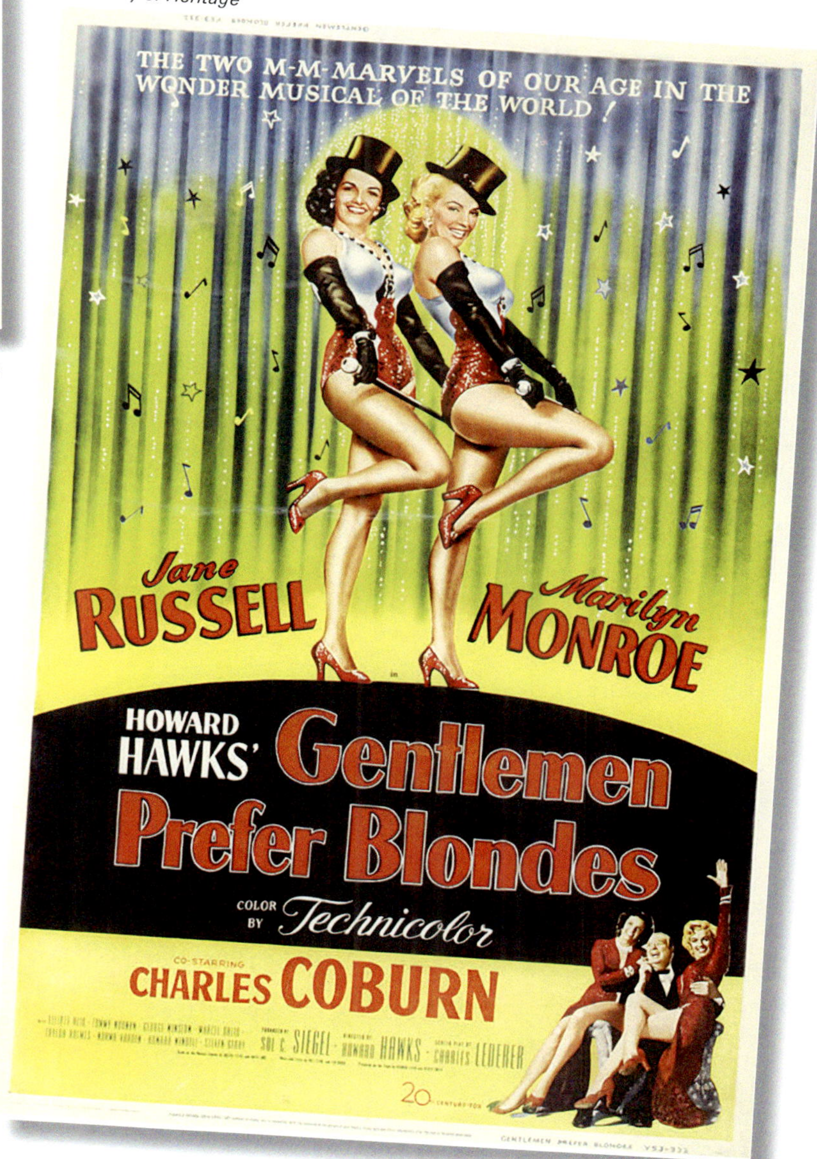

Gentlemen Prefer Blondes—Style Y	1953	40x60	
Heritage	$3,220	FN-	11/05
Heritage	$2,760	FN	03/03
Heritage	$3,680	FN	03/02
Private	$3,788	VF	04/99
Christie's	$5,500	FN	12/92

- There are 6 known to exist.
- There is no *Gentlemen Prefer Blondes* 40x60 Style Z known to exist.

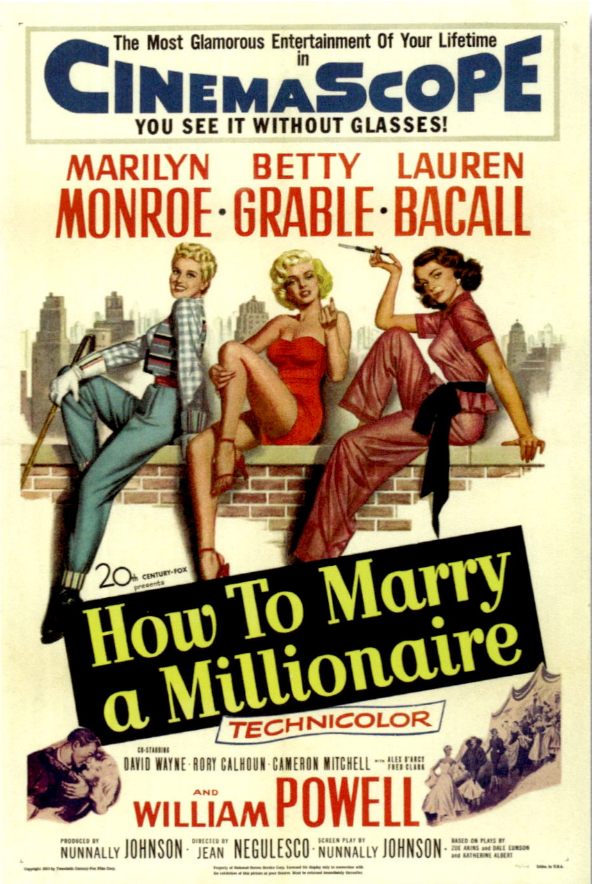

Courtesy of Heritage

How to Marry a Millionaire		1953	27x41
Heritage	$1,533	VF	07/07
eMoviePoster	$896	VF	12/06
Profiles in History	$950	VF+	07/06
Heritage	$690	VG/FN	03/06
eMoviePoster	$760	VF	02/06

Highest Price realized:

Christie's	$3,055	VF	11/01

Price in 1993:

Camden House	$850	VF	06/93

• This poster has appeared at auction 14 times since 1989.

Courtesy of Heritage

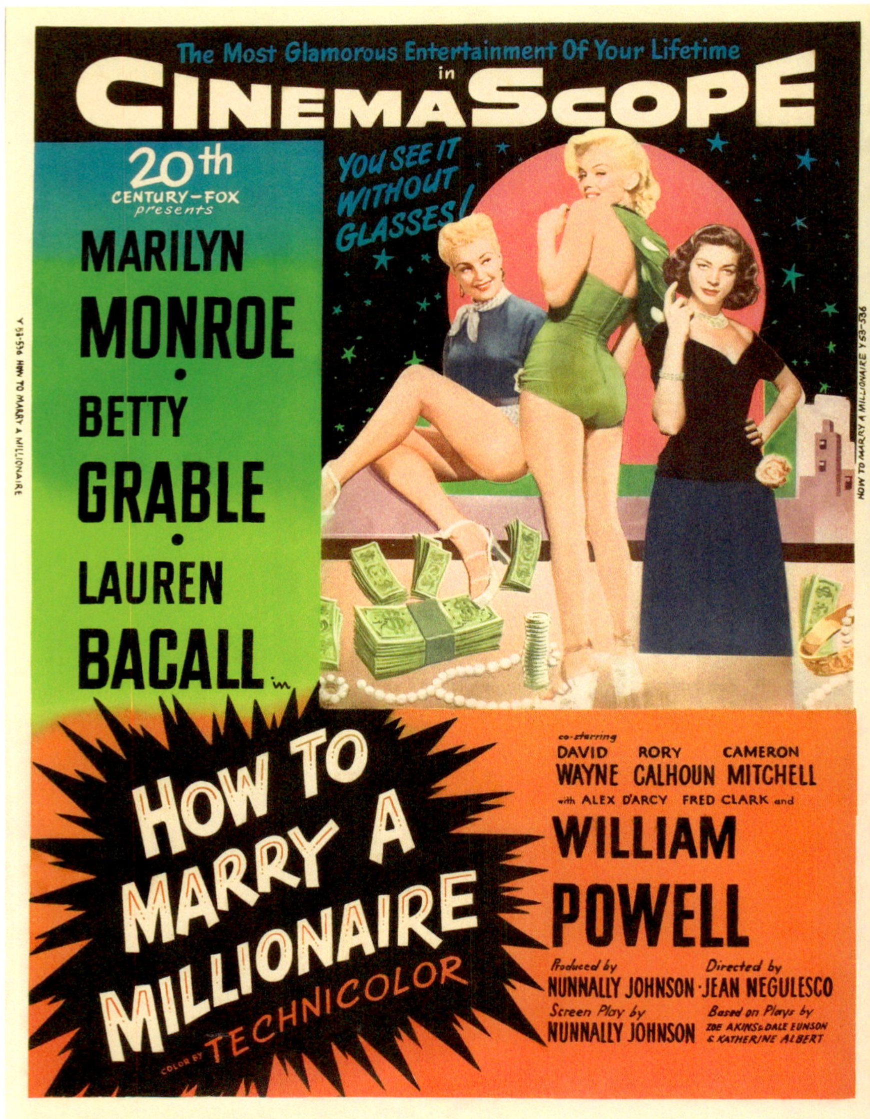

How to Marry a Millionaire—Style Y		1953	30x40
Heritage	$836	FN	07/09

• There is 1 known to exist.
• There is no *How to Marry a Millionaire* 30x40 style Z known to exist.
• There is no *How to Marry a Millionaire* 40x60 known to exist.

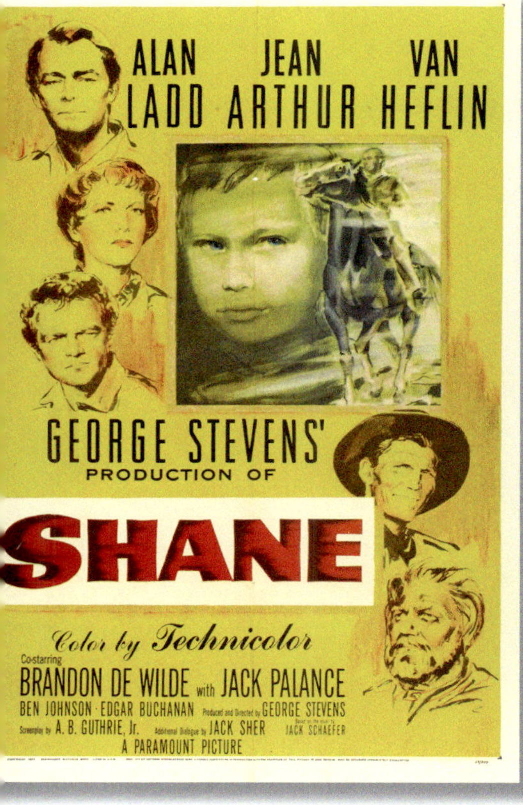

Courtesy of Heritage

Shane 1953 27x41

Heritage	$896	FN/VF	11/09
Hollywood Poster	$1,320	VF+	10/09
eMoviePoster	$737	VG	07/09
Heritage	$1,015	VF+	03/09
Heritage	$1,673	VF	07/08

Highest price realized:

Heritage	$2,390	FN/VF	07/07

Price in 1990:

Camden House	$250	FN	03/90

- This poster has appeared at auction 29 times since 1989.
- There is no *Shane* 30x40 known to exist.

Courtesy of Heritage

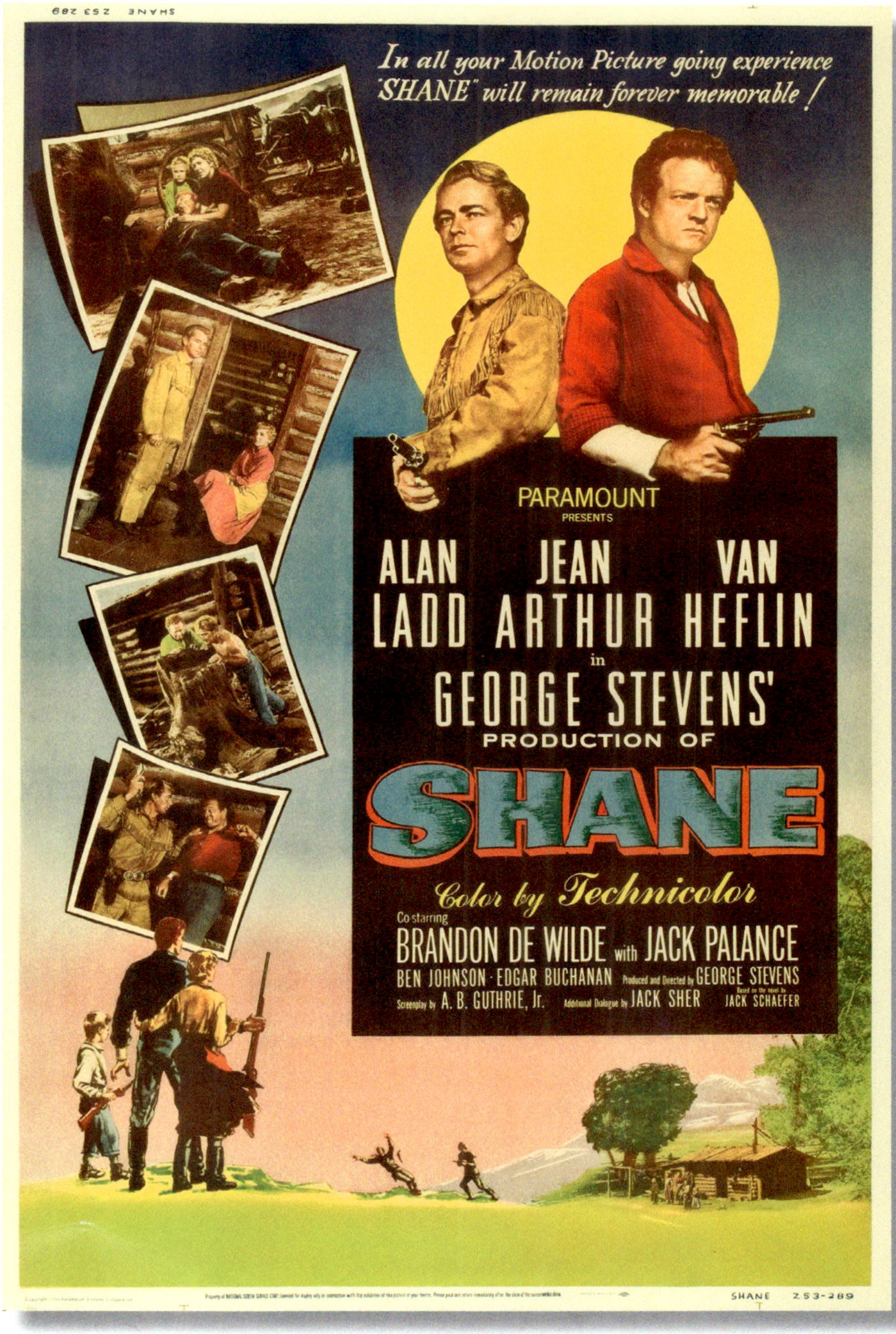

Shane—Style Z 1953 40x60

Heritage	$5,676	FN/VF	11/08

- There is 1 known to exist.

Shane—Style Y 1953 40x60
Estimate: $5,000 - $6,000

• There is 1 known to exist.

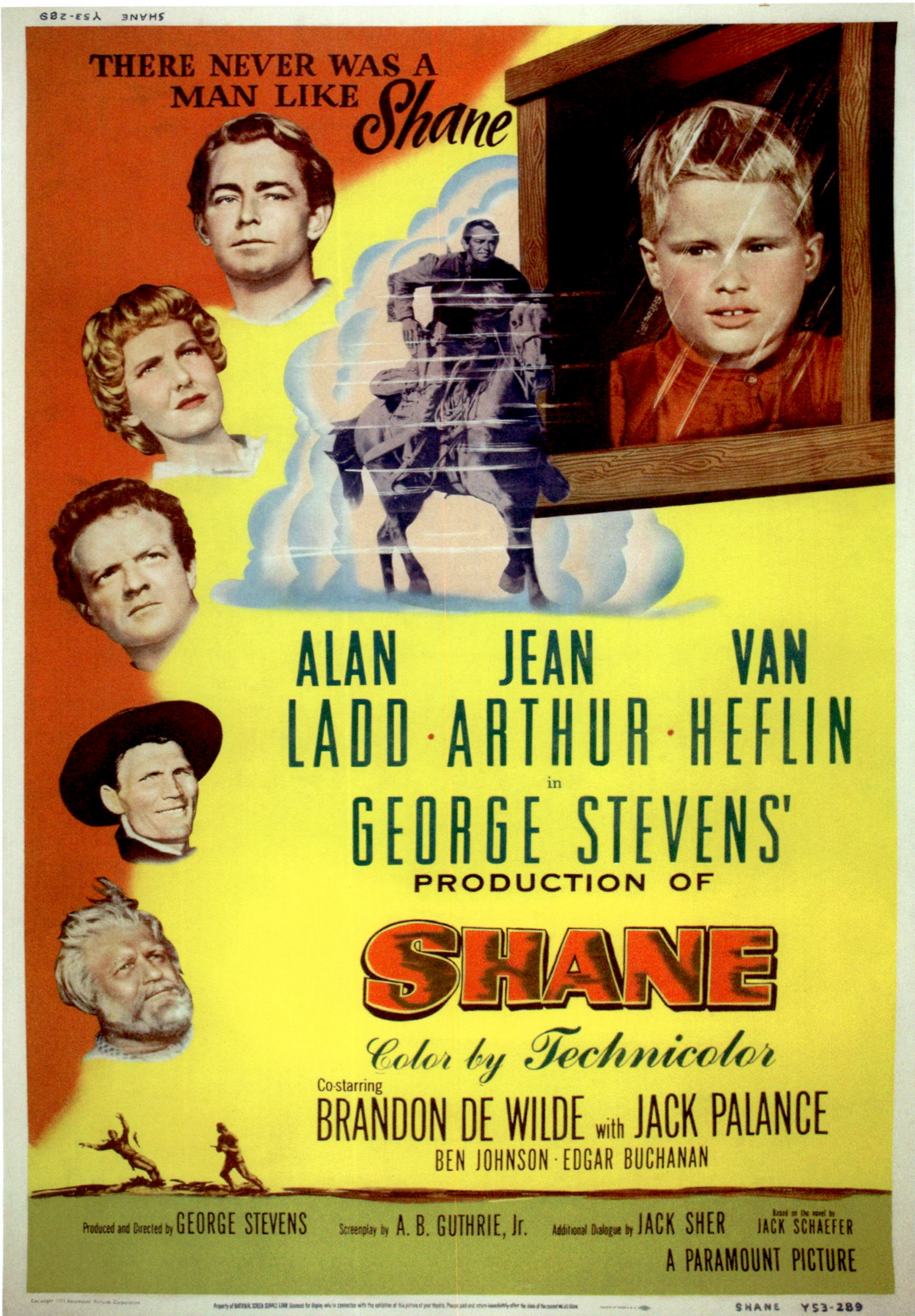

Photo by R. Aaron Raymond

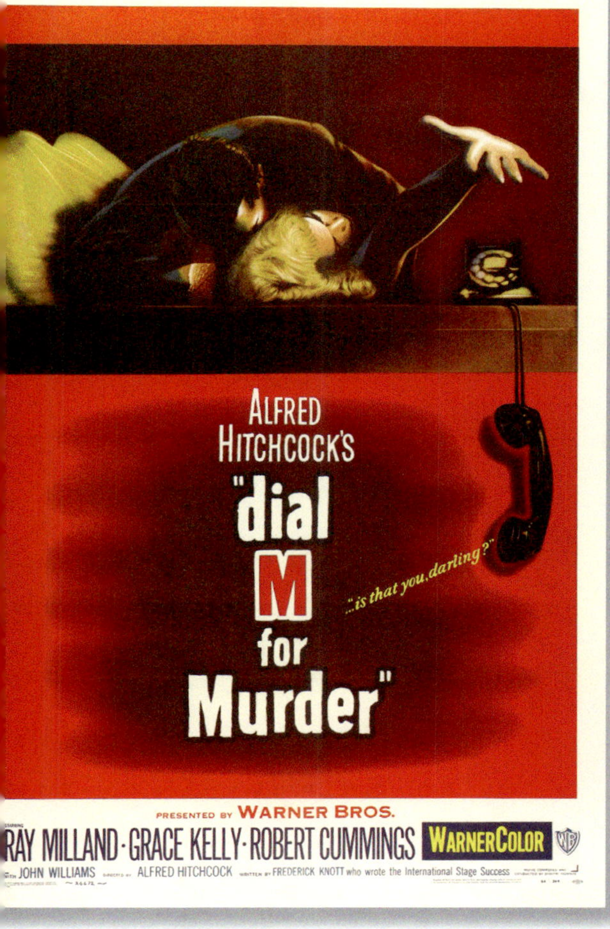

Courtesy of Heritage

Dial M for Murder	1954	27x41	
Heritage	$2,390	FN/VF	11/09
Heritage	$1,912	FN	03/09
Christie's	$1,376	VF	03/09
Heritage	$2,031	FN	11/08
Heritage	$2,390	FN+	03/08

Highest price realized:

CineMasterpieces	$3,495	VF	02/08

Price in 1989:

Camden House	$325	VF	05/89

- This poster has appeared at auction 41 times since 1989.
- There is no *Dial M for Murder* 30x40 known to exist.

Dial M for Murder—Style Z	1954	40x60	
Heritage	$3,883	FN	11/08

- There is 1 known to exist.
- There is no *Dial M for Murder* 40x60 Style Y known to exist.

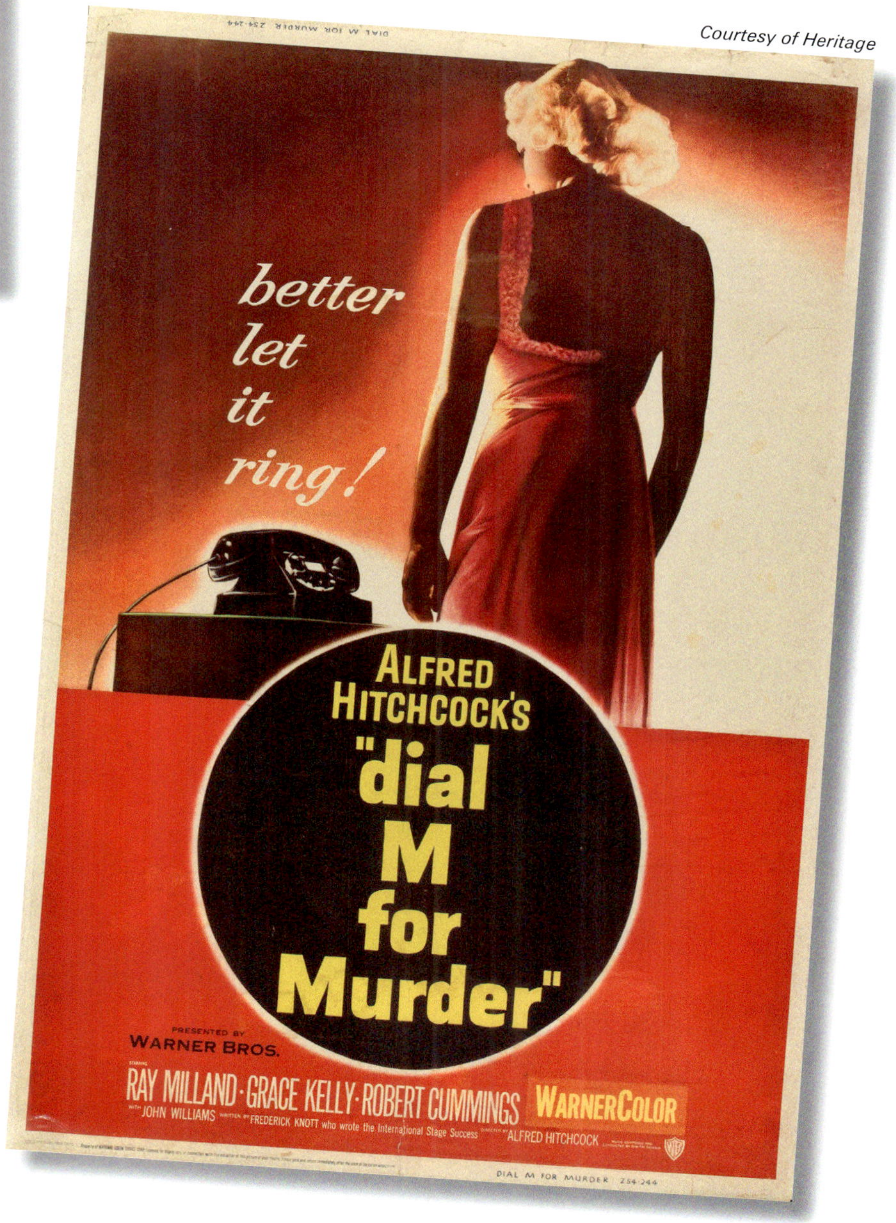

Courtesy of Heritage

Rear Window	1954	27x41	
Heritage	$6,572	VF+	11/09
Heritage	$3,883	FN/VF	07/09
Heritage	$2,868	FN/VF	03/09
eMoviePoster	$4,200	VG	12/08
Heritage	$5,078	VF-	07/08

Highest price realized:

Heritage	$8,962	VF/NM	07/07

Price in 1992:

Camden House	$300	FN	03/92

• This poster has appeared at auction 38 times since 1989.

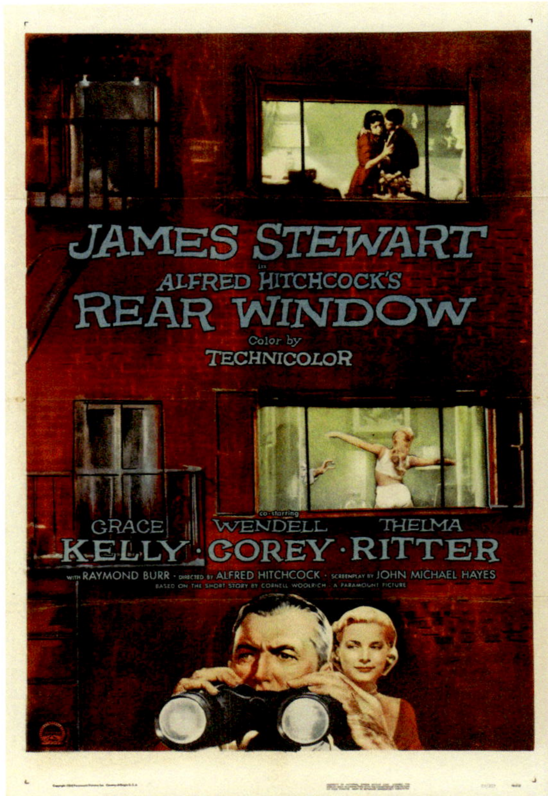

Courtesy of Heritage

Rear Window—Style Y	1954	30x40	
WalterFilm	$9,500	VF	03/06
Christie's	$4,174	FN	09/99

• There are 2 known to exist.

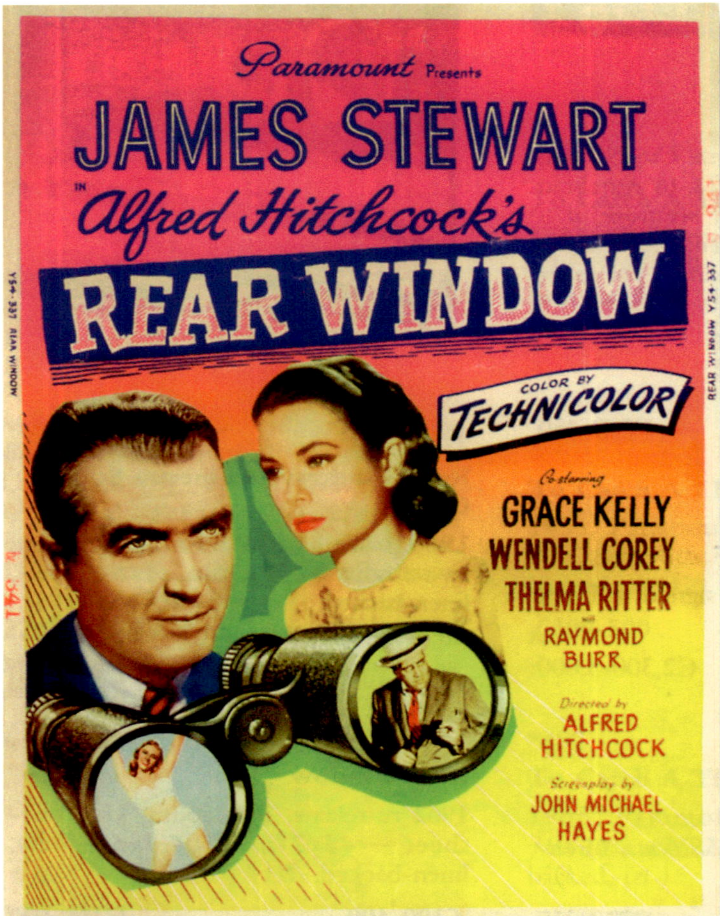

Courtesy of WalterFilm

Rear Window— Style Z	1954	30x40	
WalterFilm	$9,500	VF	05/06

• There is 1 known to exist
• There is no *Rear Window* 40x60 Style Y or Z known to exist.

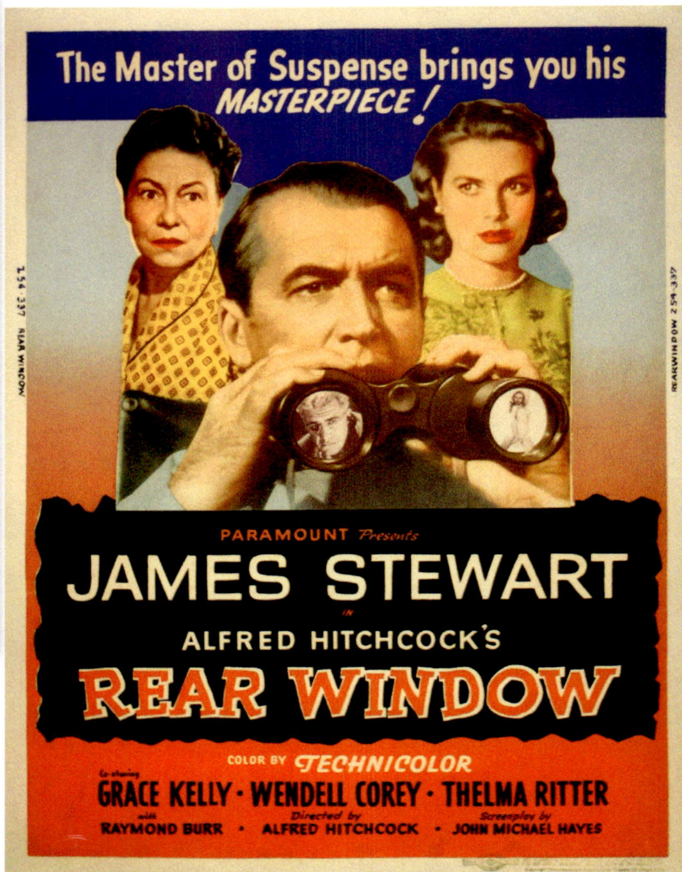

Courtesy of WalterFilm

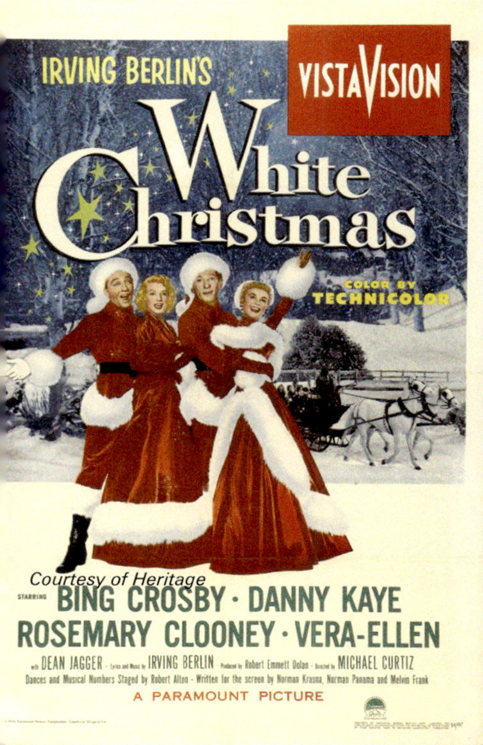

Courtesy of Heritage

White Christmas	1954	27x41	
eMoviePoster	$625	GD/VG	12/09
eMoviePoster	$700	GD	12/09
Heritage	$1,314	VF	11/09
eMoviePoster	$263	PR	08/09
Heritage	$1,075	FN/VF	05/09

Highest price realized:

CineMasterpieces	$1,895	VF	06/08

Price in 1990:

Camden House	$110	VF	10/90

• This poster has appeared at auction 31 times since 1989.

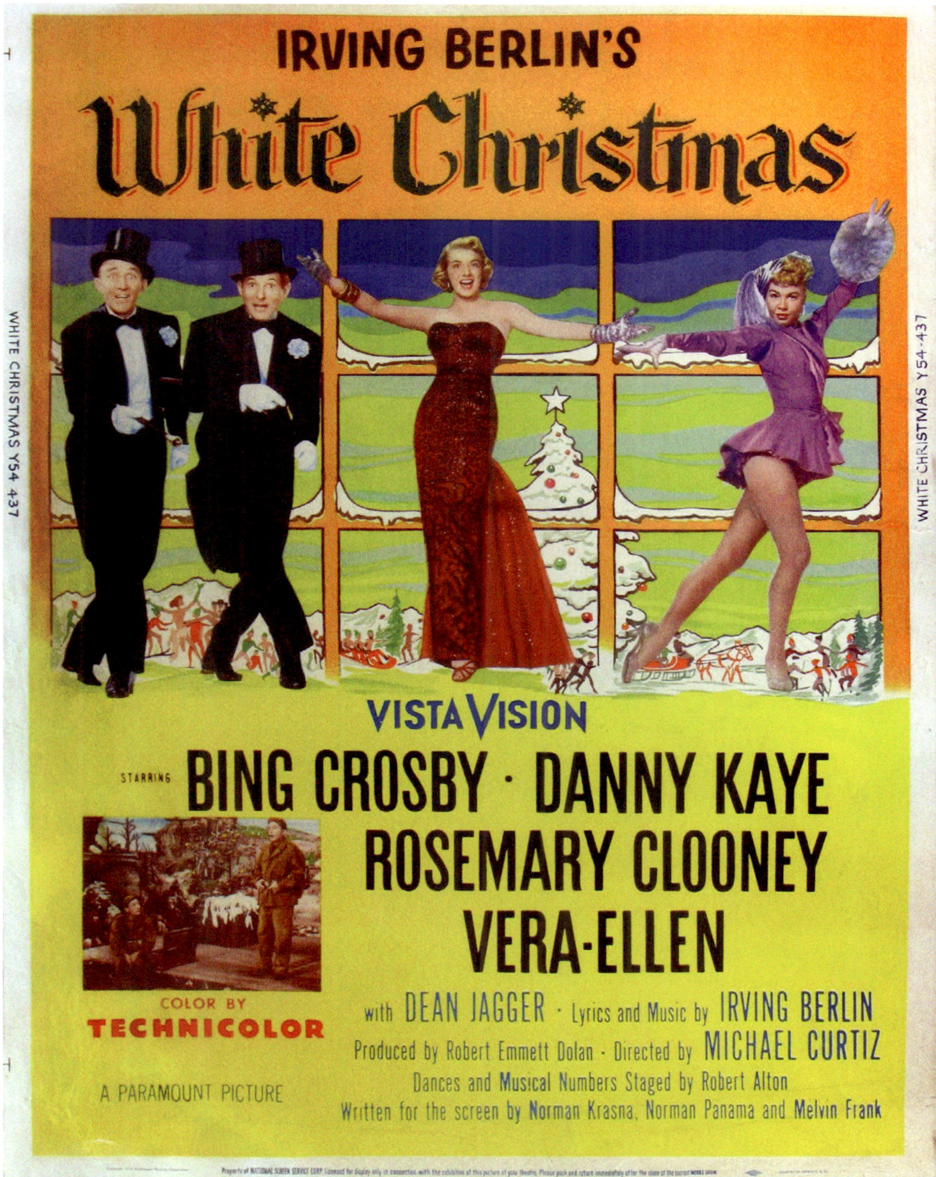

Courtesy of Hershenson/Allen Archive

White Christmas—Style Y	1954	30x40	
eMoviePoster	$800	VG	12/09*
eMoviePoster	$1,111	VG	12/06

Estimate: $1,500 - $2,000

• There are 2 known to exist

* This is the same poster that was sold in 2006.

White Christmas— Style Z 1954 30x40
Estimate: $1,500 - $2,000

• There is 1 known to exist.

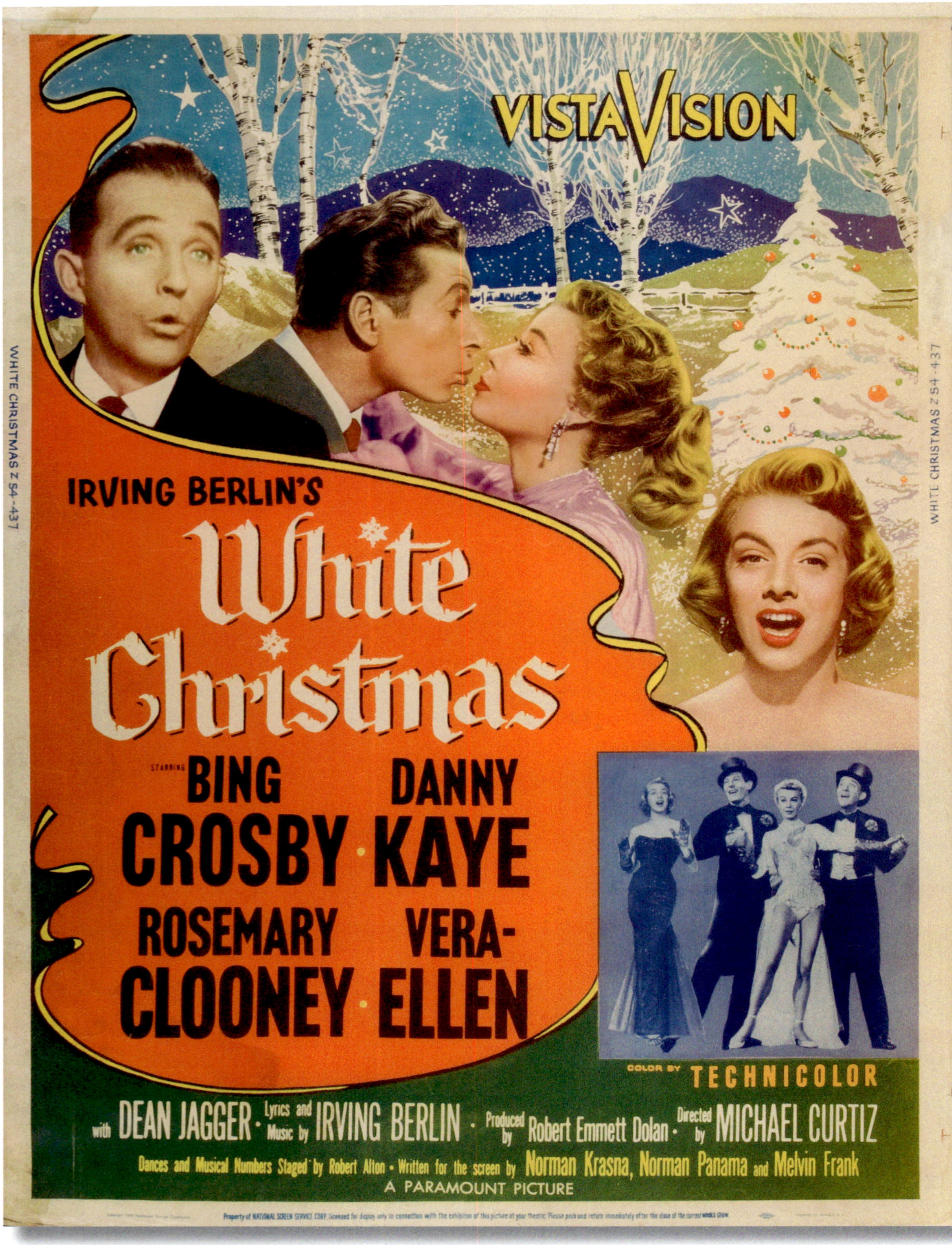

Photo by R. Aaron Raymond & Stephen Allard

White Christmas—Style Y 1954 40x60
eMoviePoster $510 VG 12/06
Estimate: $1,500 - $2,500

- There is 1 known to exist.
- There is no *White Christmas* 40x60 Style Z known to exist.

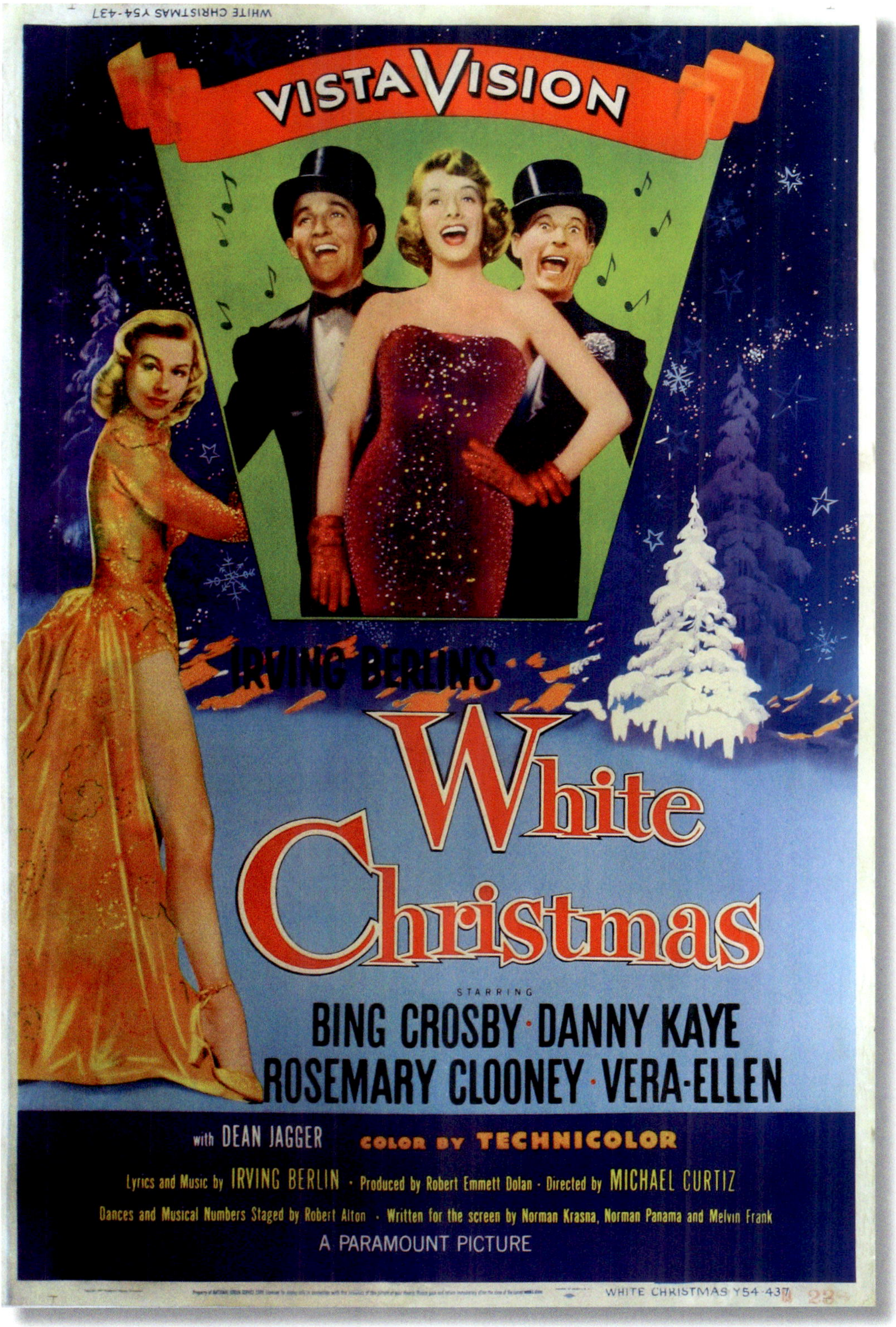

Courtesy of Hershenson/Allen Archive

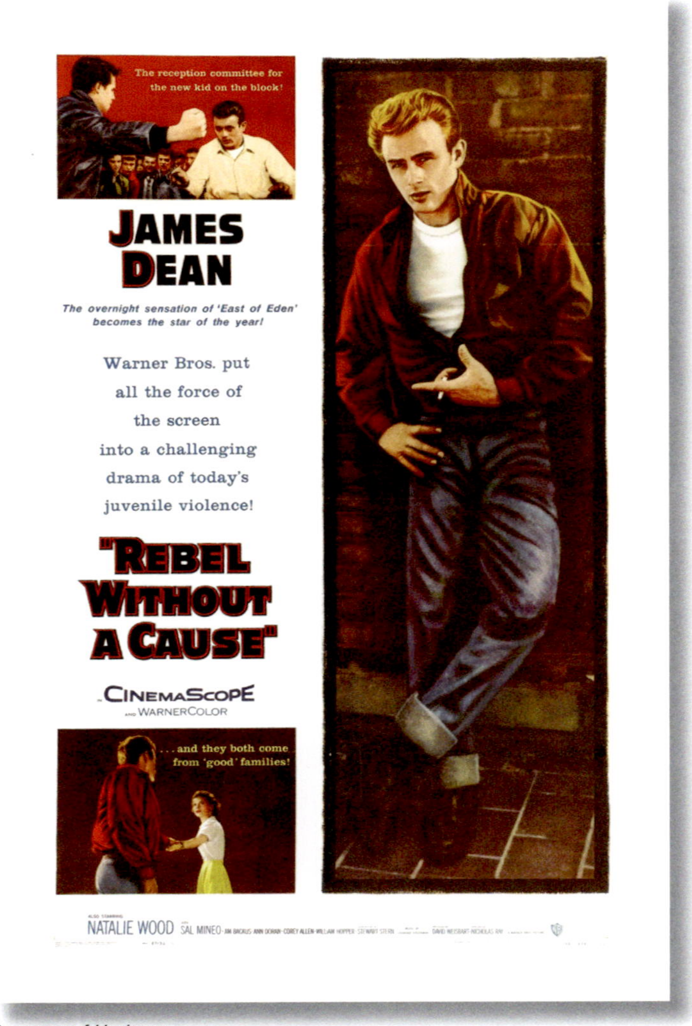

Courtesy of Heritage

Rebel without a Cause 1955 27x41

Heritage	$1,673	VF	03/09
Christie's	$1,118	VF	03/09
Heritage	$1,434	FN+	11/08
Heritage	$2,031	FN+	03/08
Christie's	$2,382	VF	06/07

Highest price realized:

MPA	$5,000	VF	10/01

Price in 1990:

Camden House	$750	FN	03/90

• This poster has appeared at auction 36 times since 1989.

Courtesy of Sotheby's

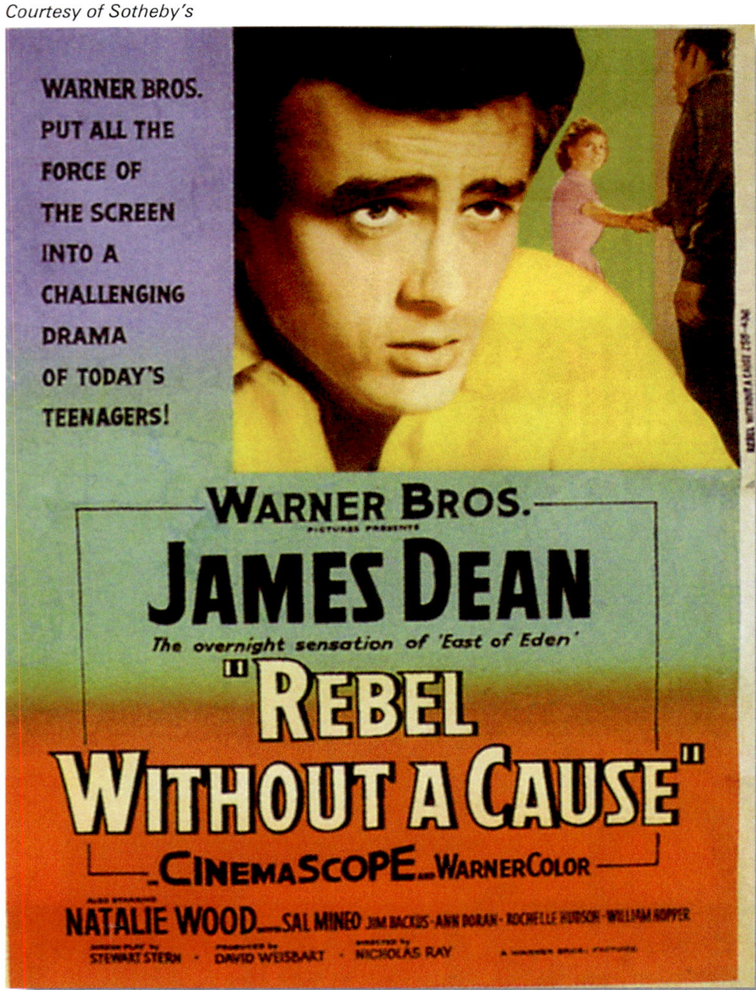

Rebel without a Cause—Style Z 1955 30x40

Sotheby's	$4,600	VF+	04/98

• There are 2 known to exist.
• There is no *Rebel without a Cause* 30x40 style Y known to exist.

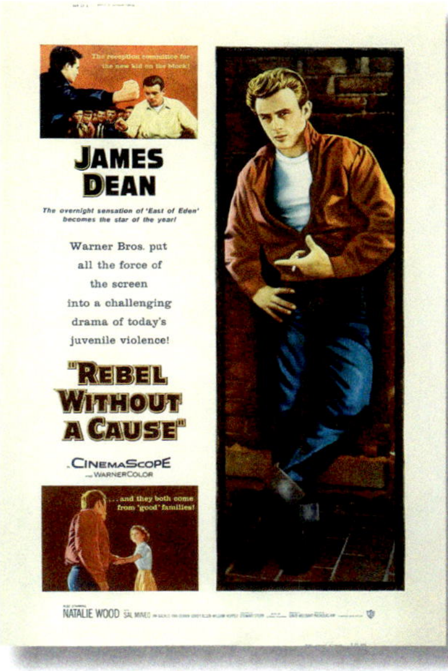

Courtesy of Heritage

Rebel without a Cause—Style Y 1955 40x60

Bonhams & Butterfields	$1,076	GD	12/06
Heritage	$1,380	GD	07/06
Heritage	$5,750	VF+	11/05
Heritage	$4,140	FN	07/02
Christie's	$2,530	VG	12/97

• There are 5 known to exist.

Rebel without a Cause— Style Z 1955 40x60

Heritage	$2,868	GD	03/09*
Heritage	$1,195	VG+	07/08
eMoviePoster	$1,265	VG	12/07
Heritage	$2,629	GD	11/07*
eMoviePoster	$2,122	GD/VG	04/07

• There are 6 known to exist.
* This poster is the same one that appeared in the Heritage Auction in 2006 and sold for $2,300. It had major restoration.

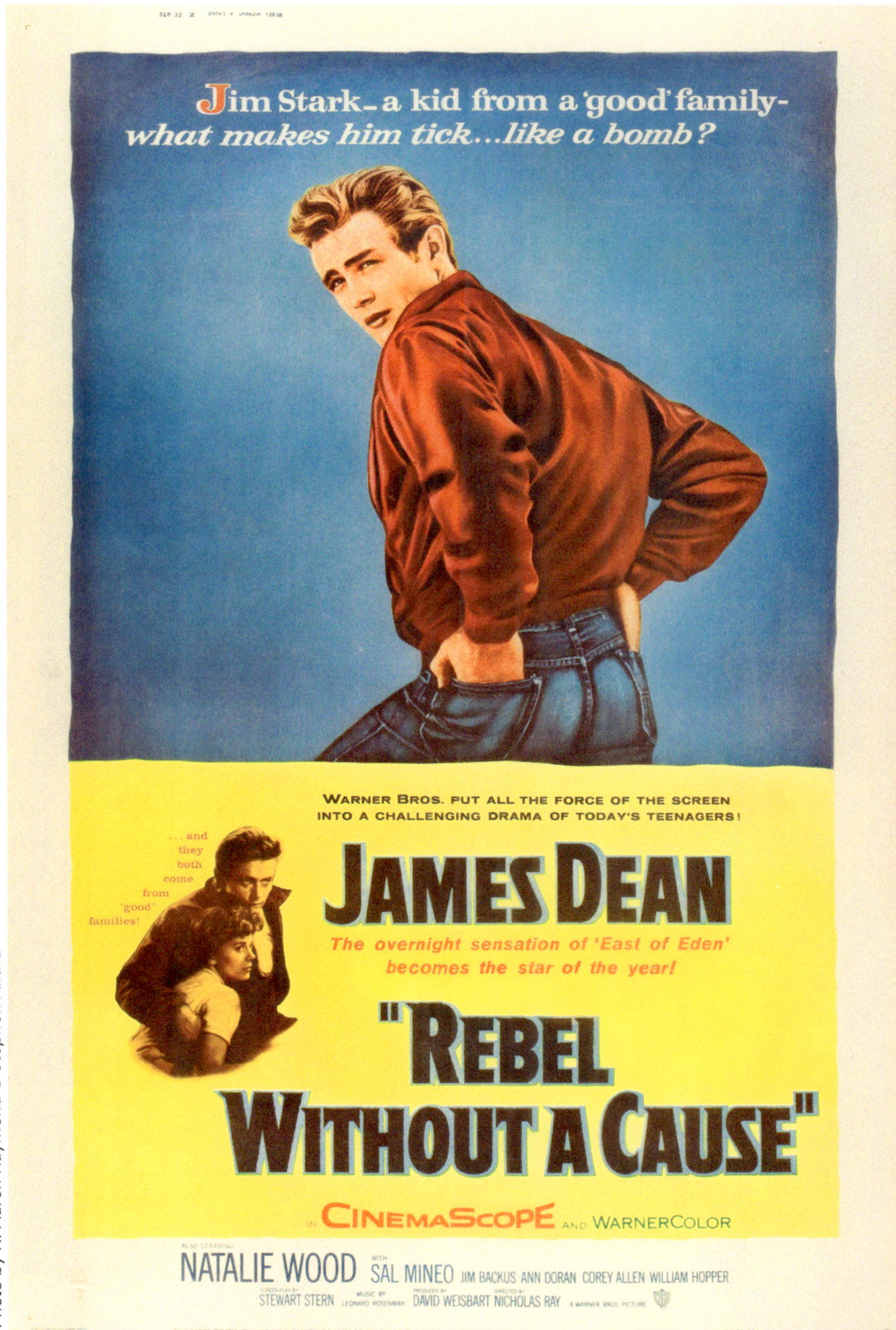

Photo by R. Aaron Raymond & Stephen Allard

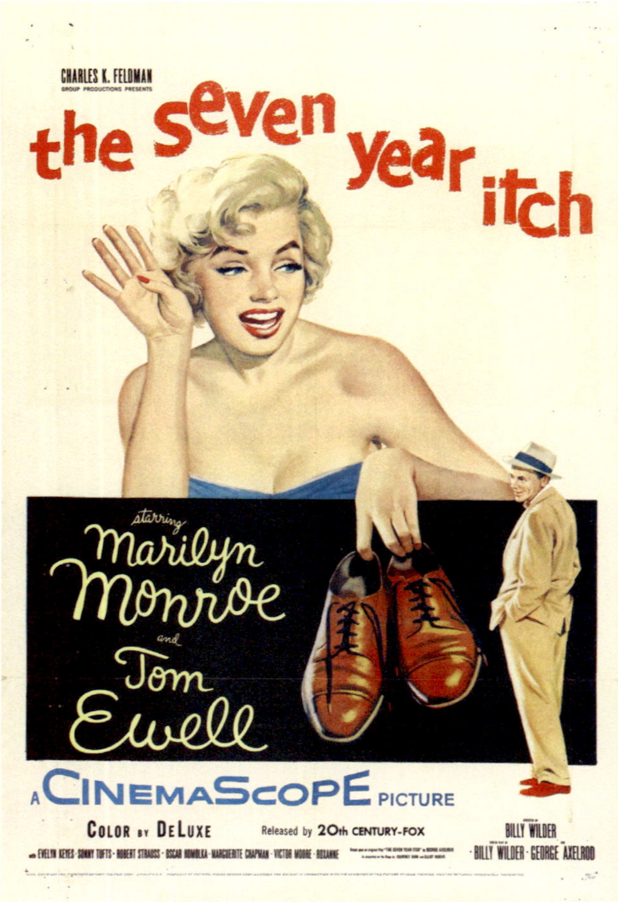

Courtesy of Heritage

Seven Year Itch	1955	27x41	
Heritage	$1,075	FN/VF	07/09
eMoviePoster	$1,270	GD	06/09
Heritage	$657	FN+	12/08
Heritage	$2,509	VF+	11/08
Christie's	$1,074	VF	09/08

Highest price realized:

Heritage	$2,760	VF+	11/03

Price in 1990:

Camden House	$325	VF	03/90

• This poster has appeared at auction 42 times since 1989.

Courtesy of Christie's

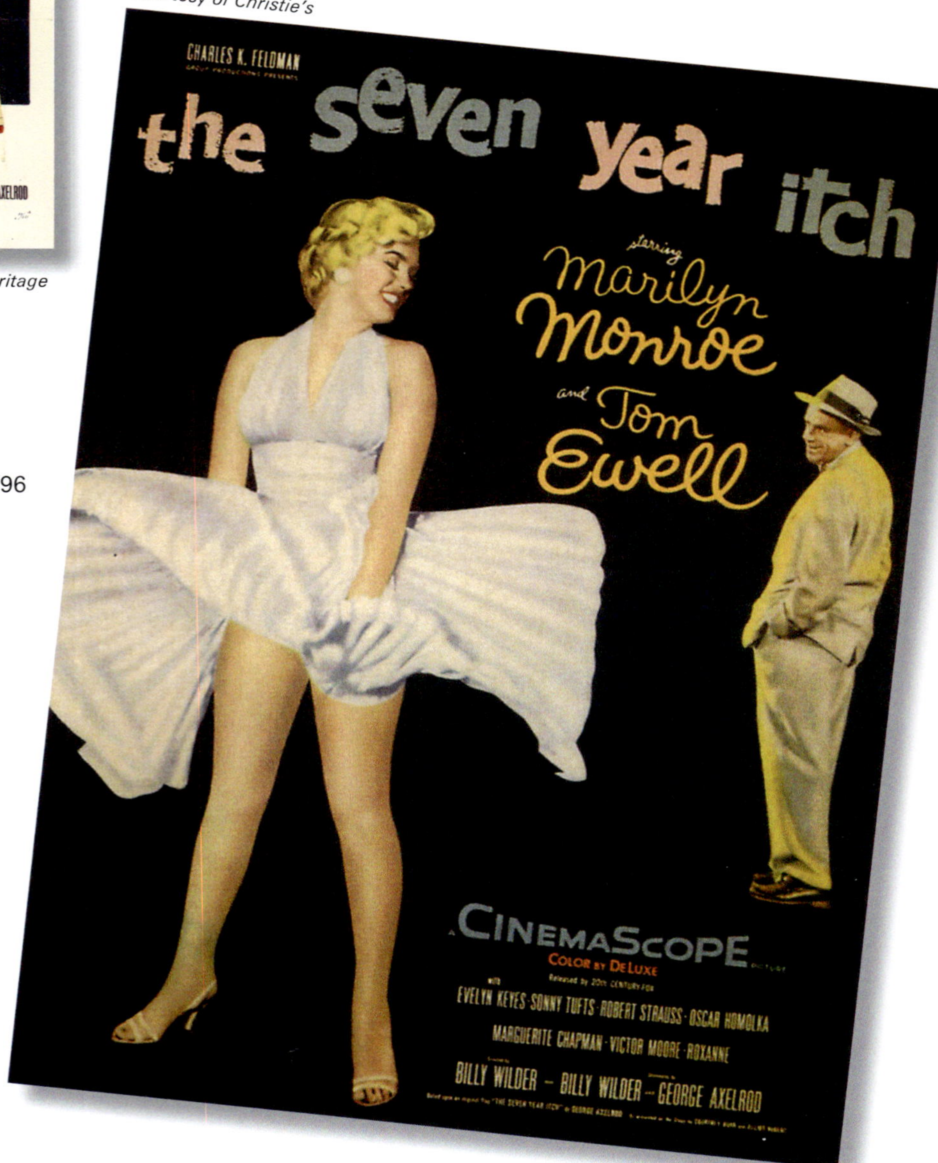

Seven Year Itch	1955	30x40	
Christie's	$3,680	FN+	12/96

Estimate: $5,000 - $6,000

• There is 1 known to exist.

Seven Year Itch—Style Y 1955 40x60

Heritage	$5,078	VG/FN	07/09
Skinner	$3,220	VF	11/98

- There are 2 known to exist.
- There is no *Seven Year Itch* 40x60 Style Z known to exist.

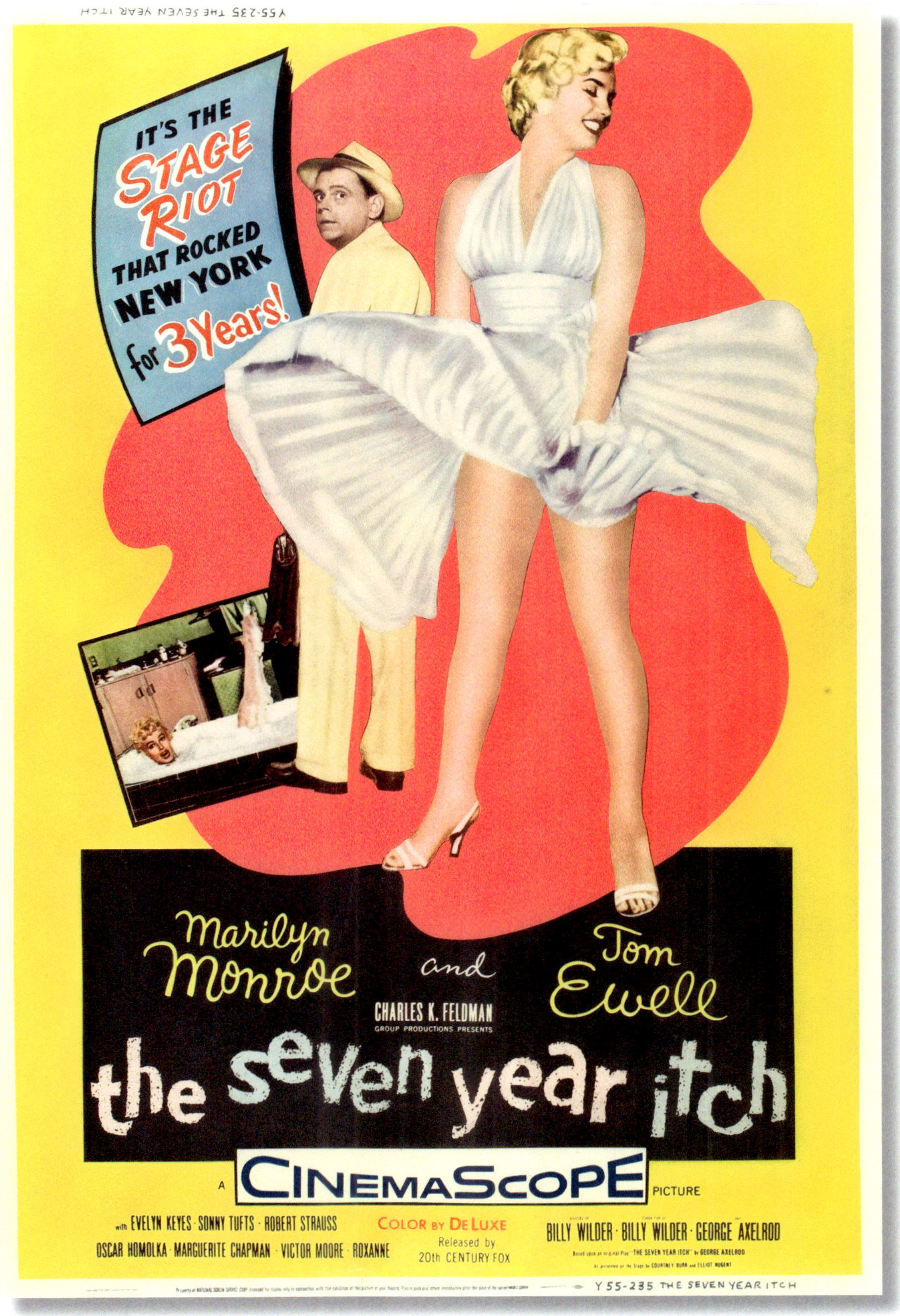

Courtesy of Heritage

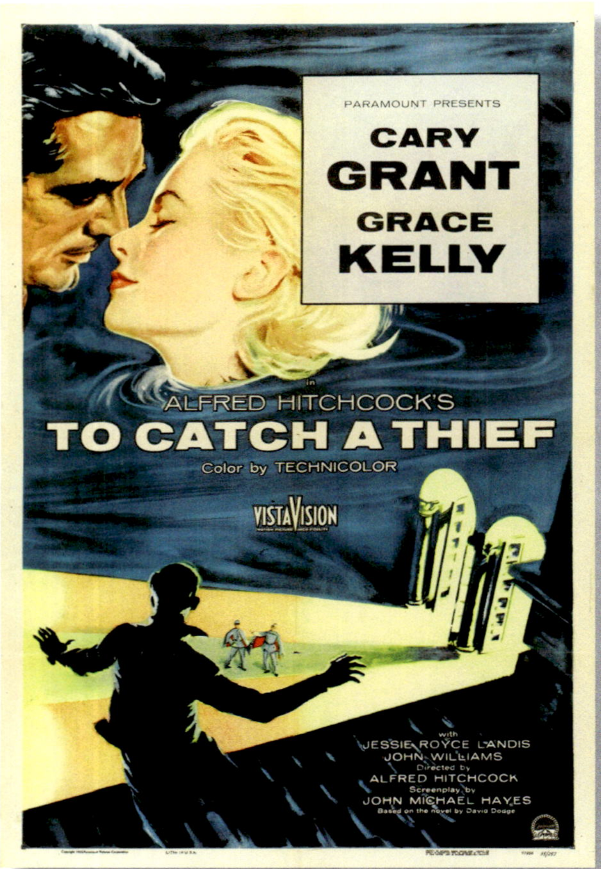

Courtesy of Heritage

To Catch a Thief	1955	27x41	
Heritage	$1,912	VF	07/09
Heritage	$1,075	FN/VF	06/09
Heritage	$1,434	VF	03/09
Christie's	$1,376	VF-	03/09
Heritage	$1,314	VF-	11/08

Highest price realized:

Profiles in History	$5,000	VF-	07/06

Price in 1992:

Camden House	$130	VG	03/92

• This poster has appeared at auction 21 times since 1989.

To Catch a Thief—Style Z	1955	30x40	
eMoviePoster	$2,100	GD	05/07

• There are 2 known to exist.
• There is no *To Catch a Thief* 30x40 Style Y known to exist.

Courtesy of Hershenson/ Allen archive

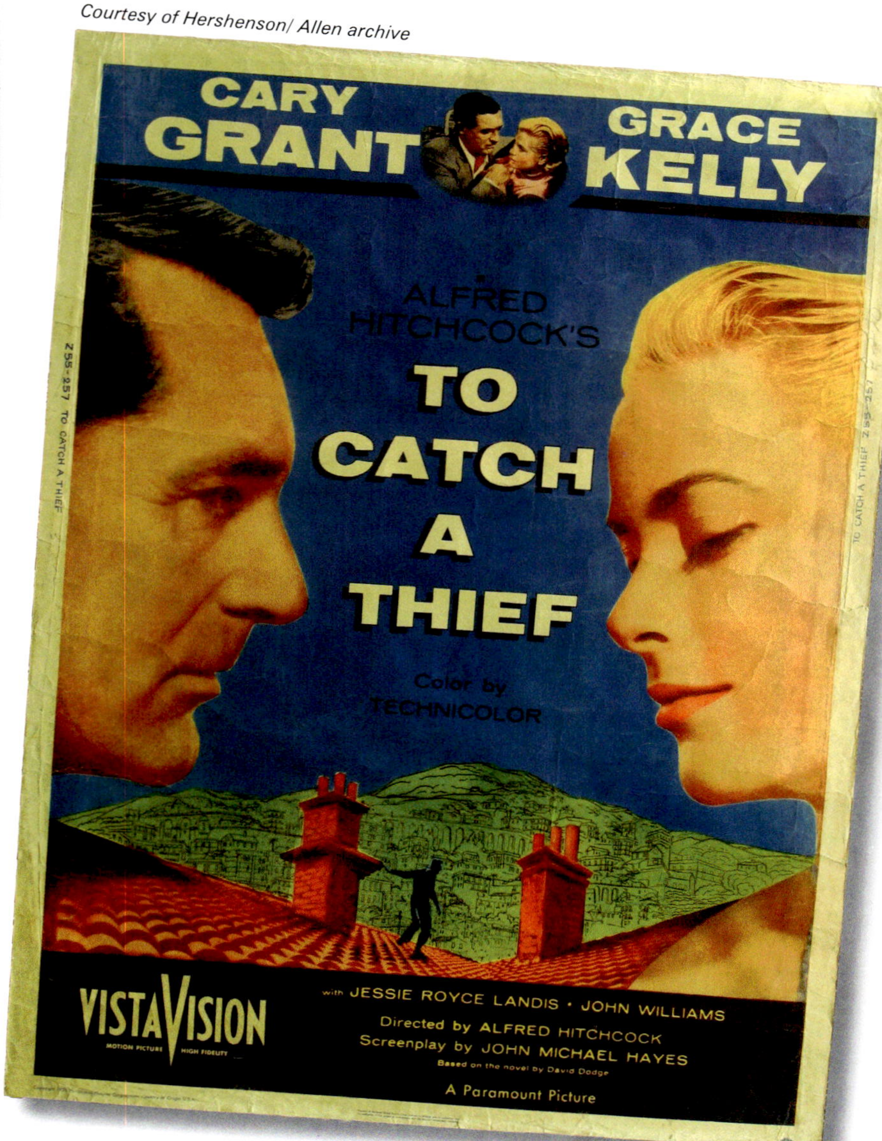

To Catch a Thief—Style Y	1955	40x60
Heritage	$2,868	FN 03/09
Private	$350	VF 02/97

- There are 2 known to exist.
- There is no *To Catch a Thief* 40x60 style Z known to exist.

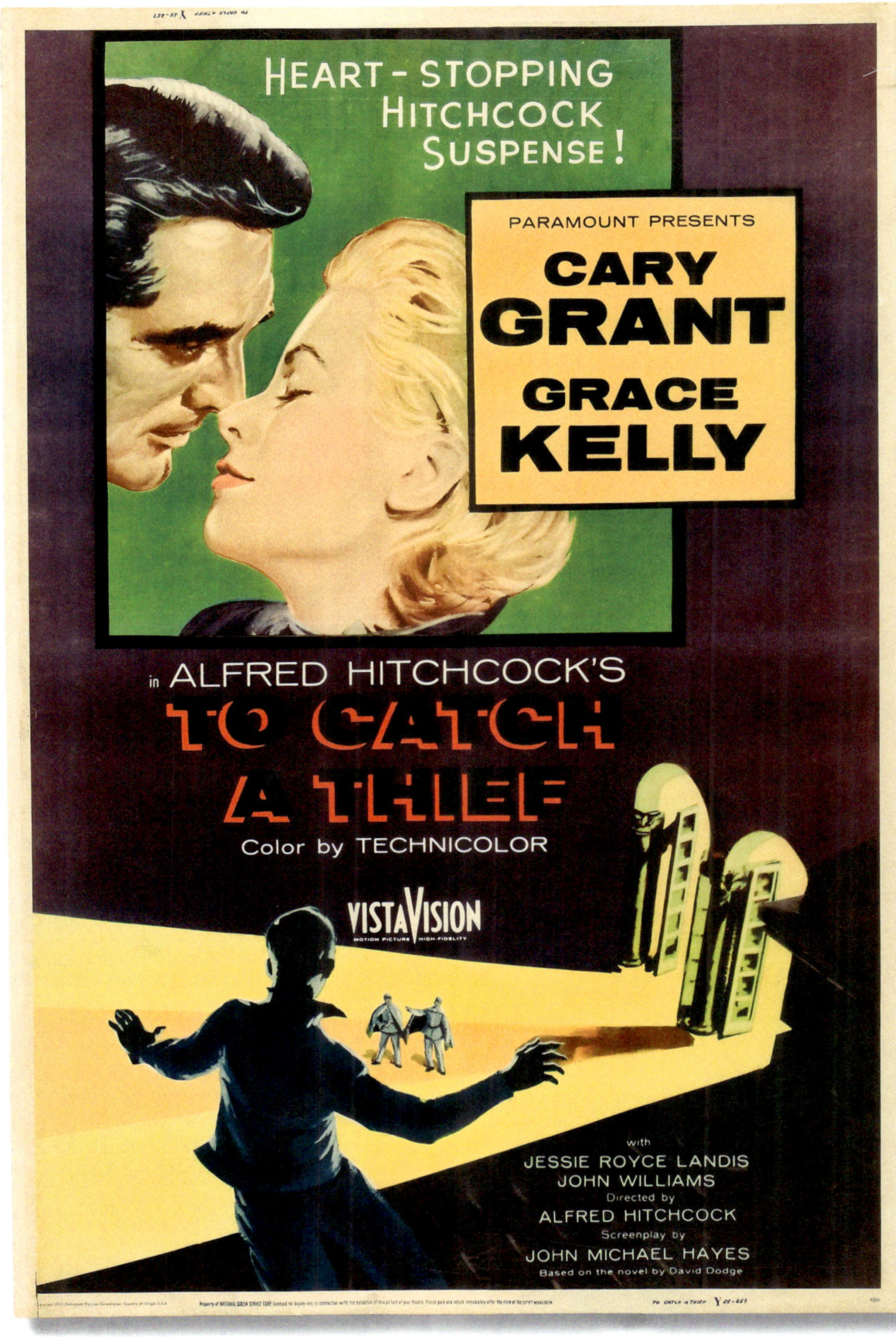

Courtesy of Heritage

Bus Stop 1956 27x41			
eMoviePoster	$262	GD/VG	09/09
eMoviePoster	$310	VG	08/09
Heritage	$262	VF+	02/09
Heritage	$358	VF	11/08
eMoviePoster	$655	VG	11/08

Highest price realized:

Christie's	$699	VG	07/97

Price in 1989:

Camden House	$325	VF	05/89

• This poster has appeared at auction 53 times since 1989.

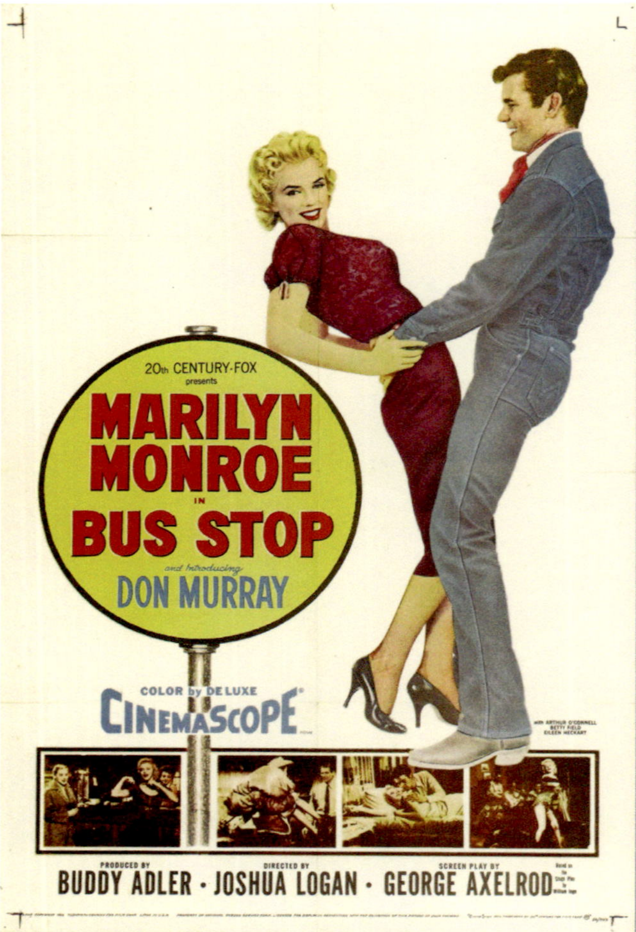

Courtesy of Heritage

Bus Stop**—Style Z** 1956 30x40			
Heritage	$956	VF	07/09
Camden House	$375	FN+	11/94

• There are 2 known to exist.

Courtesy of Heritage

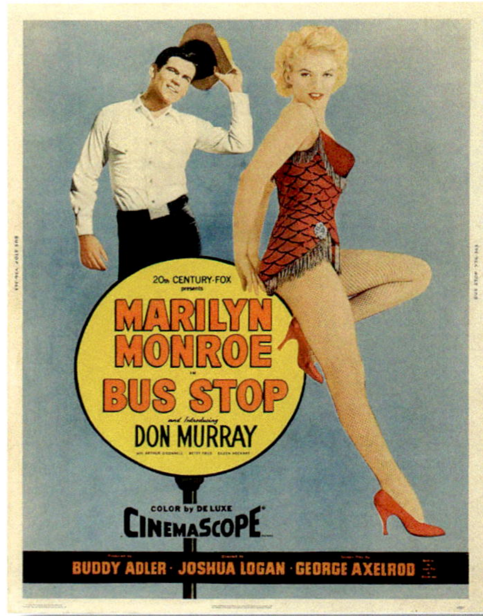

Bus Stop**—Style Y** 1956 30x40			
Heritage	$2,760	FN	11/05

• There is 1 known to exist.

Courtesy of Heritage

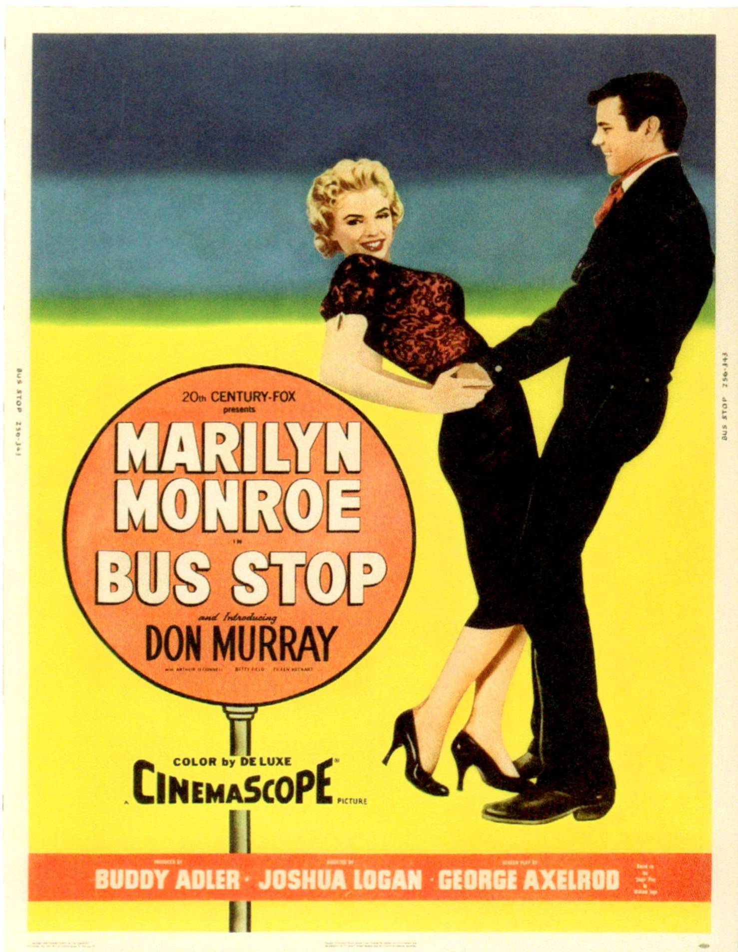

Bus Stop—Style Z	1956	40x60	
Christie's	$3,133	VF	11/08
Heritage	$2,300	VF	03/06

- There are 2 known to exist.
- There is no *Bus Stop* 40x60 Style Y known to exist.

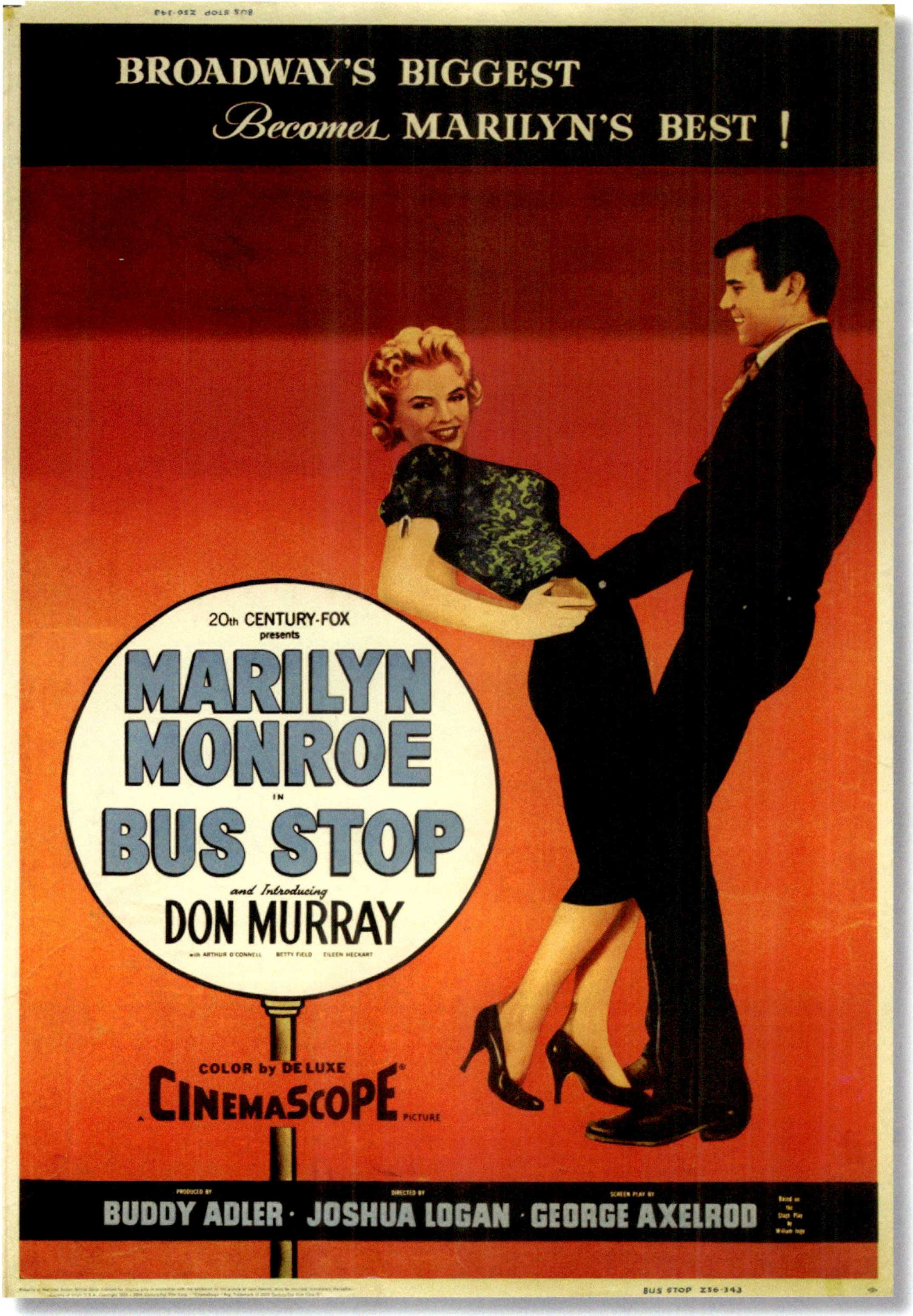

Courtesy of Heritage

Giant 1956 27x41			
Heritage	$262	VF-	11/09
Heritage	$286	VF-	05/09
eMoviePoster	$132	FR	04/09
Heritage	$310	FN/VF	03/09
Heritage	$418	VF	01/09

Highest price realized:

Profiles in History	$650	VF	12/08

Price in 1989:

Camden House	$350	VG	05/89

• This poster has appeared at auction 36 times since 1989.

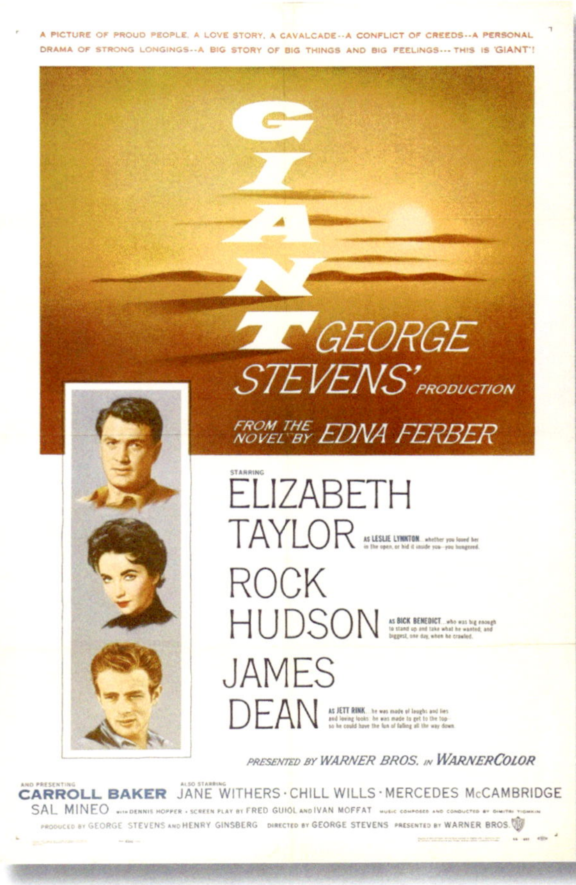

Courtesy of Heritage

Giant—Style Y 1956 30x40			
Heritage	$657	VF	07/07
Sotheby's	$1,092	VF	04/98

• There are 2 known to exist.

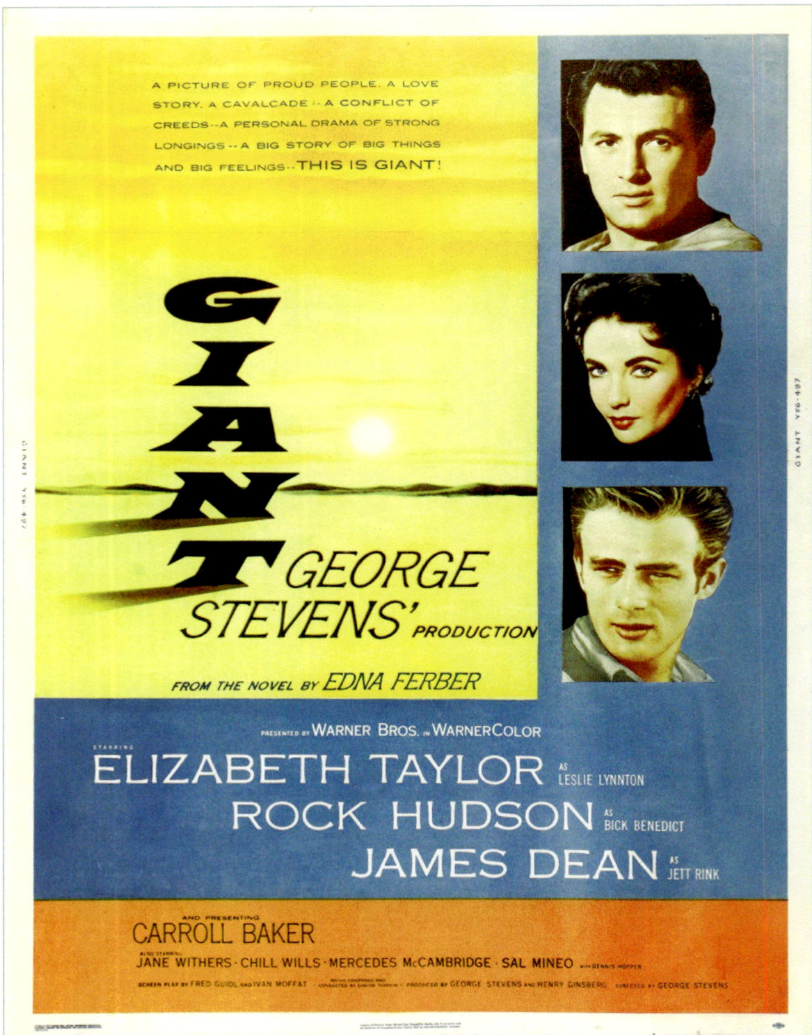

Courtesy of Heritage

Giant—Style Z 1956 30x40			
Sotheby's	$2,185	FN	12/93

• There is 1 known to exist.

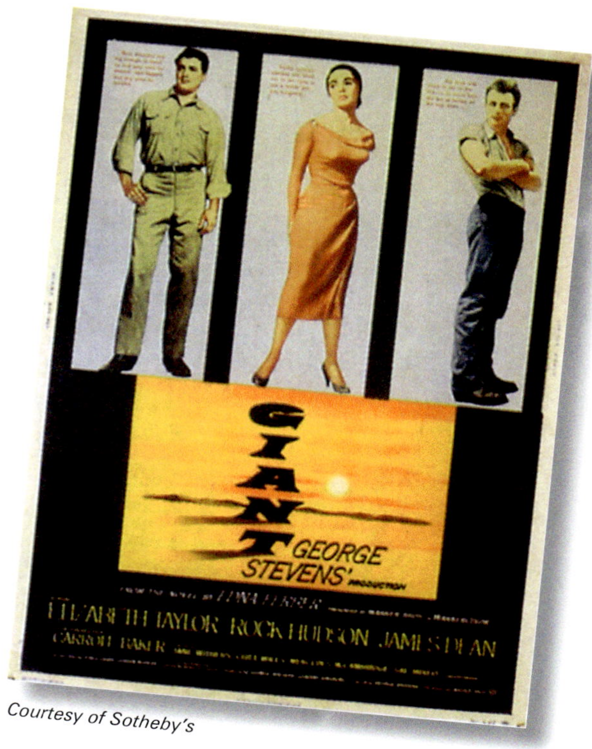

Courtesy of Sotheby's

Giant—Style Z 1956 40x60

eMoviePoster	$415	FR	04/07*
eMoviePoster	$494	FR	12/05*
Private	$1,200	FN+	02/05
eMoviePoster	$416	FR	12/04
Christie's	$978	VF	12/97

- There are 4 known to exist.
- There is no *Giant* 40x60 Style Y known to exist.

* This is the same poster that was sold by eMoviePoster in 2004. It had major restoration.

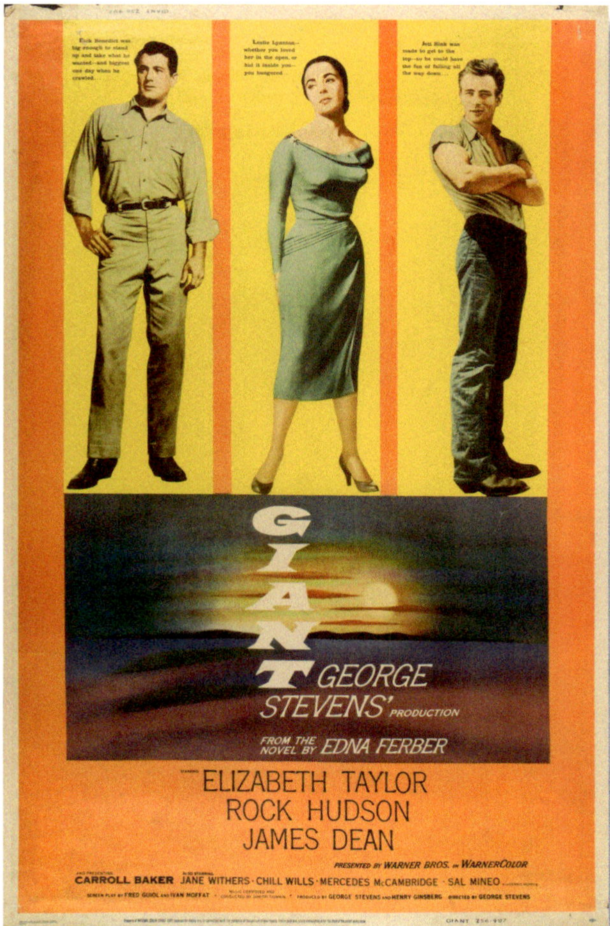

Courtesy of R. Aaron Raymond

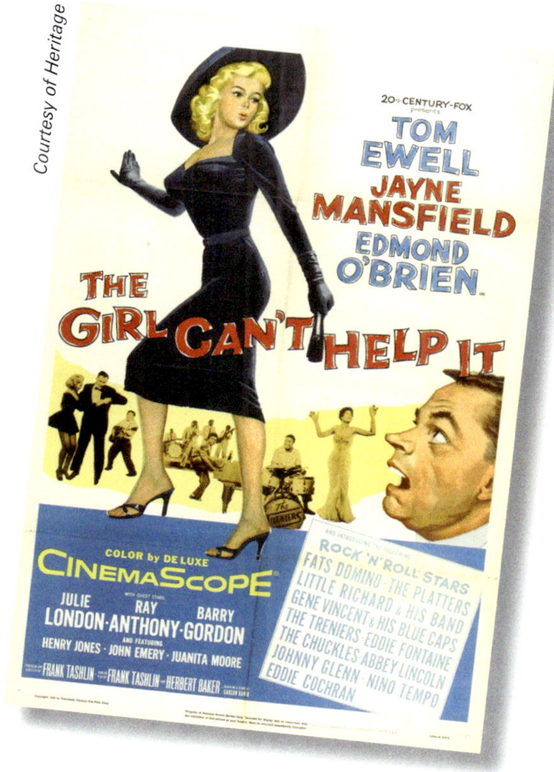

Courtesy of Heritage

The Girl Can't Help It 1956 27x41

Highest price realized:

Heritage	$507	NM	11/08

- This poster sells for $50- $200
- This poster has appeared at auction over 75 times since 1989.
- There is no *The Girl Can't Help It* 30x40 known to exist.

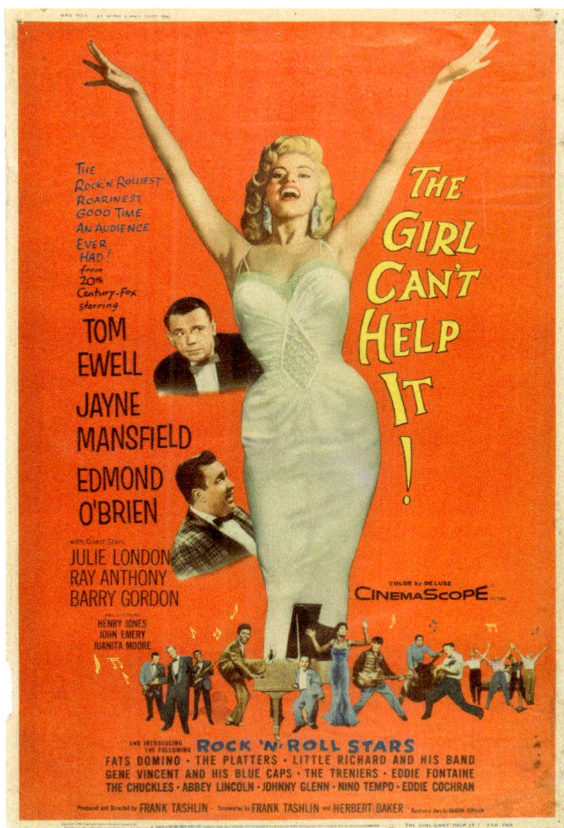

Courtesy of Heritage

The Girl Can't Help It—Style Y 1956 40x60

Heritage	$5,377	FN+	11/08

- There is 1 known to exist.
- There is no *The Girl Can't Help It* 40x60 style Z known to exist.

High Society—Style Z 1956 40x60

Christie's	$1,790	FN+	09/08

• There is 1 known to exist.

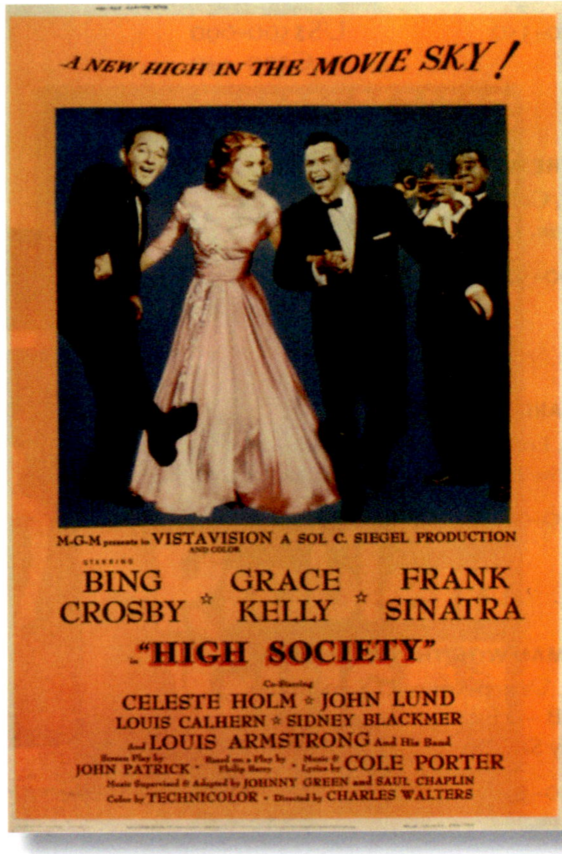

Courtesy of Christie's

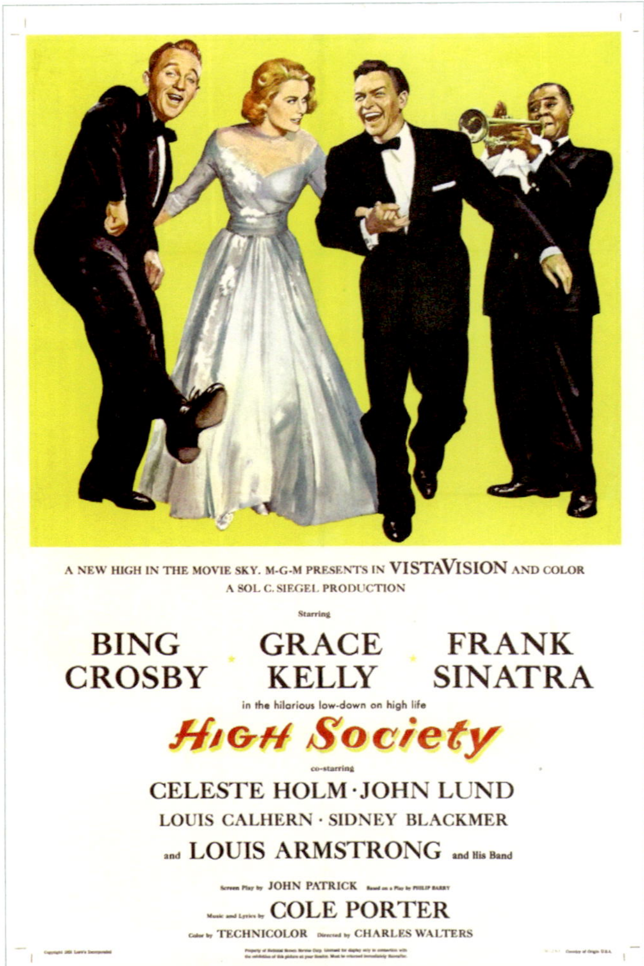

Courtesy of Heritage

High Society 1956 27x41

Christie's	$991	VF-	11/09
eMoviePoster	$338	GD	09/09
Heritage	$537	FN/VF	03/09
Christie's	$1,790	VF	11/08
Heritage	$896	VG	11/08

Highest price realized:

Christie's	$3,525	NM	11/00

Price in 1992:

Camden House	$150	FN	03/92

•This poster has appeared at auction 26 times since 1989.
• There is no *High Society* 30x40 known to exist.

High Society—Style Y 1956 40x60

Christie's	DNS	VF	03/09

• There is 1 known to exist.

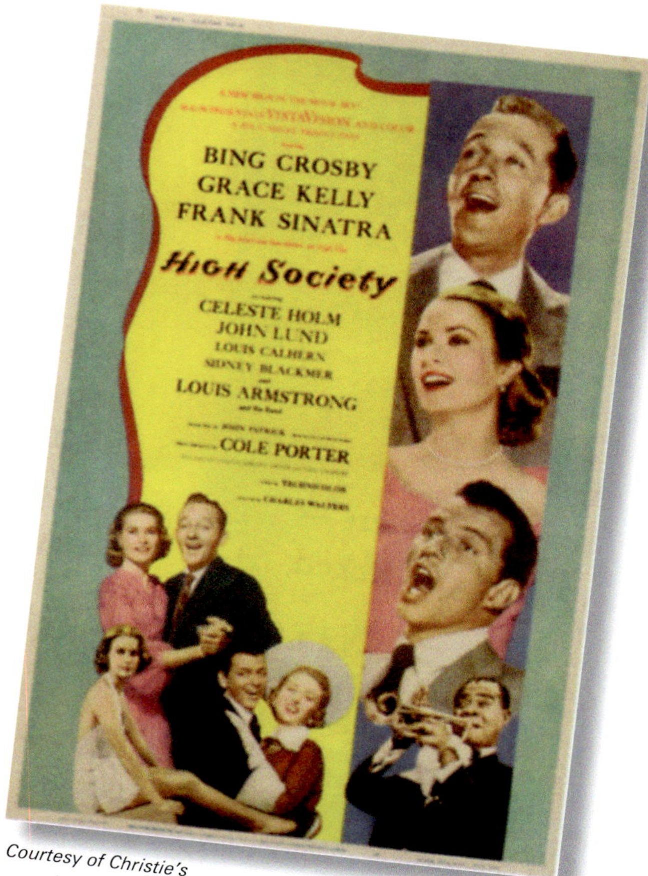

Courtesy of Christie's

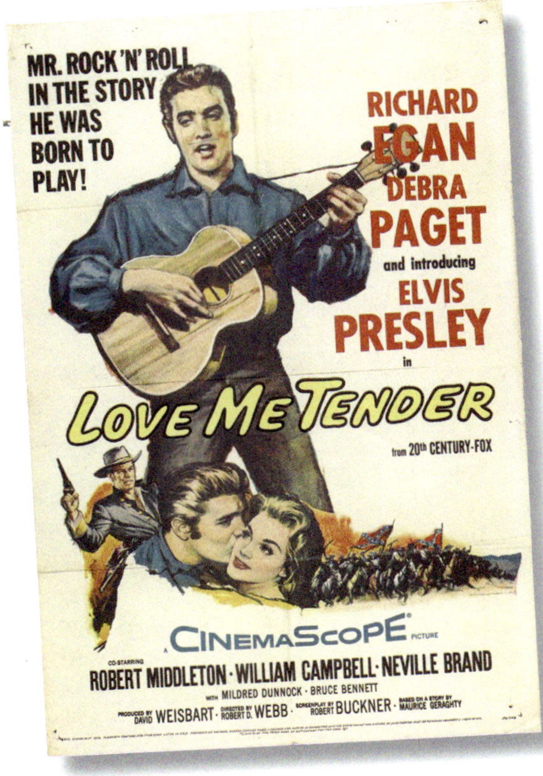

Courtesy of Heritage

Love Me Tender	1956	27x41	
Heritage	$448	VF	11/09
Hollywood Poster	$480	VF-	10/09
Heritage	$358	VF-	11/08
Heritage	$388	FN-	05/08
Heritage	$448	VF	11/07

Highest price realized:

Heritage	$718	NM	03/03

Price in 1989:

Camden House	$225	VF	05/89

- This poster has appeared at auction 39 times since 1989.
- There is no *Love Me Tender* 30x40 known to exist.

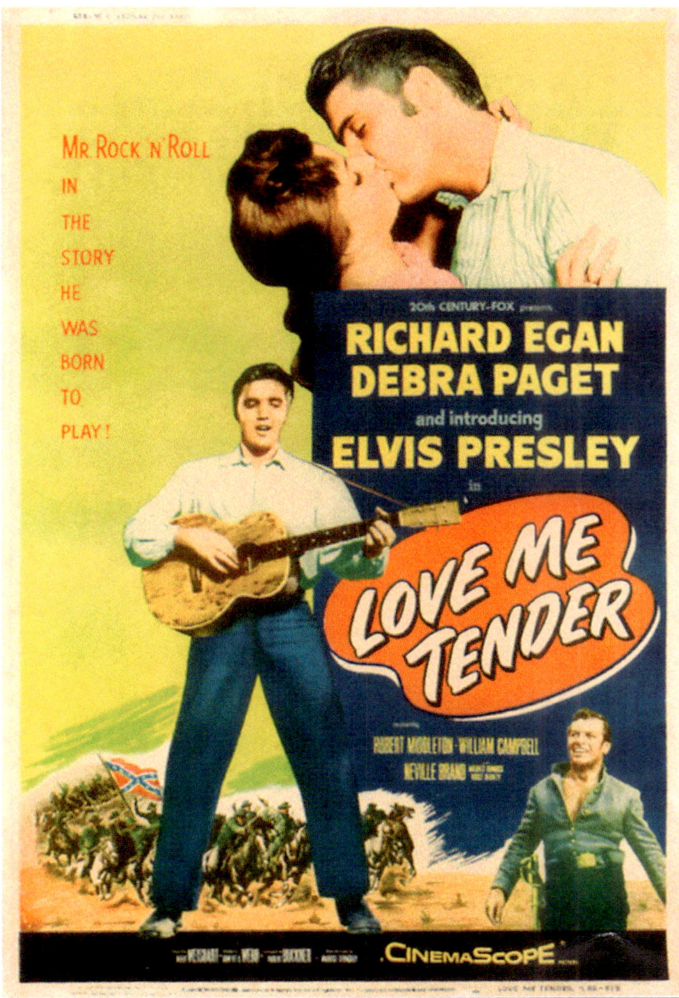

Courtesy of Christie's

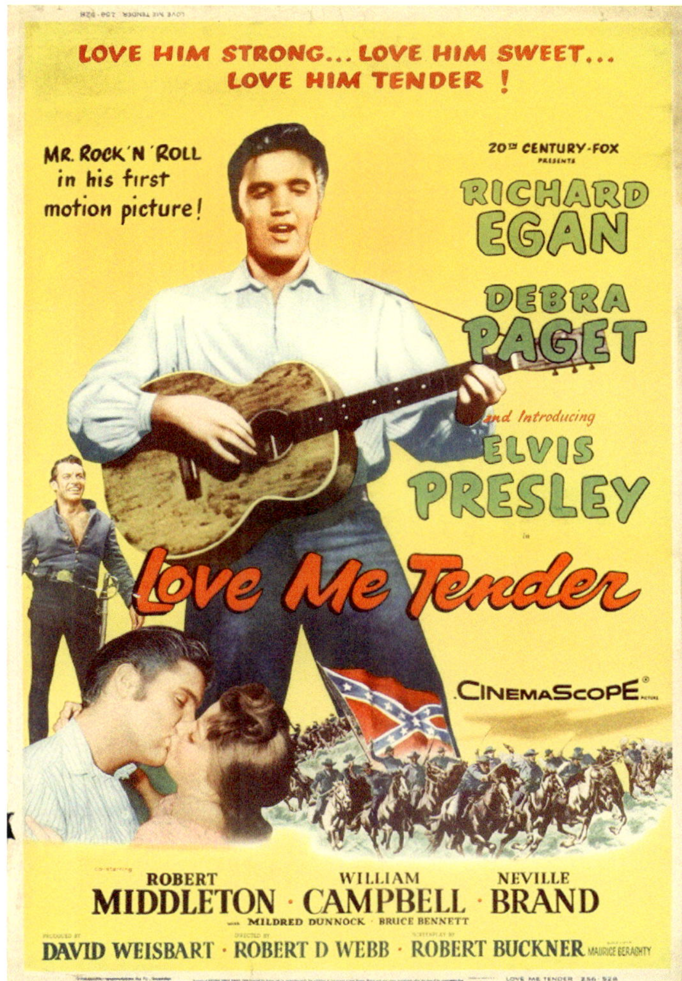

Courtesy of Heritage

Love Me Tender**—**Style Z	1956	40x60	
Heritage	$862	FN	03/04

Estimate: $1,000 - $2,000

- There is 1 known to exist.

Love Me Tender **—**Style Y	1956	40x60	
Christie's	$880	FN	03/00

Estimate: $1,500 - $2,000

- There is 1 known to exist.

Man Who Knew Too Much—Style Y 1956 30x40

Heritage	$460	FN-	03/06*
Private	$375	FN	11/97*
Private	$250	VG	07/97*

• There are 3 known to exist.
* There were two Private sales in 1997, there is no way to tell if they were Style "Y" or "Z'" or if these posters appeared in these later auctions. The "known to exist" is also most likely incorrect due to these unknown private sales.

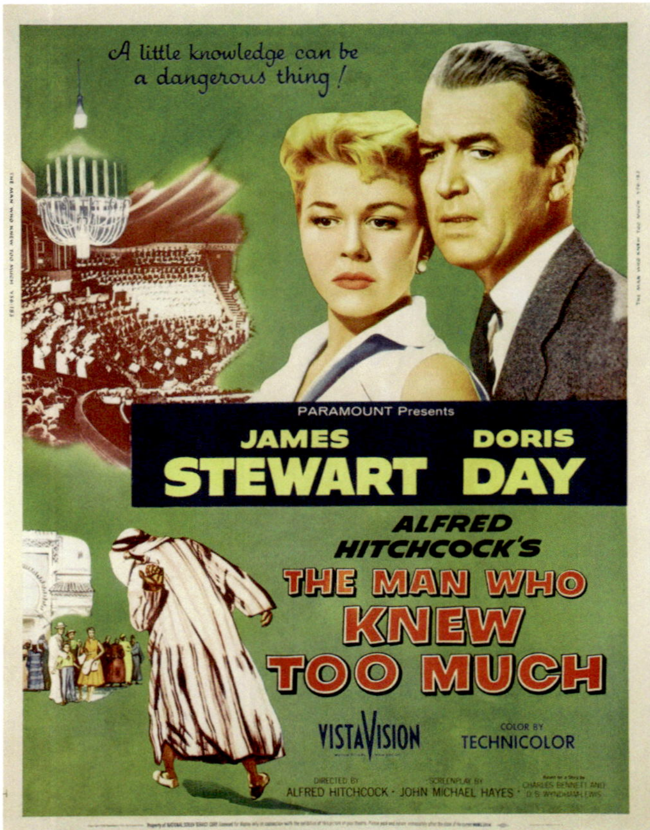

Courtesy of Heritage

Man Who Knew Too Much—Style Z 1956 30x40

Butterfield's	$690	VF	10/00*
Christie's	$1,243	VF-	09/98*

• There are 2 known to exist. *

* There were two Private sales in 1997, there is no way to tell if they were Style "Y" or "Z'" or if these posters appeared in these later auctions. The "known to exist" is also most likely incorrect due to these unknown private sales.

The Man Who Knew Too Much—Style Y & Z 1956 40x60
No image available

Private	$250	FN	07/97*
Private	$425	FN	03/97*
Butterfield & Butterfield	$475	NM	11/96*

• There are 3 known to exist.
* There is no way to tell if they were the Style Y or Z and the Butterfield auction does not specify.

Man Who Knew Too Much 1956 27x41
This poster typically sells for $95- $400

Highest price realized:

Private	$695	VF	01/01

• This poster has appeared at auction more than 75 times since 1989.

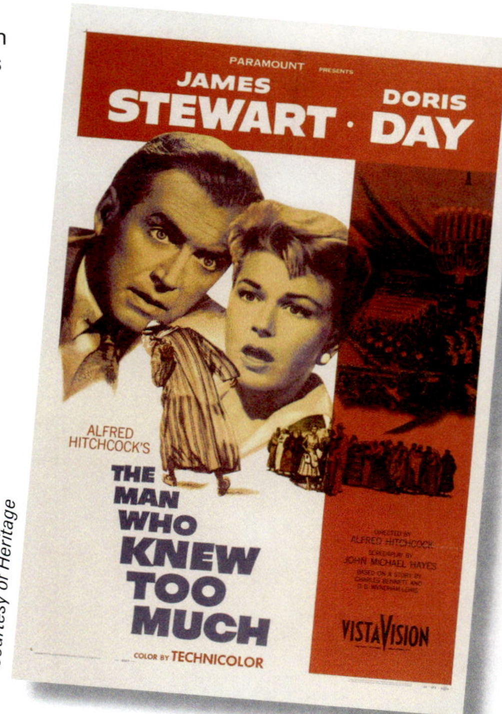

Courtesy of Heritage

Courtesy of Butterfield's

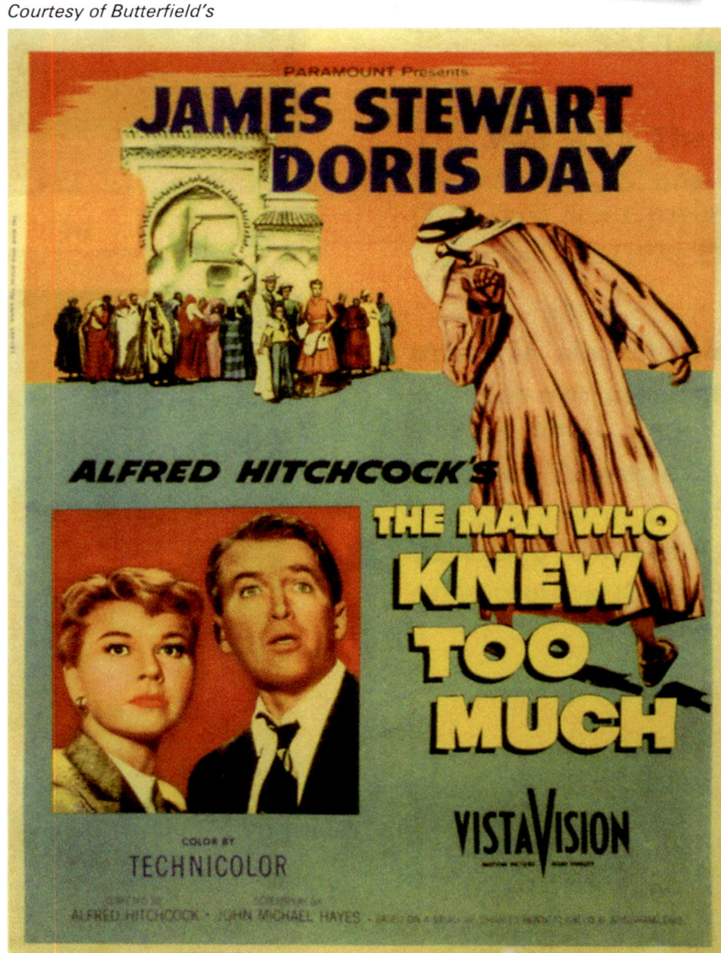

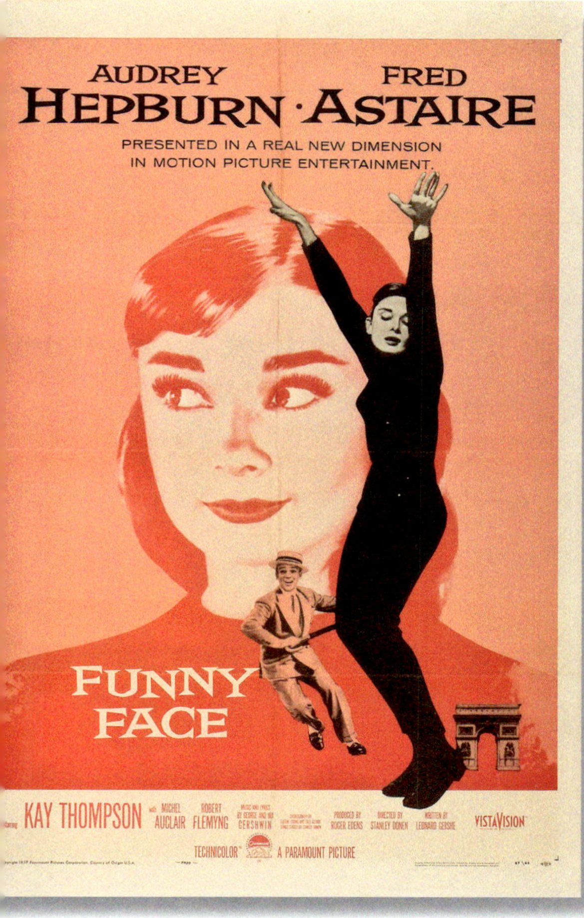

Courtesy of Heritage

Funny Face 1957 27x41

Heritage	$418	FN+	11/09
Heritage	$489	FN/VF	11/09
Heritage	$418	VF	04/09
Heritage	$776	VF/NM	03/09
Heritage	$478	VF	07/09

Highest price realized:
Bonhams & Butterfields $1,645 VF 12/05

Price in 1995:
Camden House $125 FN 01/95

• This poster has appeared at auction 32 times since 1989.

Funny Face 1957 30x40.
No image available
Vintage Poster Art $748 FN 05/96
Estimate: $2,000 - $4,000

• There is 1 known to exist.

Funny Face—Style Y 1957 40x60
Estimate: $2,500 - $4,500

• There is 1 known to exist.

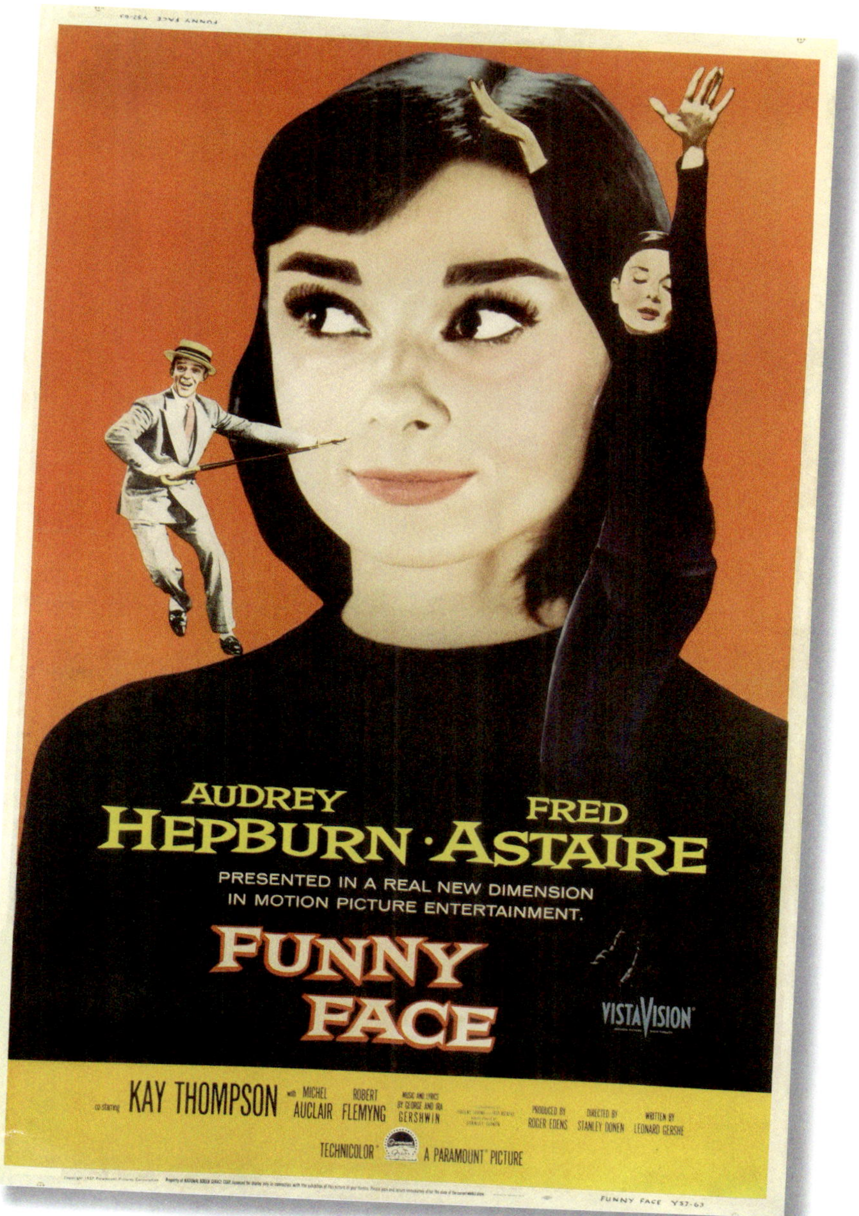

Courtesy of the Reel Poster Gallery, London

Funny Face—Style Z 1957 40x60
Estimate: $2,500 - $4,500

• There is 1 known to exist.

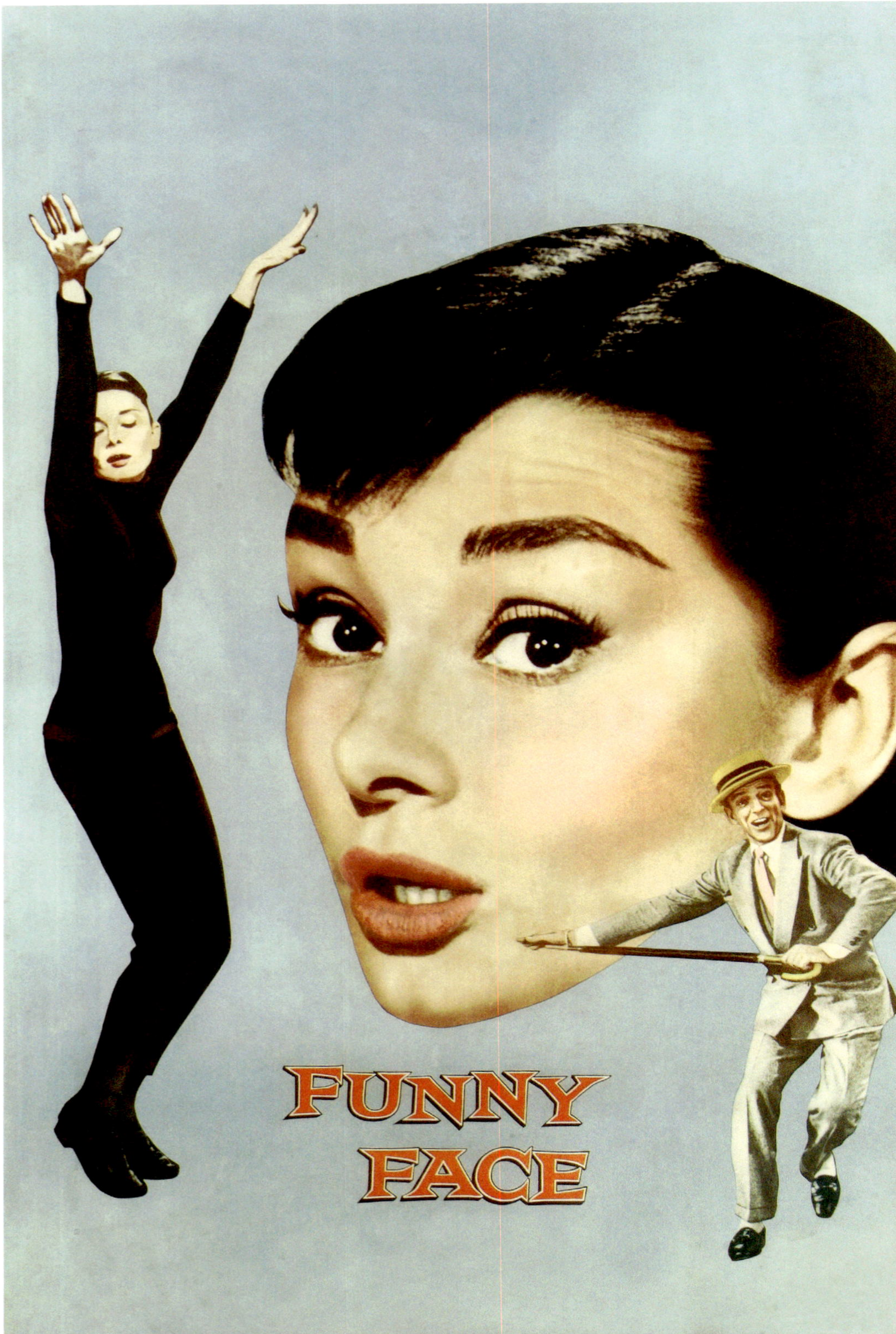

Courtesy of the Reel Poster Gallery, London

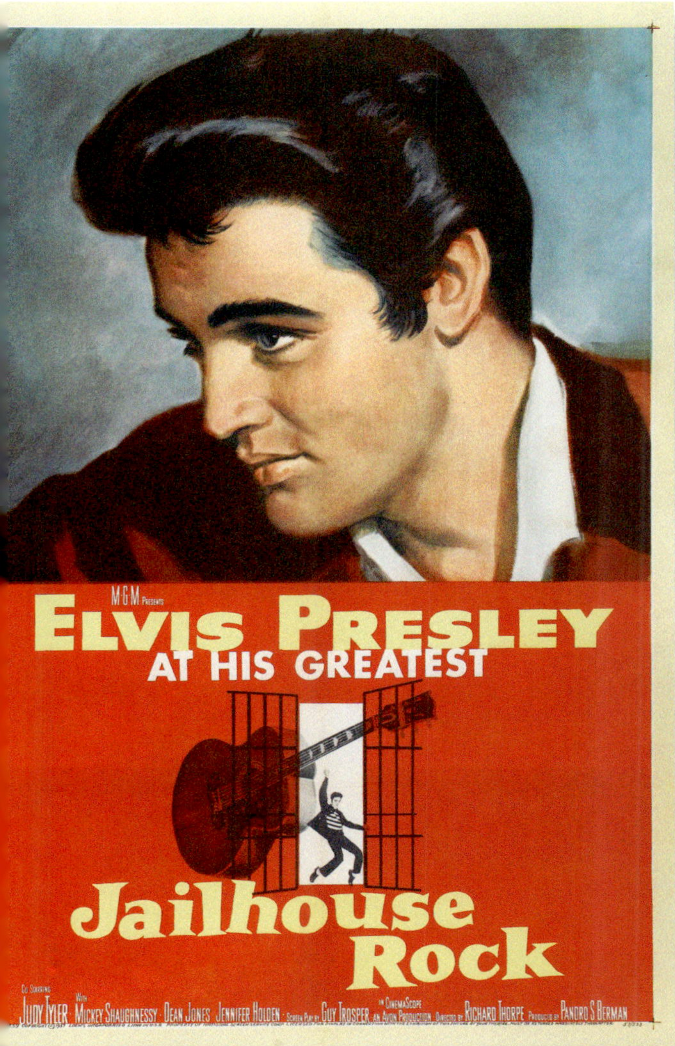

Courtesy of Heritage

Jailhouse Rock	1957	27x41	
Heritage	$1,075	VF+	07/09
eMoviePoster	$1,411	FN	04/09
Heritage	$1,673	VF	03/09
Heritage	$1,434	VF	11/08
eMoviePoster	$1,850	FN	09/08

Highest price realized:

eMoviePoster	$3,300	NM	12/03

Price in 1990:

Camden House	$1,500	NM	03/90

- This poster has appeared at auction 44 times since 1989.
- There is no *Jailhouse Rock* 30x40 known to exist

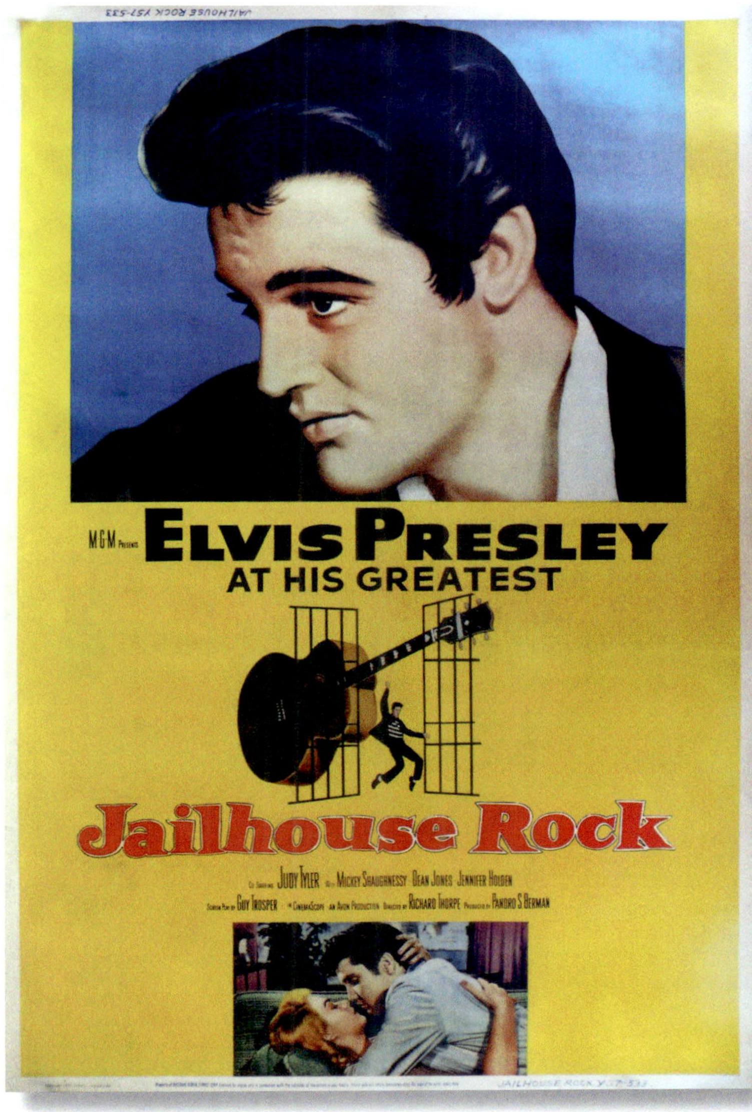

Courtesy of Sotheby's

Jailhouse Rock—Style Y	1957	40x60	
Sotheby's	$747	VF-	04/99

Estimate: $5,000 - $8,000

- There are 3 known to exist.
- There is no *Jailhouse Rock* 40x60 Style Z known to exist.

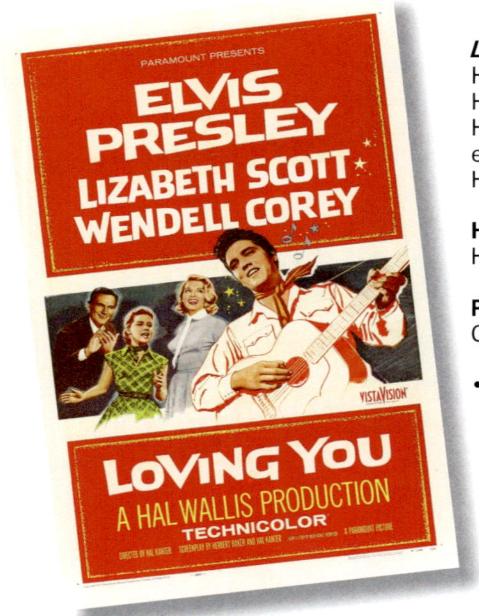

Courtesy of Heritage

Loving You 1957 27x41			
Heritage	$388	VF-	11/09
Heritage	$310	VF-	07/09
Heritage	$448	VF	05/09
eMoviePoster	$112	FR	05/09
Heritage	$346	VF-	11/08

Highest price realized:

Heritage	$1,314	VF-	11/06

Price in 1990:

Camden House	$150	FN	10/90

- This poster has appeared at auction 36 times since 1989.

Loving You—Style Y 1957 40x60			
Heritage	$2,151	VF	03/08

- There is 1 known to exist.
- There is no *Loving You* Style Z 40x60 known to exist.

Courtesy Sotheby's

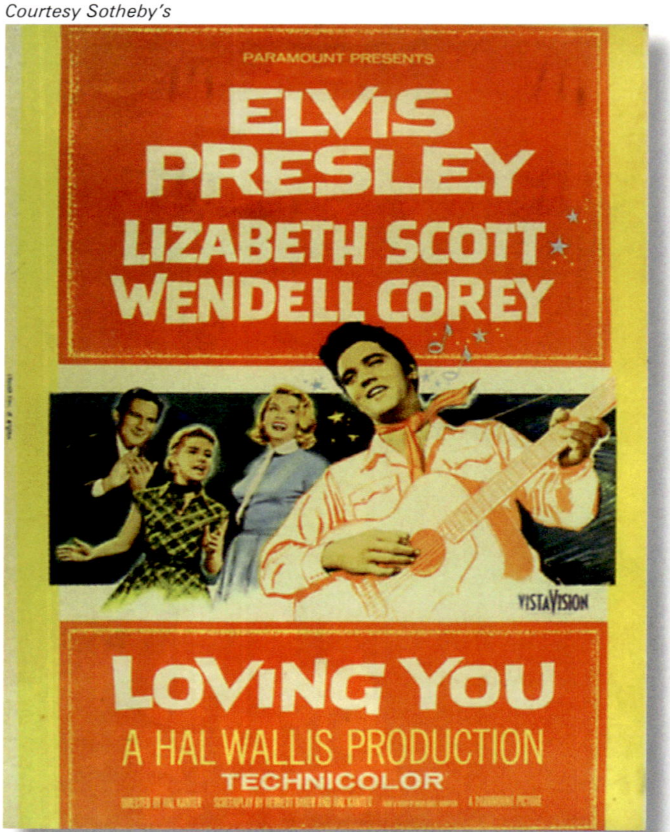

Loving You—Style Y 1957 30x40			
Sotheby's	DNS	VF	12/95

Estimate: $2,000 - $3,000

- There is 1 known to exist.
- There is no *Loving You* Style Z 30x40 known to exist.

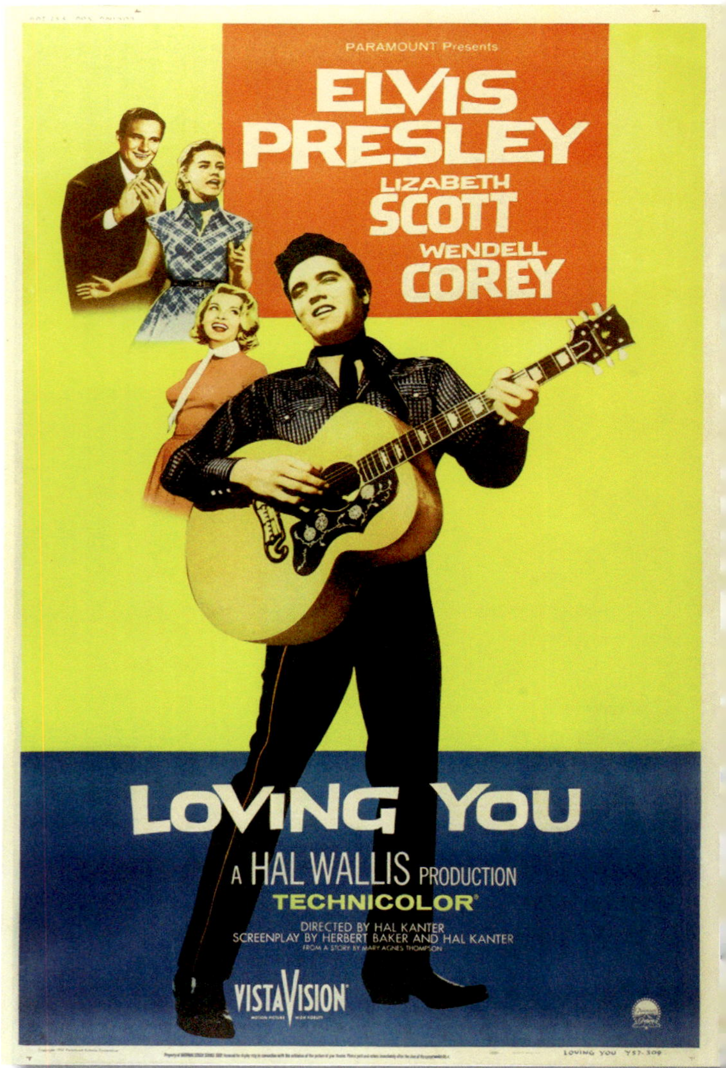

Courtesy of Heritage

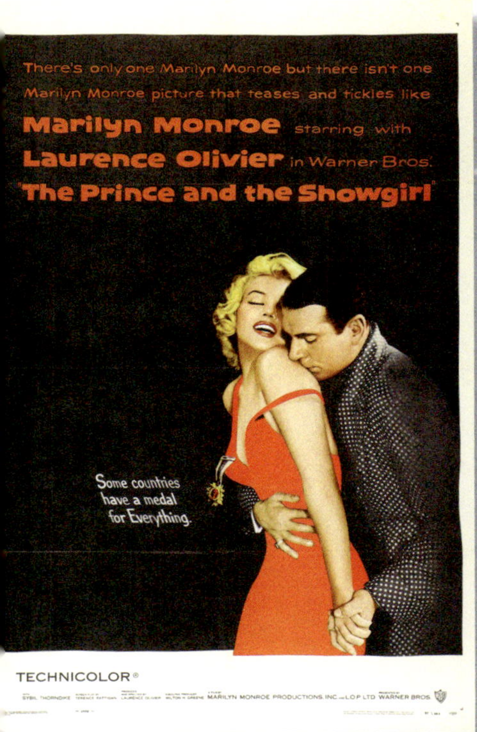

Courtesy of Heritage

Prince and the Showgirl	1957	27x41	
Christie's	$1,549	VF-	11/09
Heritage	$717	VF	11/09
Heritage	$956	VF+	04/09
eMoviePoster	$521	GD/VG	04/09
Christie's	$1,290	VF	03/09

Highest price realized:

Christie's	$1,549	VF-	11/09

Price in 1990:

Camden House	$200	FN	10/90

•This poster has appeared at auction 47 times since 1989.

Prince and the Showgirl 1957 30x40.
No image available

eMoviePoster	$203	FR	11/06

• There are 2 known to exist.

Photo by R. Aaron Raymond & Stephen Allard

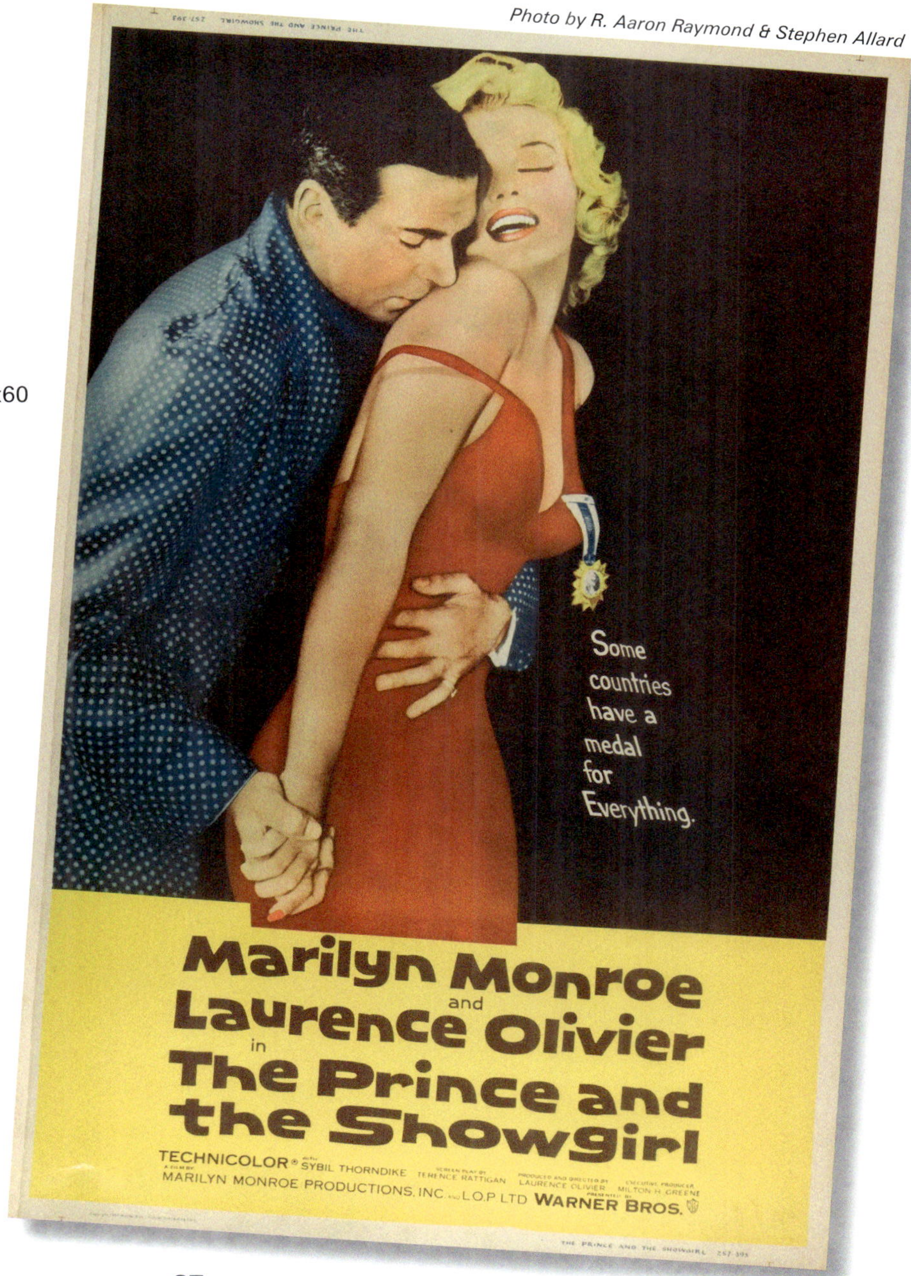

Prince and the Showgirl—Style Z 1957 40x60

Private	$2,200	VF	11/08

• There is 1 known to exist.
• There is no *Prince and the Showgirl* Style Y known to exist.

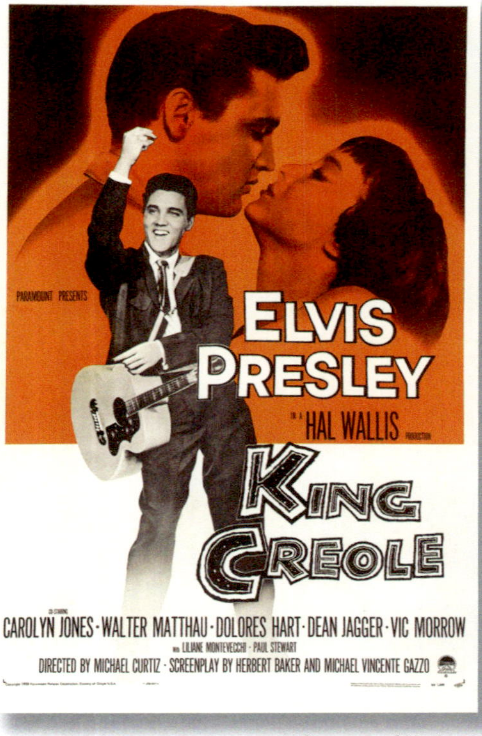

Courtesy of Heritage

King Creole 1958 27x41

Heritage	$448	FN+	05/09
CineMasterpieces	$1,500	NM	02/09
Heritage	$478	VF+	07/08
CineMasterpieces	$1,400	EX	07/08
Heritage	$507	VF	03/08

Highest price realized:

CineMasterpieces	$1,500	NM	02/09

Price in 1993:

Camden House	$500	FN	11/93

- This poster has appeared at auction 28 times since 1989.
- There is no *King Creole* 30x40 known to exist.

Courtesy of Christie's

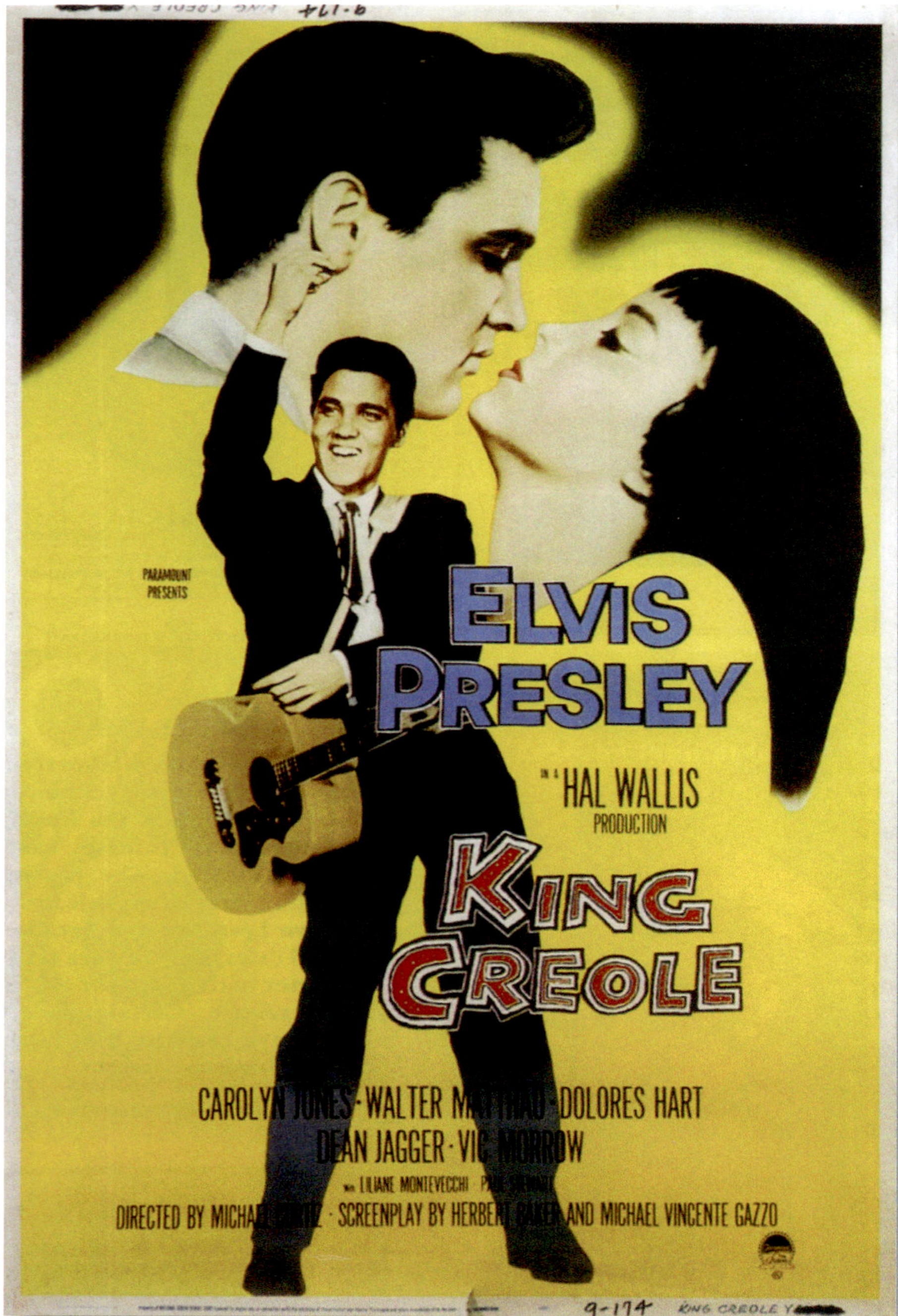

King Creole—Style Y 1958 40x60

Skinner	$2,645	VF	11/98*
Christie's	$2,208	VF	03/96
Private	$1,500	NM	01/96

Estimate: $7,000 - $10,000

- There are 2 known to exist.
- There is no *King Creole* 40x60 Style Z known to exist.

* This is the same poster that was offered at the Christie's auction in 1996.

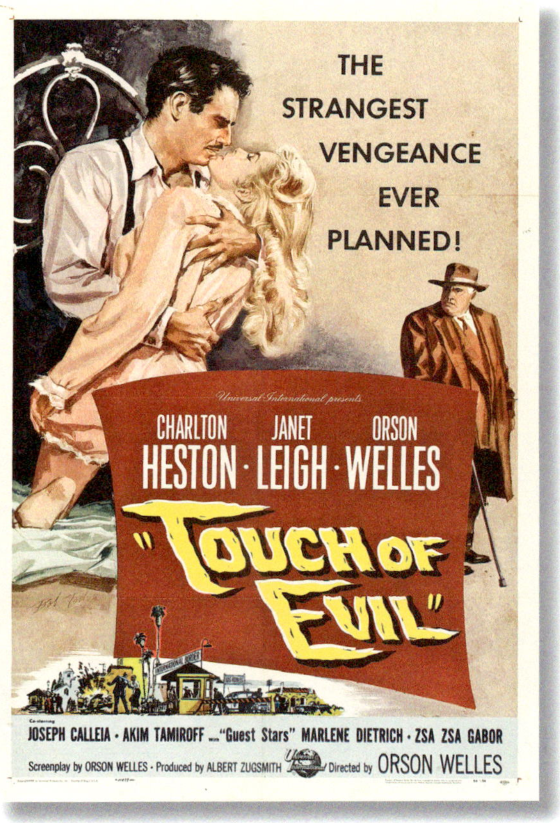

Courtesy of Heritage

Touch of Evil	1958	27x41	
Heritage	$836	FN+	11/09
Heritage	$836	VF-	07/09
eMoviePoster	$1,000	VG	07/09
eMoviePoster	$900	GD/VG	05/09
eMoviePoster	$1,050	VG	04/09

Highest price realized:
Bonhams & Butterfields $2,115 VF 12/05

Price in 1992:
Camden House $10 FN 03/92

- This poster has appeared at auction 32 times since 1989.

Courtesy of Heritage

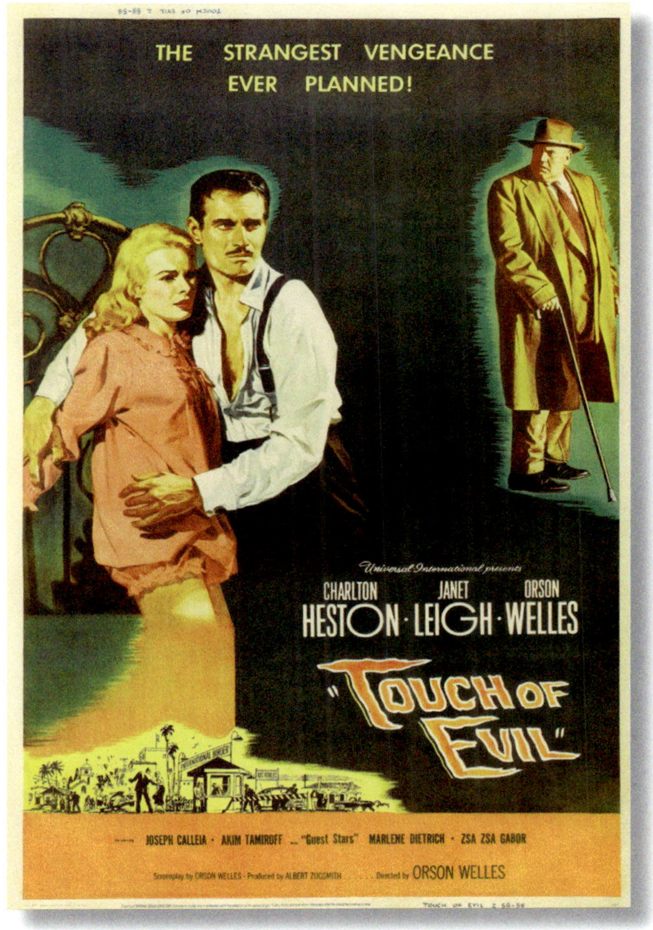

Touch of Evil**—Style Z**	1958	40x60	
Heritage	$2,629	FN/VF	07/09
Heritage	$2,390	VF	03/08

- There are 2 known to exist.
- There is no *Touch of Evil* 40x60 Style Y known to exist.

Courtesy of Sotheby's

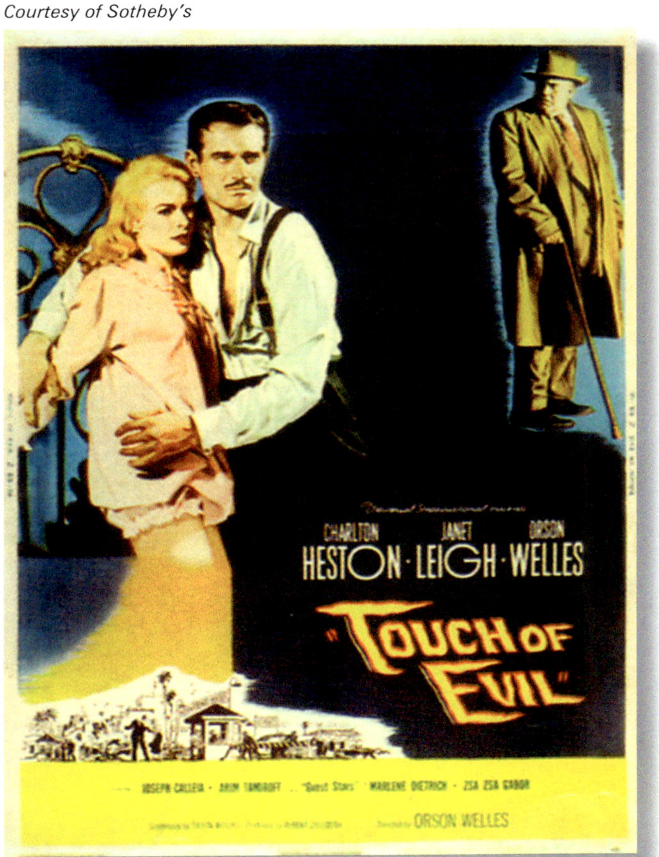

Touch of Evil**—Style Z**	1958	30x40	
Heritage	$989	FN/VF	07/04
Sotheby's	$550	VG	12/94

- There are 2 known to exist.
- There is no *Touch of Evil* 30x40 Style Y known to exist.

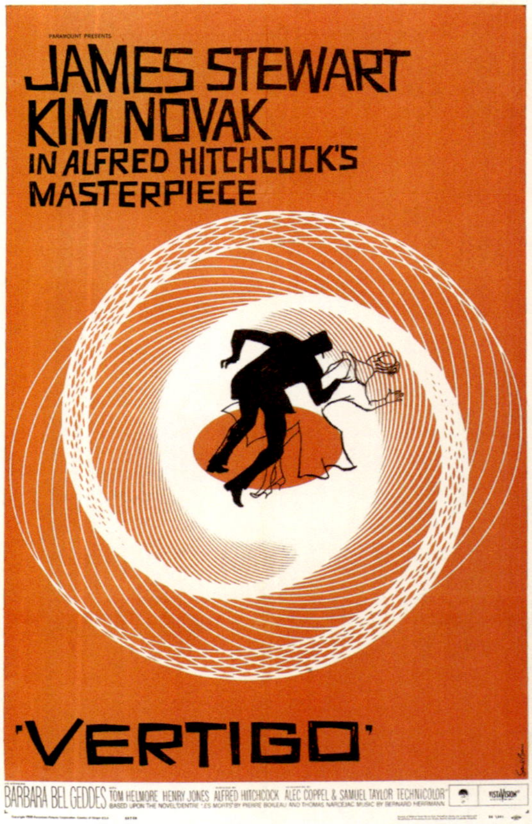

Courtesy of Heritage

Vertigo 1958 27x41

Christie's	$3,717	VF-	11/09
Heritage	$5,078	VF	07/09
Heritage	$3,883	VF+	03/09
Christie's	$3,440	VF	03/09
Profiles in History	$4,000	VF	12/08

Highest price realized:

Christie's	$5,444	VF-	03/06

Price in 1990:

Camden House	$325	NM	05/89

- This poster has appeared at auction 62 times since 1989.

Vertigo—Style Y 1958 30x40

Movieart.net	$10,500	NM	10/02
Movieart.net	$7,500	FN	08/02
Movieart.net	$2,500	FN	11/96

Estimate: $12,000 - $15,000

- There are 4 known to exist.

Courtesy of the Reel Poster Gallery, London

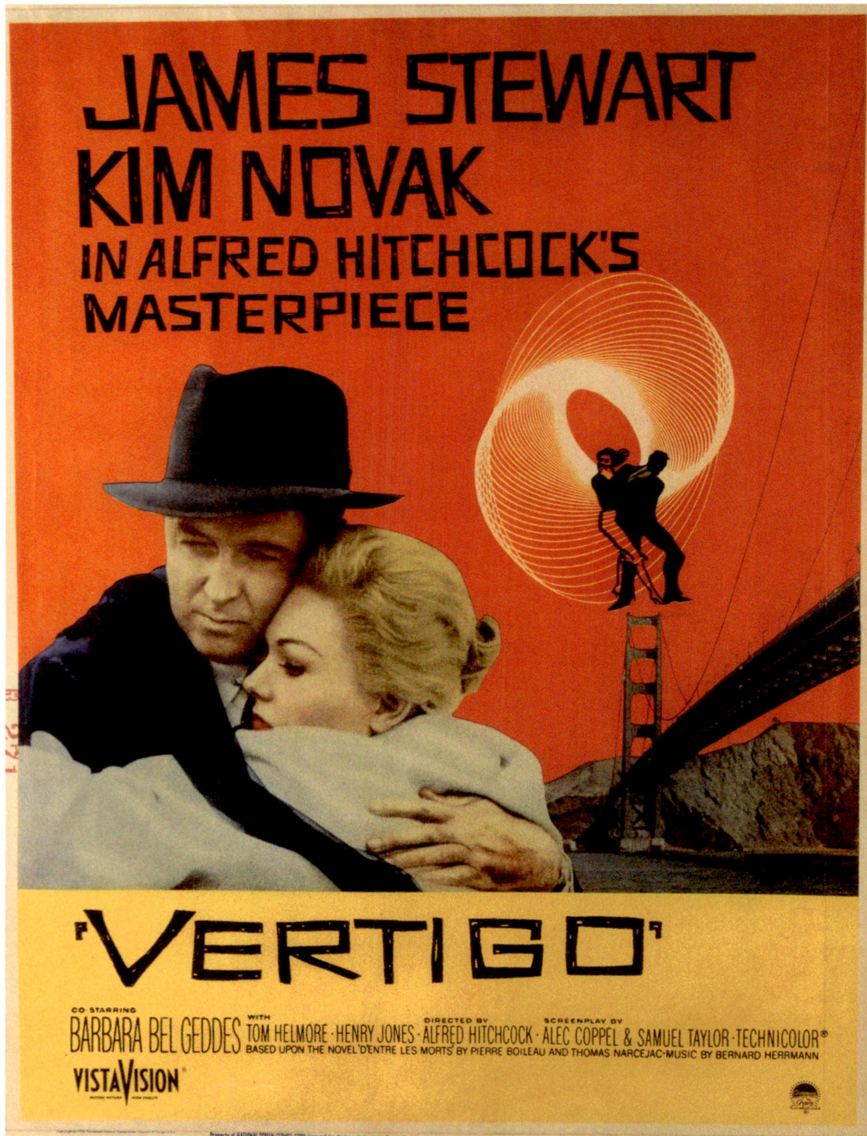

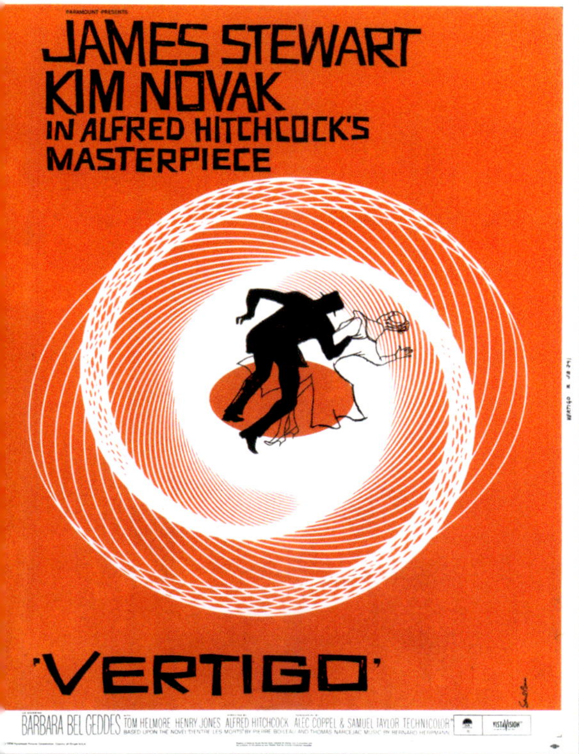

Courtesy of the Reel Poster Gallery, London

Vertigo—Style Z 1958 30x40

Private	$5,000	VF	10/02

Estimate: $6,000 - $7,500

- There are 3 known to exist.

Vertigo—Style Y 1958 40x60

Heritage	$2,151	FN	03/07
Movie Art	$5,500	VF	03/05
Christie's	$3,793	VF	11/03
Christie's	$3,249	VF	11/02
Christie's	$4,770	VF	03/01

- There are 8 known to exist.

Photo by R. Aaron Raymond & Stephen Allard

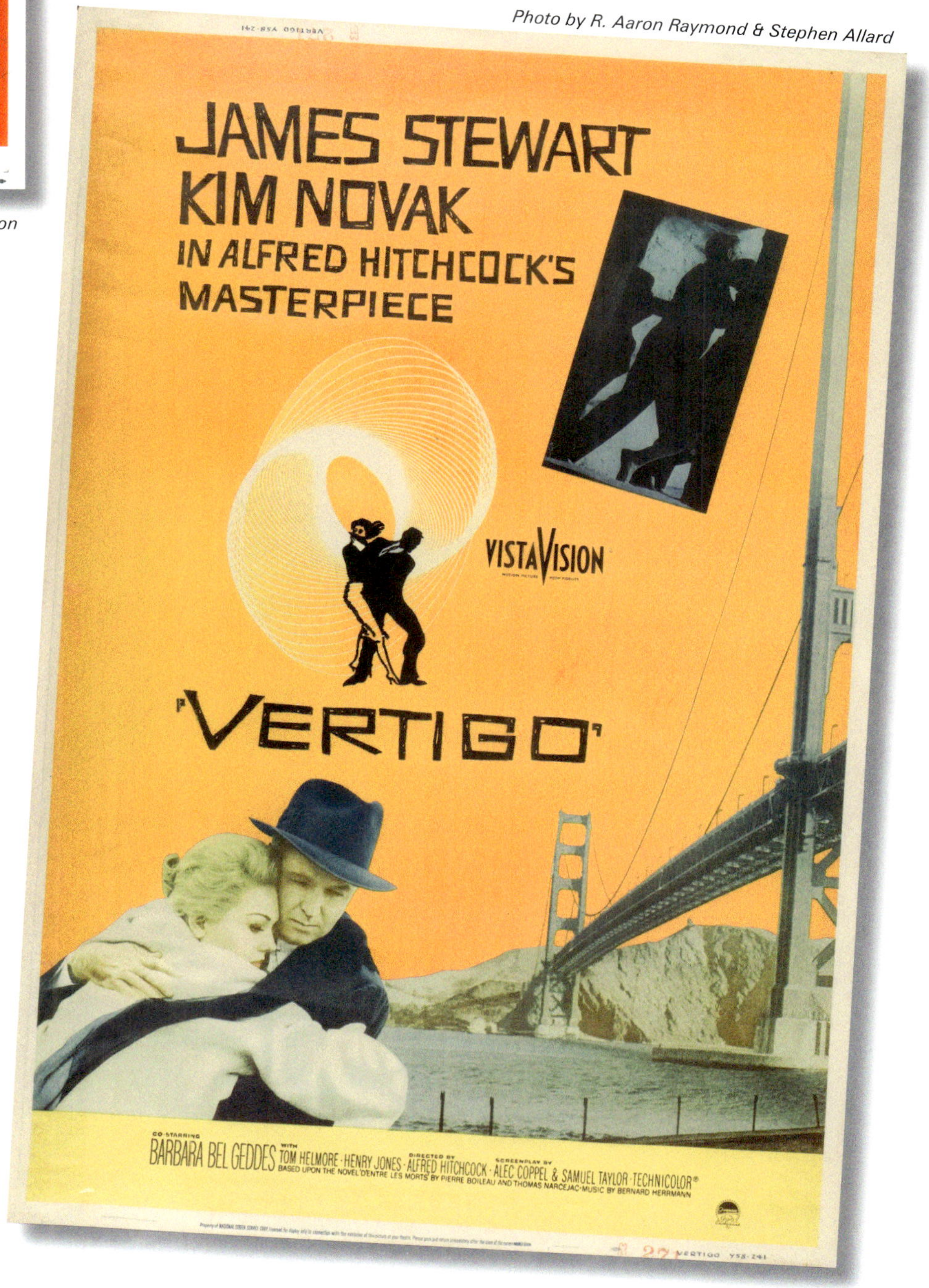

Vertigo—Style Z 1958 40x60
Heritage $7,767 FN/VF 11/08

- There are 2 known to exist.

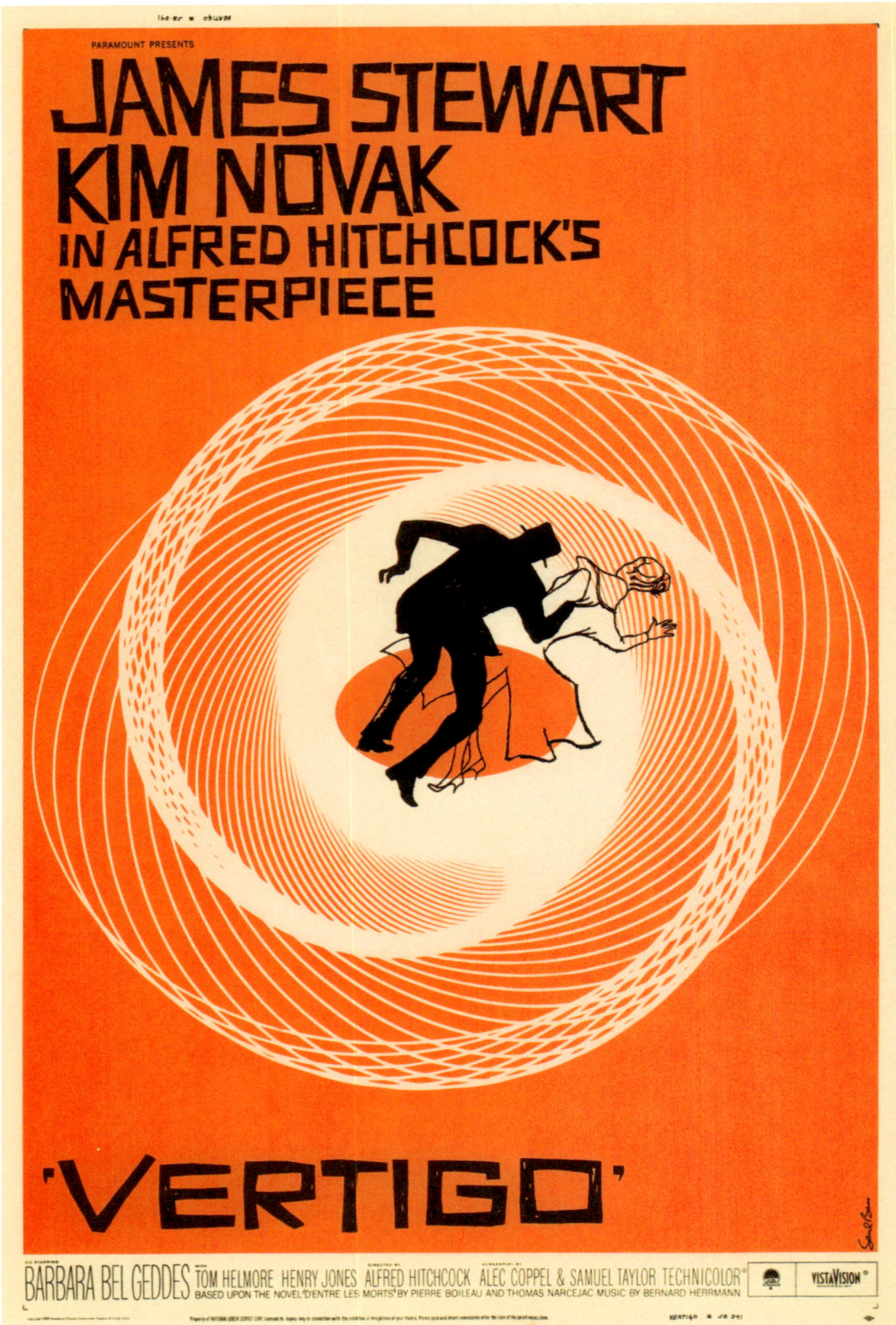

Courtesy of Heritage

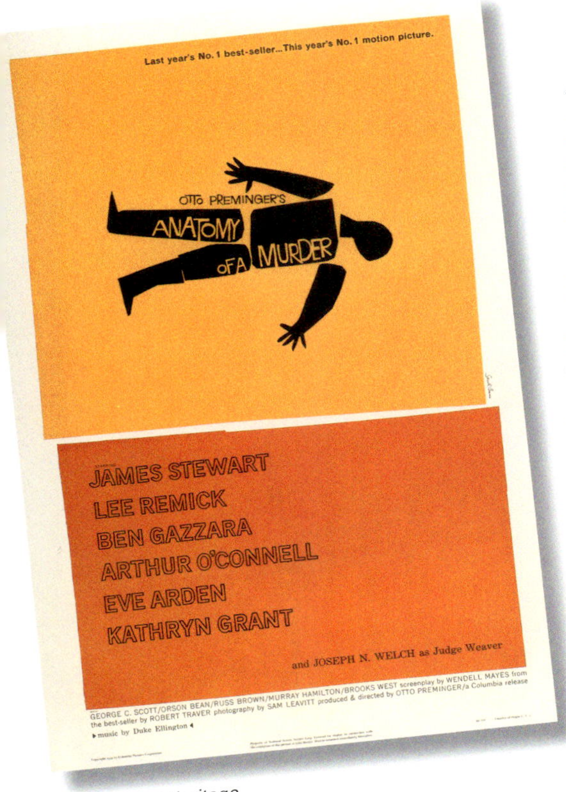

Courtesy of Heritage

Anatomy of a Murder—Style B 1959 27x41

eMoviePoster	$2,477	VG	12/09
Heritage	$2,270	VF	07/09
Heritage	$2,270	VF	03/09
Heritage	$2,390	VF	07/08
Bonhams & Butterfields	$2,400	VF	12/07

Highest price realized:

Bonhams & Butterfields	$2,400	VF	12/07

Price in 1990:

Camden House	$30	FN	03/90

- This poster has appeared at auction 31 times since 1989.

Courtesy of the Reel Poster Gallery, London

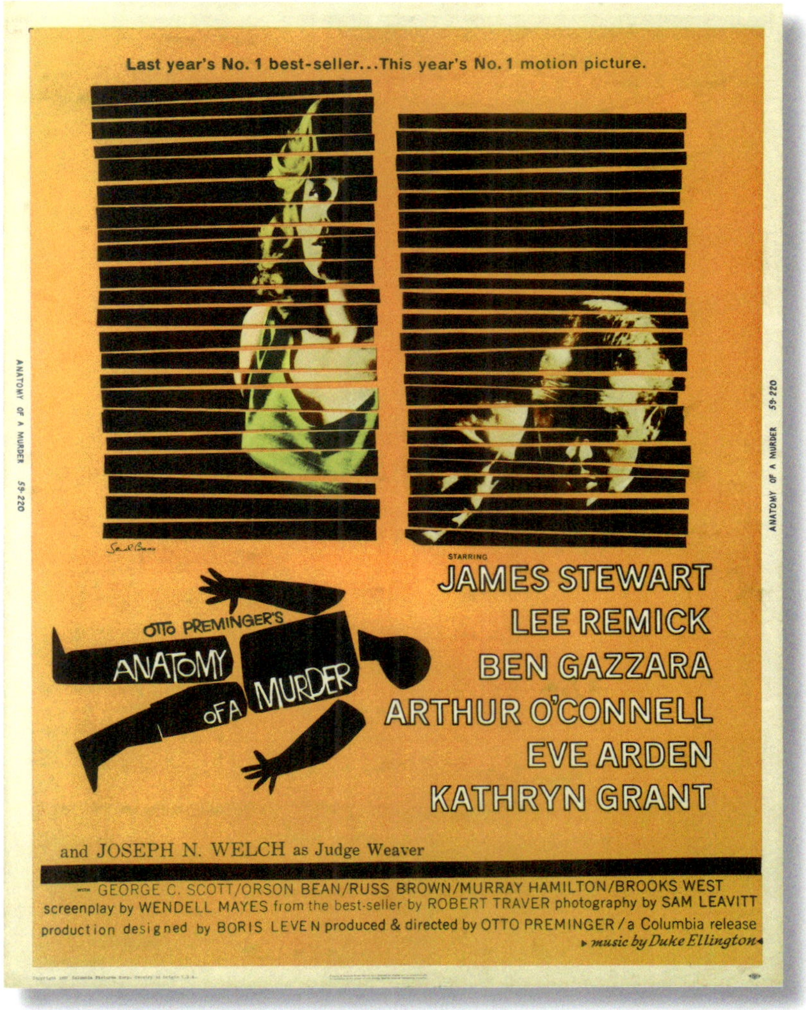

Anatomy of a Murder 1959 30x40
Estimate: $3,000 - $5,000

- There are 2 known to exist.

Courtesy of the Reel Poster Gallery, London

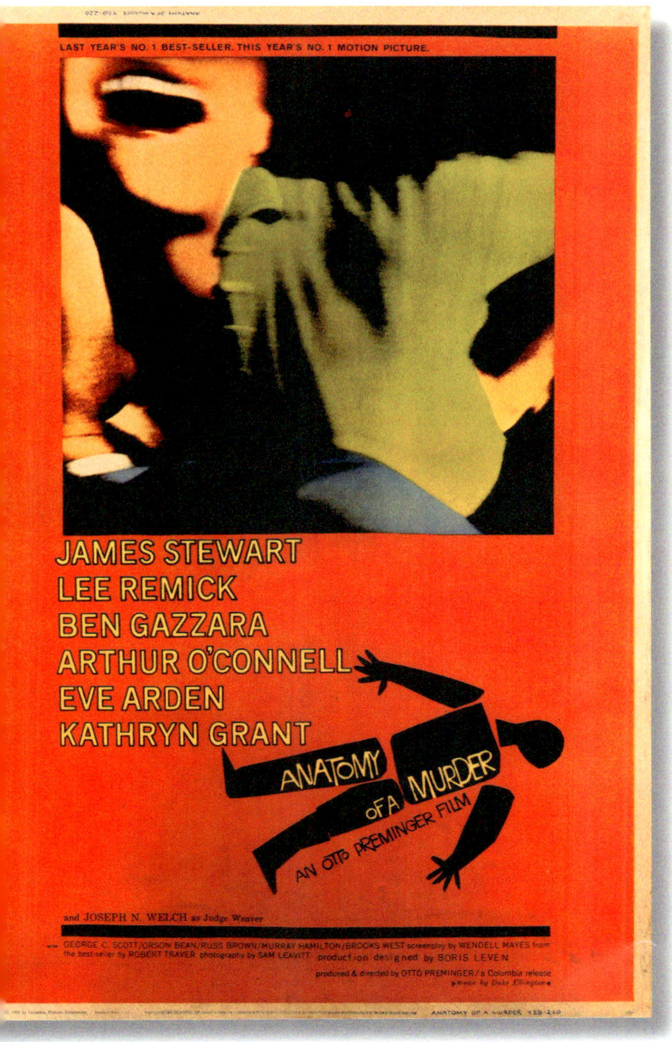

Anatomy of a Murder—Style Y 1959 40x60

Christie's	$1,200	FN+	09/02

Estimate: $3,000 - $5,000

- There are 2 known to exist.
- There is no *Anatomy of a Murder* 40x60 Style Z known to exist.

North by Northwest	1959	27x41	
Heritage (autographed)	$5,377	FN	11/09
Christie's	$860	VF	03/09
Heritage	$866	VF+	09/08
Heritage	$310	VG/FN	10/08
Heritage	$717	FN/VF	03/08

Highest price realized:

Heritage (Autographed)	$5,377	FN	11/09

Price in 1994:

Camden House	$450	VF	06/94

• This poster has appeared at auction 39 times since 1989.

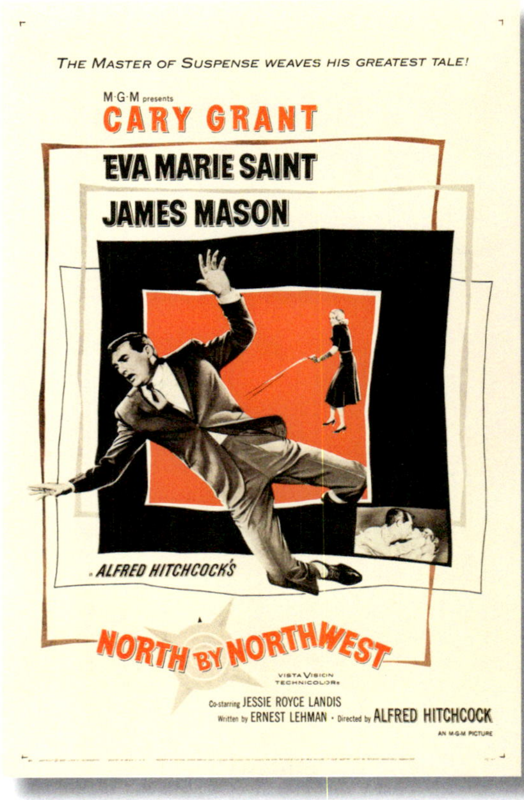

Courtesy of Heritage

Courtesy of Heritage

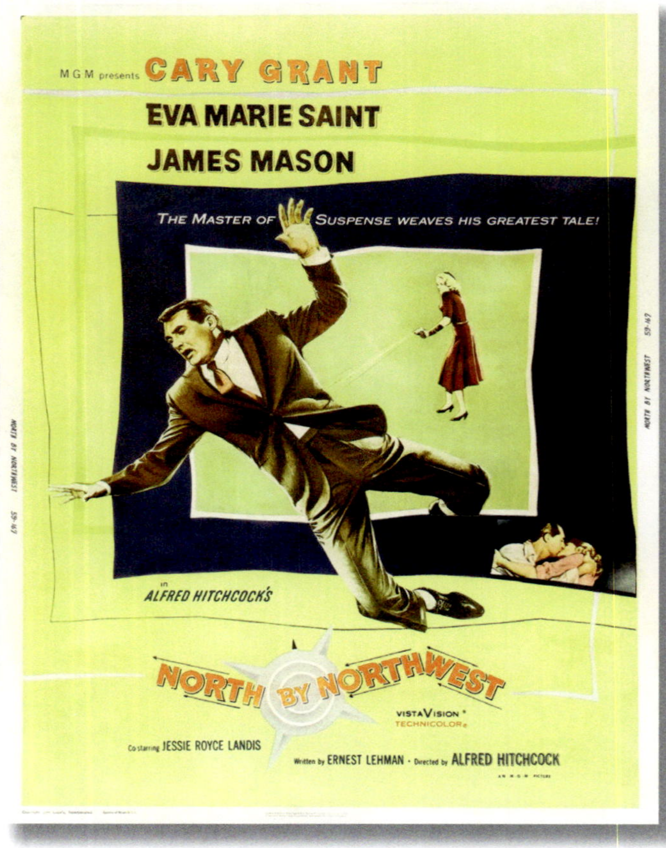

North by Northwest	1959	30x40	
Heritage	$1,553	FN-	07/09*
Heritage	$1,912	FN/VF	03/07*
Christie's	$750	FN	05/00*
Private	$900	VF	05/97*
Private	$300	FN	02/97*

• There are 5 known to exist.
* There is no way to know if the two poster from the private sales in 1997 appeared in these later auctions. The "known to exist" is also most likely incorrect due to these unknown private sales.

Courtesy of Heritage

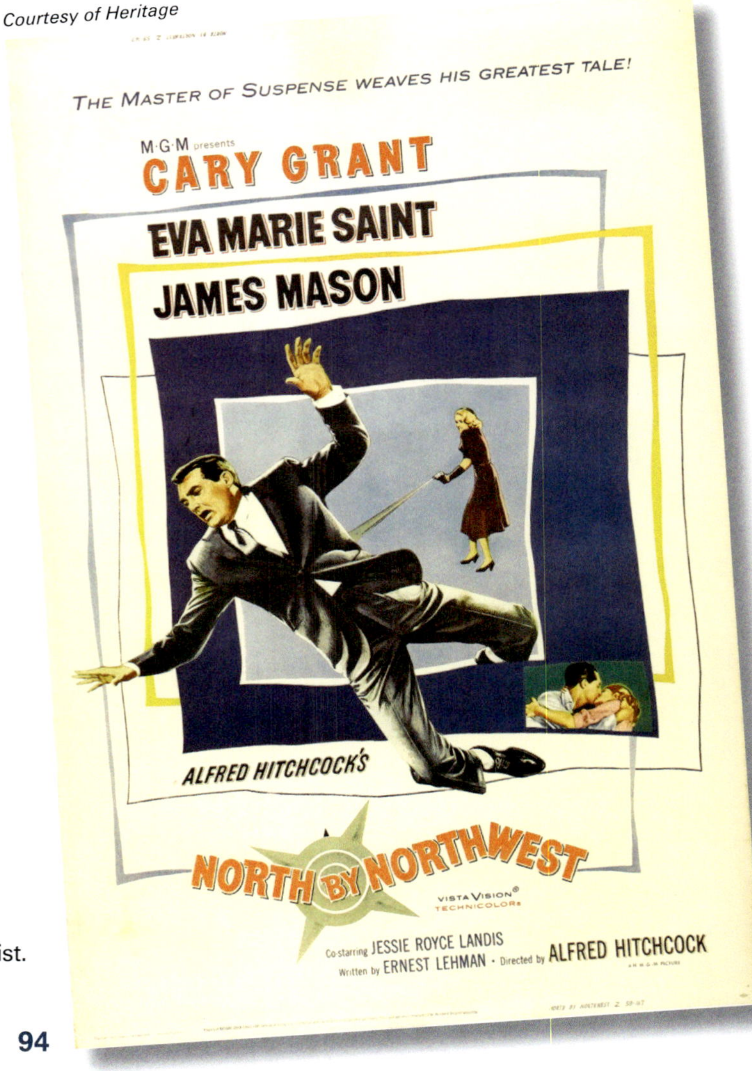

North by Northwest—Style Z	1959	40x60	
Heritage	$2,151	VF+	11/06
eMoviePoster	$290	GD	12/05

• There are 3 known to exist.
• There is no *North by Northwest* 40x60 Style Y known to exist.

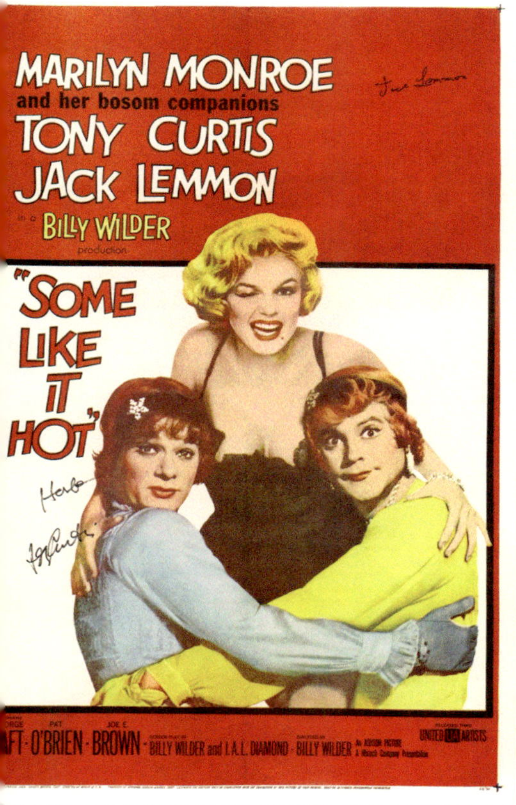

Courtesy of Heritage

Some Like it Hot	1959	27x41	
Christie's	$1,662	VF-	11/09
Heritage	$776	FN	11/09
Heritage	$1,015	FN	07/09
eMoviePoster	$775	GD/VG	07/09
eMoviePoster	$880	GD/VG	06/09

Highest price realized:
Heritage (autographed) $3,585 VF + 07/07

Price in 1990:
Camden House $325 VF 10/90

• This poster has appeared at auction 58 times since 1989.

Courtesy of Hershenson/Allen Archive

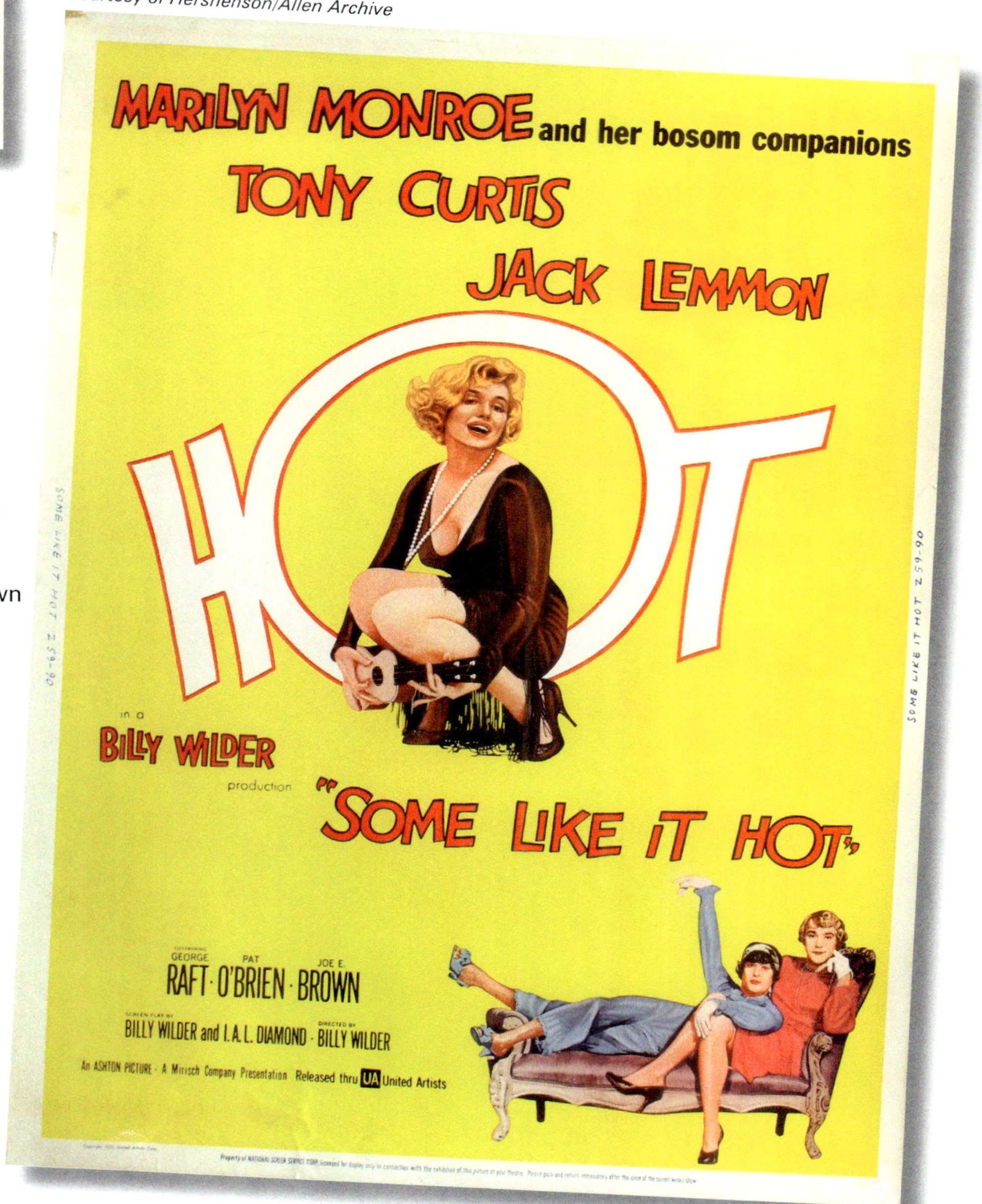

Some Like It Hot—Style Z	1959	30x40
eMoviePoster	$4,350	VG/FN 12/07

• There is 1 known to exist.
• There is no *Some Like it Hot* Style Y known to exist

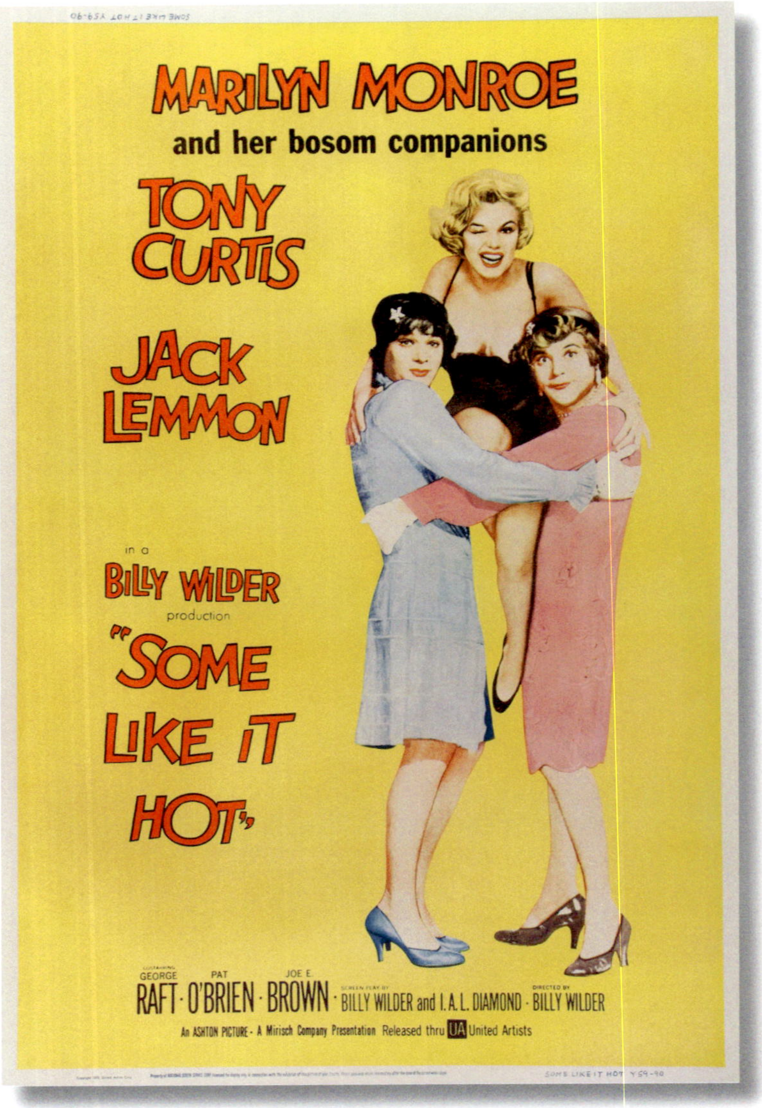

Photo by R. Aaron Raymond & Stephen Allard

Some Like It Hot—Style Y 1959 40x60

Private	$3,600	VF+	05/02

Estimate: $5,000 - $6,500

• There are 2 known to exist.

Some Like It Hot—Style Z 1959 40x60

Heritage	$4,481	VF-	03/09
Christie's	$2,103	VF-	09/99
Butterfield & Butterfields	$1,495	NM	10/98

• There are 3 known to exist.

Photo by R. Aaron Raymond & Stephen Allard

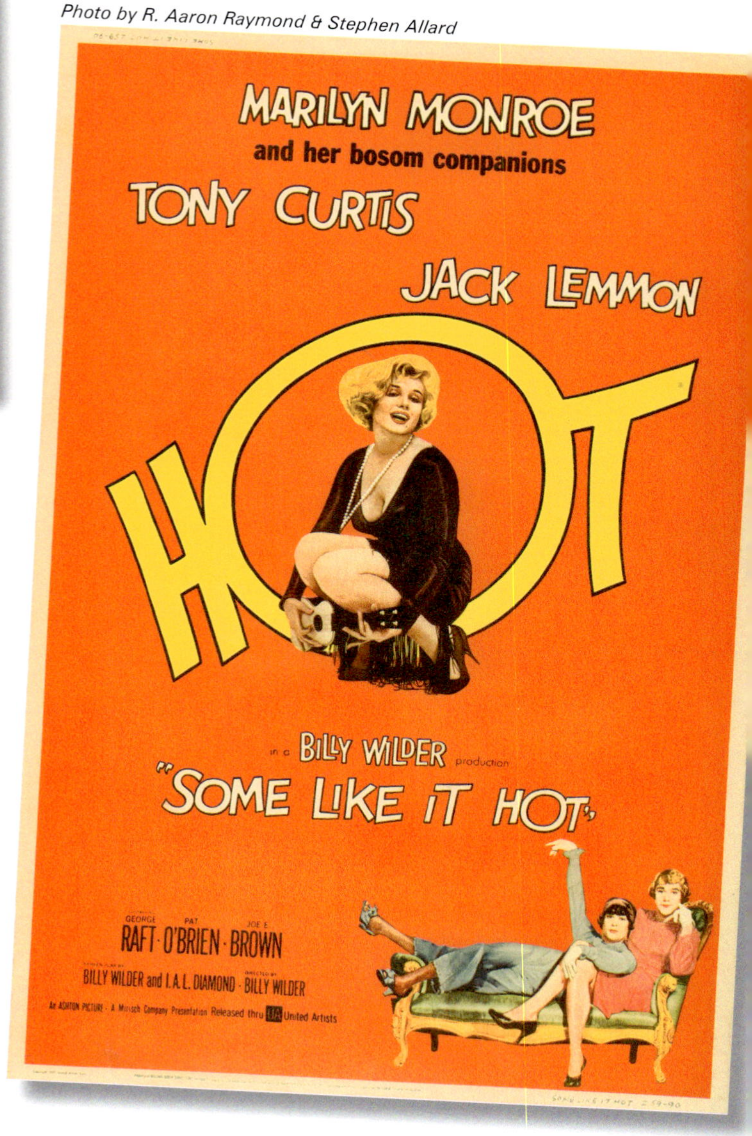

SCIENCE FICTION & HORROR MOVIE POSTERS OF THE 1950s

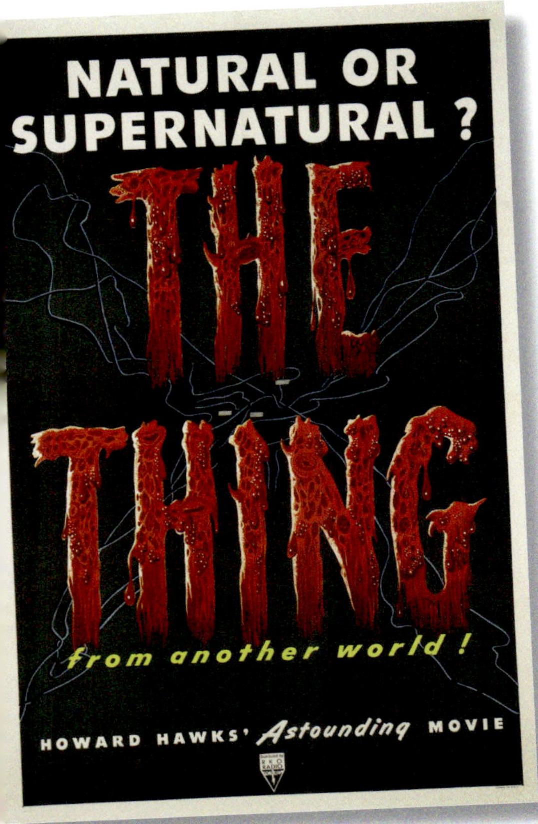

Courtesy of Heritage

Thing from Another World		1951	27x41
Heritage	$776	FN-	11/09
Heritage	$1,553	VF+	03/09
Heritage	$1,075	VF-	07/08
Christie's	$582	VF	09/08
Heritage	$956	FN	03/08

Highest price realized:

Heritage	$2,185	VF/NM	03/06

Price in 1990:

Camden House	$400	VF	10/90

- This poster has appeared at auction 37 times since 1989.
- There is no *Thing from Another World* 30x40 known to exist.

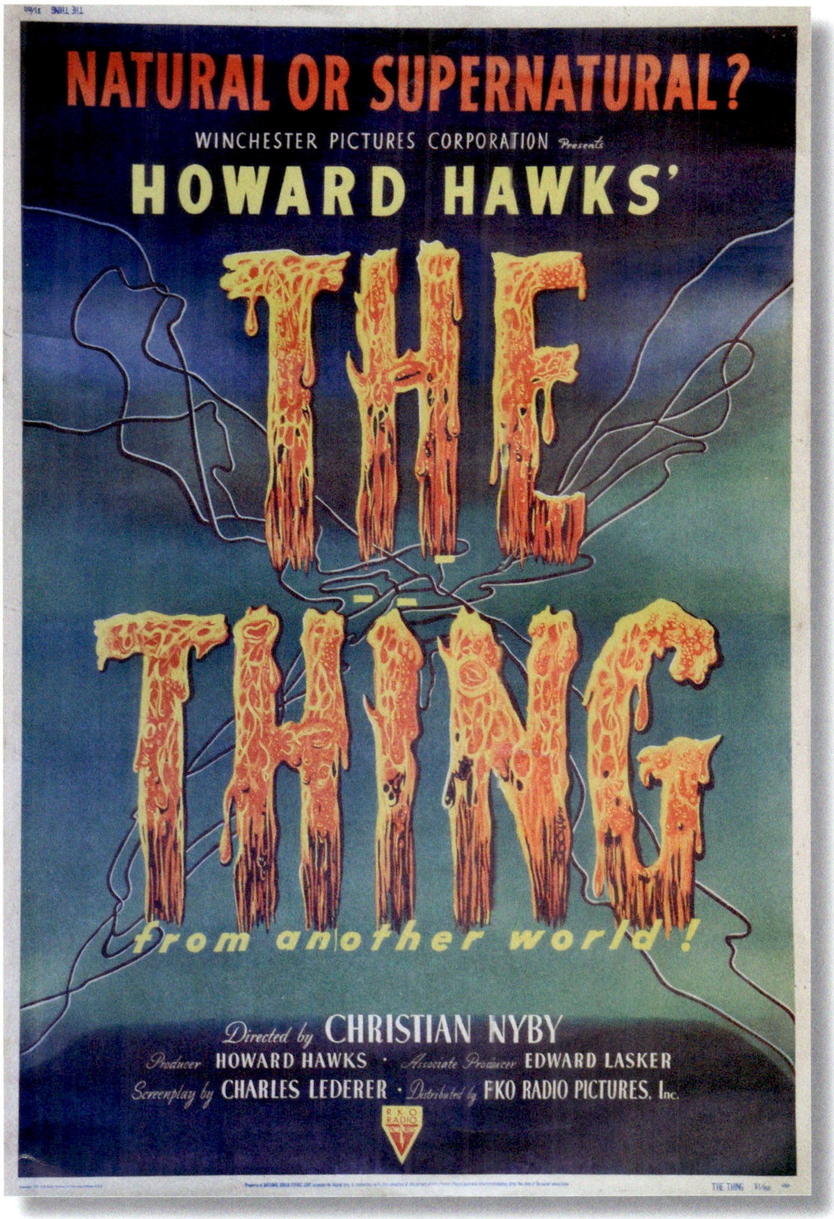

Courtesy of Marc Zubatkin, Photo by Bill Mitchell

Thing from Another World		1951	40x60
Heritage	$1,314	VF	07/09

- There are 3 known to exist.

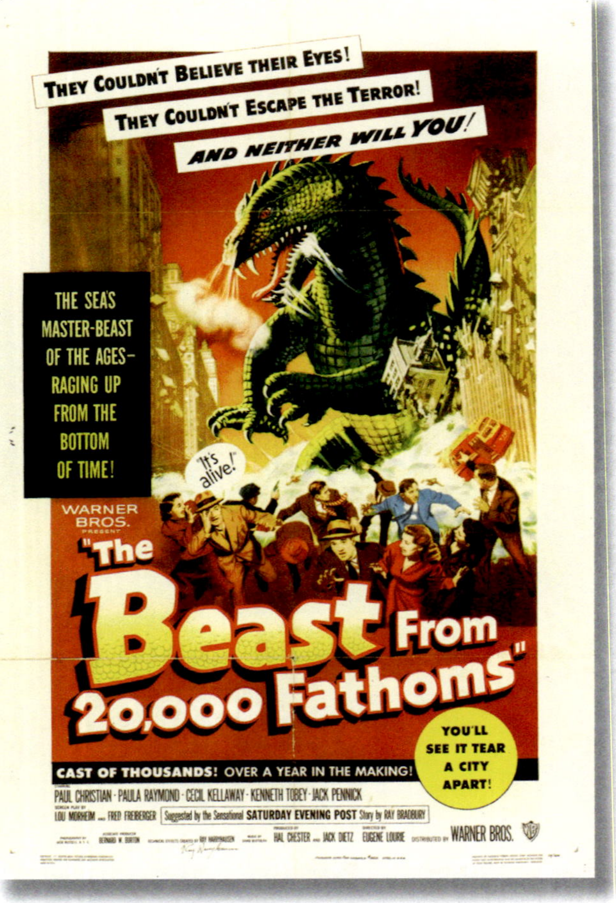

Courtesy of Heritage

Beast from 20,000 Fathoms		1953	27x41
Heritage	$1,912	VF	07/09
Heritage	$1,314	FN/VF	03/09
Christie's	$895	VF	09/08
Heritage	$2,390	VF	03/08
Profiles in History	$1,800	VF+	08/07

Highest price realized:

Heritage	$3,680	NM	11/03

Price in 1991:

Camden House	$375	VF	11/91

• This poster has appeared at auction 24 times since 1989.

Courtesy of Heritage

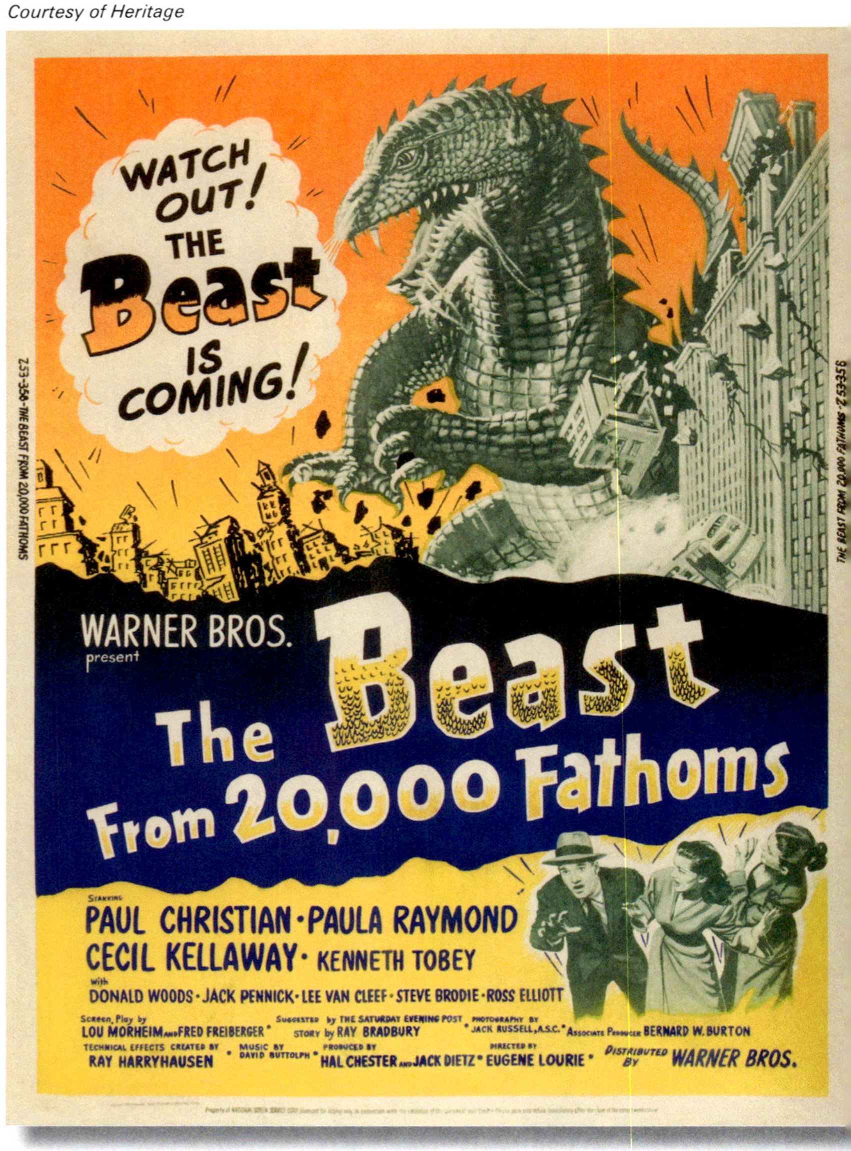

Beast from 20,000 Fathoms—Style Z		1953	30x40
Heritage	$1,434	FN	11/06

• There is 1 known to exist.
• There is no *Beast from 20,000 Fathoms* 30x40 Style Y known to exist.
• There is no *Beast from 20,000 Fathoms* 40x60 known to exist.

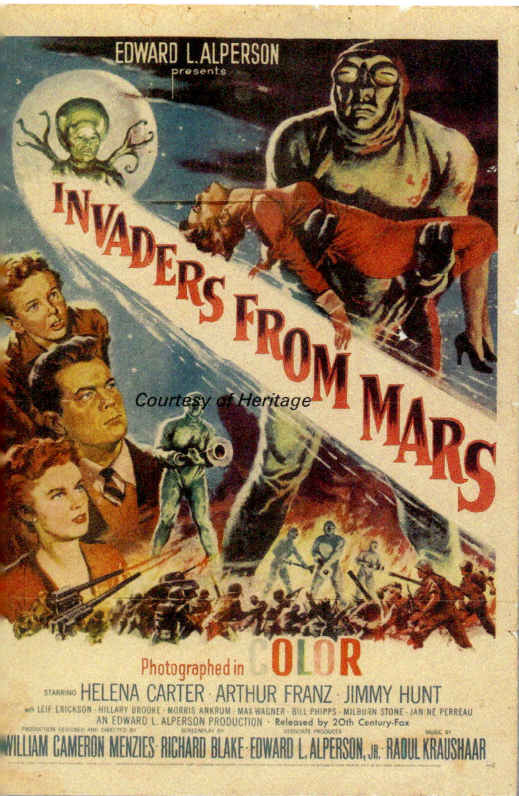

Courtesy of Heritage

Invaders from Mars	1953	27x41	
Heritage	$956	VF+	11/09
Heritage	$507	GD	05/09
Heritage	$985	FN	11/08
Heritage	$1,015	FN/VF	10/08
Heritage	$717	VF+	07/08

Highest price realized:

Heritage	$2,629	VF+	11/07

Price in 1991:

Christie's	$880	NM	12/91

- This poster has appeared at auction 34 times since 1989.
- There is no *Invaders from Mars* 30x40 known to exist.

Courtesy of Heritage

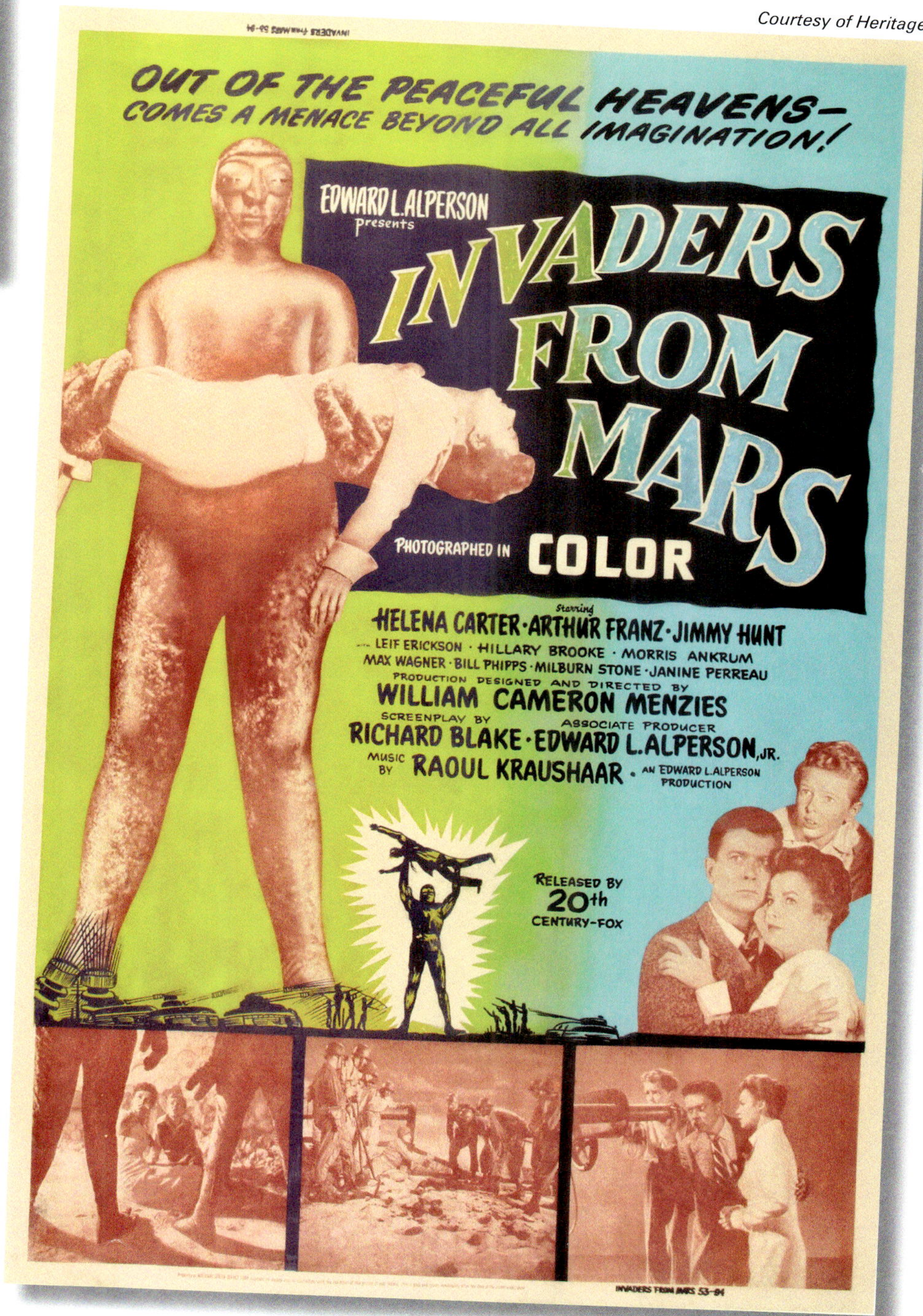

Invaders from Mars	1953	40x60	
Heritage	$1,912	FN/VF	11/09

- There are 2 known to exist.

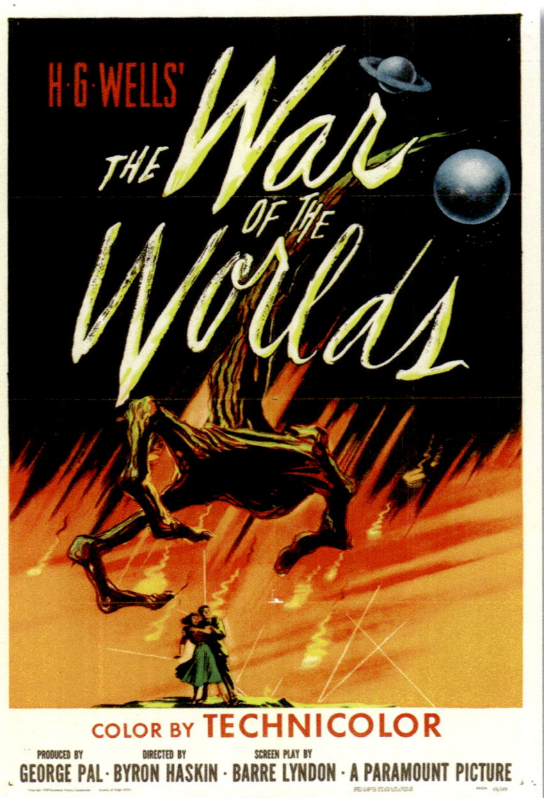

Courtesy of Heritage

War of the Worlds	1953	27x41	
Heritage	$2,151	VF	11/09
Christie's	$2,065	VF-	11/09
Heritage	$2,629	VG/FN	07/09
Heritage	$3,346	FN	03/09
Heritage	$10,157	VF+	07/08

Highest price realized:			
Heritage	$10,157	VF+	07/08

Price in 1990:			
Camden House	$800	FN	10/90

• This poster has appeared at auction 34 times since 1989.

Courtesy of Heritage

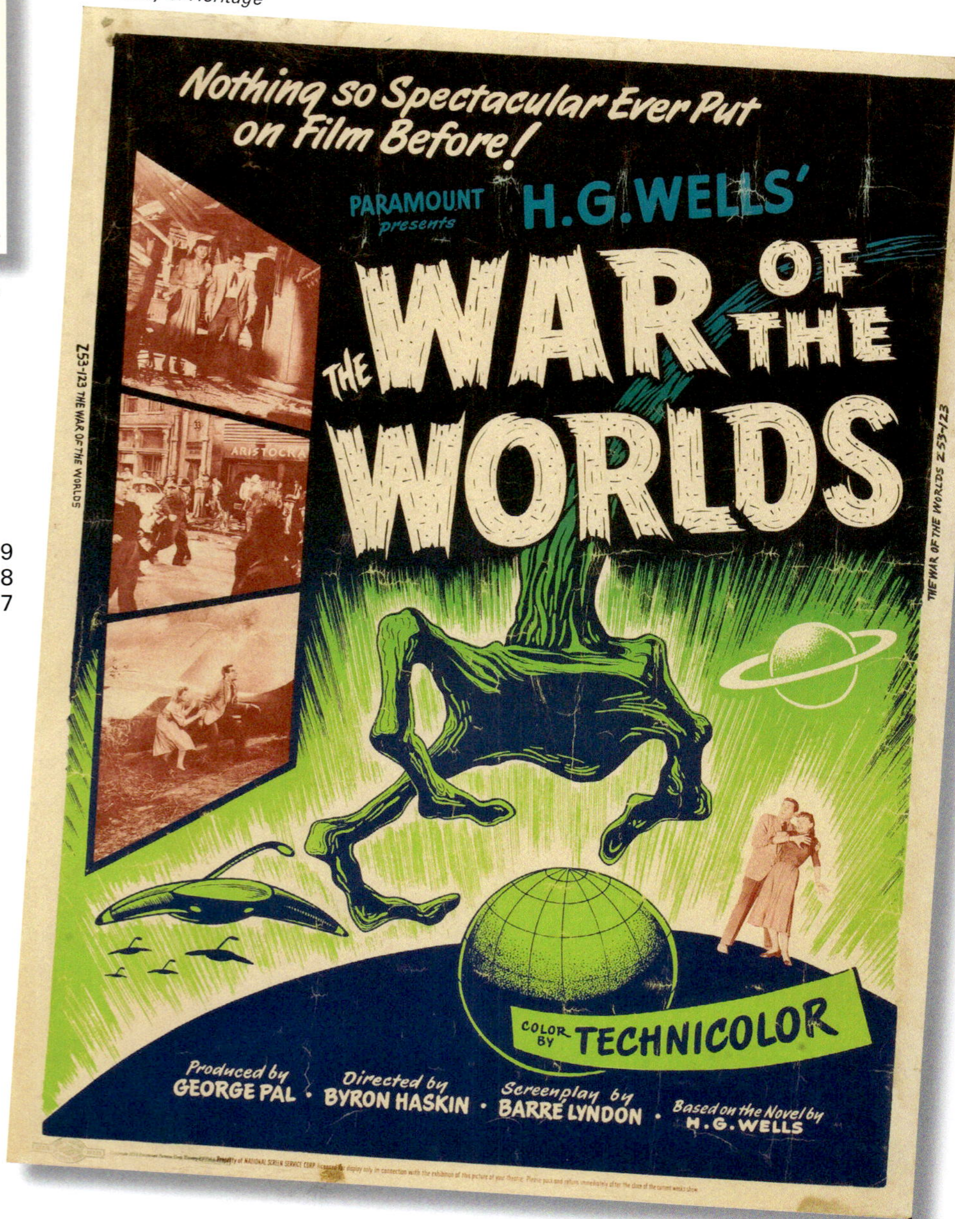

***War of the Worlds*—Style Z**	1953	30x40	
Heritage	$4,481	FN	07/09
Heritage	$5,377	FN+	11/08
Bonhams & Butterfields	$4,200	PR	12/07

• There are 3 known to exist.
• There is no *War of the World* 30x40 Style Y known to exist.

War of the Worlds—Style Y 1953 40x60
Heritage $5,377 FN+ 11/08

- There are 2 known to exist.
- There is no *War of the Worlds* 40x60 Style Z known to exist.

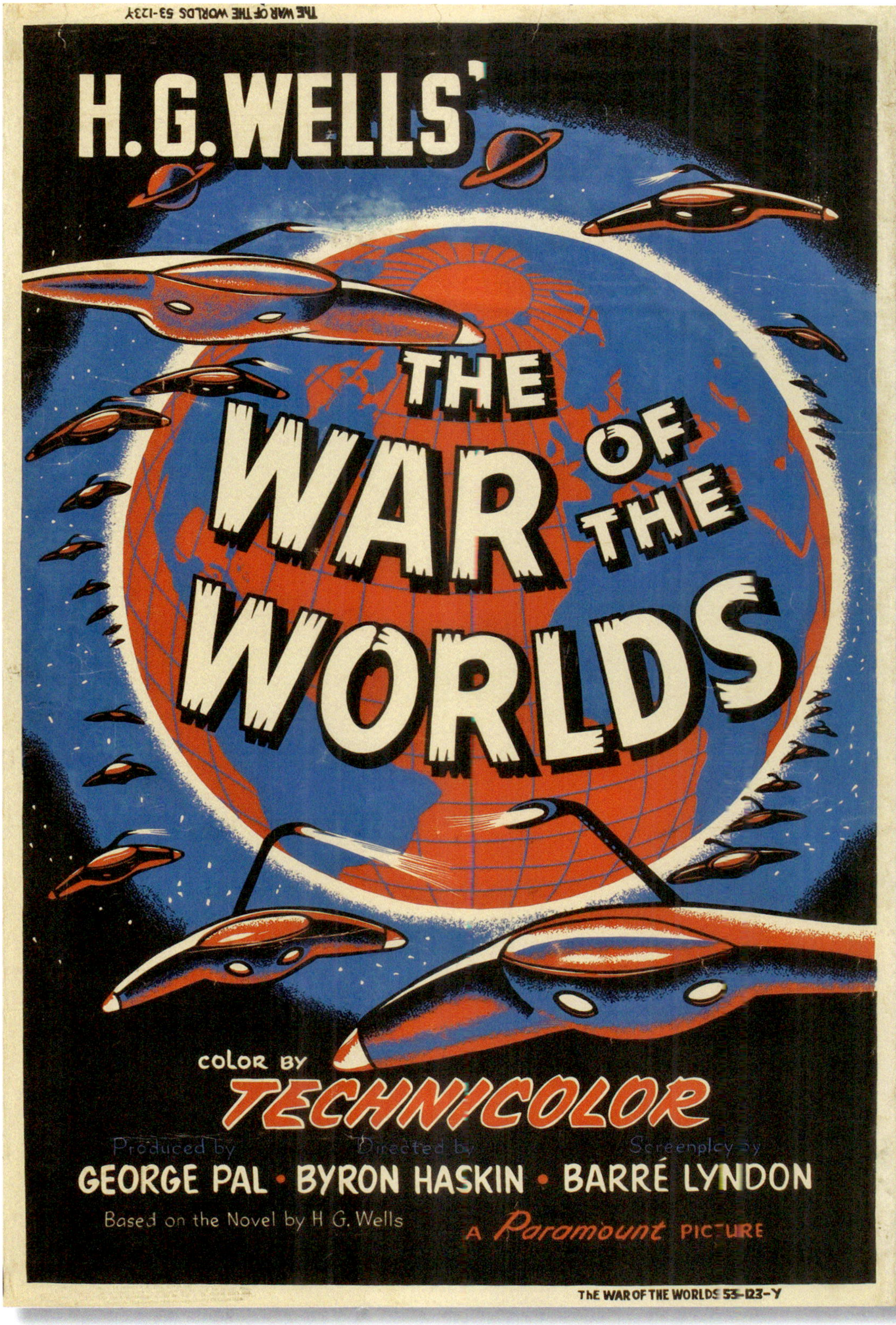

Courtesy of Heritage

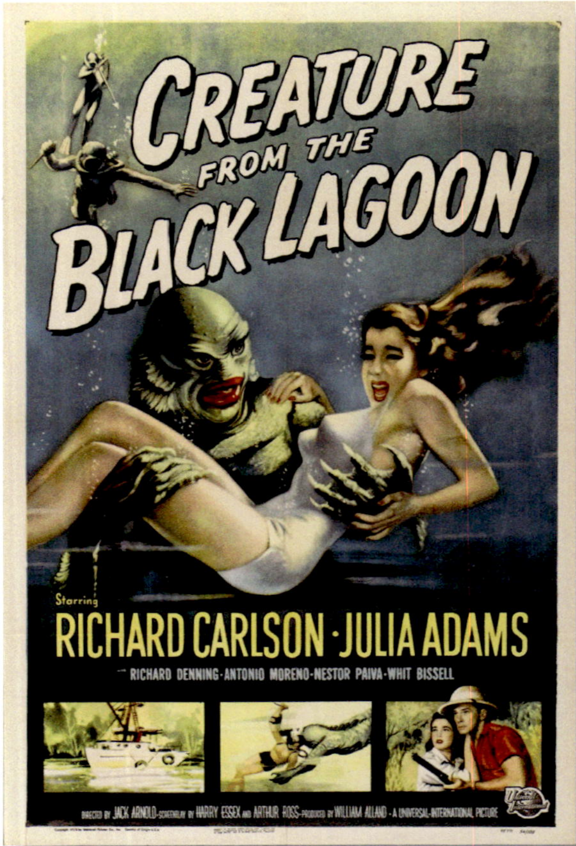

Courtesy of Heritage

Creature from the Black Lagoon 1954 27x41

Heritage	$10,775	VF-	11/09
Heritage	$22,705	VF/NM	03/09
Profiles in History	$13,600	VF-	12/08
Heritage	$25,095	NM	07/08
CineMasterpieces	$17,500	FN	06/08

Highest price realized:

Heritage	$25,095	NM	07/08

Price in 1991:

Christie's	$4,620	FN	12/91

This poster has appeared at auction 26 times since 1989.

- There is no *Creature from the Black Lagoon* 30x40 known to exist.

***Creature from the Black Lagoon*—** Style Y 1954 40x60

Heritage	$4,780	VF	03/08

- There are 2 known to exist.
- There is no *Creature from the Black Lagoon* 40x60 Style Z known to exist.

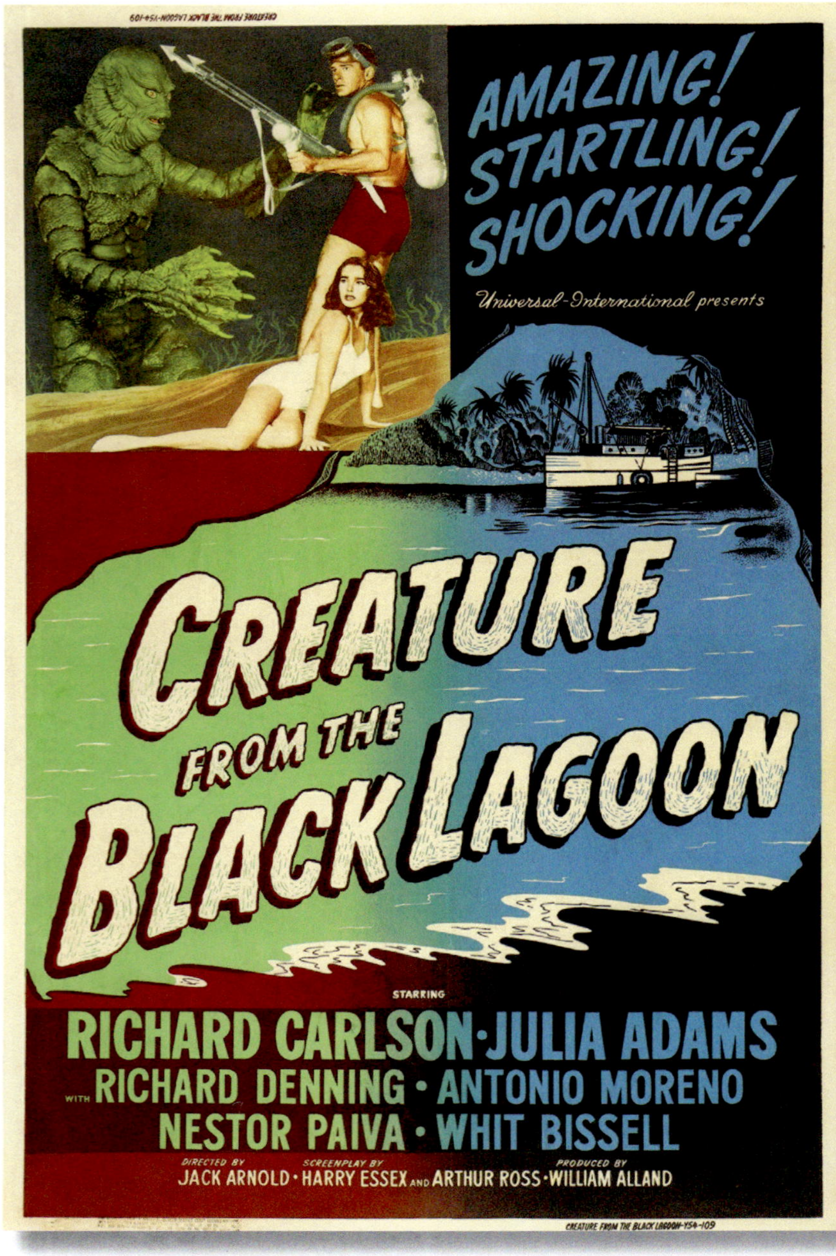

Courtesy of Heritage

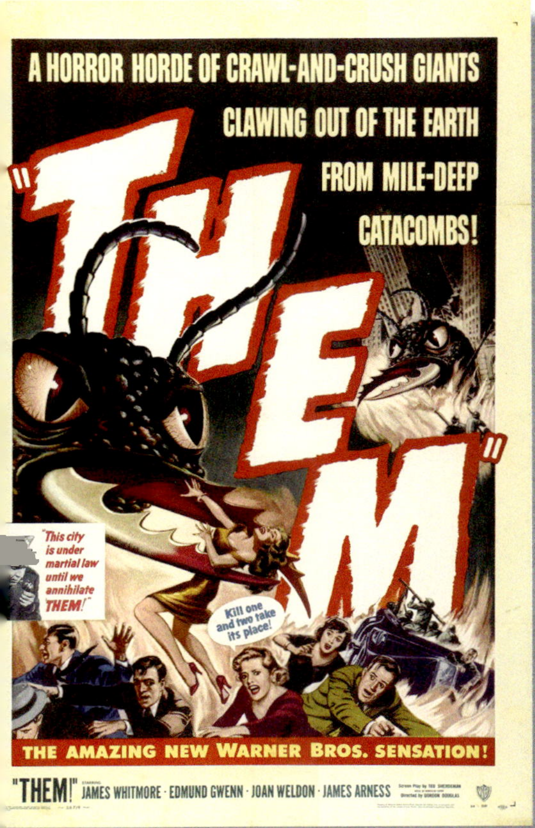

Courtesy of Heritage

Them 1954 27x41

eMoviePoster	$2,100	VF	10/09
eMoviePoster	$1,300	GD/VG	10/08
Heritage	$2,031	VF-	07/08
Profiles in History	$2,500	NM	12/07
Heritage	$2,629	VF	11/06

Highest price realized:

Heritage	$2,629	VF	11/06

Price in 1990:

Camden House	$300		10/90

This poster has appeared at auction 26 times since 1989.

Them— Style Y 1954 30x40
Estimate: $1,500 - $2,500

- There is 1 known to exist.
- There is no *Them* 30x40 Style Z known to exist.

Courtesy of Marc Zubatkin, Photo by Bill Mitchell

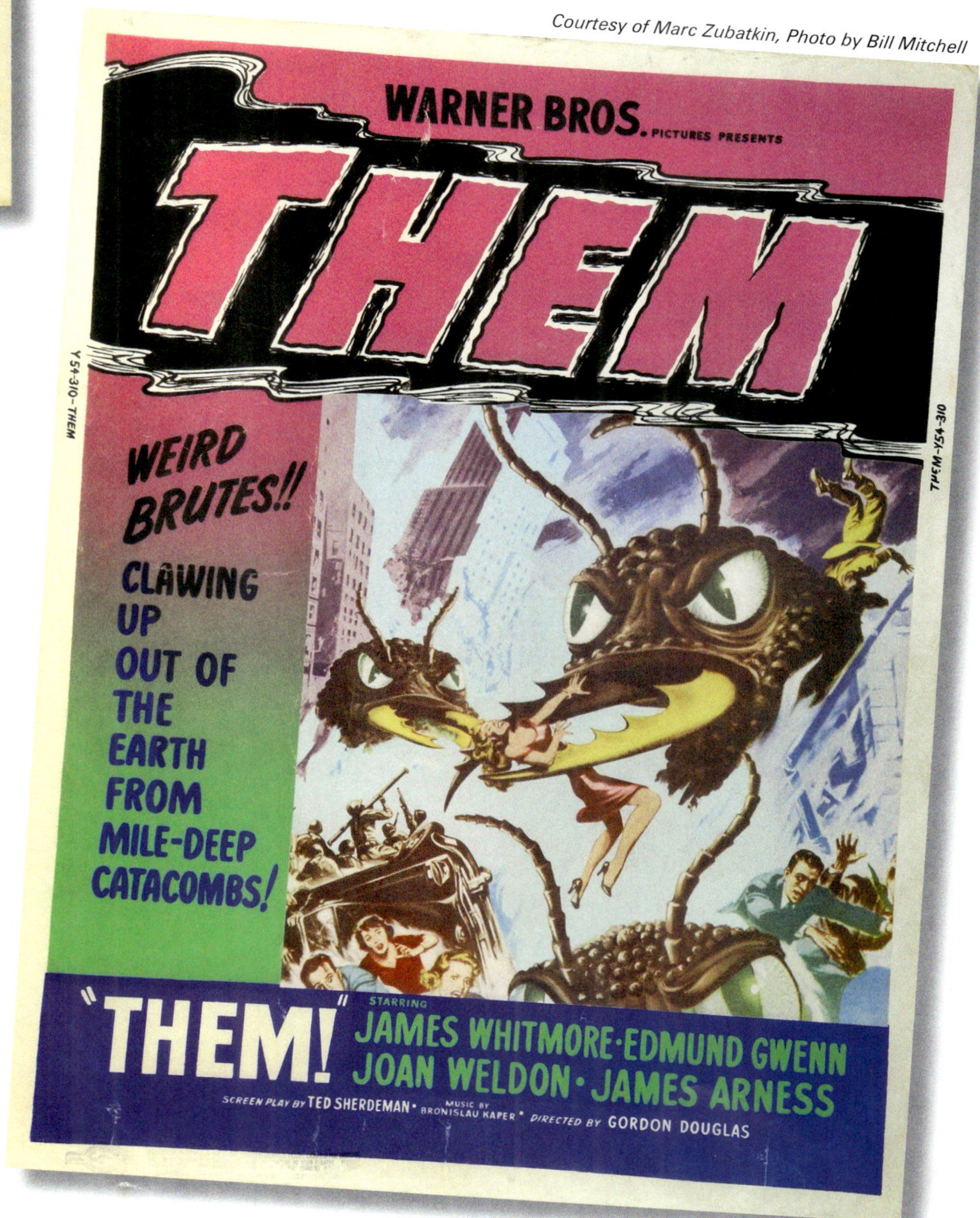

Them—Style Y 1954 40x60
Heritage $1,314 FN+ 11/08

- There is 1 known to exist.
- There is no *Them* 40x60 Style Z known to exist.

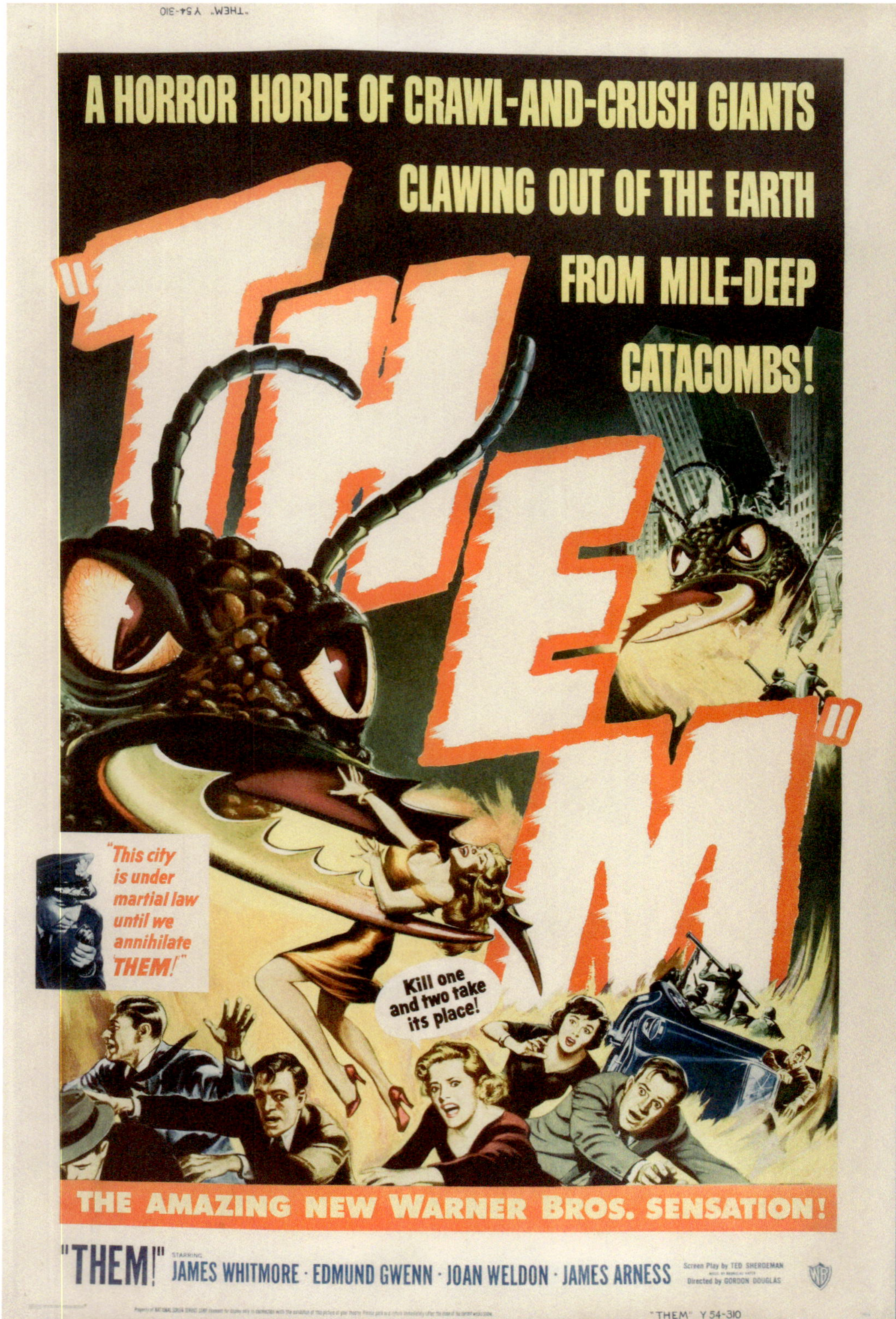

Photo by R. Aaron Raymond & Stephen Allard

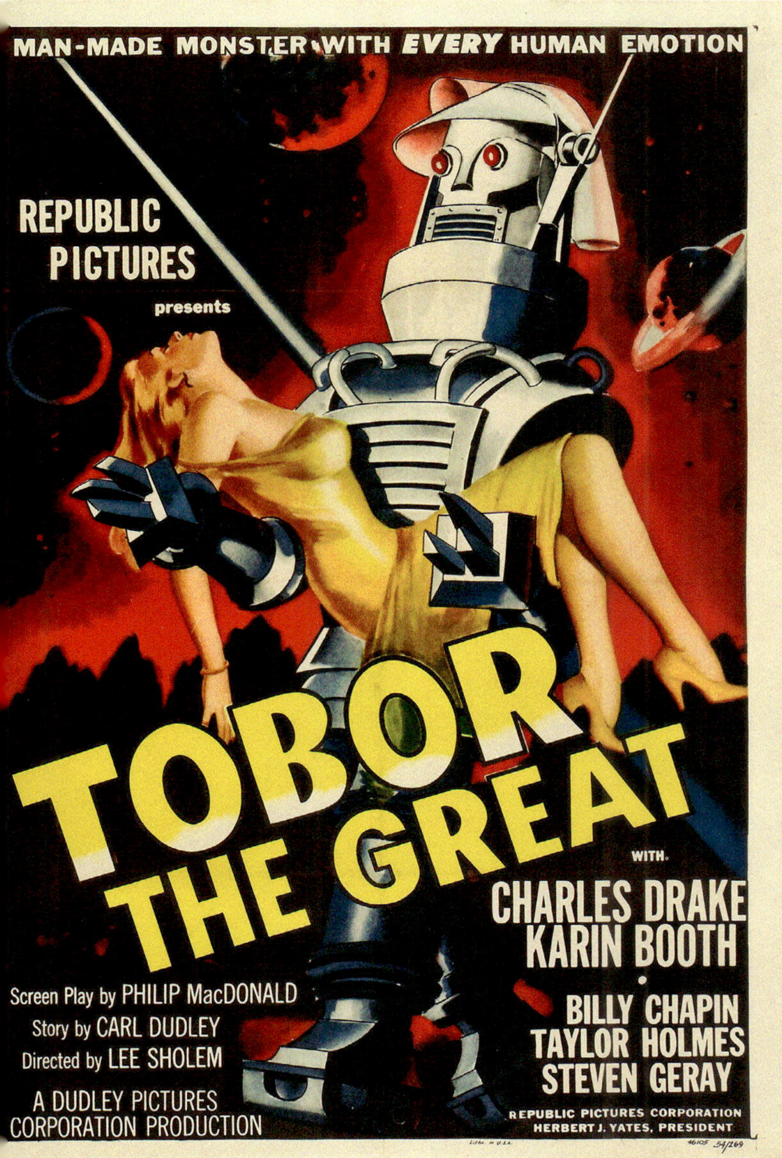

Courtesy of Heritage

Tobor the Great	1954	27x41	
Heritage	$2,390	VF+	03/09
Heritage	$2,279	NM	11/08
Heritage	$1,195	VF	03/08
Heritage	$1,434	NM	11/07
eMoviePoster	$1,125	GD/VG	11/06

Highest price realized:

Heritage	$4,025	VF	07/02

Price in 1991:

Camden House	$1,000	NM	05/91

- This poster has appeared at auction 31 times since 1989.
- There is no *Tobor the Great* 30x40 known to exist.

Courtesy of Camden House

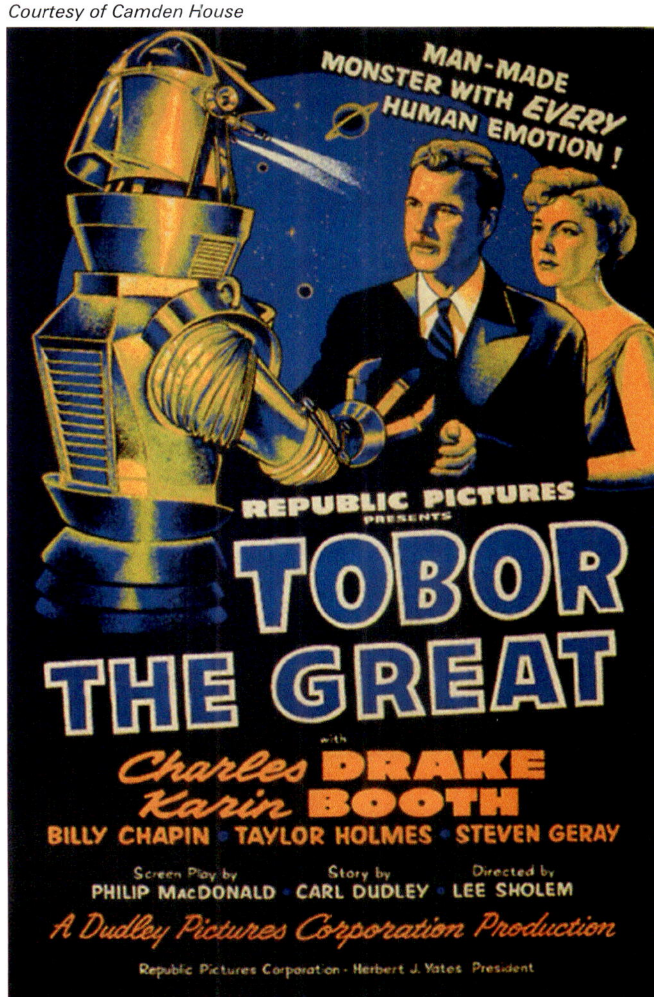

Tobor the Great	1954	40x60	
Private	$1,000	FN	07/97
Camden House	$600	FN	06/94

- There are 2 known to exist.

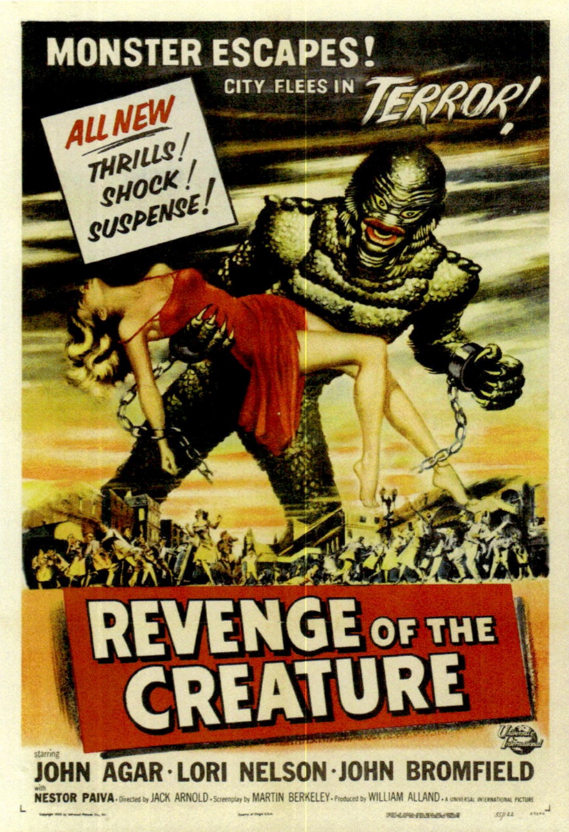

Courtesy of Heritage

Revenge of the Creature 1955 27x41

Heritage	$1,673	VF-	11/09
eMoviePoster	$1,600	VF	10/09
Heritage	$2,031	FN/VF	07/09
Heritage	$2,270	VF	03/09
Heritage	$3,346	VF	11/08

Highest price realized:

eMoviePoster	$3,800	FN	12/05

Price in 1994:

Butterfield & Butterfield	$850	FN	10/94

- This poster has appeared at auction 24 times since 1989.
- There is no *Revenge of the Creature* 30x40 known to exist.

Courtesy of Marc Zubatkin, Photo by Bill Mitchell

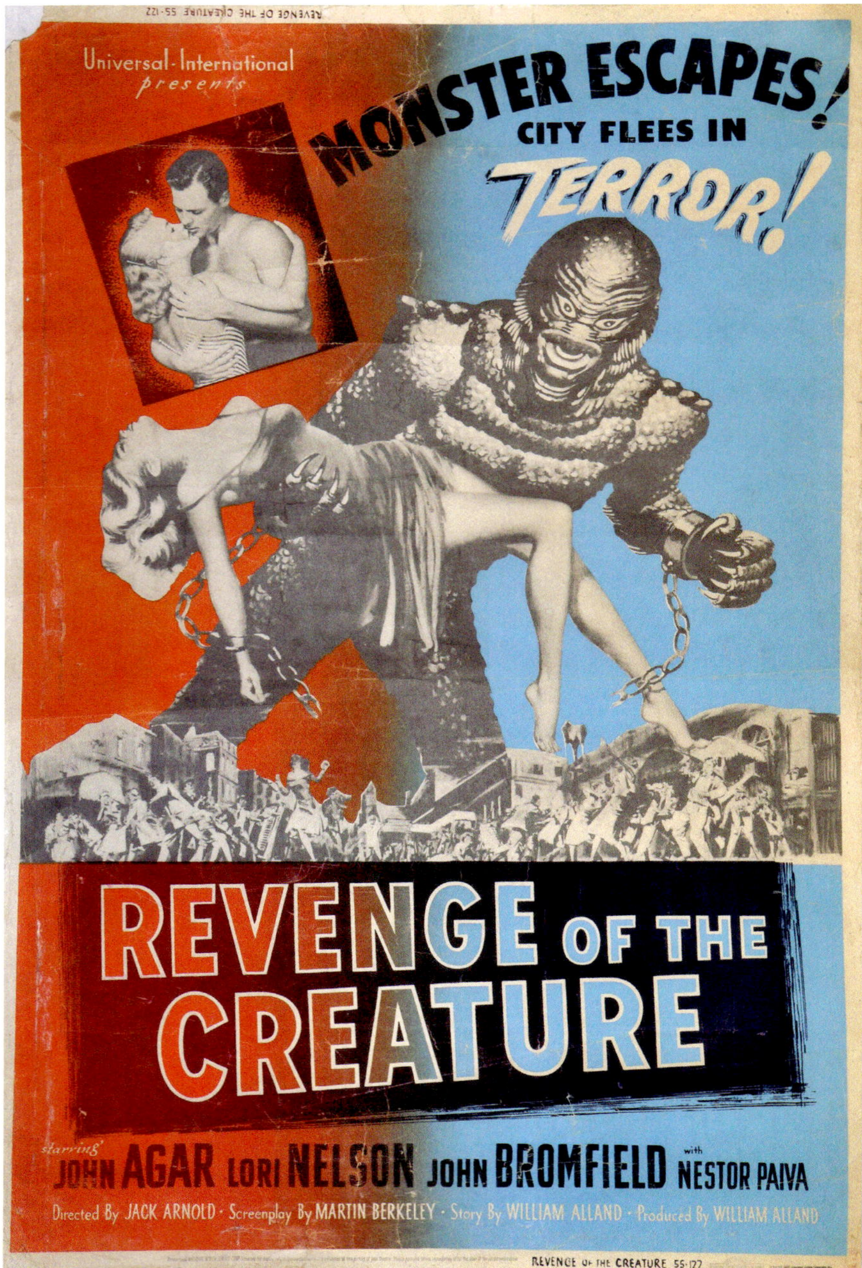

Revenge of the Creature 1955 40x60
Estimate: $4,000 - $5,000

- There is 1 known to exist.

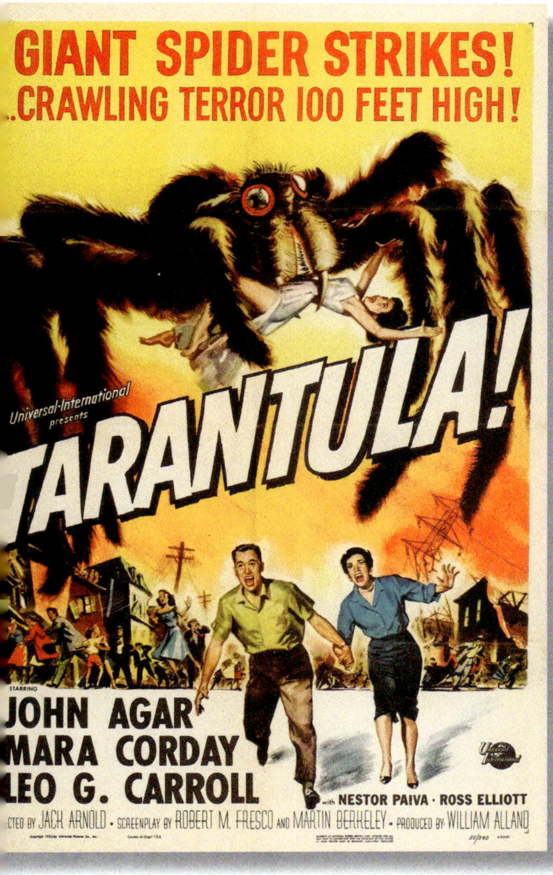

Courtesy of Heritage

Tarantula 1955 27x41			
Heritage	$956	FN+	11/09
Heritage	$2,629	NM-	03/09
Heritage	$836	FN+	11/08
eMoviePoster	$978	FN	10/08
Heritage	$1,553	FN/VF	03/08

Highest price realized:

Heritage	$2,629	NM-	03/09

Price in 1992:

Camden House	$500	FN	11/92

•This poster has appeared at auction 26 times since 1989.

Tarantula 1955 30x40			
Hollywood Poster Auction	$480	FN	10/09

•There is 1 known to exist.

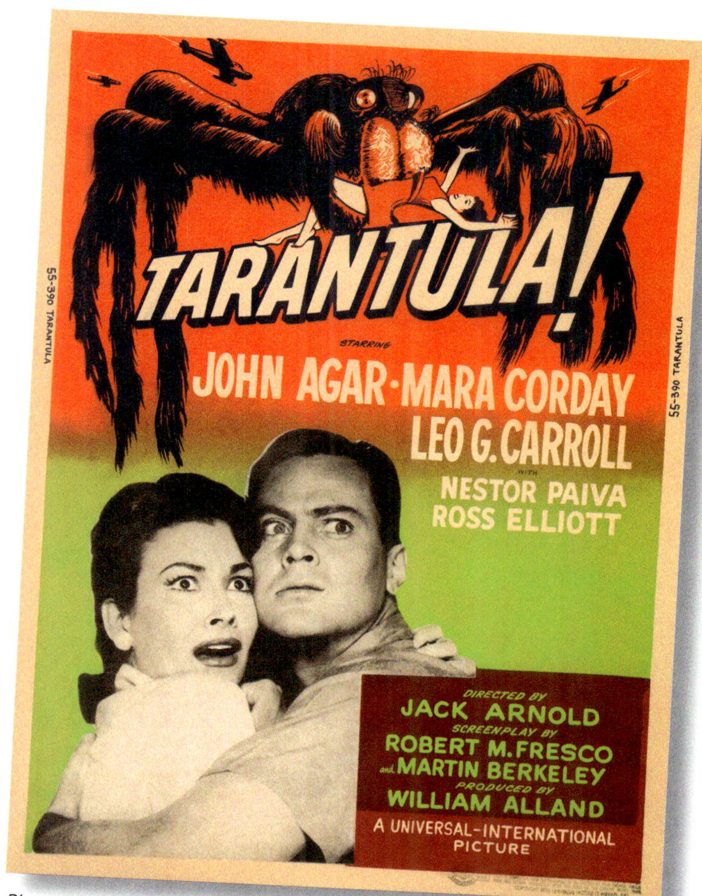

Photo by R. Aaron Raymond

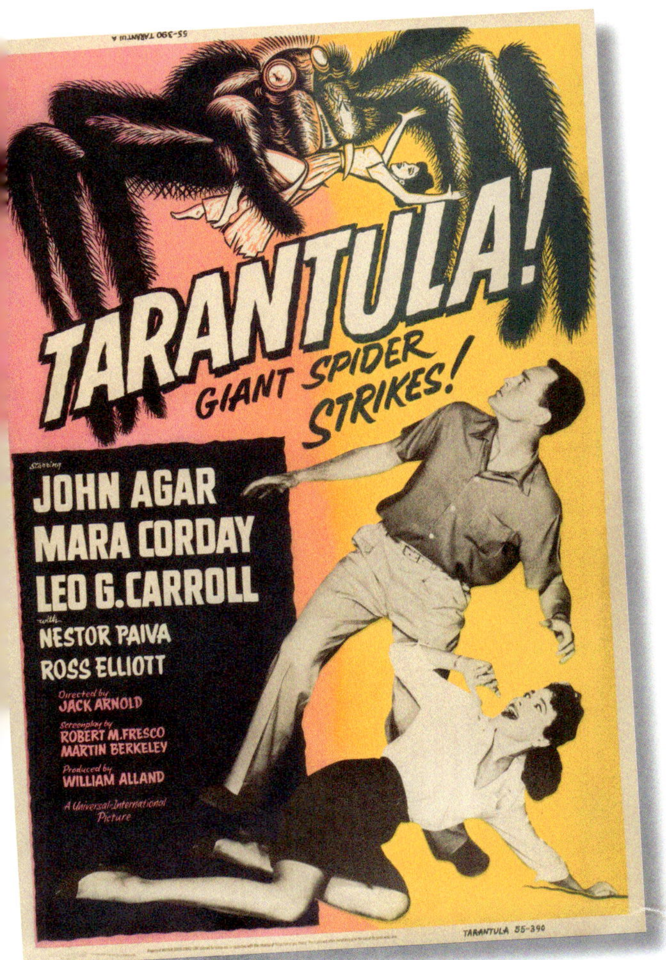

Photo by R. Aaron Raymond & Stephen Allard

Tarantula 1955 40x60			
Heritage	$1,015	VF-	07/09
Private	$900	FN	02/09
eMoviePoster	$305	FN	07/04
Sotheby's	$690	VF-	12/99
Christie's	$437	VF	12/96

• There are 6 known to exist.

This Island Earth—Style Z 1955 30x40
Heritage $5,676 FN 07/09

- There is 1 known to exist.
- There is no *This Island Earth* 30x40 Style Y known to exist.

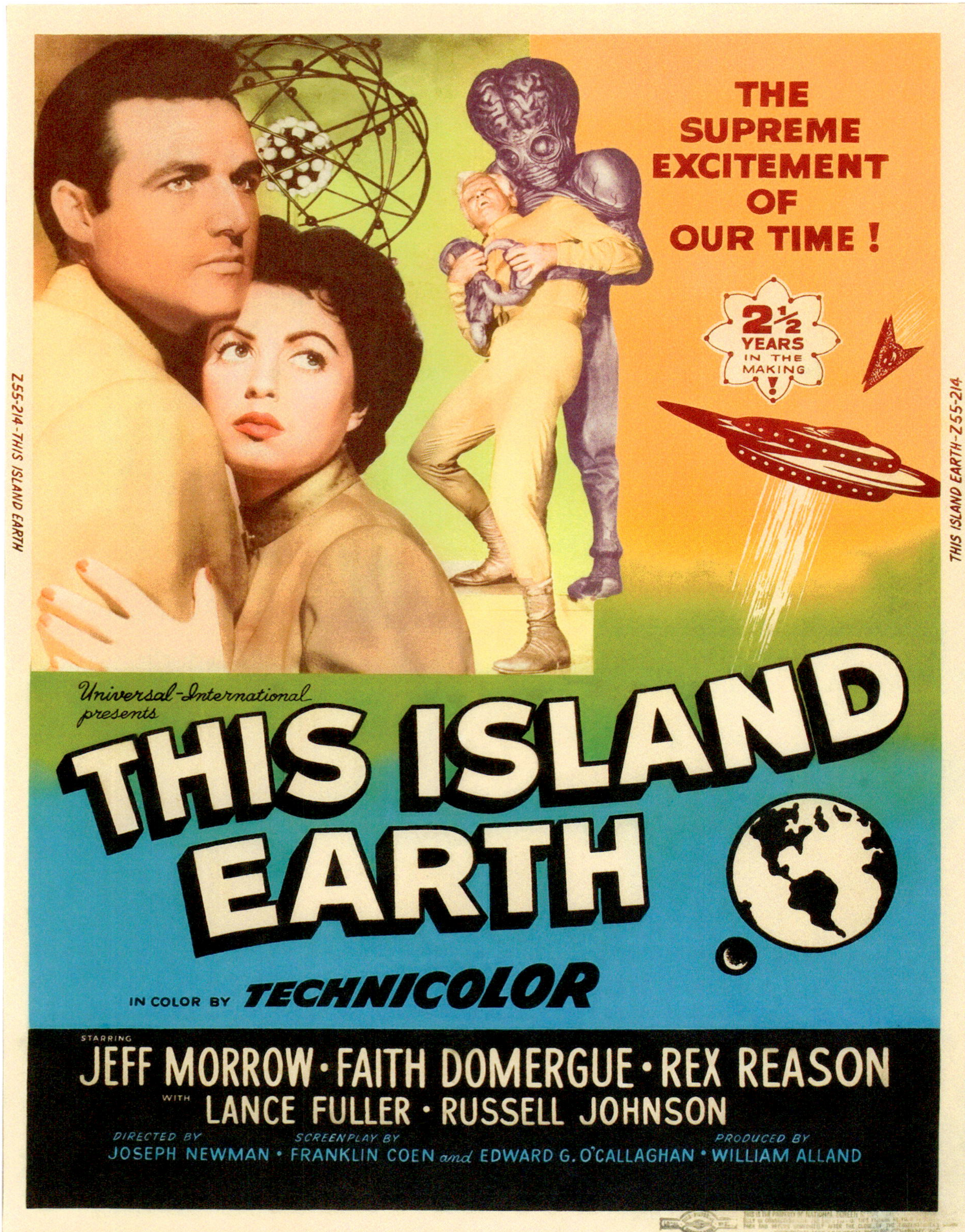

Courtesy of Heritage

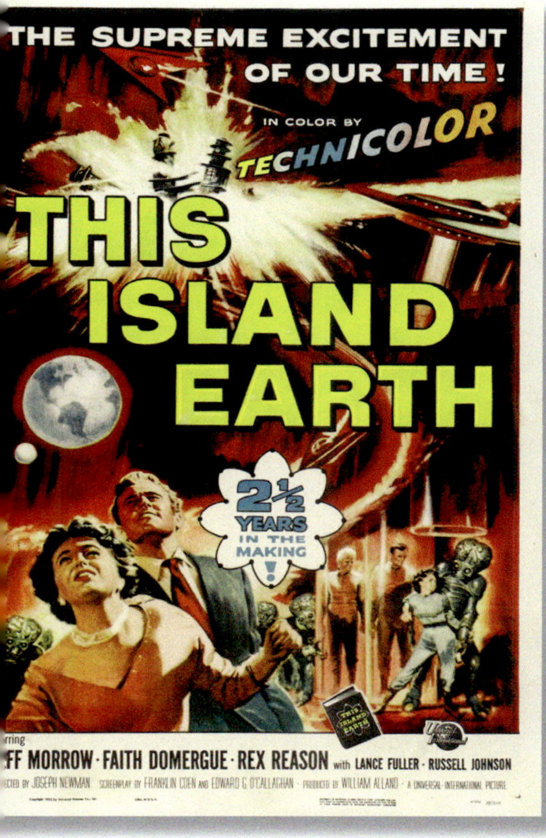

Courtesy of Heritage

This Island Earth	1955	27x41		
Heritage		$1,314	FN	11/09
Heritage		$1,195	VF	03/09
Heritage		$1,493	VF	11/08
Heritage		$1,434	FN+	07/08
Heritage		$1,015	FN/VF	03/08

Highest price realized:

Lowery (Autographed)	$2,185	FN	06/00

Price in 1993:

Camden House	$850	NM	11/93

•This poster has appeared at auction 35 times since 1989.

Courtesy of Marc Zubatkin, Photo by Bill Mitchell

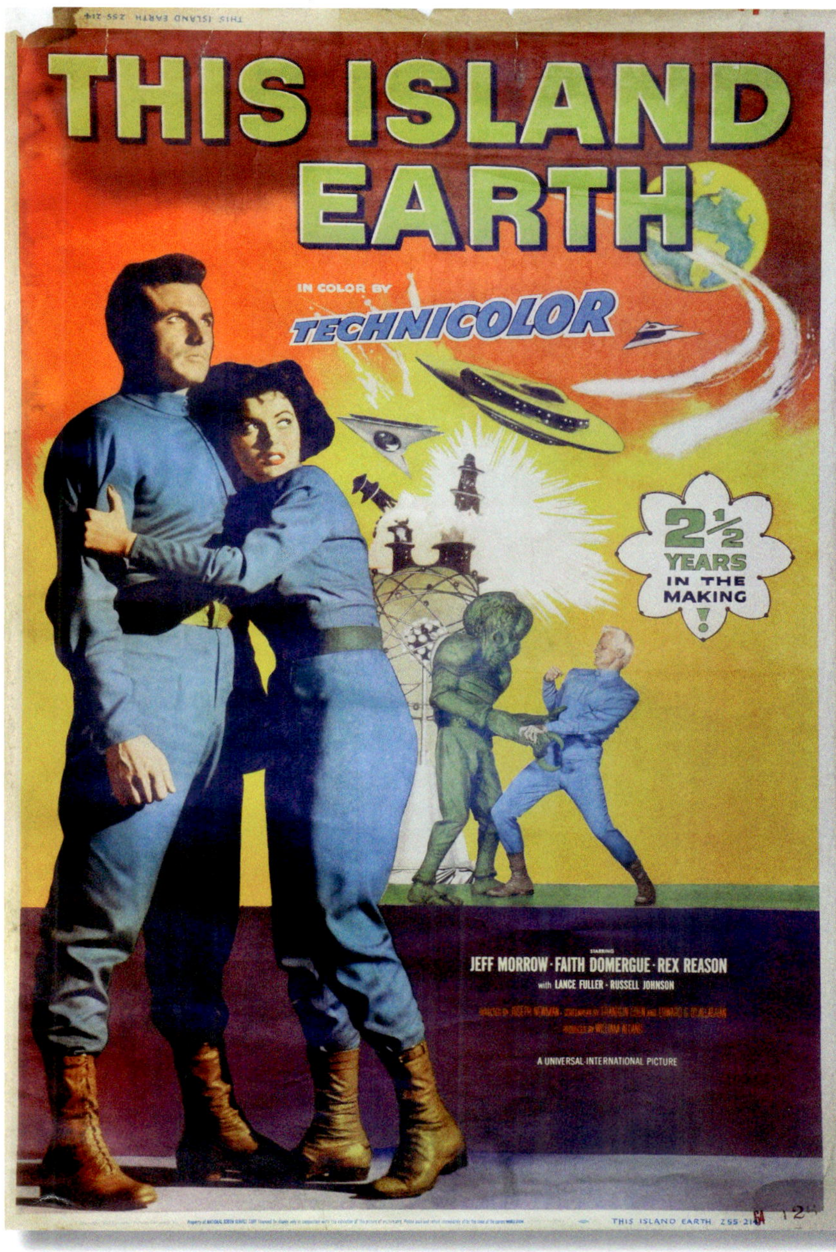

This Island Earth—Style Z 1955 40x60
Estimate: $9,000 - $12,000

• There are 4 known to exist.

This Island Earth—Style Y	1955	40x60
Private $12,500	VF	07/06
Christie's $3,680	VF	12/97
Christie's $2,090	VF	12/92

Estimate: $15,000 - $18,500

- There are 4 known to exist.

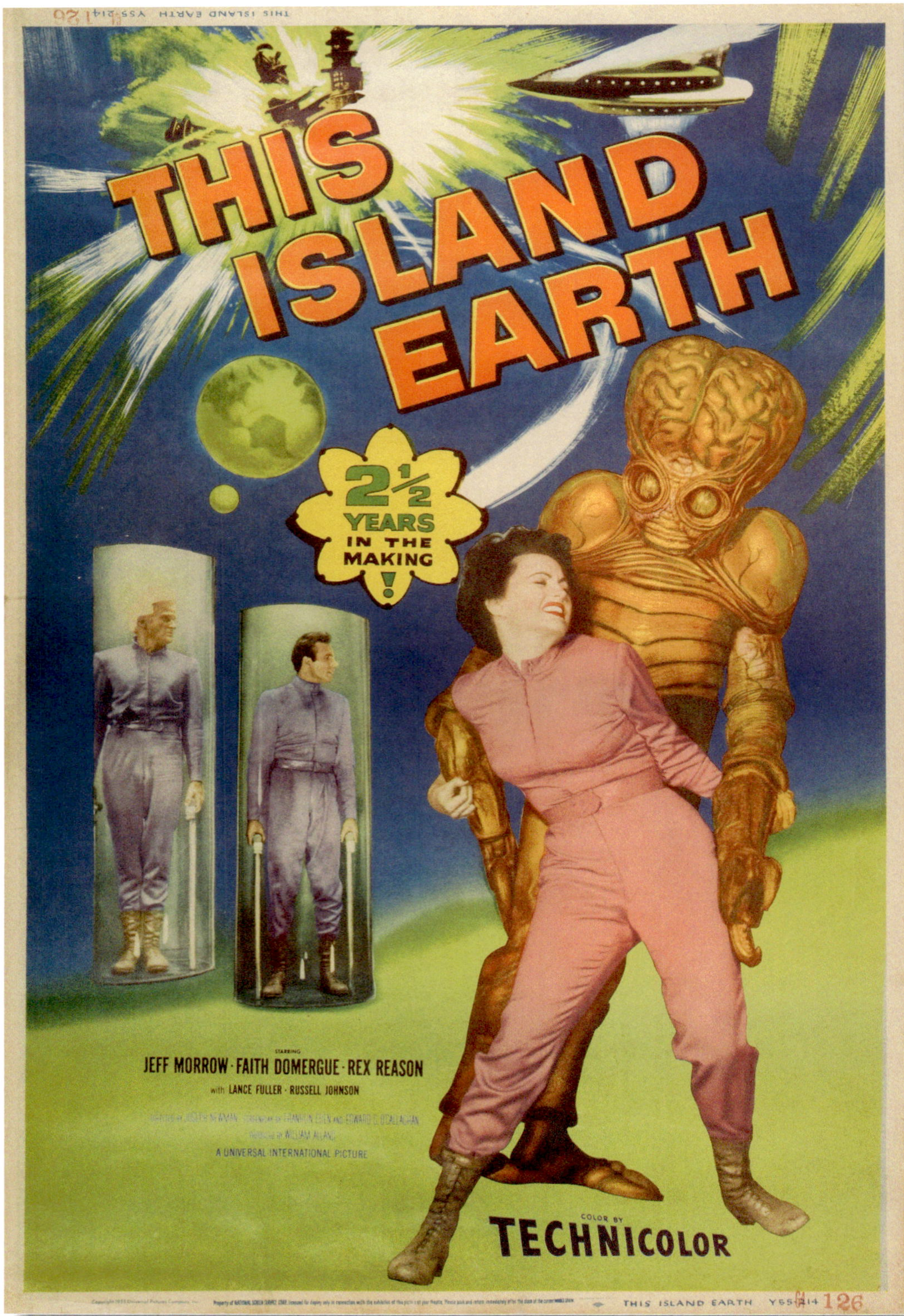

Photo by R. Aaron Raymond & Stephen Allard

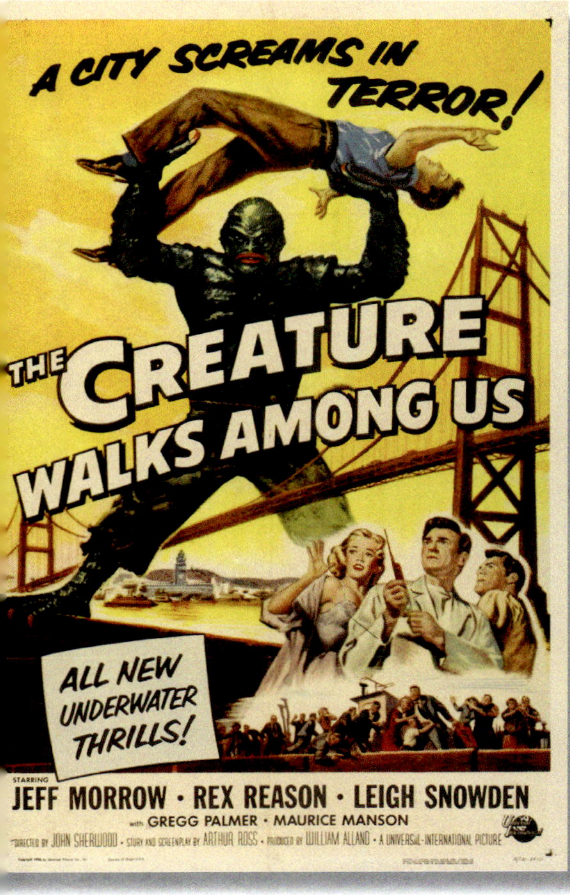

Courtesy of Heritage

Creature Walks Among Us	1956	27x41	
eMoviePoster	$975	VF	10/09
Heritage	$806	FN+	07/09
Heritage	$657	FN	11/08
Heritage	$1,434	VF+	07/08
eMoviePoster	$837	VF	07/08
Highest price realized:			
eMoviePoster	$2,510	NM	03/05
Price in 1991:			
Camden House	$425	FN	05/91

- This poster has appeared at auction 39 times since 1989.

Courtesy of Heritage

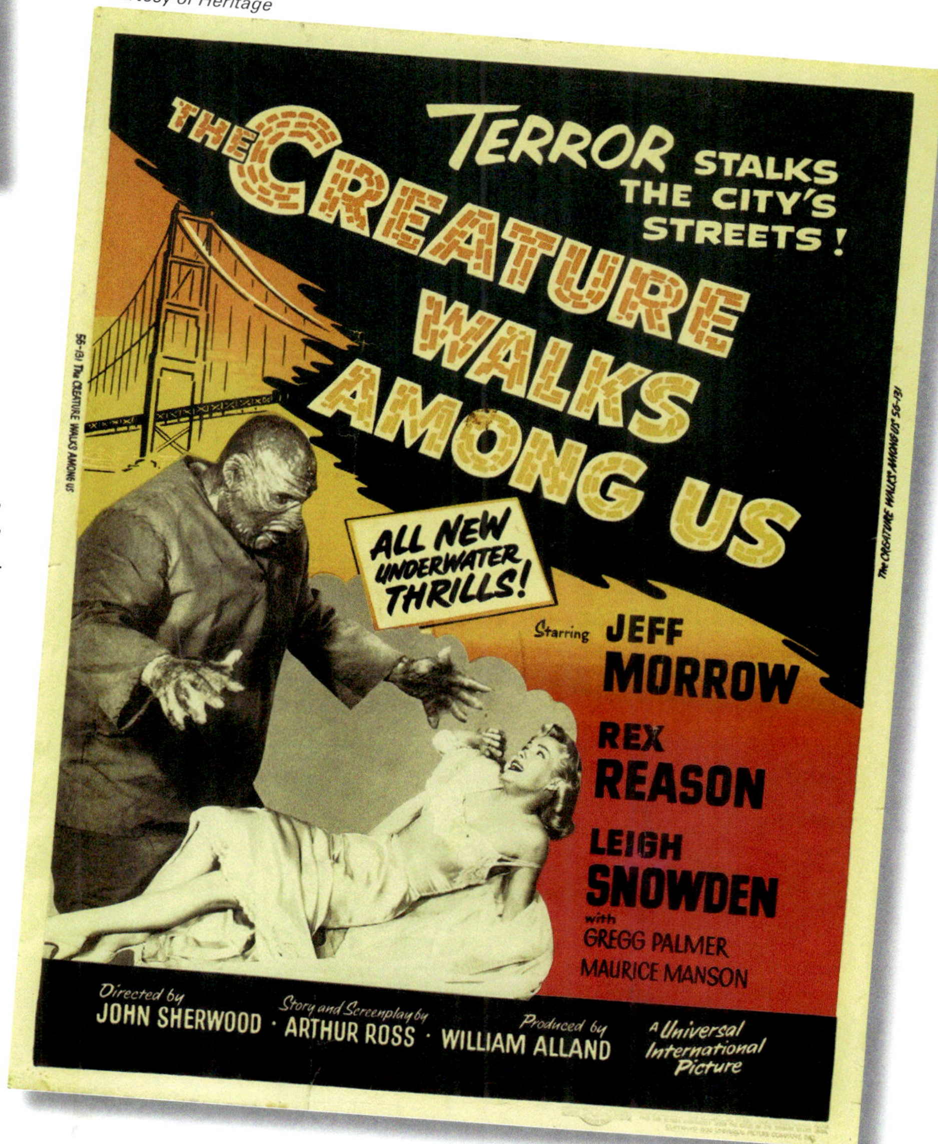

Creature Walks Among Us	1956	30x40	
Heritage	$1,015	FN-	03/07
Private	$350	VF	02/97
Camden House	$125	FN	11/94

- There are 3 known to exist.

Creature Walks Among Us	1956	40x60
Heritage $2,390	VF	11/08

• There is 1 known to exist.

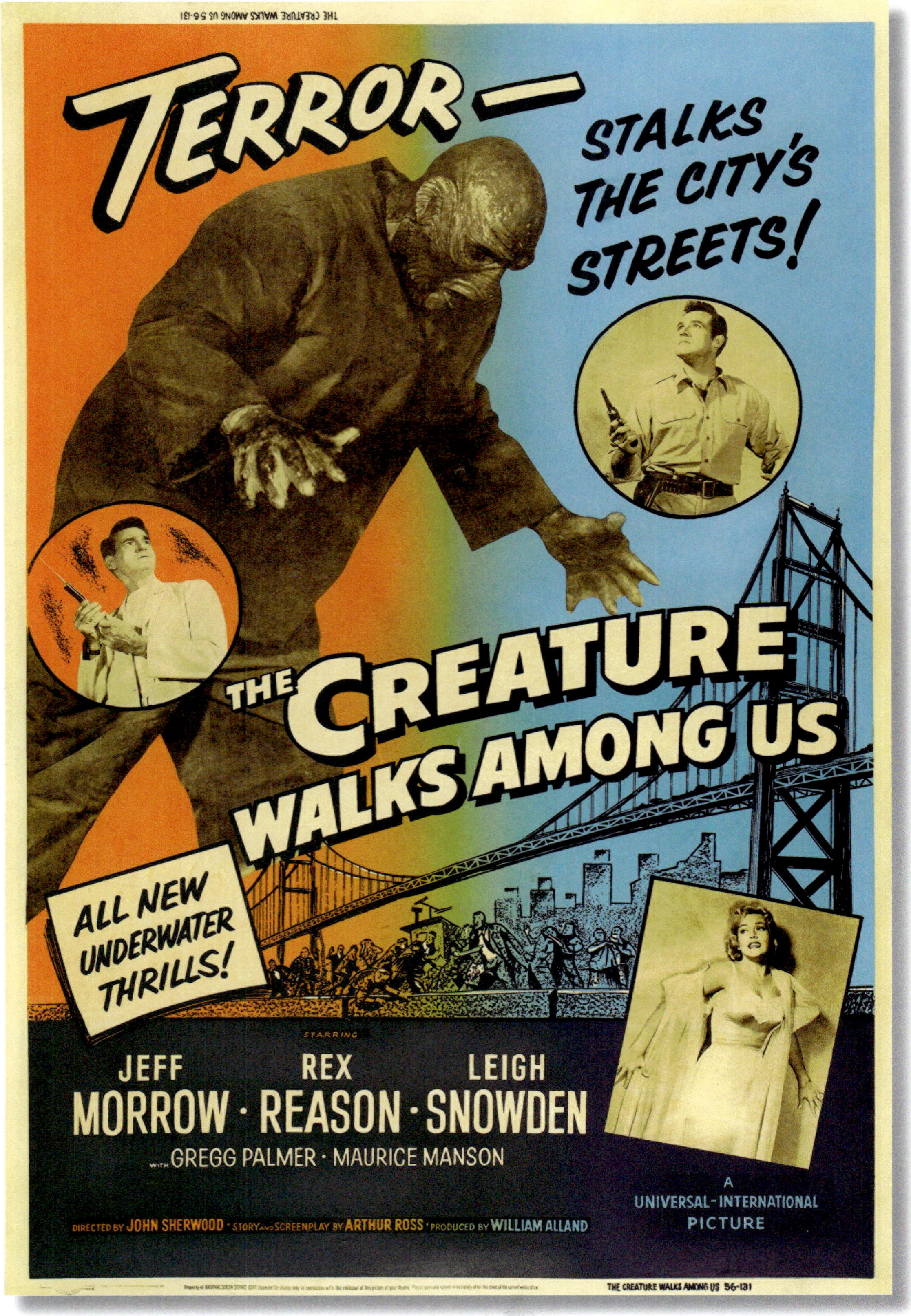

Courtesy of Heritage

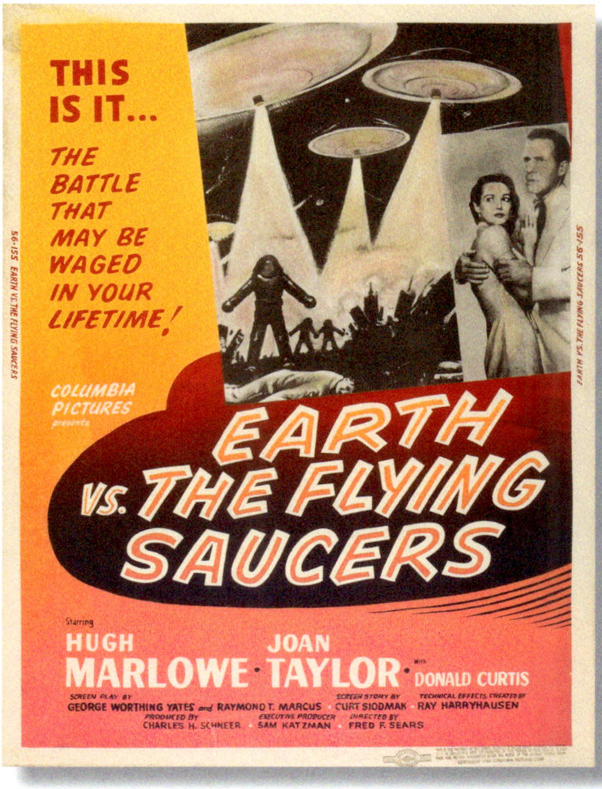

Courtesy of Heritage

Earth vs. the Flying Saucers	1956	30x40	
Heritage	$690	VF+	07/02

- There is 1 known to exist.

Earth vs. the Flying Saucers	1956	40x60	
Heritage	$977	G/VG	07/06
eMoviePoster	$845	VG	12/05
Christie's	$1,265	VG	12/97

- There are 3 known to exist.

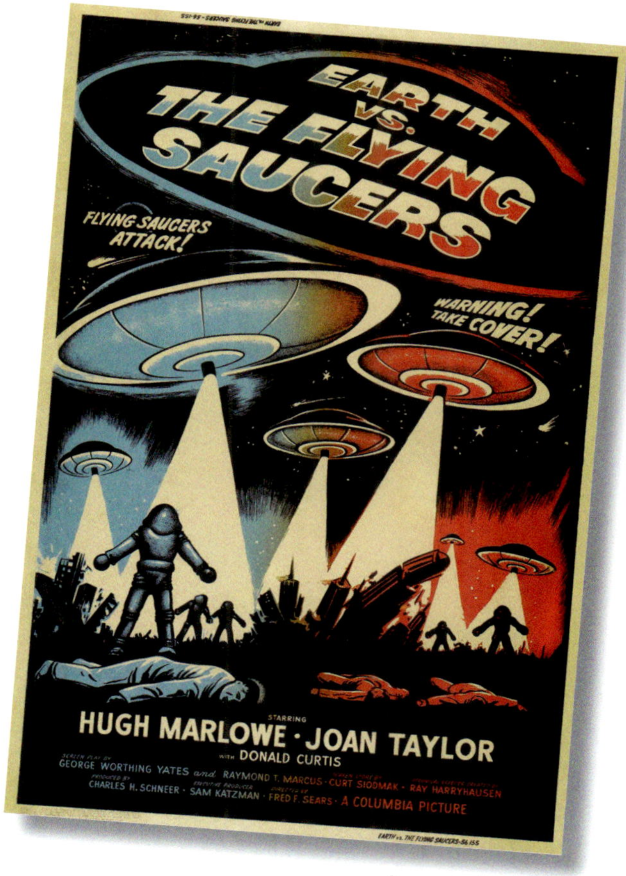

Courtesy of Heritage

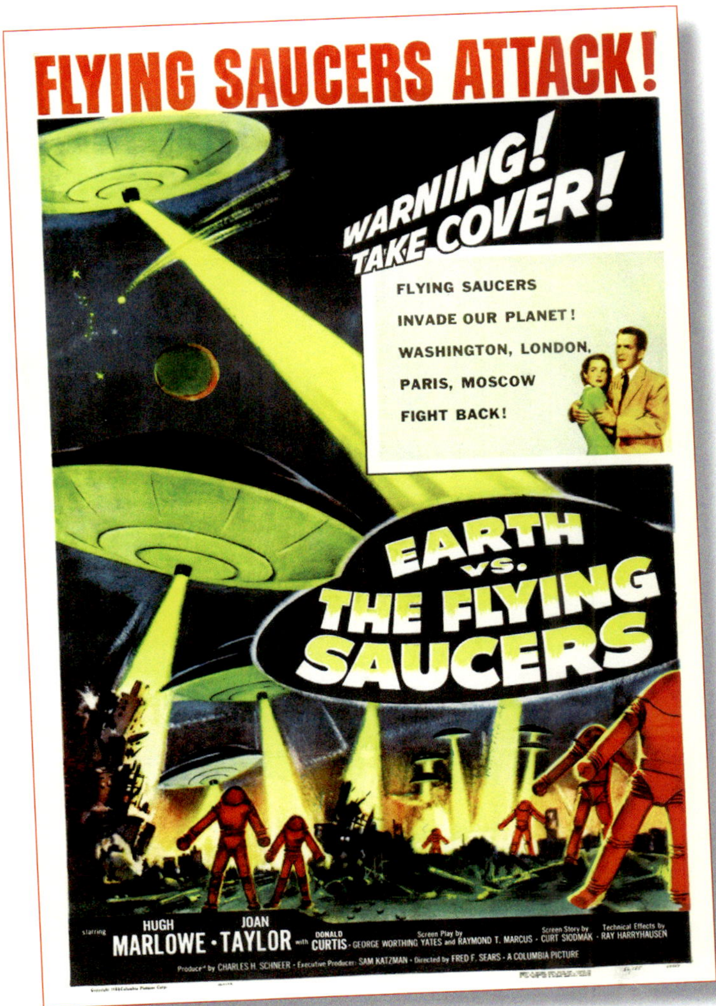

Courtesy of Heritage

Earth vs. the Flying Saucers	1956	27x41	
Heritage	$1,195	VF+	07/09
Heritage	$1,434	VF	03/09
Heritage	$1,434	NM	11/08
Heritage	$1,792	VF	03/08
Profiles in History	$1,400	NM	12/07

Highest price realized:

Heritage	$1,792	VF	03/08

Price in 1990:

Camden House	$200	VF	03/90

- This poster has appeared at auction 28 times since 1989.

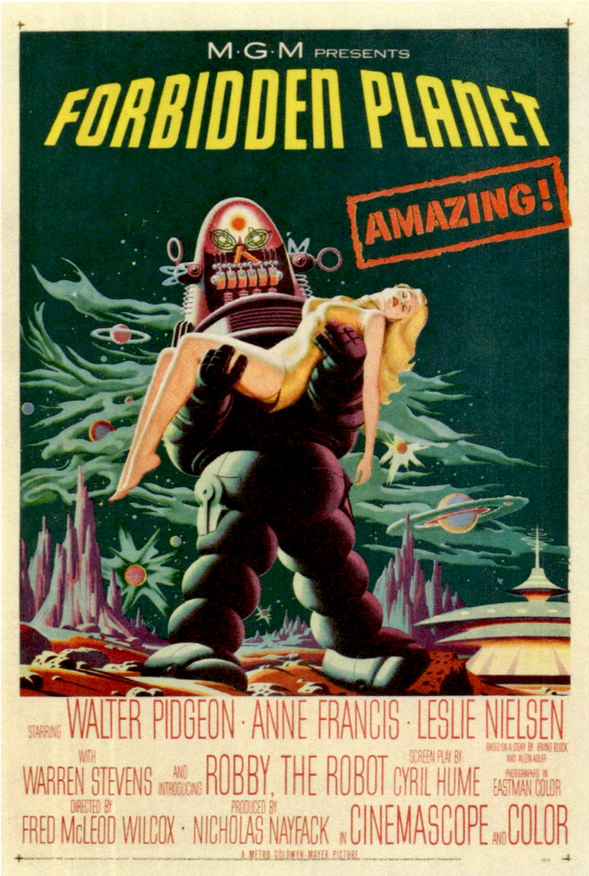

Courtesy of Heritage

Forbidden Planet	1956	27x41	
Heritage	$6,273	VF	11/09
Heritage	$6,572	FN-	07/09
Heritage	$8,962	VF+	03/09
Christie's	$8,950	VF	09/08
Christie's	$9,890	VF	03/08

Highest price achieved:

Christie's	$18,800	NM	06/00

Price in 1989:

Camden House	$850	NM	05/89

• This poster has appeared at auction 46 times since 1989.

Photo by R. Aaron Raymond & Stephen Allard

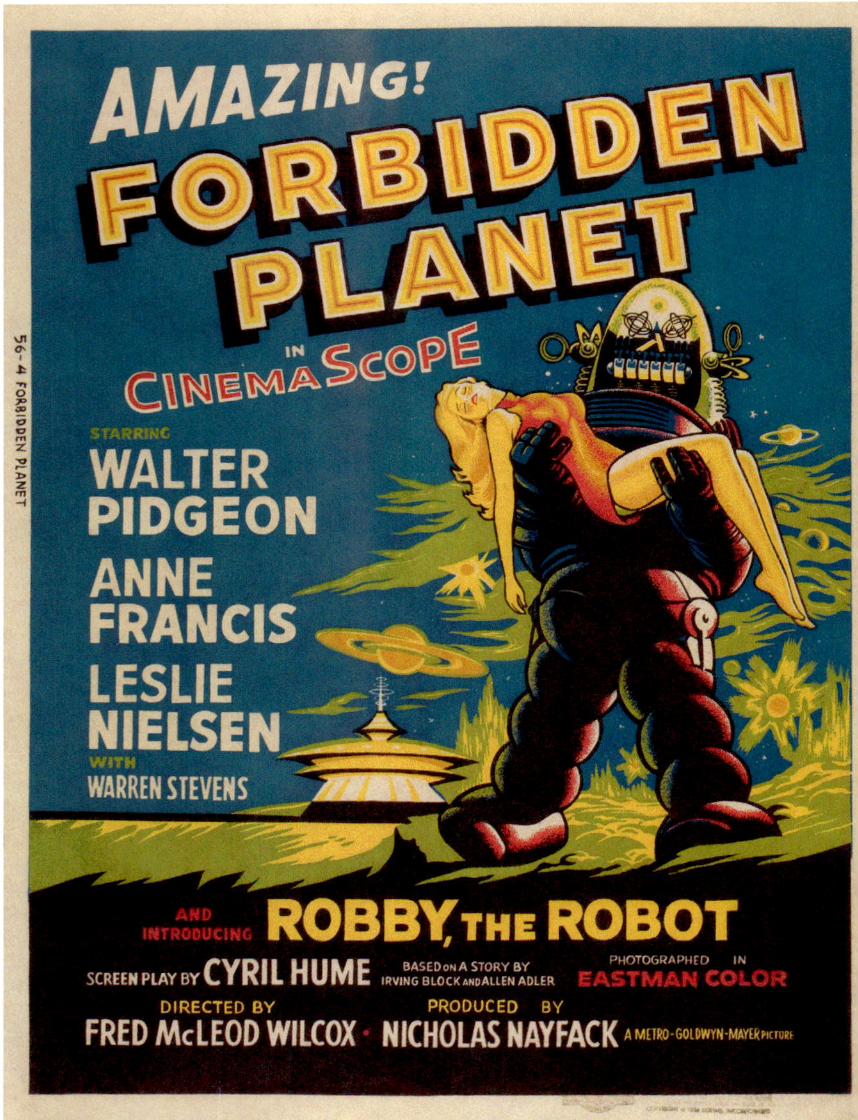

Forbidden Planet	1956	30x40	
Private	$11,500	VF	06/05
Butterfield & Butterfield	$3,162	FN	02/99
Sotheby's	$1,700	VF	12/94
Christie's	$2,750	FN	12/92

• There are 5 known to exist.

Forbidden Planet	1956	40x60	
Heritage	$7,475	FN-	03/06
Camden House	DNS	FN	06/94

• There are 3 known to exist.

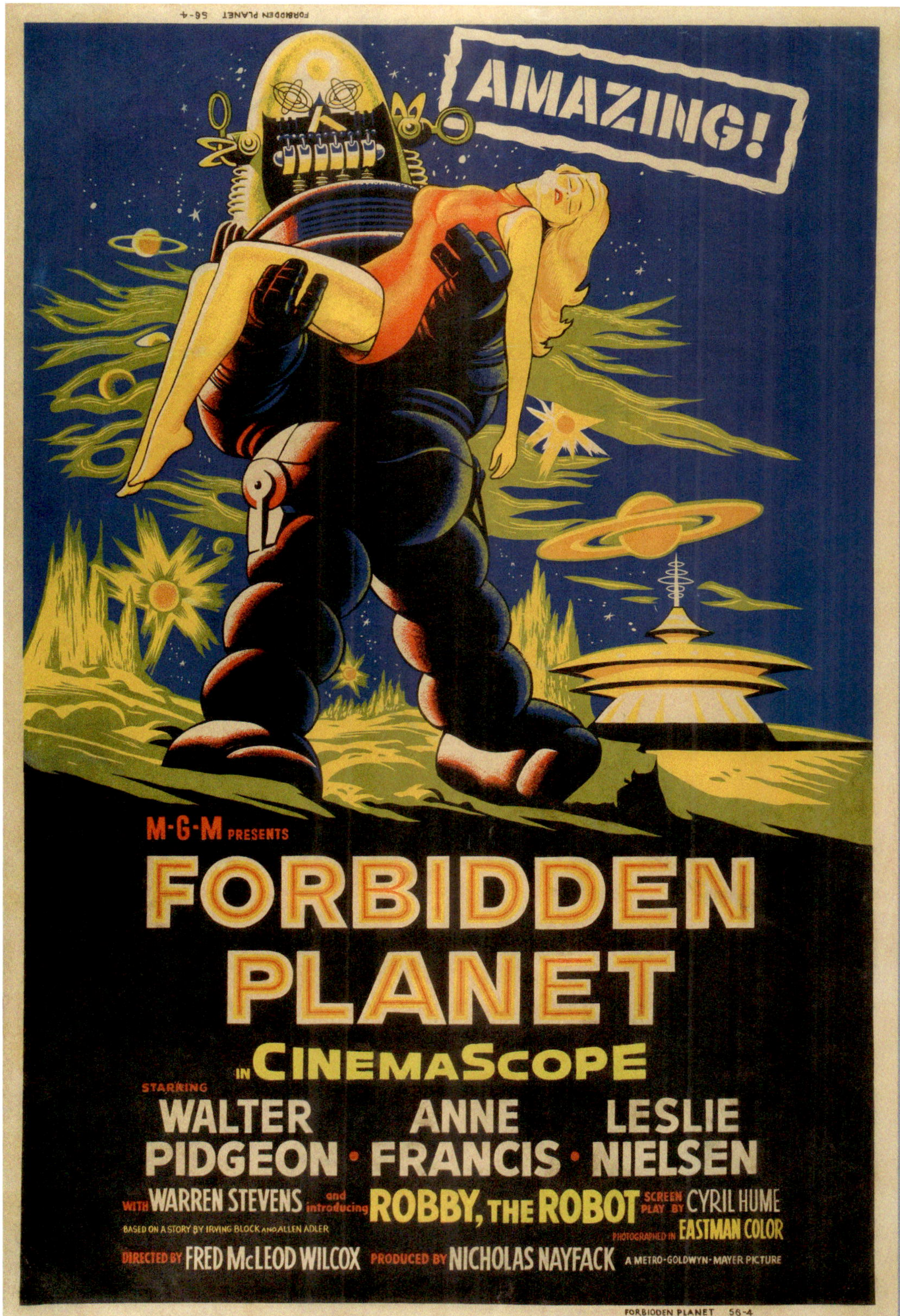

Photo by R. Aaron Raymond & Stephen Allard

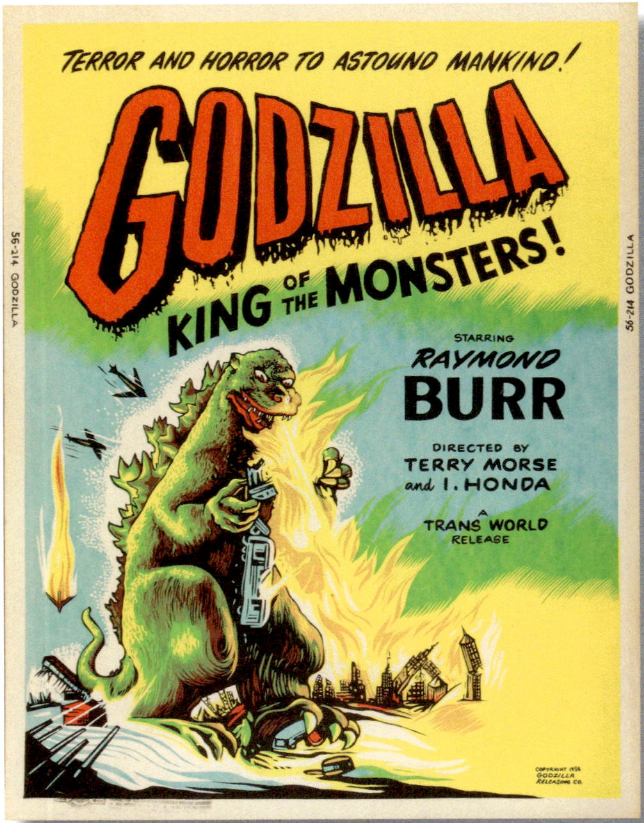

Courtesy of David Frediani, Photo by R. Aaron Raymond & Stephen Allard

Godzilla 1956 30x40

Lowery	$4,140	FN	06/00

Estimate: $5,000 - $6,500

- There are 3 known to exist.

Godzilla 1956 40x60

Private	$2,750	VF	08/01
Camden House	$1,200	FN	06/94

Estimate: $4,500 – $6,500

- There are 4 known to exist.

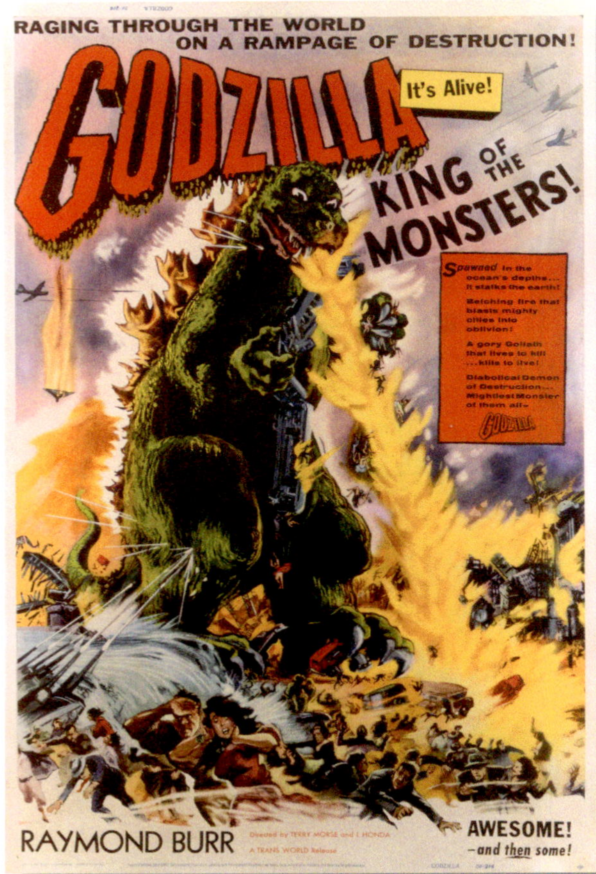

Courtesy of Reel Poster Gallery, London

Courtesy of Heritage

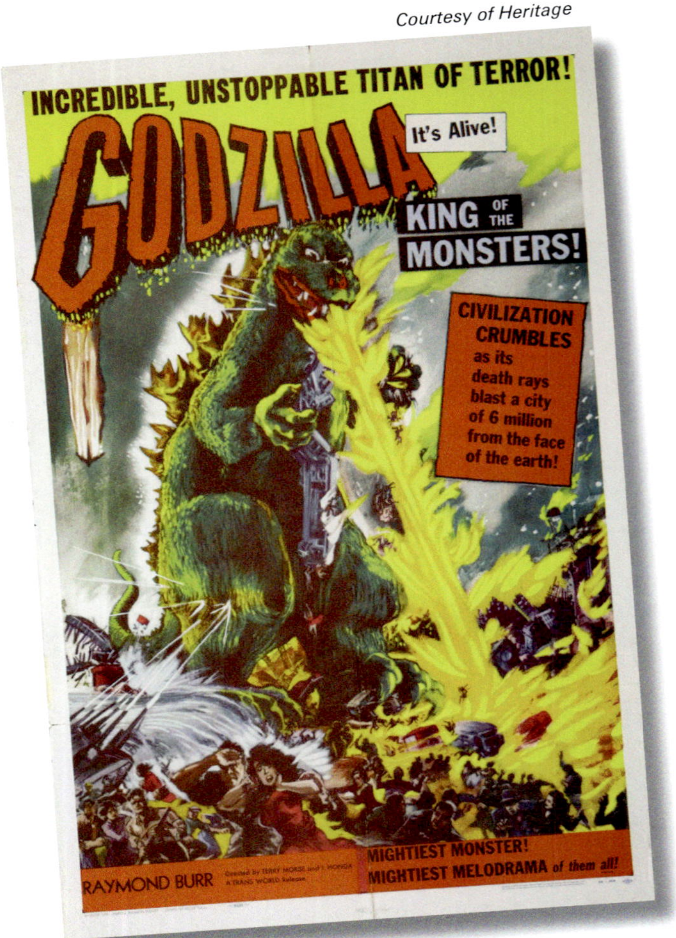

Godzilla 1956 27x41

Heritage	$2,031	FN/VF	11/09
Heritage	$2,131	VF+	07/09
Heritage	$1,792	FN/VF	03/09
Heritage	$2,031	FN	11/08
Bonhams & Butterfields	$2,400	VF-	12/07

Highest price realized:

Christie's	$5,288	NM	05/00

Price in 1990:

Christie's	$1,430	NM	12/90

- This poster has appeared at auction 17 times since 1989.

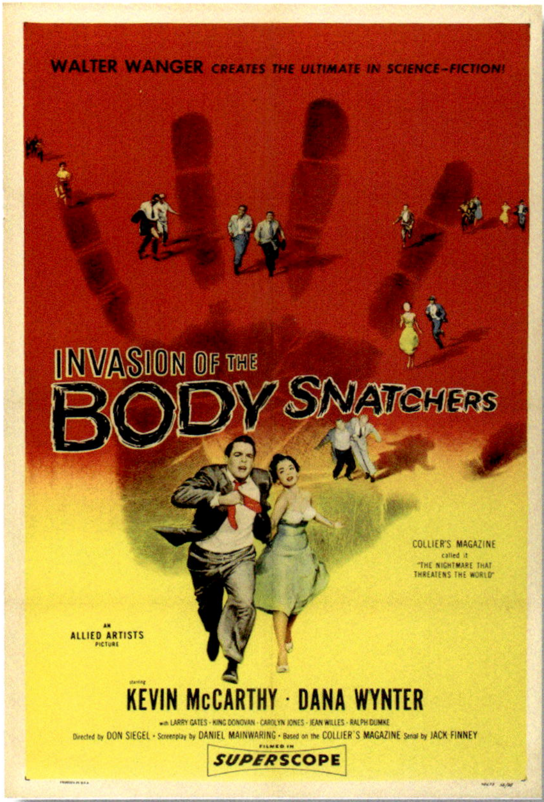

Courtesy of Heritage

Invasion of the Body Snatchers 1956 27x41

Heritage	$1,792	FN+	11/09
eMoviePoster	$927	VG	10/09
eMoviePoster	$1,150	GD/VG	07/09
Heritage	$1,533	VF+	03/09
Heritage	$1,553	VF-	07/08

Highest price realized:
Profiles in History $4,500 NM 12/07

Price in 1990:
Camden House $200 FN 10/90

• This poster has appeared at auction 42 times since 1989.

Invasion of the Body Snatchers 1956 30x40
Private $1,400 VF 05/00
Estimate: $3,500 - $5,500

• There is 1 known to exist.

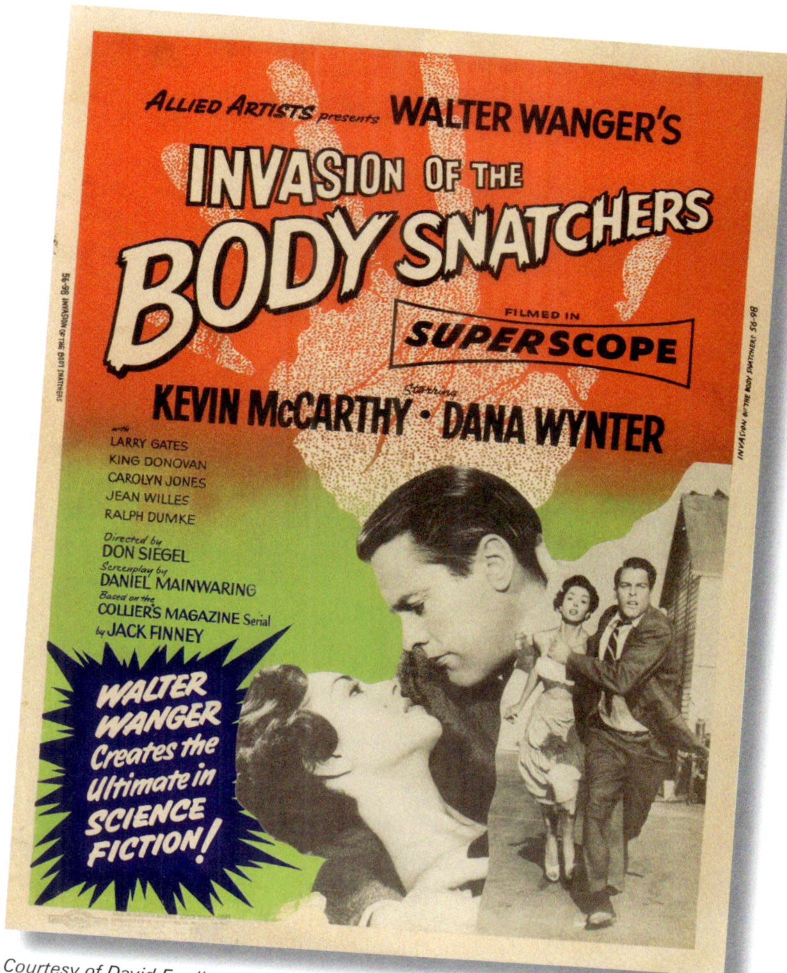

Courtesy of David Frediani, Photo by R. Aaron Raymond & Stephen Allard

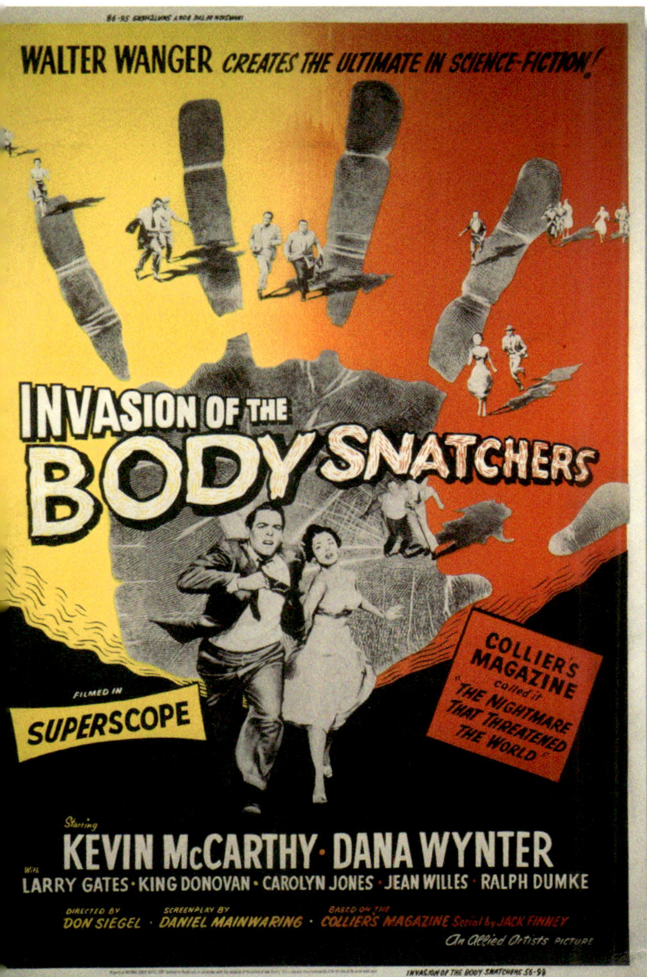

Courtesy of Camden House

Invasion of the Body Snatchers 1956 40x60
Camden House $400 FN 06/94
Estimate: $4,500 - $6,500

•There are 2 known to exist.

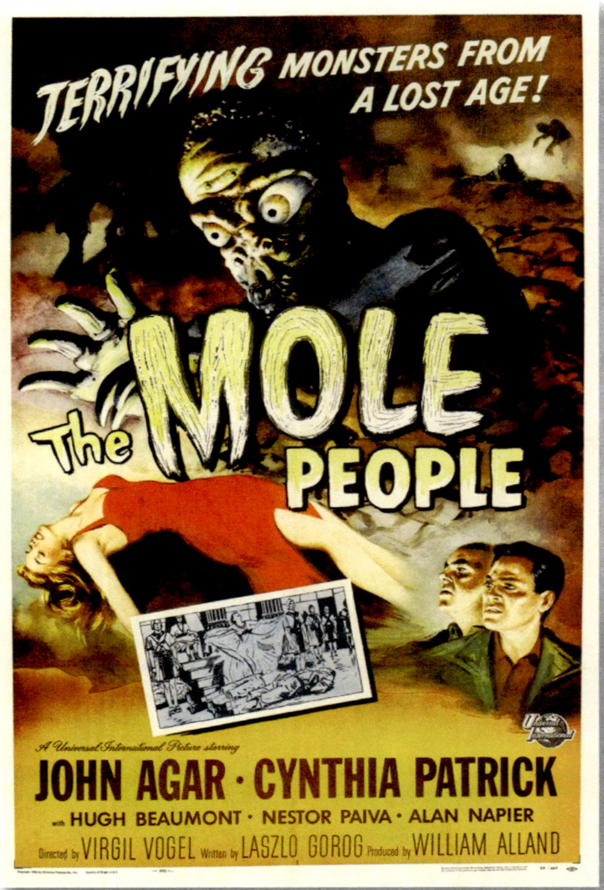

Courtesy of Heritage

Mole People			1956	27x41
Heritage	$657	VF	11/09	
Heritage	$956	NM	07/09	
Heritage	$746	FN/VF	03/09	
Profiles in History	$800	VF	12/08	
Heritage	$1,195	NM+	11/08	
Highest price realized:				
Heritage	$1,434	VF-	03/08	
Price in 1992:				
Camden House	$400	FN	11/92	

• This poster has appeared at auction 26 times since 1989.

Photo by R. Aaron Raymond & Stephen Allard

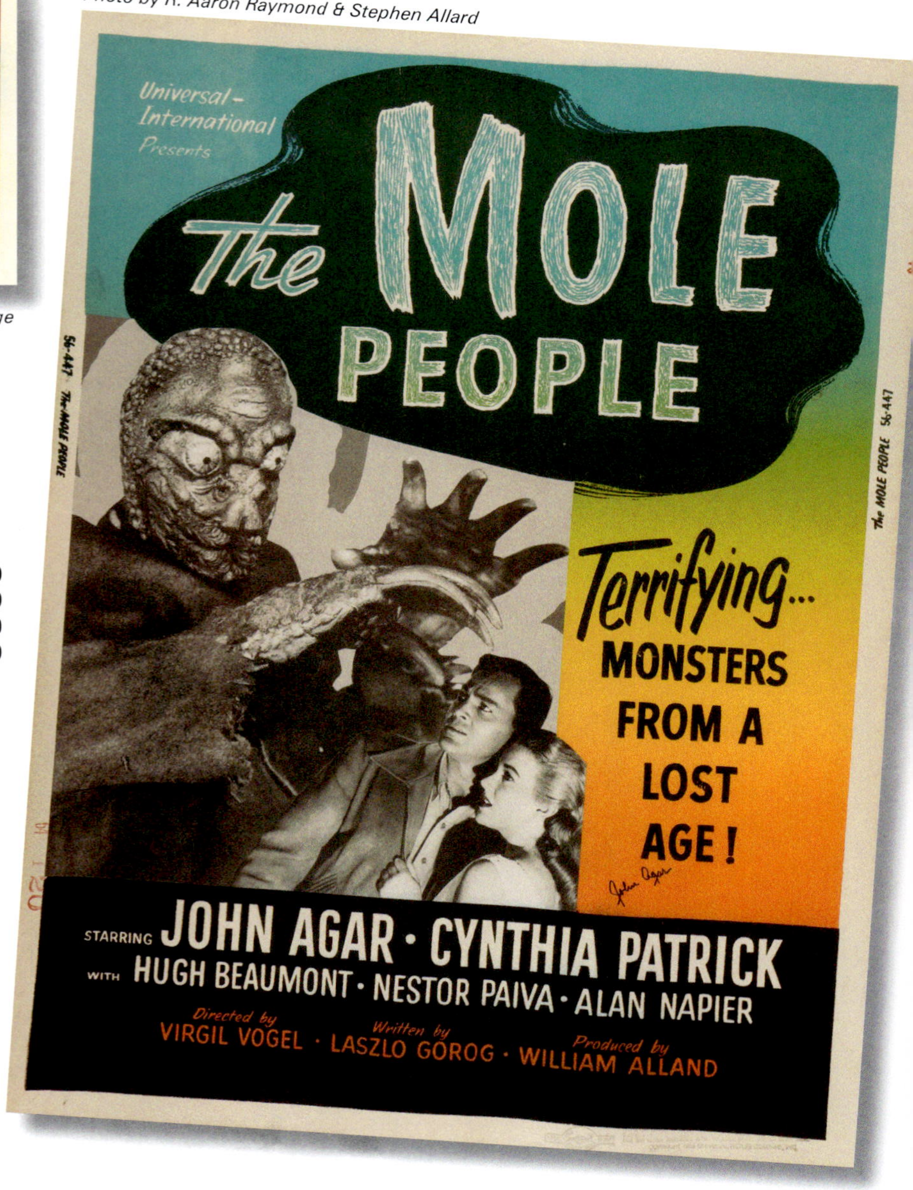

Mole People	1956		30x40
Private (Autographed)	$2,000	NM	03/09
Private	$850	VF	10/00
Sotheby's (Autographed)	$575	VF	04/99

• There are 8 known to exist.

Mole People	1956	40x60	
Private	$950	VF	01/09
eMoviePoster	$430	FN	01/01
Private	$500	VF	07/96
Butterfield's	$287	FN	12/94

Estimate: $900 - $1,500

• There are 6 known to exist.

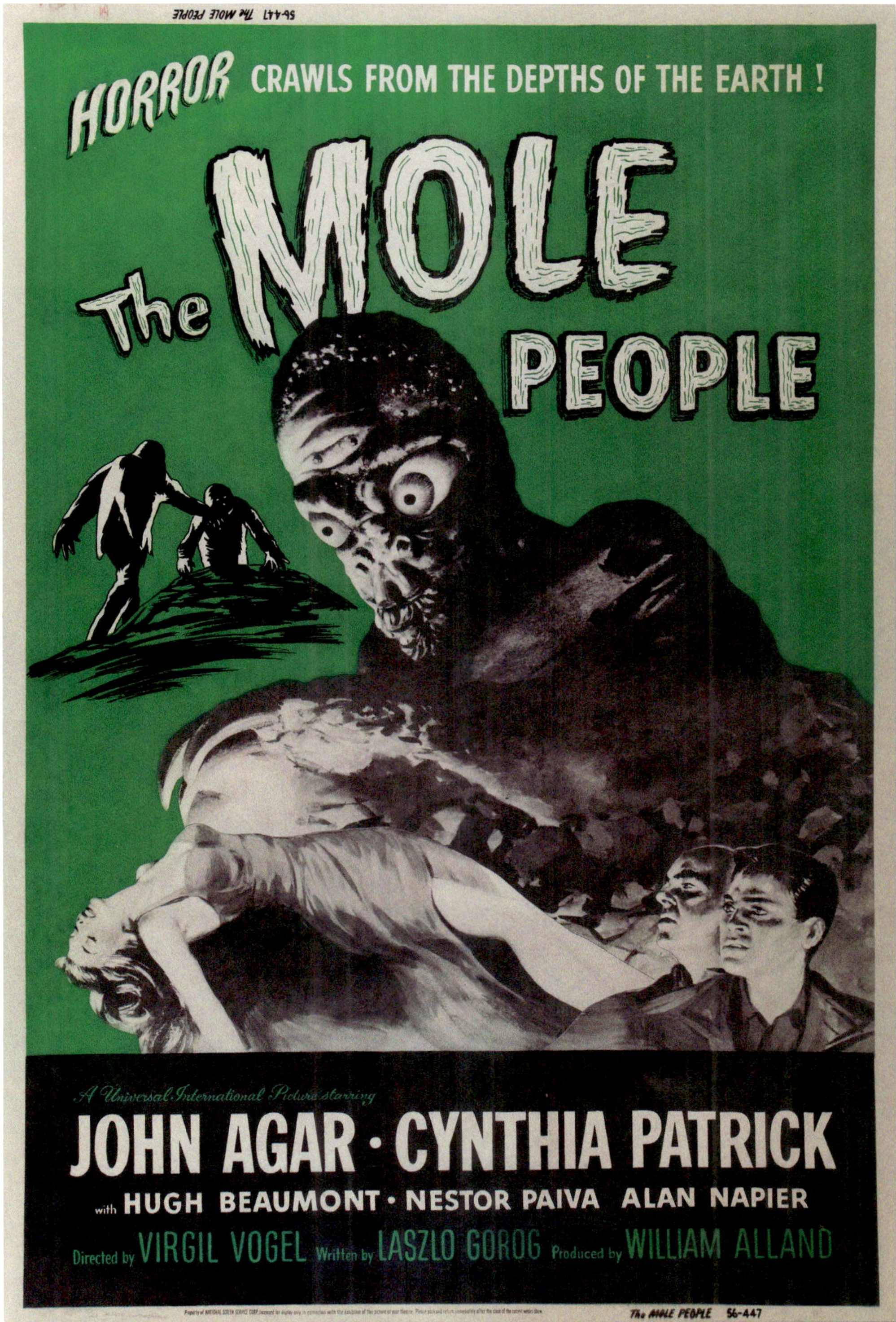

Photo by R. Aaron Raymond & Stephen Allard

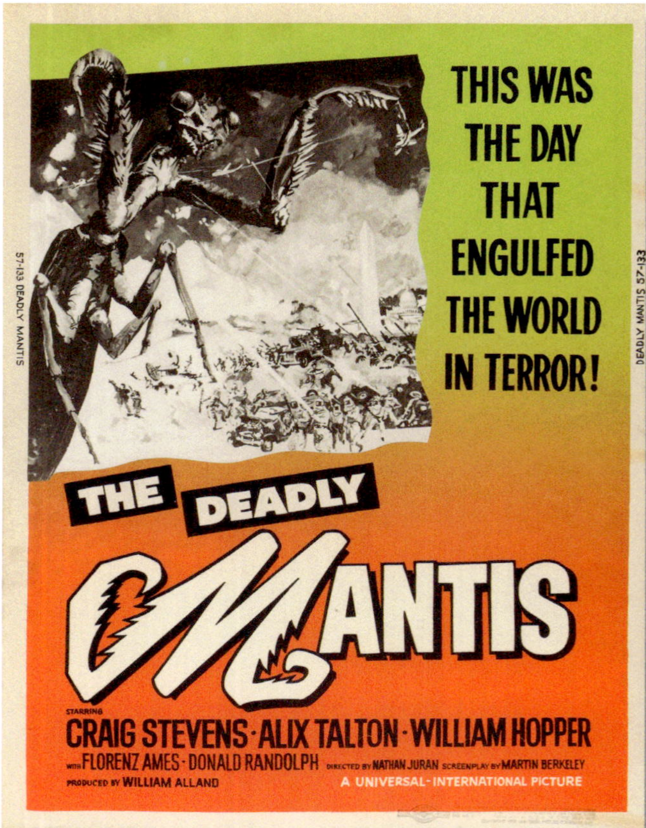

Courtesy of David Frediani, Photo by R. Aaron Raymond & Stephen Allard

Deadly Mantis 1957 30x40			
Private	$750	VF	05/02
Estimate: $1,500 - $2,000			

• There are 2 known to exist.

Deadly Mantis 1957 40x60			
Private	$800	VF	02/09
Private	$200	VG	06/95

• There are 4 known to exist.

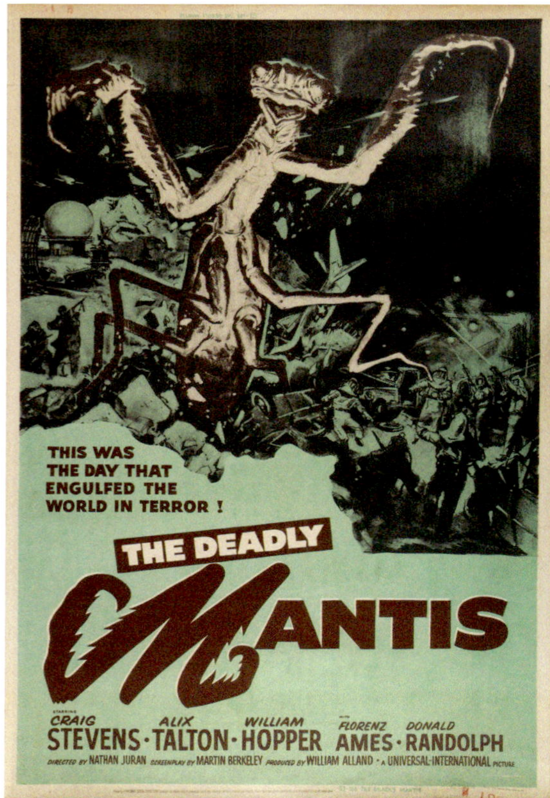

Photo by R. Aaron Raymond & Stephen Allard

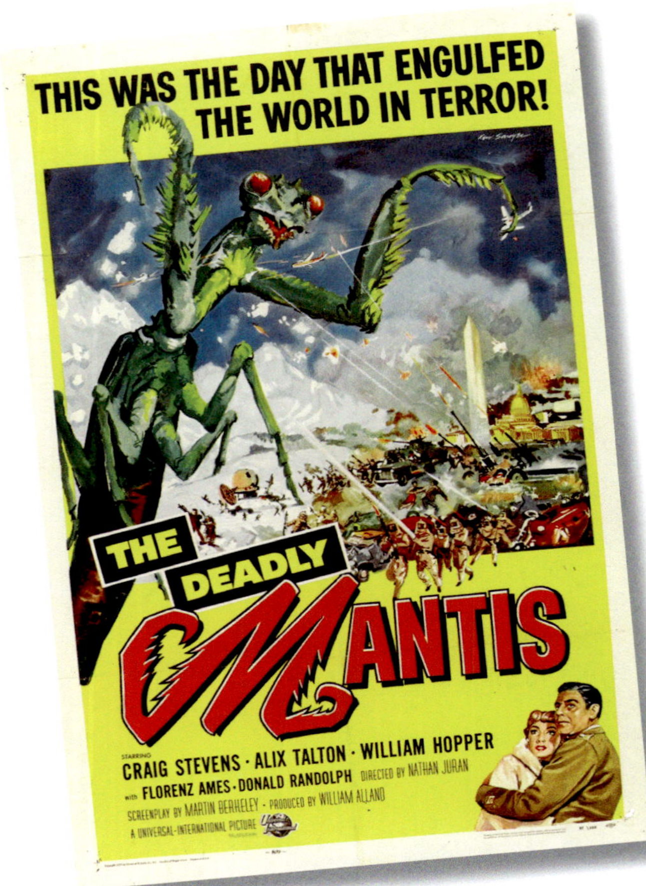

Courtesy of Heritage

Deadly Mantis 1957 27x41			
eMoviePoster	$459	VG	10/09
Heritage	$507	VF	03/09
Heritage	$374	VF-	11/08
Heritage	$478	VF-	07/08
eMoviePoster	$630	VG/FN	06/08

Highest price achieved:

Heritage	$776	VF	03/08

Price in 1993:

Camden House	$175	VF	11/93

• This poster has appeared at auction 31 times since 1989.

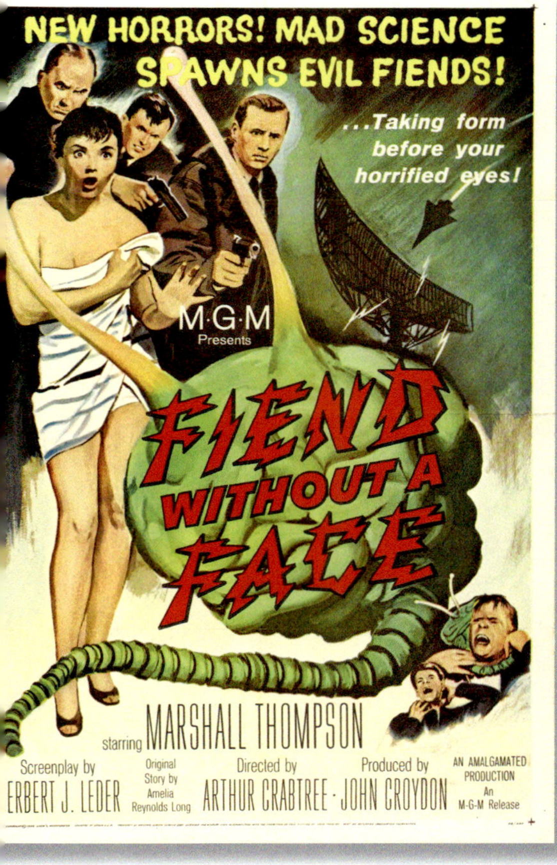

Courtesy of Heritage

Fiend without a Face	1957	27x41	
eMoviePoster	$330	VG	10/09
eMoviePoster	$381	VF	08/09
Heritage	$896	MT	07/09
eMoviePoster	$201	GD/VG	04/09
Profiles in History	$375	VF	12/07

Highest price realized:

Heritage	$896	MT	07/09

Price in 1993:

Camden House	$225	NM	11/93

- This poster has appeared at auction 32 times since 1989.

Photo by R. Aaron Raymond & Stephen Allard

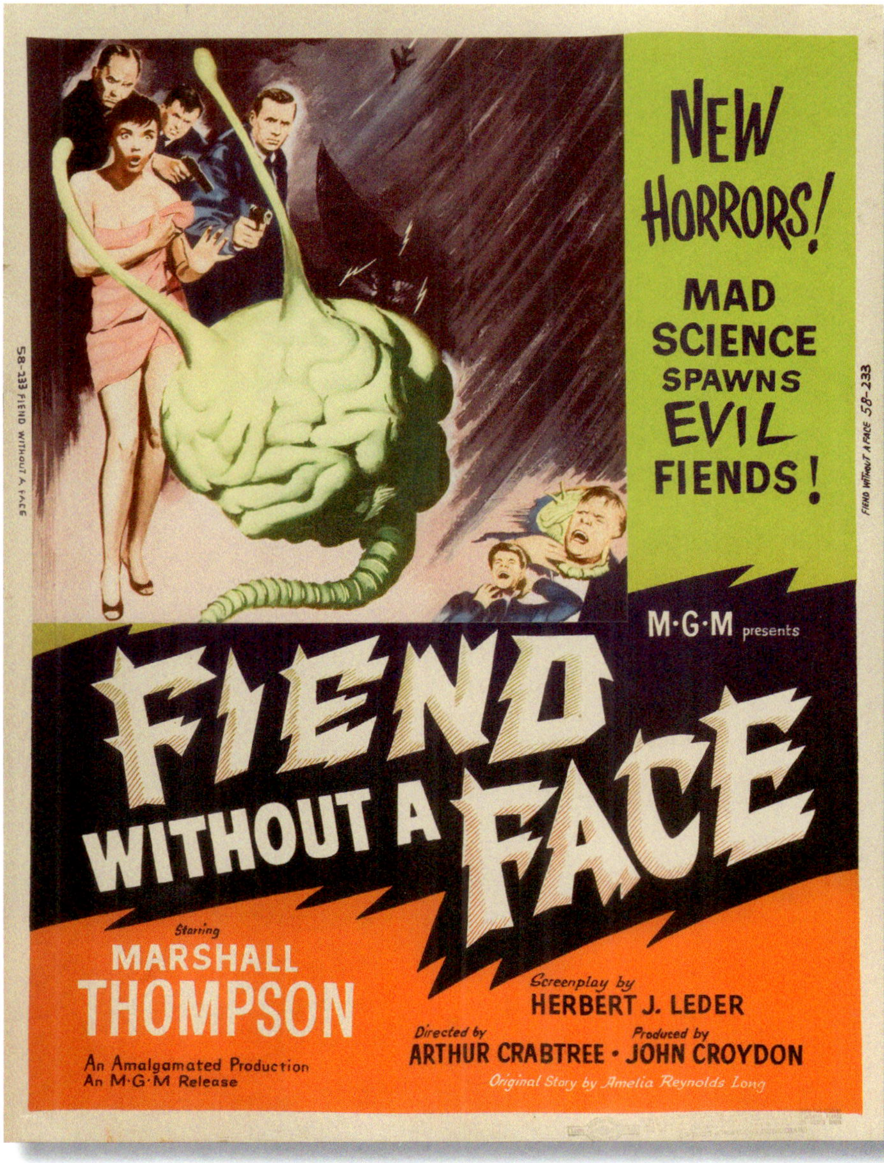

Fiend without a Face	1957	30x40	
Private	04/07	NM	$475
Poster City	12/00	VF	$300

Estimate: $800 - $1,200

- There are 6 known to exist.
- There is 1 *Fiend without a Face* 40x60 known to exist. Image not available.

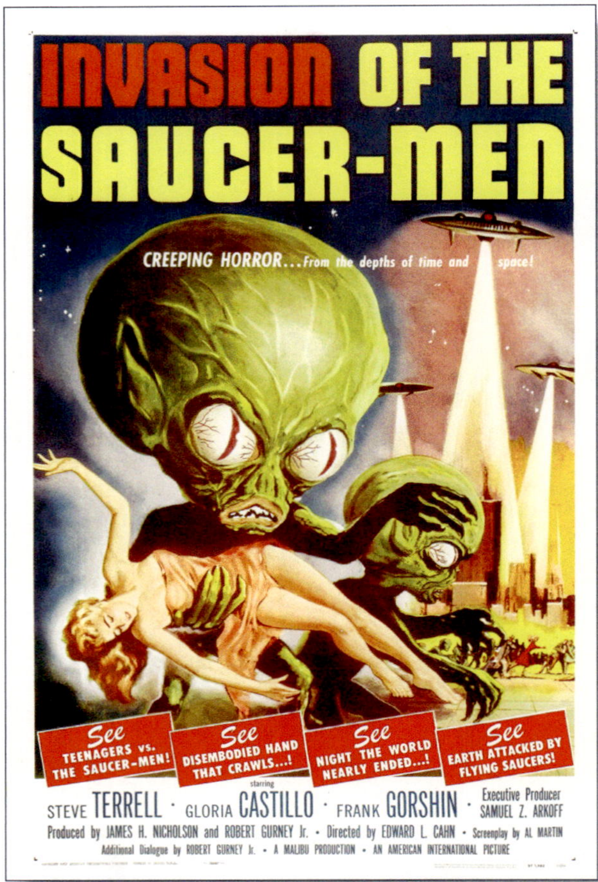

Courtesy of Heritage

Invasion of the Saucer-Men		1957	27x41
Heritage	$4,780	VF	11/09
Heritage	$5,377	FN/VF	07/09
Heritage	$3,346	VF-	03/09
Heritage	$5,676	NM	11/08
eMoviePoster	$4,600	VG/FN	11/08

Highest price realized:

Heritage	$6,572	VF+	03/08

Price in 1993:

Sotheby's	$1,093	FN	12/93

• This poster has appeared at auction 34 times since 1989.

Courtesy of David Frediani, Photo by R. Aaron Raymond & Stephen Allard

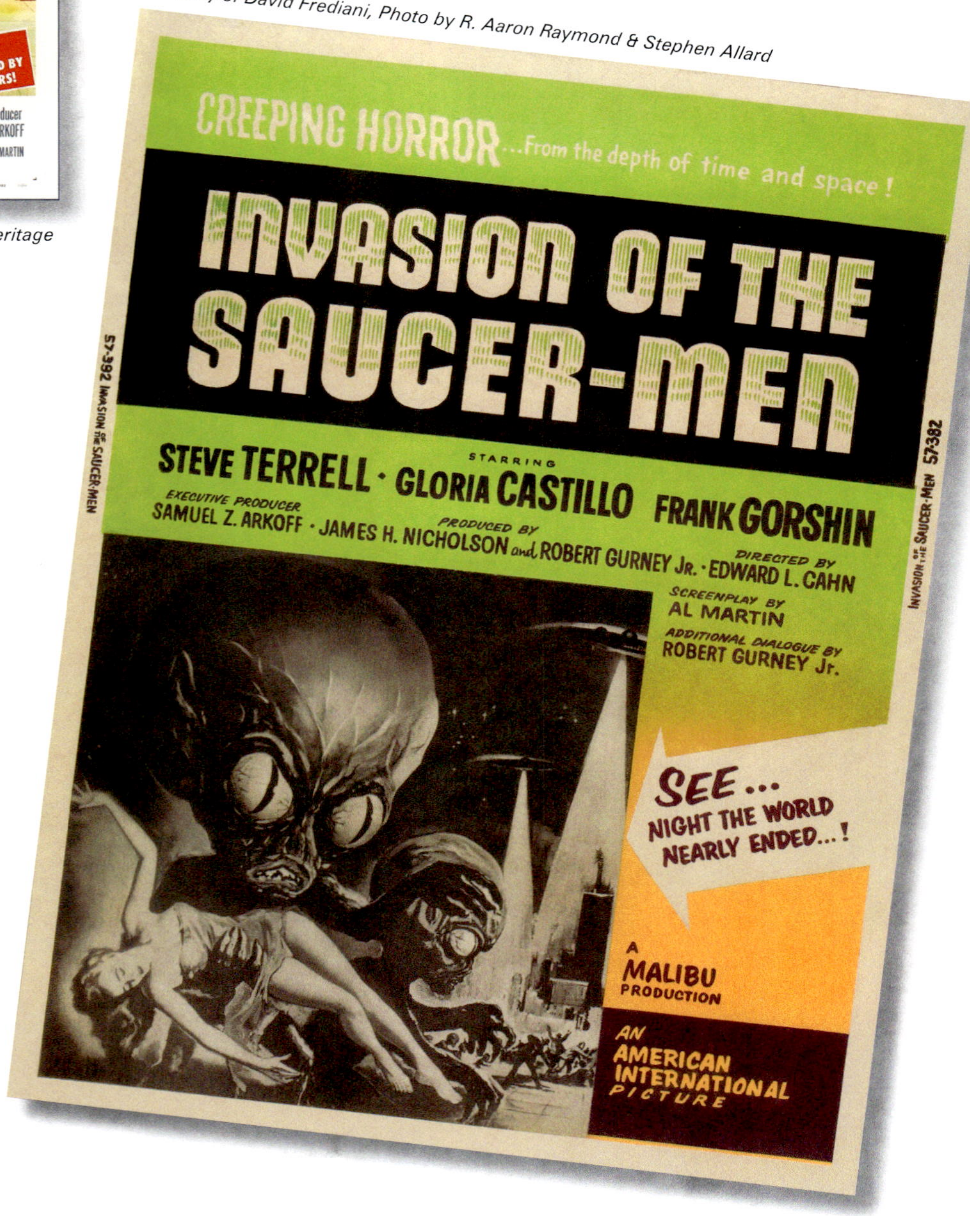

Invasion of the Saucer-Men		1957	30x40
Private	$2,400	VF	04/01

Estimate: $5,500 - $8,500

• There is 1 known to exist.

Invasion of the Saucer-Men 1957 40x60
Private $9,500 NM 03/03
Estimate: $12,000 - $15,000

• There is 1 known to exist.

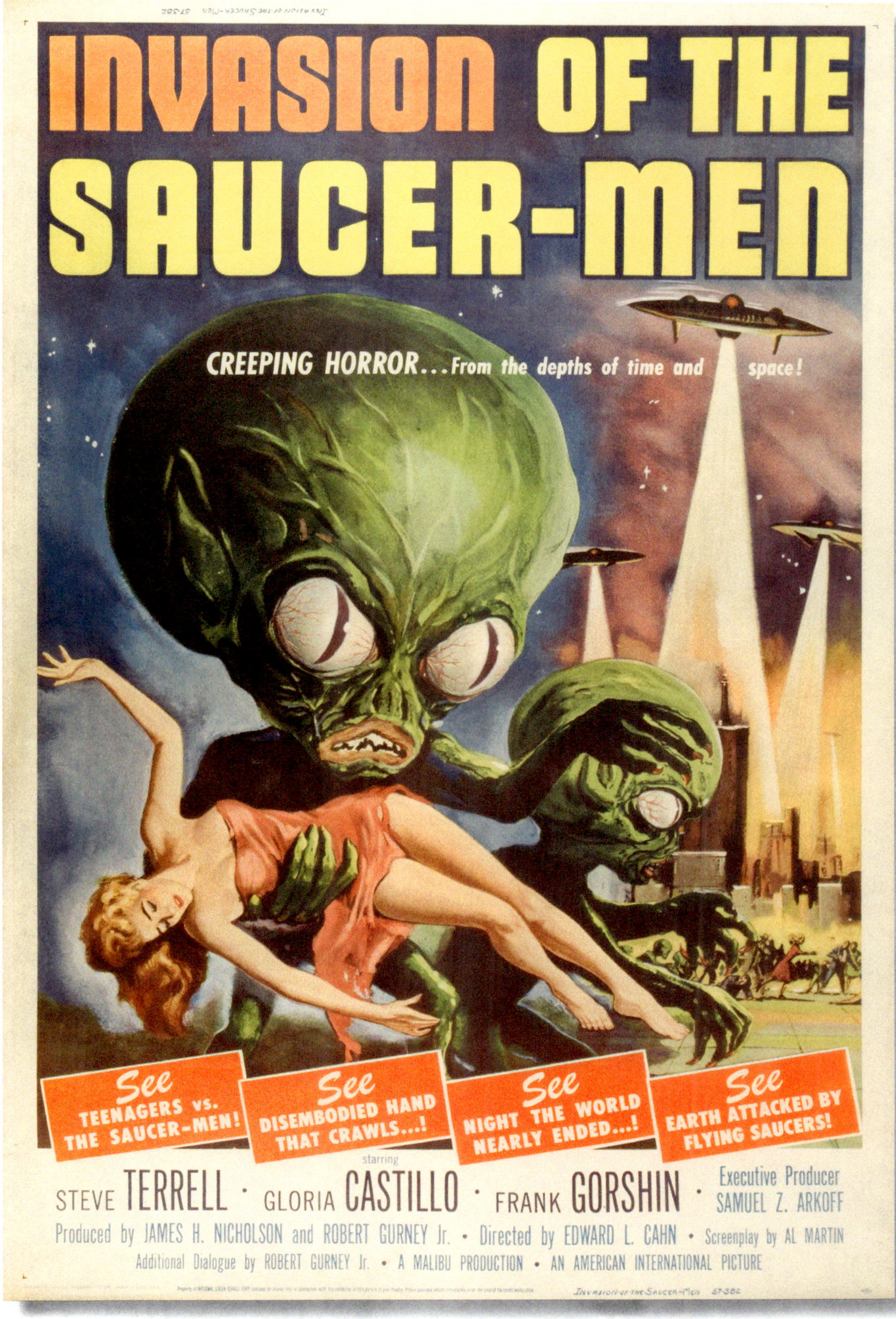

Photo by R. Aaron Raymond & Stephen Allard

20 Million Miles to Earth 1957 30x40
Heritage $3,910 FN+ 07/04
Estimate: $4,500 - $6,500

• There is 1 known to exist.

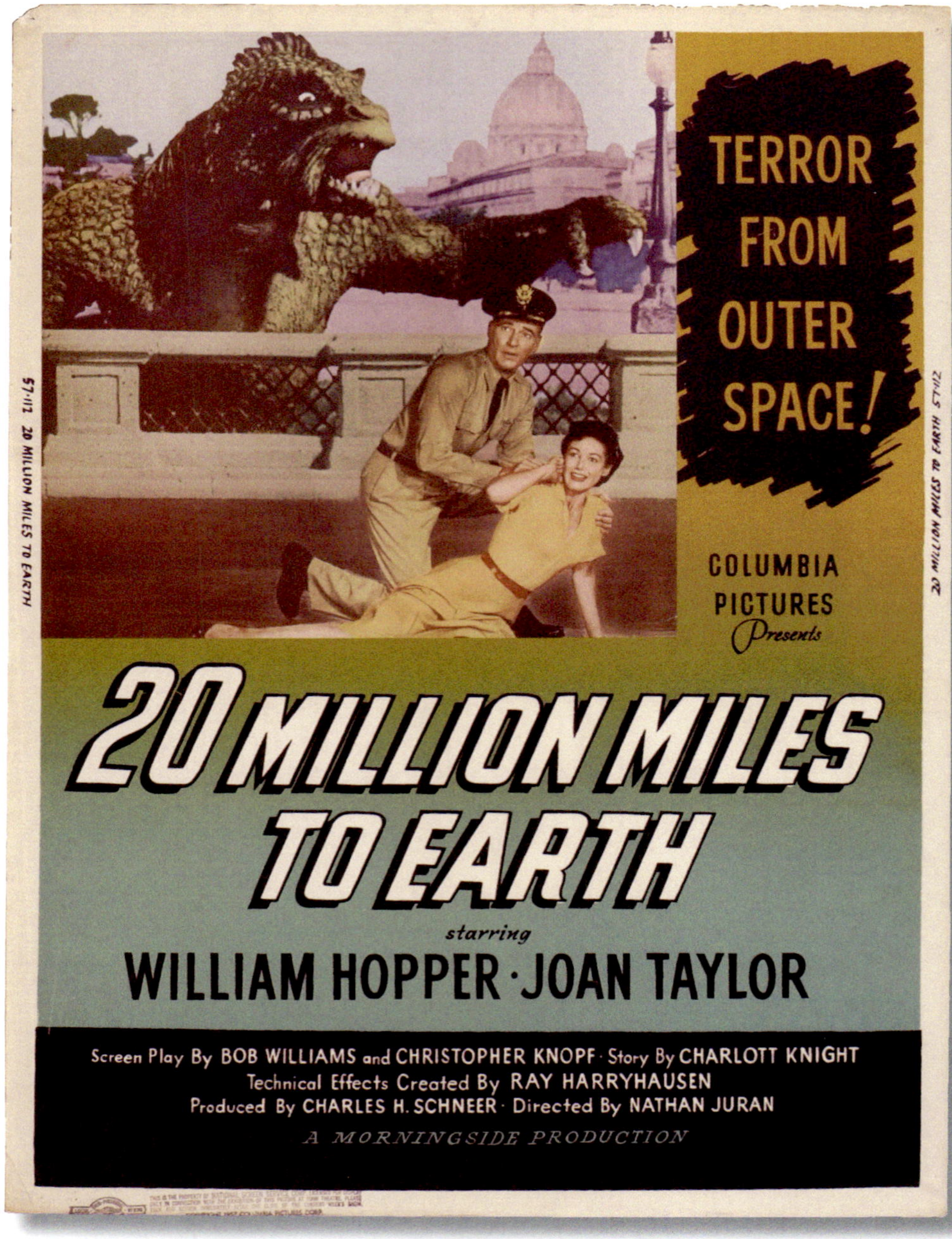

Courtesy of Heritage

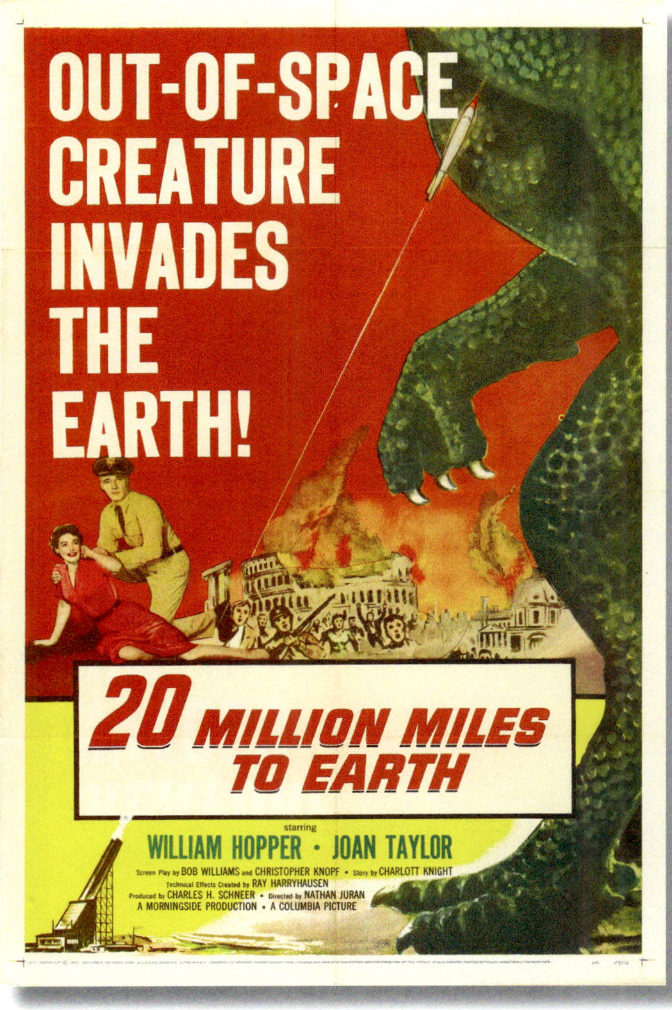

Courtesy of Heritage

20 Million Miles to Earth—Style A		1957	27x41
eMoviePoster	$194	GD	10/09
Heritage (Autographed)	$388	FN+	10/09
CineMasterpieces (Autographed)	$1,195	VF	09/08
Profiles in History	$400	NM	12/07
Heritage	$328	VF/NM	07/07

Highest price realized:

CineMasterpieces (Autographed)	$1,195	VF	09/08

Price in 1996:

Butterfield & Butterfield	$172	NM	02/96

• This poster has appeared at auction 26 times since 1989.

20 Million Miles to Earth		1957	40x60
Heritage	$ 657	VG	11/09

• There are 2 known to exist.

Courtesy of Heritage

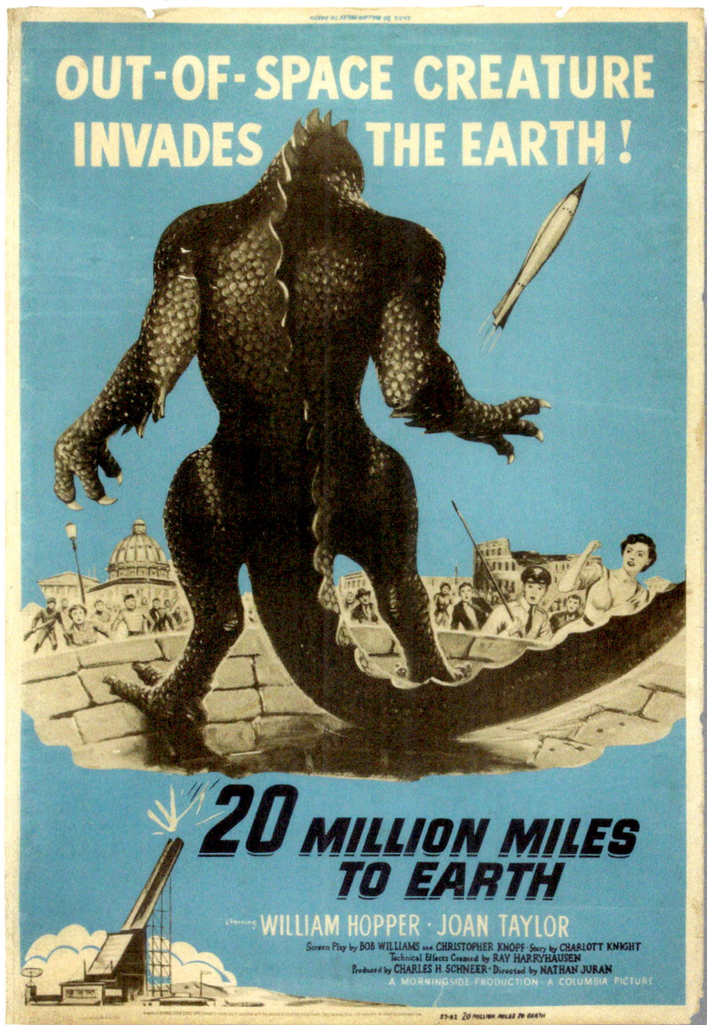

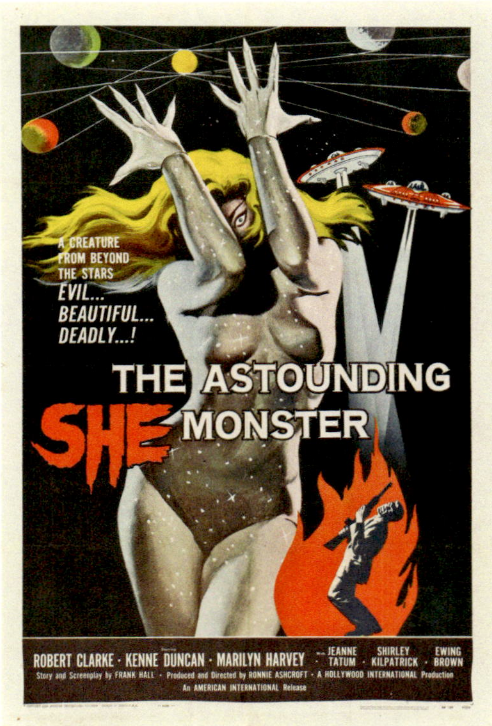

Courtesy of Heritage

Astounding She Monster	1958	27x41	
Heritage	$1,673	VF+	11/09
Heritage	$2,629	VF	03/09
Christie's	$2,720	VF	03/08
Profiles in History	$1,600	NM	12/07
eMoviePoster	$1,525	FN	04/07

Highest price realized:

Christie's	$2,720	VF	03/08

Price in 1992:

Hollywood Poster Art Auction	$400	NM	12/92

•This poster has appeared at auction 32 times since 1989.

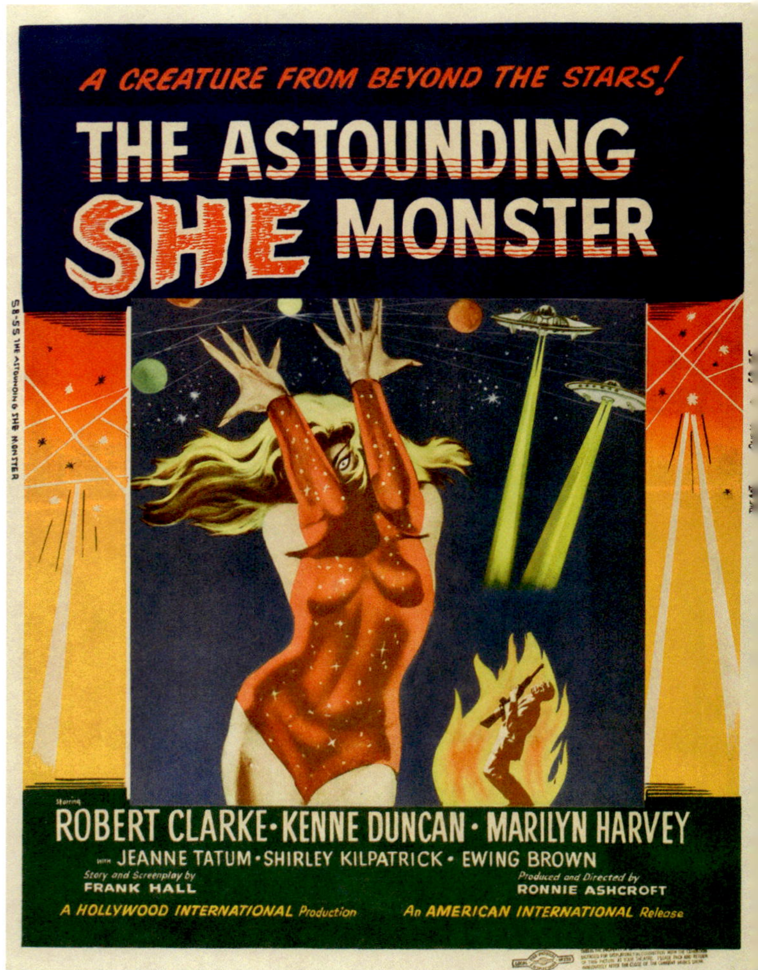

Courtesy of Heritage

Astounding She Monster	1958	30x40	
Heritage	$1,792	VF	11/08
Lowery	$1,150	VF	06/00
Private	$500	VG	03/96

• There are 3 known to exist.

Courtesy of Heritage

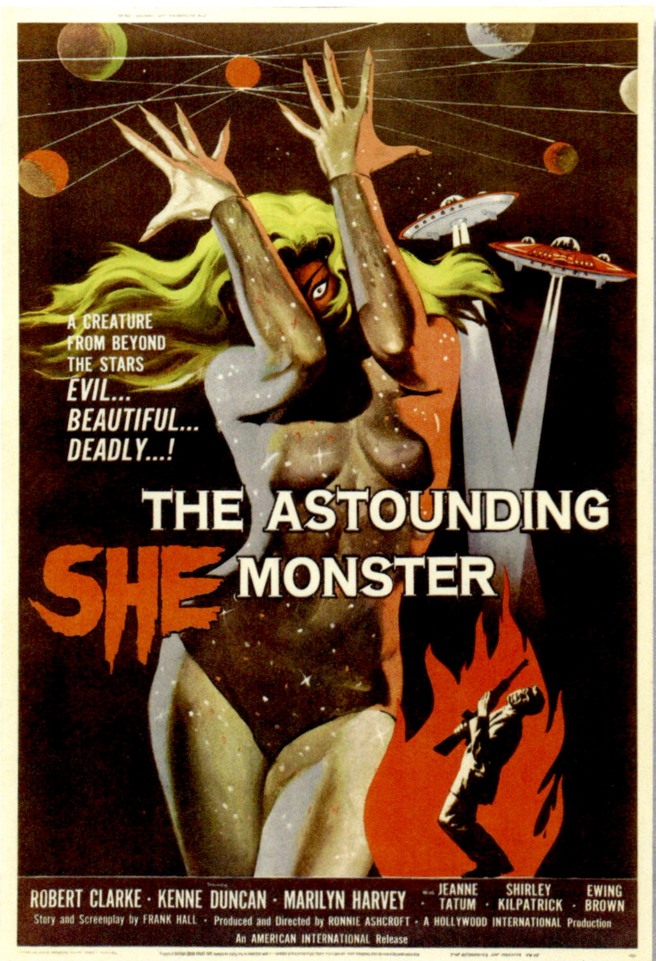

Astounding She Monster	1958	40x60	
Heritage	$2,091	VF-	11/09
Heritage	$1,135	FN	11/06

• There are 3 known exist.

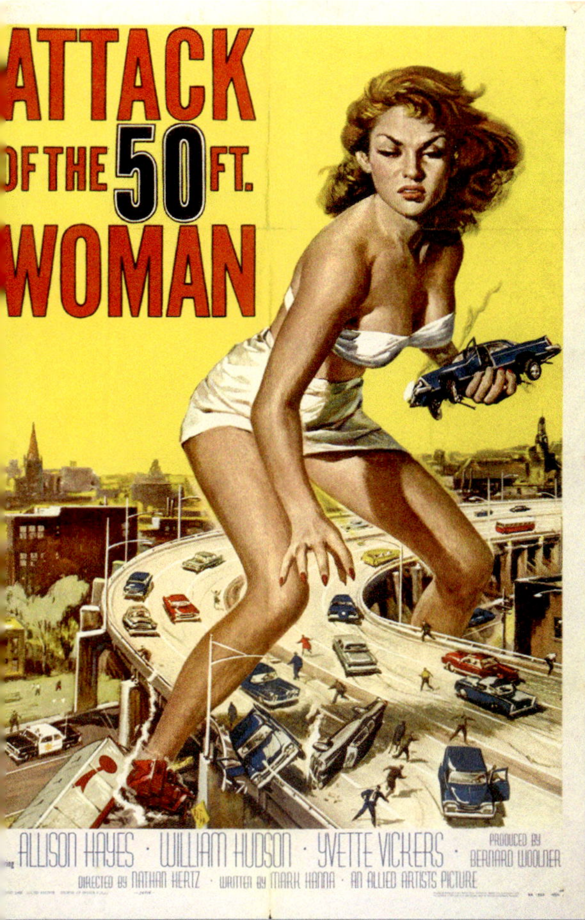

Courtesy of Heritage

Attack of the 50ft. Woman	1958	27x41	
Christie's	$5,639	FN	11/09
Heritage	$6,872	FN	07/09
Heritage	$9,560	VF+	03/09
Heritage	$13,145	VF	11/08
Heritage	$15,535	VF+	03/08

Highest price realized:

Christie's	$23,489	VF	03/08

Price in 1992:

Christie's	$2,090	VF	12/92

- This poster has appeared at auction 23 times since 1989.
- There is no *Attack of the 50ft. Woman* 30x40 known to exist.

Attack of the 50ft. Woman	1958	40x60	
Heritage	$2,629	FN	11/09*
Heritage	$3,170	FN	11/08

- There are 3 known to exist.

* This is the same poster that appeared in the Heritage 11/08 auction.

Courtesy of Heritage

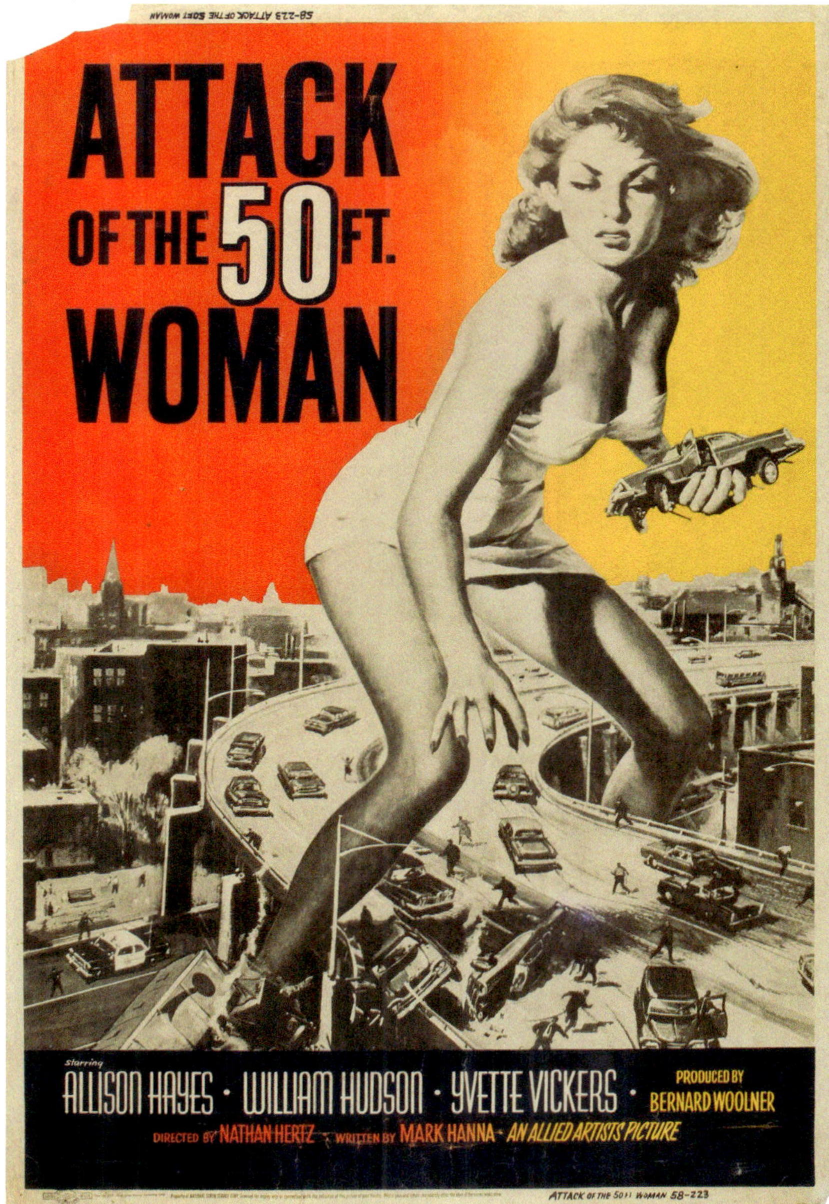

The Fly 1958 27x41

High price realized:

Lowery	$518	VF	06/00

- This poster currently sells for $75-$300
- This poster has appeared at auction over 75 times since 1989.
- There is no *Fly* 30x40 known to exist.

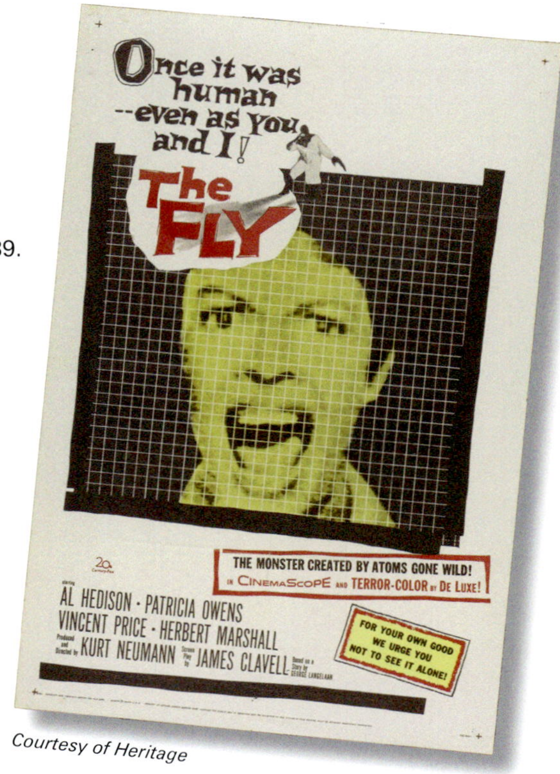

Courtesy of Heritage

Courtesy of Heritage

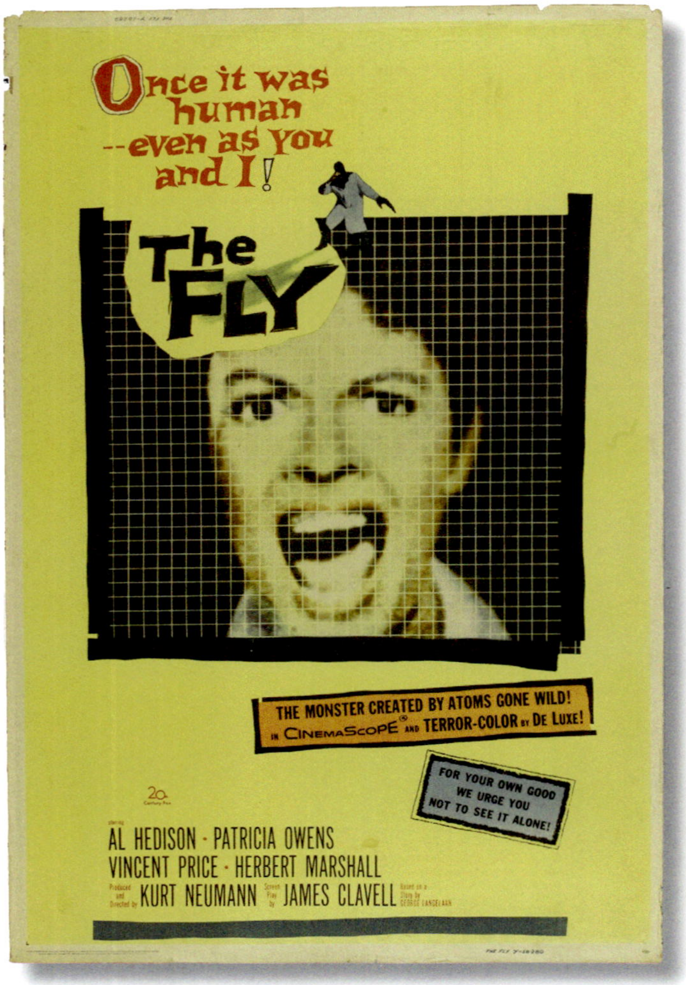

***The Fly*—Style Y** 1958 40x60

Heritage	$130	FN	04/08
Private	$500	VG	03/07

- There are 5 known to exist.

***The Fly*—Style Z** 1958 40x60

Heritage	$657	FN	11/08

- There is 1 known to exist.

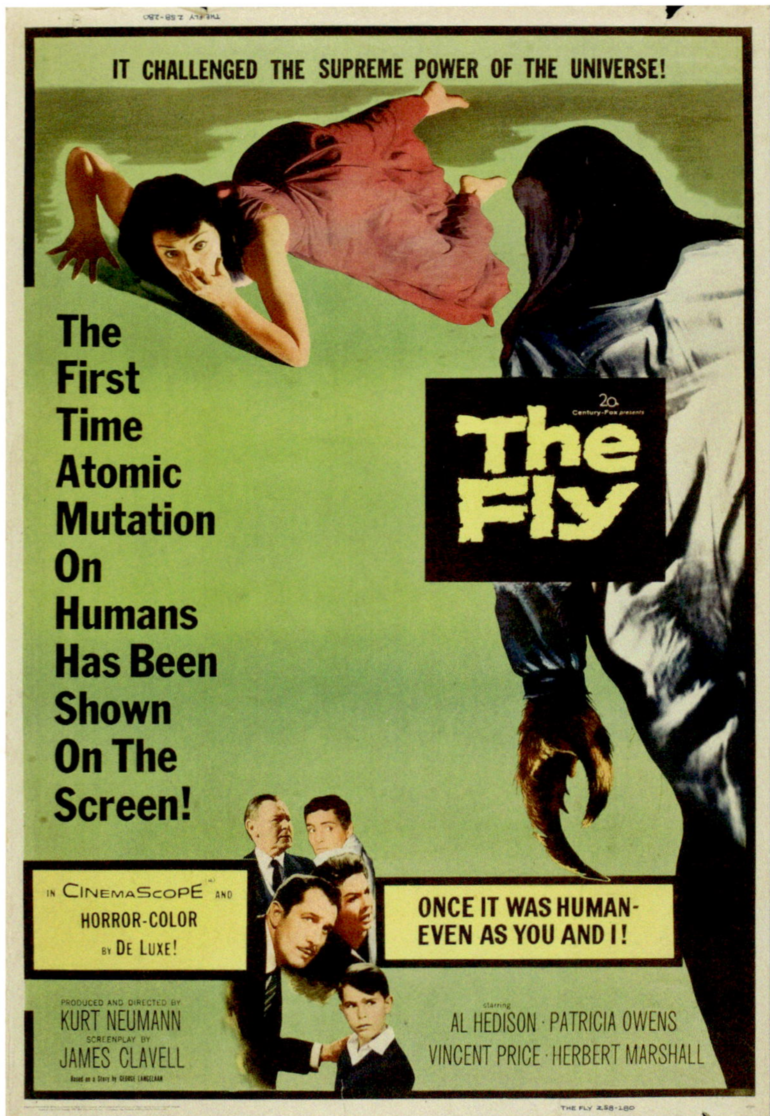

Photo by R. Aaron Raymond & Stephen Allard

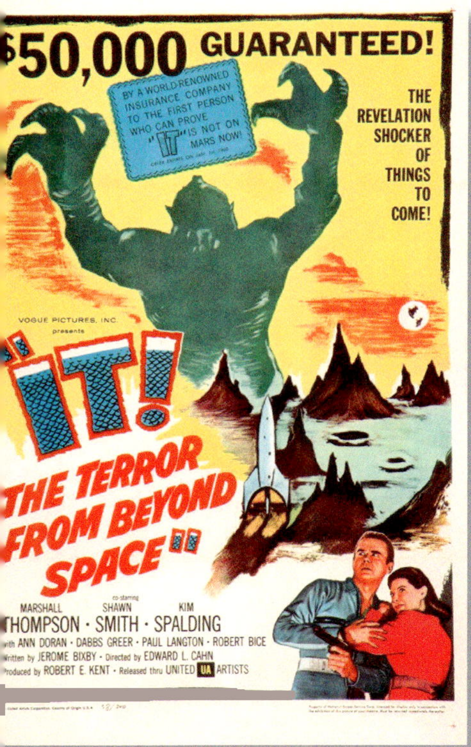

Courtesy of Heritage

It! The Terror From Beyond Space		1958	27x41
Heritage	$310	VF	03/08
Profiles in History	$375	NM	12/07
Profile in History	$450	VF	08/07
Heritage	$179	VF-	11/06
eMoviePoster	$210	VG	10/06

Highest price realized:

eMoviePoster	$890	VG/FN	06/01

Price in 1994:

Odyssey	$200	FN	10/94

- This poster has appeared at auction 18 times since 1989.
- There is no *It! The Terror From Beyond Space* 30x40 known to exist.

It! The Terror From Beyond Space		1958	40x60
Heritage	$896	FN	11/09
Heritage	$896	FN+	11/06

- There are 2 known to exist.

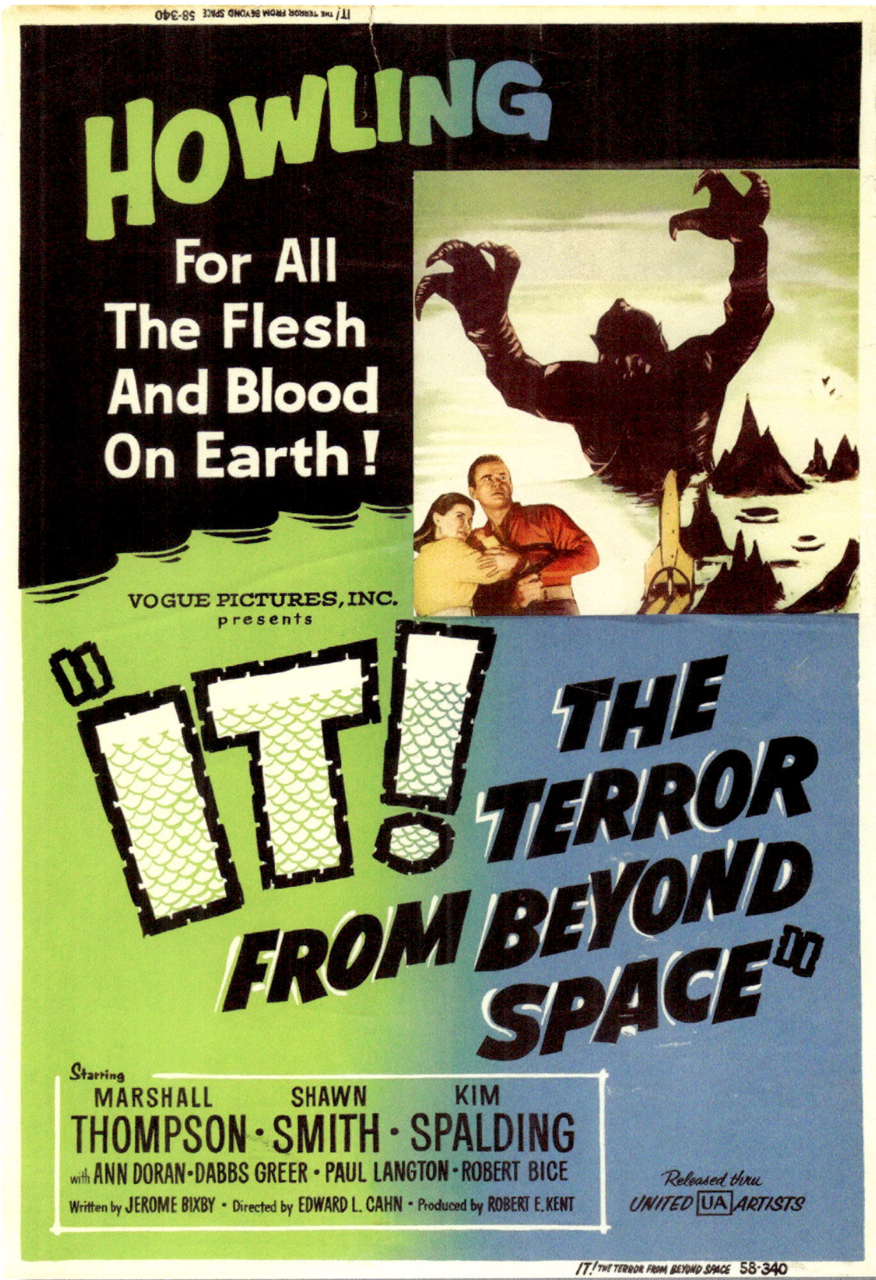

Courtesy of Heritage

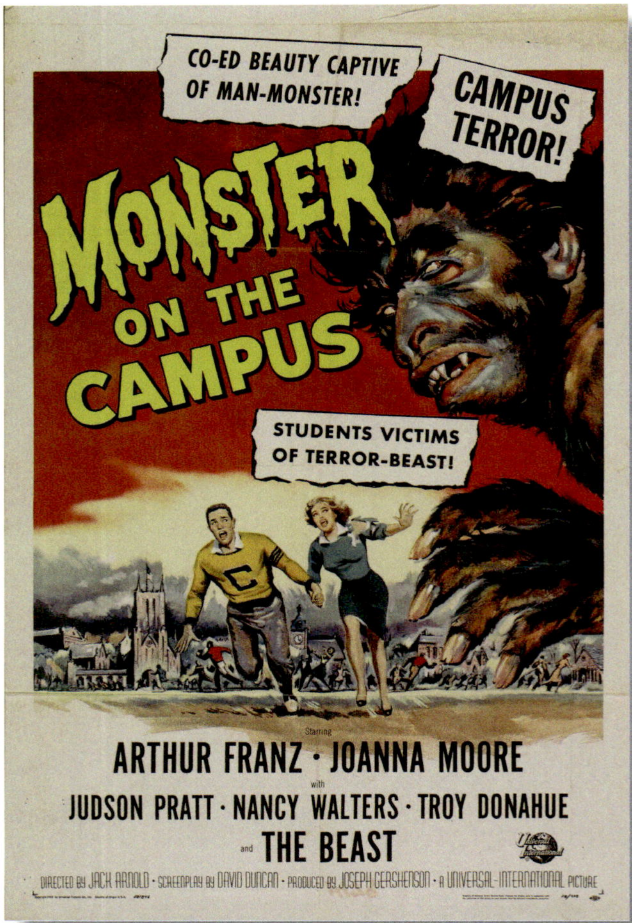

Courtesy of Heritage

Monster on the Campus 1958 27x41

- This poster typically sells for $130 - $330
- This poster has appeared at auction over 75 times since 1989.

Monster on the Campus 1958 30x40
Heritage $657 FN 07/09

- There is 1 known to exist.
- There is no *Monster on the Campus* 40x60 known to exist.

Courtesy of Heritage

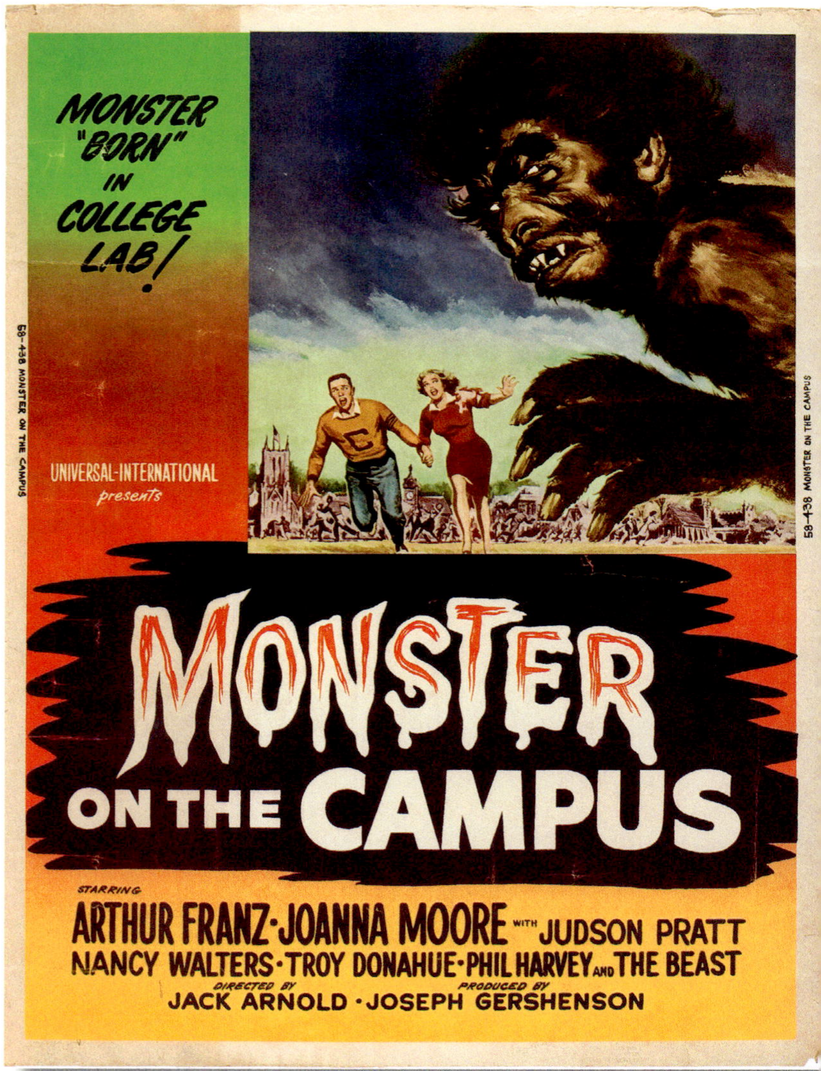

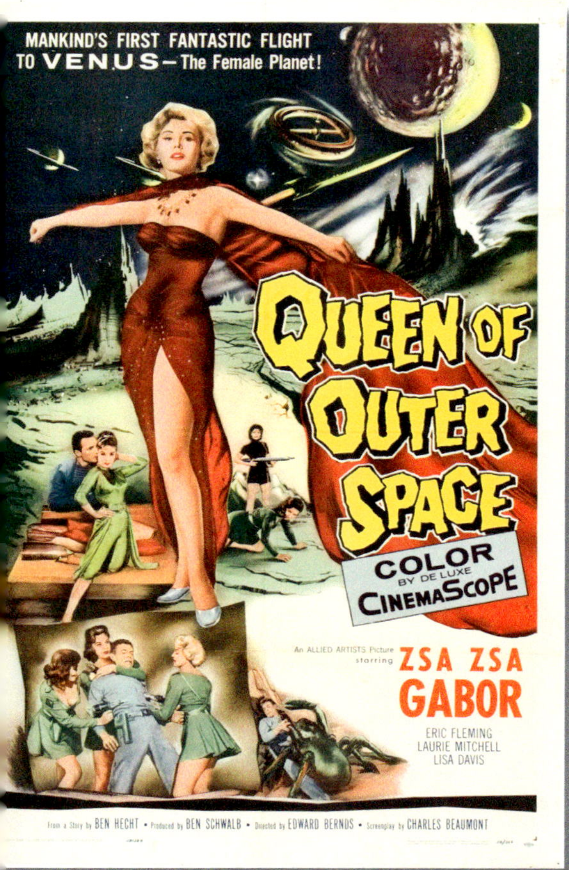

Courtesy of Heritage

Queen of Outer Space 1958 27x41			
Heritage	$961	FN/VF	07/09
Heritage	$956	VF+	03/09
Heritage	$956	VF+	11/08
Heritage	$1,075	VF/NM	03/08
eMoviePoster	$945	VG/FN	10/07

Highest price realized:

Heritage	$1,195	VF	07/07

Price in 1993:

Camden House	$250	VF	06/93

- This poster has appeared at auction 32 times since 1989.
- There is no *Queen of Outer Space* 30x40 known to exist.

Queen of Outer Space 1958 40x60			
Heritage	$1,015	VF	11/09

- There is 1 known to exist.

Courtesy of Heritage

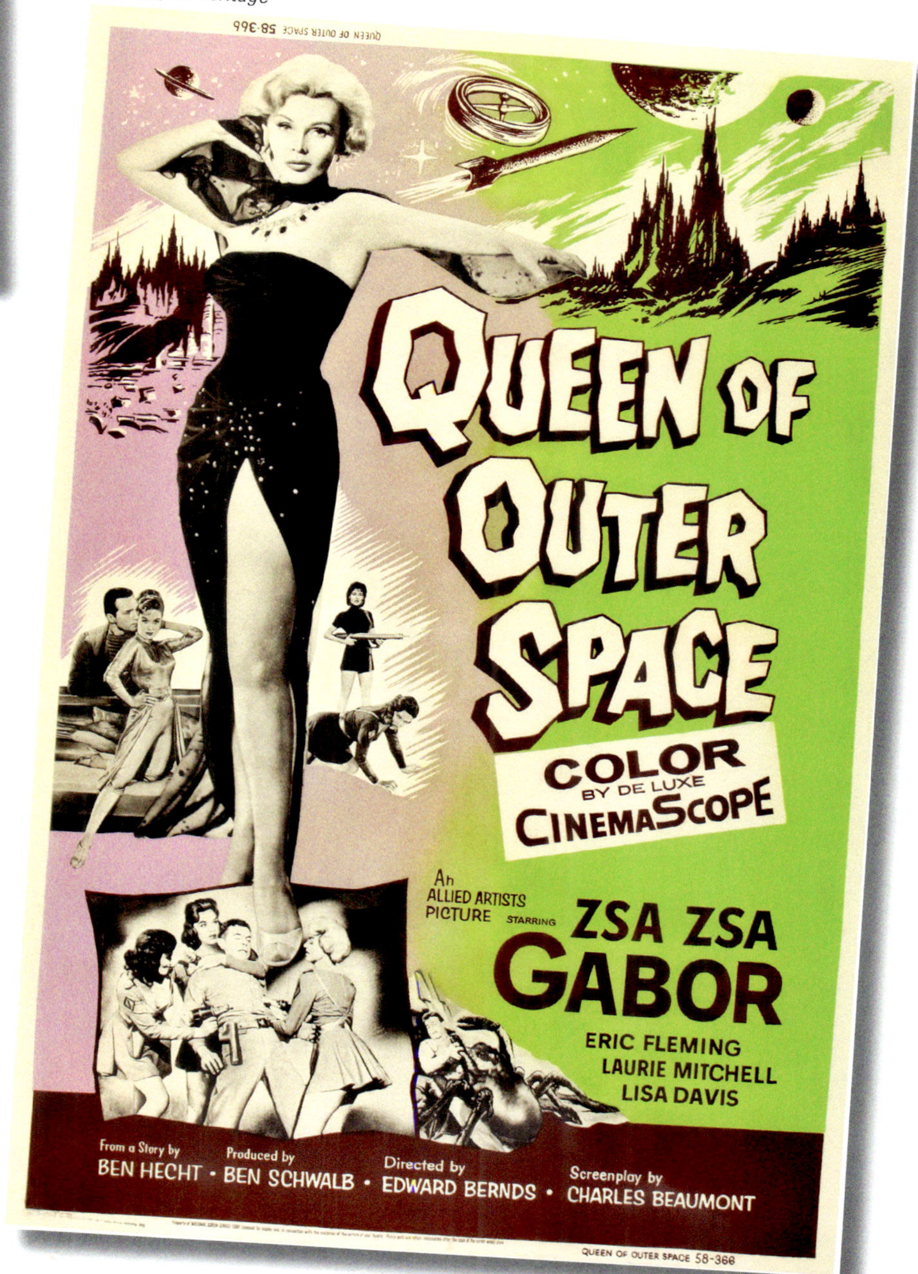

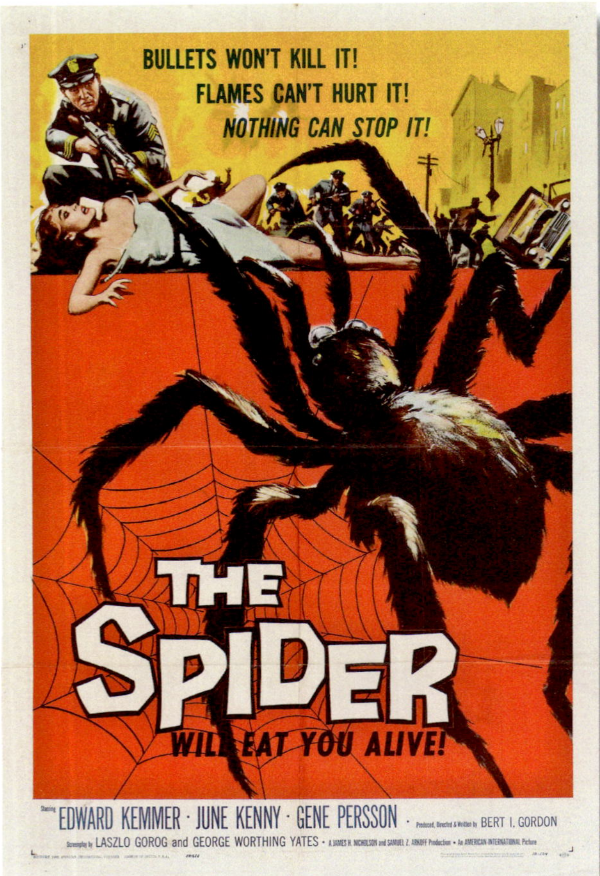

Courtesy of Heritage

Spider 1958 27x41

Heritage	$191	VG+	08/09
Heritage	$776	VF-	03/09
Heritage	$338	VF-	11/08
Heritage	$507	VF	03/08
eMoviePoster	$532	VG/FN	12/07

Highest price realized:

Heritage	$776	VF-	03/09

Price in 1994:

Butterfield & Butterfield	$175	VF	10/94

- This poster has appeared at auction 21 times since 1989.
- There is no *Spider* 30x40 known to exist.

Photo by R. Aaron Raymond & Stephen Allard

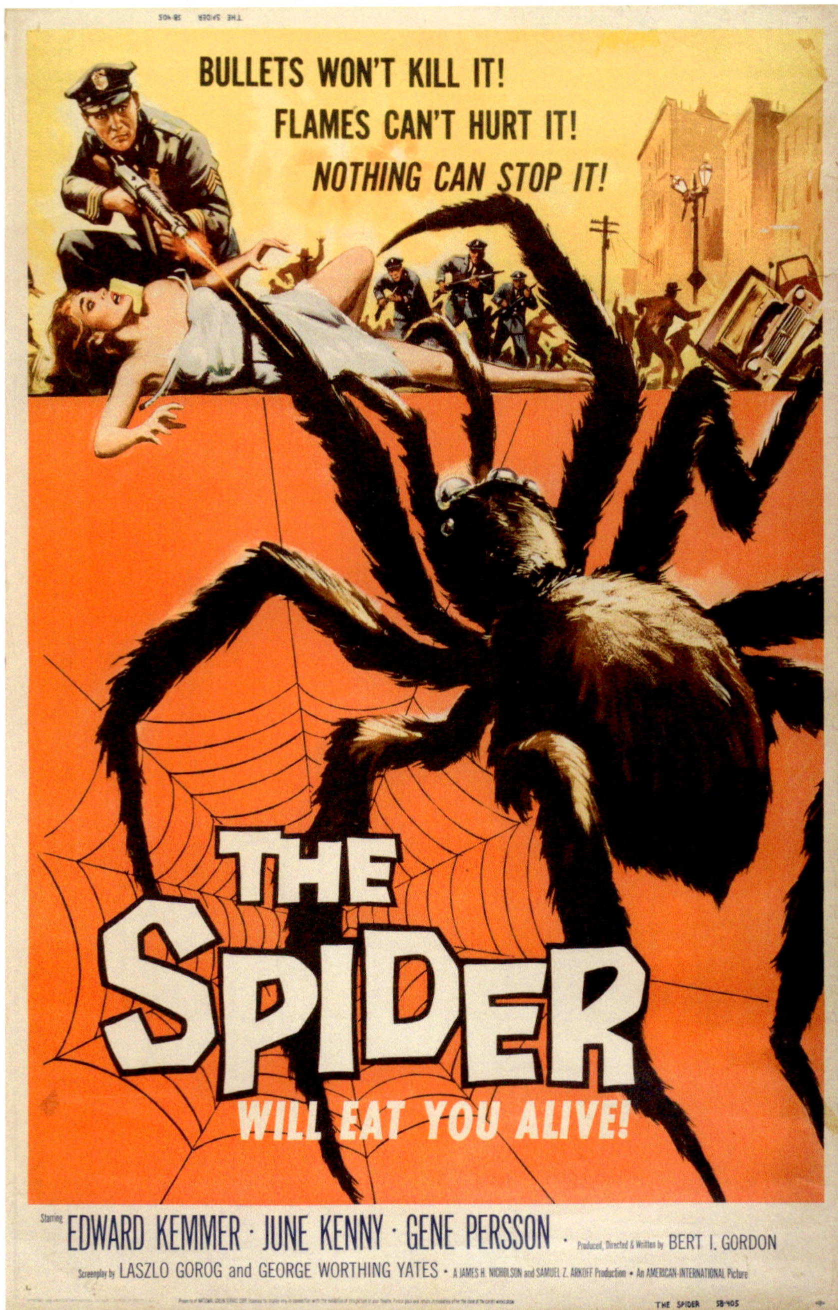

Spider 1958 40x60

Private	$1,050	VF	03/05

- There is 1 known to exist.

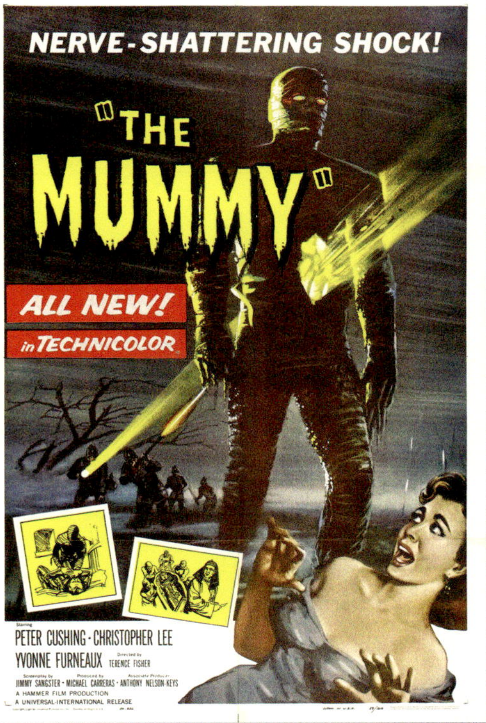

Courtesy of Heritage

Mummy 1959 27x41			
Heritage	$507	VF/NM	07/09
Heritage	$463	VF+	03/09
eMoviePoster	$311	VG	03/09
Heritage	$388	VG/FN	11/08
Heritage	$657	FN/VF	07/08
Highest price realized:			
Profiles in History	$1,500	VF+	07/06
Price in 1994:			
Camden House	$125	FN	06/94

• This poster has appeared at auction 19 times since 1989.

Photo by R. Aaron Raymond & Stephen Allard

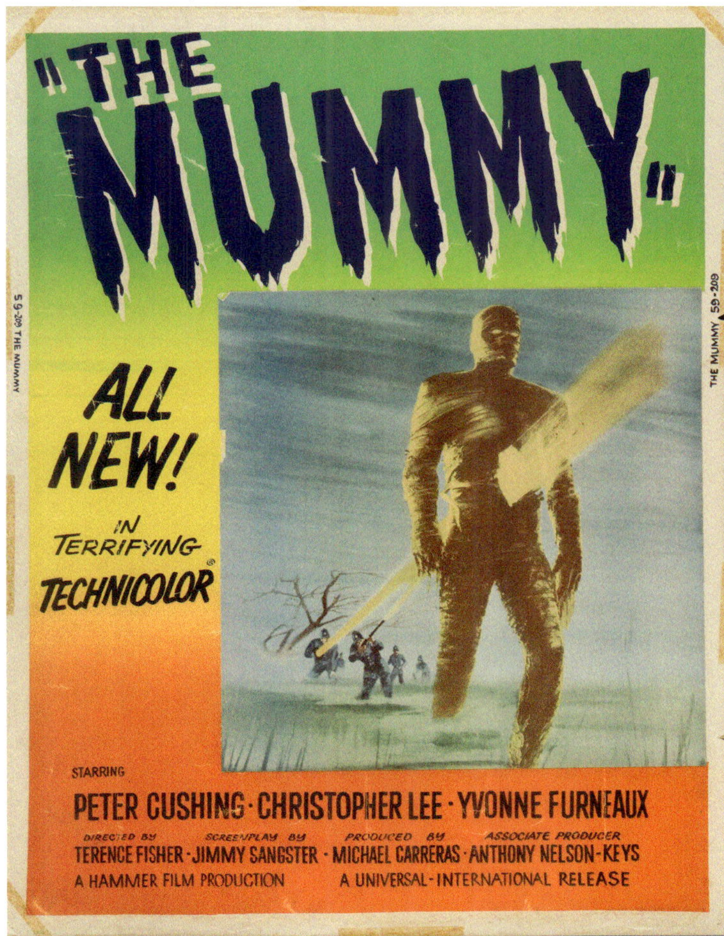

Courtesy of Heritage

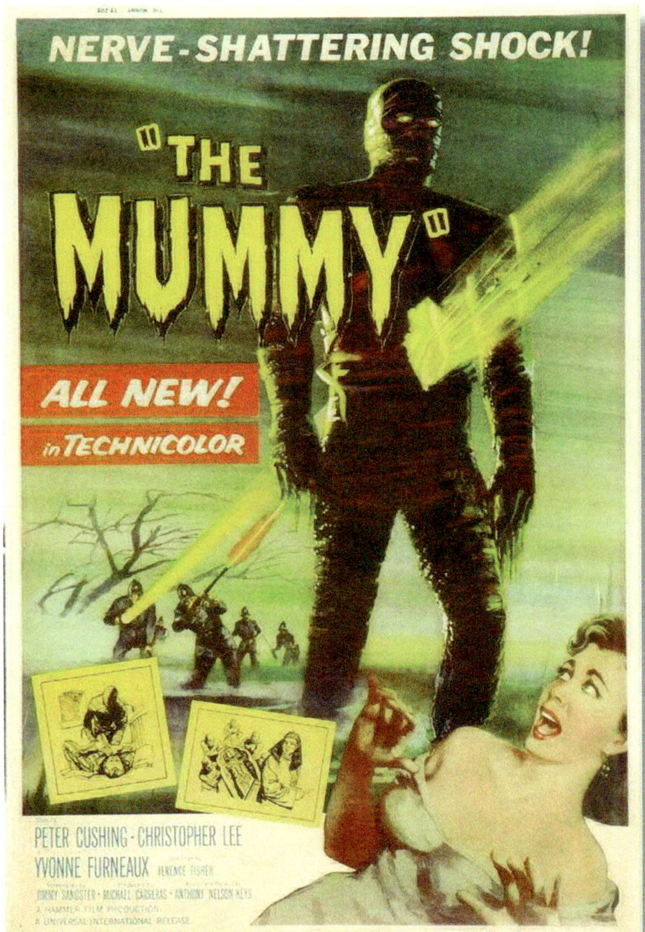

Mummy 1959 30x40			
Private	$850	VF	06/08
Christie's	$600	VF-	09/04
Private	$200	FN	02/97

• There are 3 known to exist.

Mummy 1959 40x60			
eMoviePoster	$257	FR	07/06
eMoviePoster	$610	VF	12/05
Heritage	DNS	FN-	07/03
Estimate: $800 - $1,200			

• There are 4 known to exist.

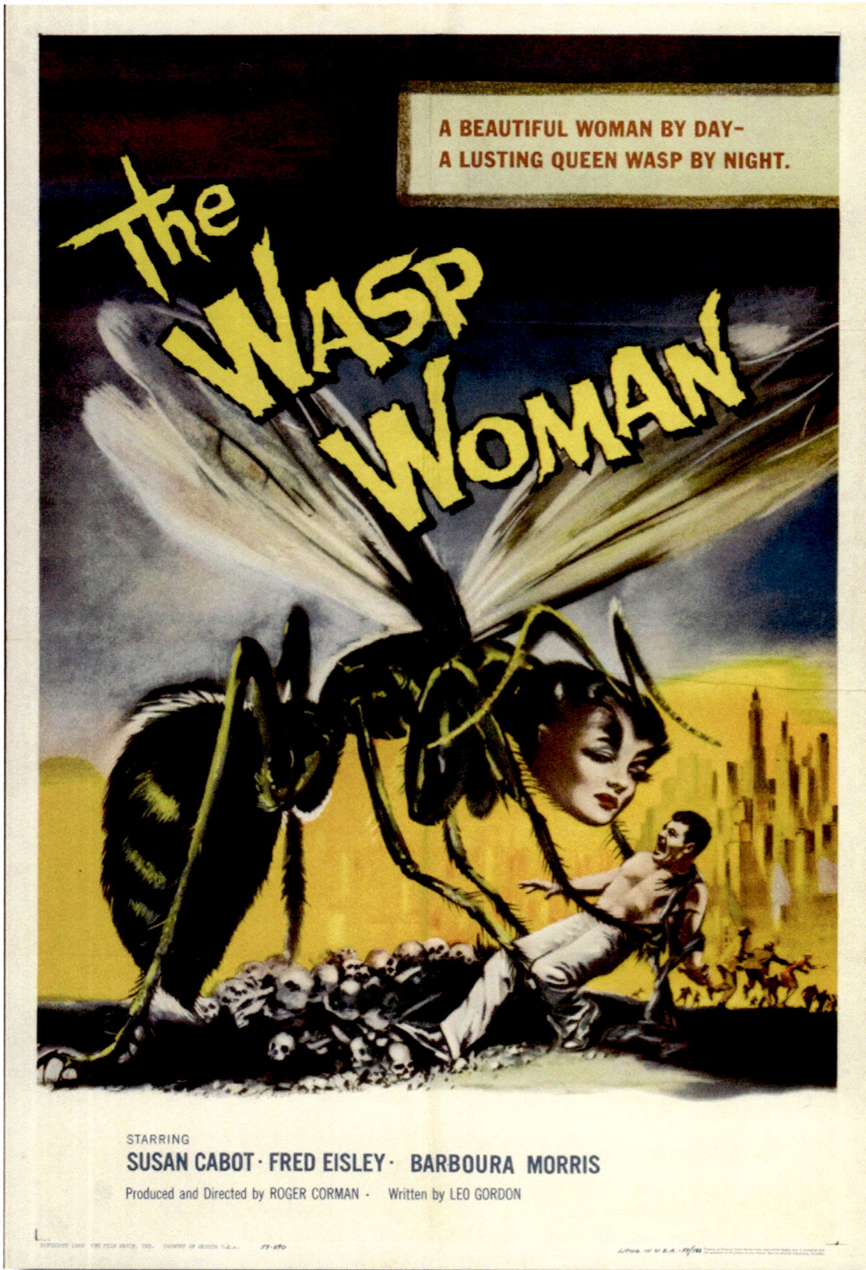

Courtesy of Heritage

Wasp Woman	1959	27x41	
Heritage	$2,390	FN/VF	11/09
Heritage	$3,107	VF	07/09
Heritage	$3,585	NM-	11/08
eMoviePoster	$1,750	GD	10/08
Heritage	$3,585	VF-	07/08

Highest Price Realized:

Heritage	$4,025	VF-	03/05

Price in 1994:

Camden House	$550	VF	06/94

• This poster has appeared at auction 26 times since 1989.
• There is no *Wasp Woman* 30x40 known to exist.

Courtesy of Sotheby's

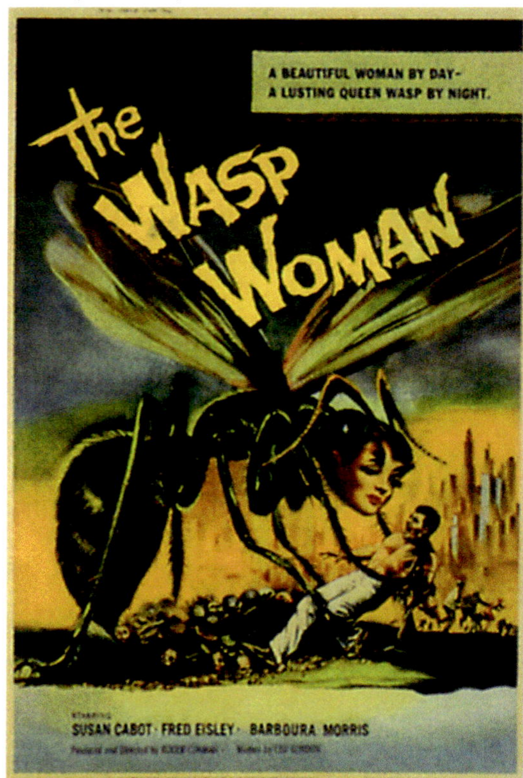

Wasp Woman	1959	40x60	
Vintage Poster Art	$863	FN	05/95
Sotheby's	$805	VF	12/93

Estimate: $3,500 - $5,500

• There are 3 known to exit.

MOVIE POSTERS OF THE 1960s

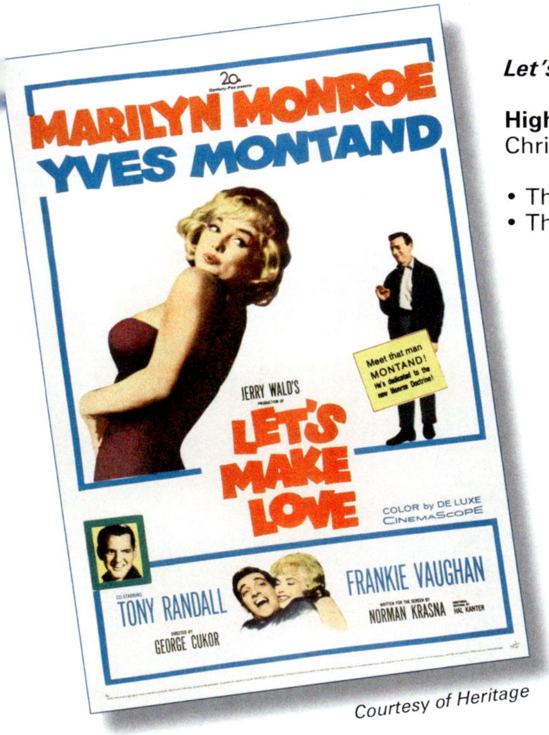

Courtesy of Heritage

Let's Make Love 1960 27x41

Highest Price Realized:
Christie's $661 FN+ 11/09

- This poster typically sells for $75 - $300
- This poster has appeared at auction over 75 times since 1989.

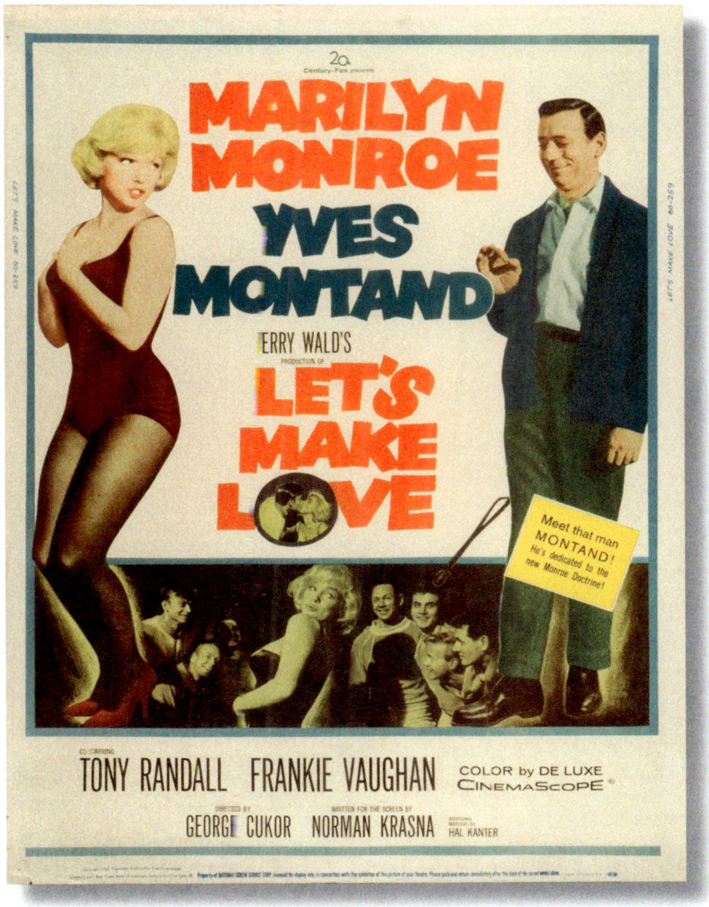

Photo by R. Aaron Raymond & Stephen Allard

Let's Make Love 1960 30x40
Private $650 VF 05/06

- There are 6 known to exist.

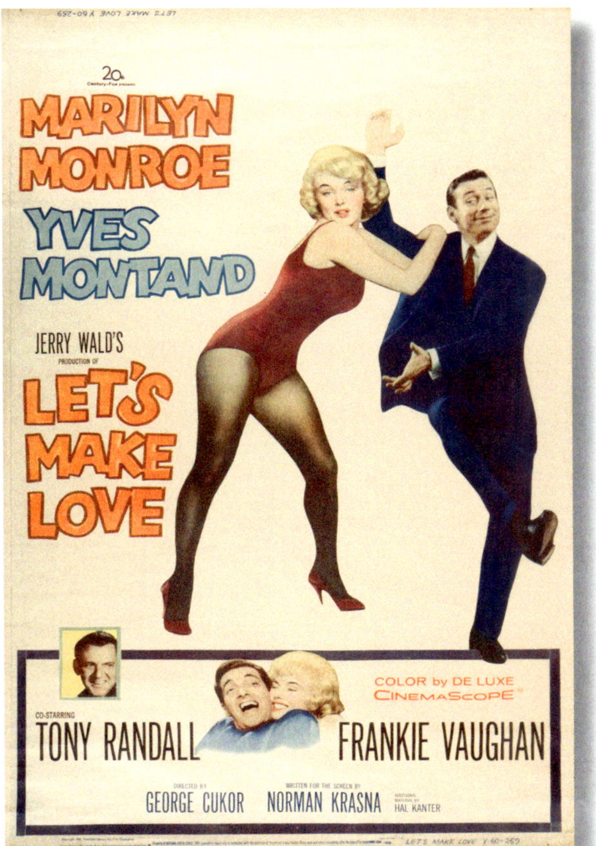

Photo by R. Aaron Raymond & Stephen Allard

Let's Make Love**—**Style Y 1960 40x60

Private	$550	VF+	08/04
eMoviePoster	$136	FN	02/01
eMoviePoster	$175	FN+	07/93

- There are 5 known to exist.
- There is no *Let's Make Love* 40x60 Style Z known to exist.

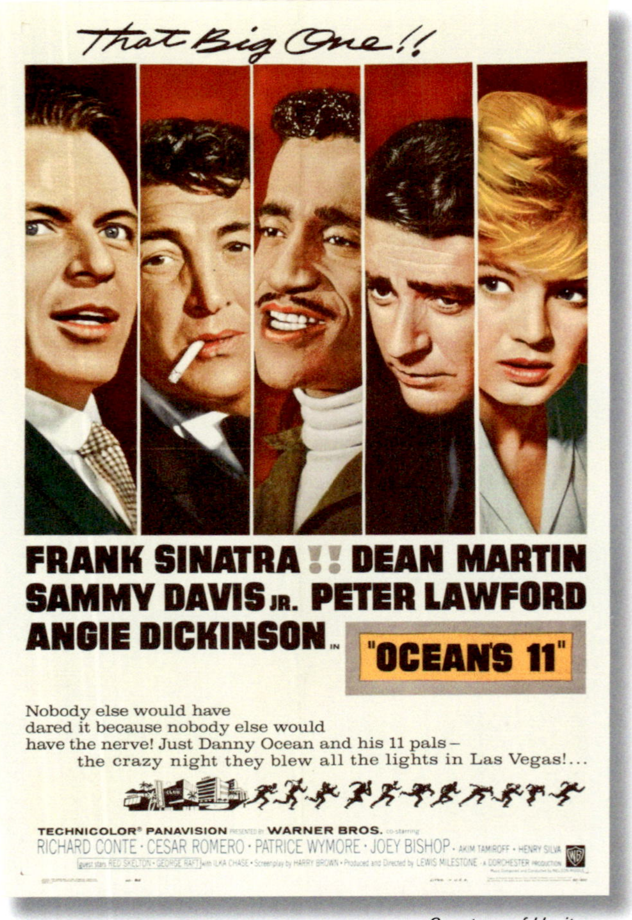

Courtesy of Heritage

Ocean's 11	1960	27x41		
Heritage		$1,015	FN/VF	11/09
eMoviePoster		$508	GD/VG	09/09
eMoviePoster		$470	GD	05/09
Heritage		$956	VF+	03/09
Heritage		$1,434	VF-	12/08

Highest price realized:

Heritage	$2,270	VF/NM	11/08

Price in 1997:

Sotheby's	$442	VF	09/97

- This poster has appeared at auction 32 times since 1989.
- There is no *Ocean's 11* 30x40 known to exist.

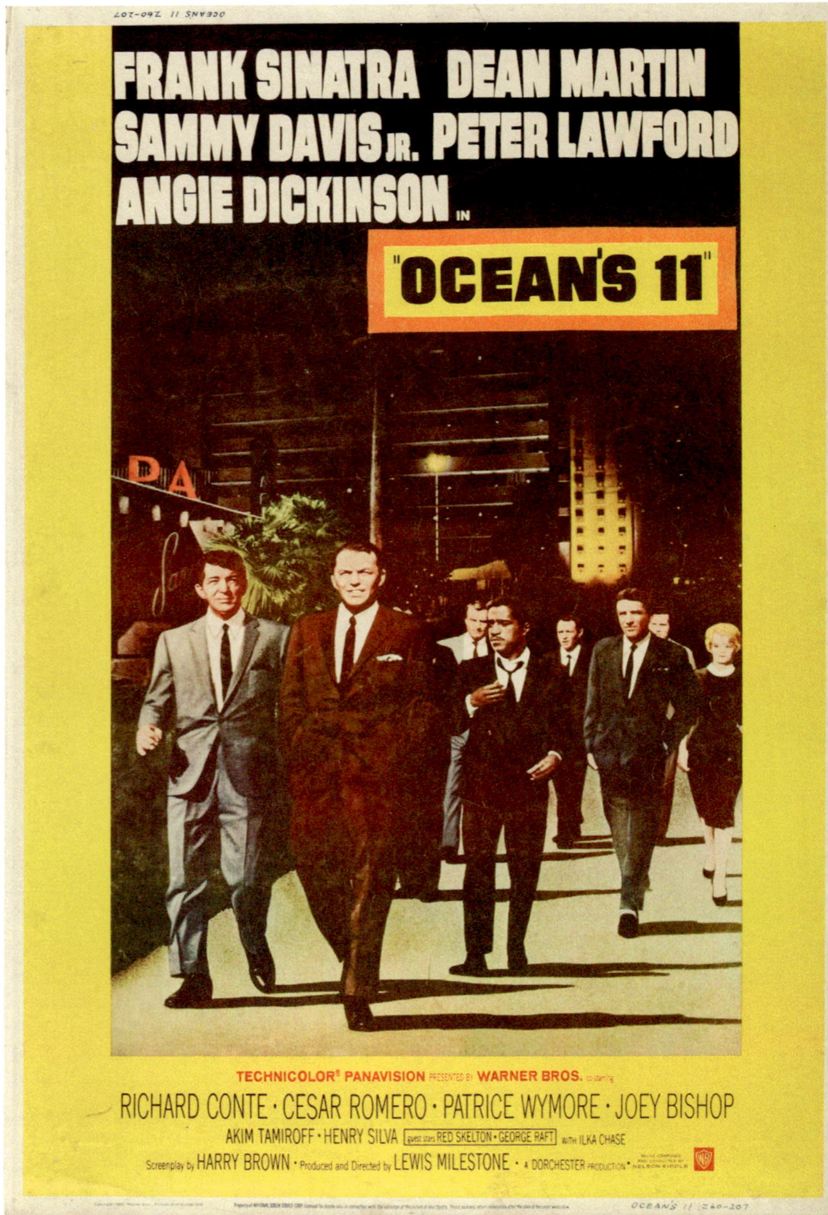

Courtesy of Heritage

Ocean's 11— Style Z	1960	40x60	
Heritage	$5,078	FN/VF	11/08
Christie's	$1,566	VF	09/08

- There are 2 known to exist.
- There is no *Ocean's 11* 40x60 Style Y known to exist.

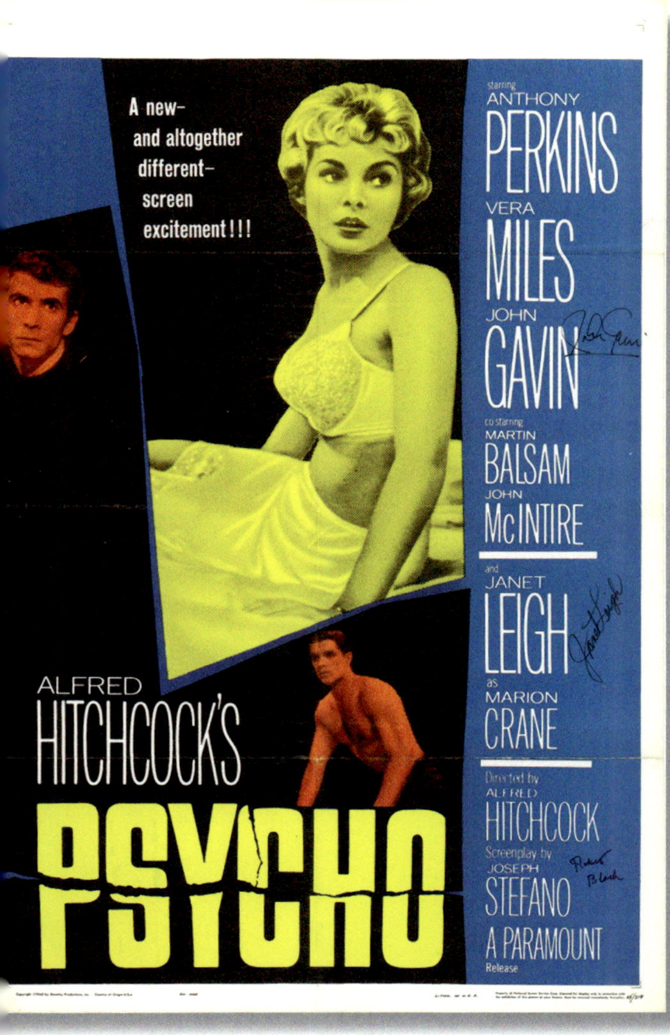

Courtesy of Heritage

Psycho 1960 27x41

eMoviePoster	$1,550	VG/FN	12/09
Heritage	$1,314	VF	11/09
Hollywood Poster Auction	$1,800	VF+	10/09
eMoviePoster	$1,317	VG	07/09
Heritage	$1,135	FN-	07/09

Highest price realized:

Heritage (Autographed)	$9,560	FN/VF	11/08

Price in 1991:

Camden House	$275	FN	05/91

- This poster has appeared at auction 63 times since 1989.
- There is no *Psycho* 30x40 known to exist.

Courtesy of Heritage

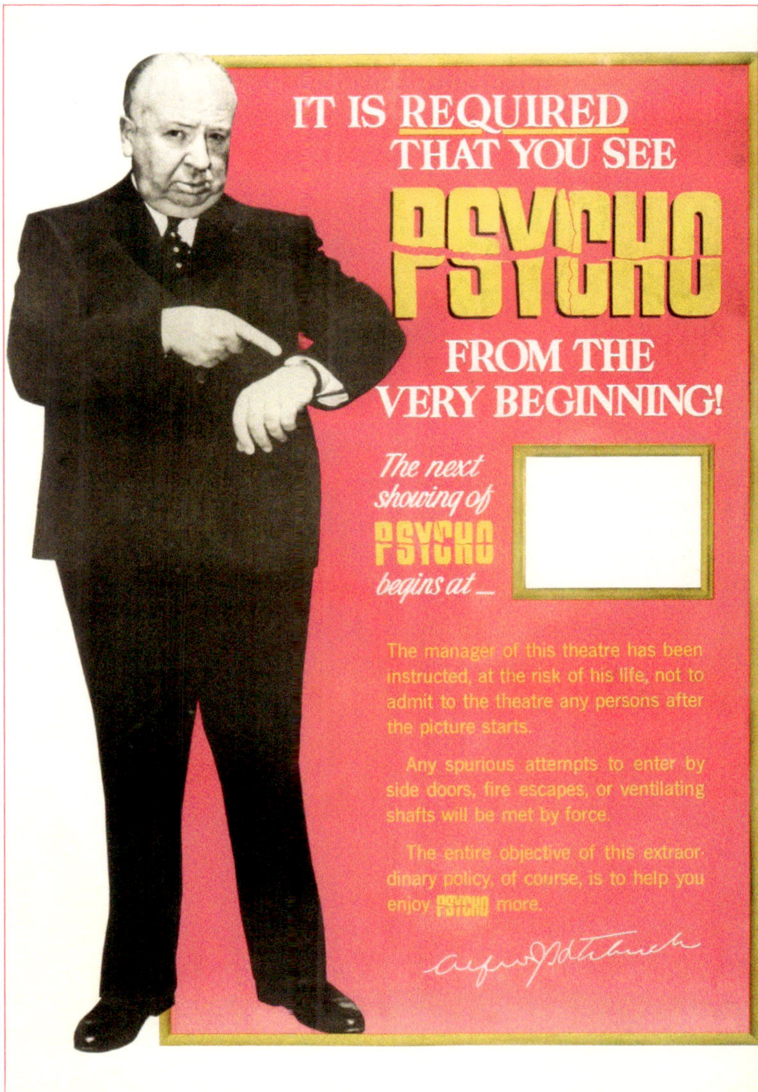

Psycho (Special) 1960 40x60

Heritage	$3,737	GD/VG	07/05
Bonhams & Butterfields	$2,115	FN+	11/04
Christie's	$3,102	VF-	03/04
Sotheby's	$3,737	VF	04/99
Butterfield & Butterfield	$1,500	VF	11/96
Christie's	$3,000	NM	12/95

- There are 7 known to exist.

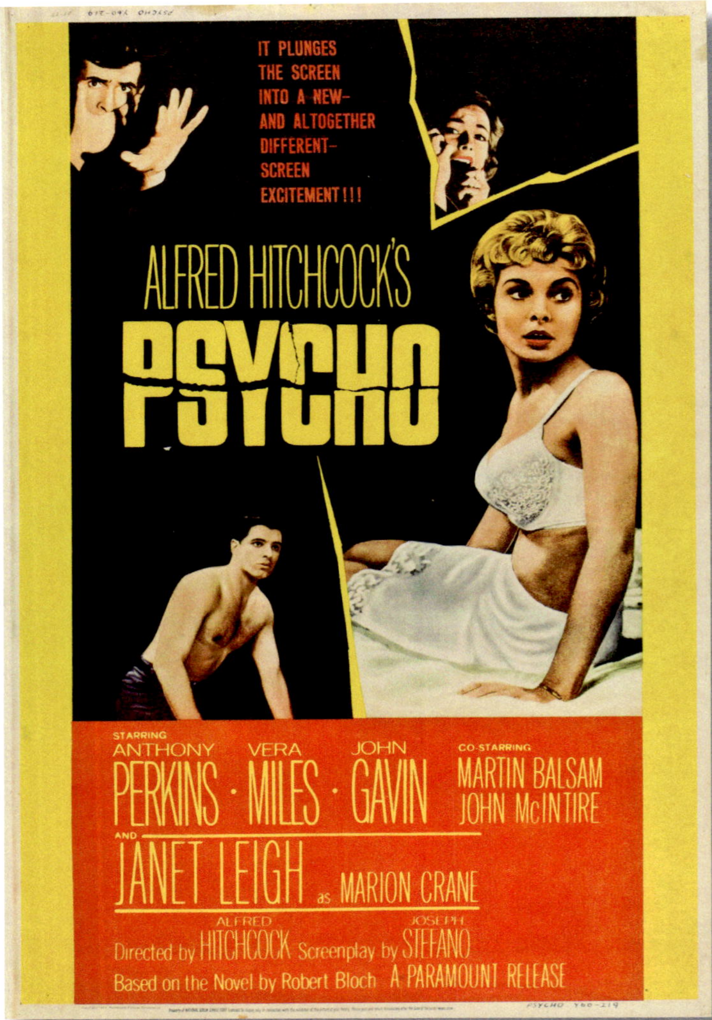

Courtesy of Heritage

Psycho—Style Y 1960 40x60

Heritage	$4,780	VF-	11/08
Camden House	$400	FN	06/94

• There are 2 known to exist.

Photo by R. Aaron Raymond & Stephen Allard

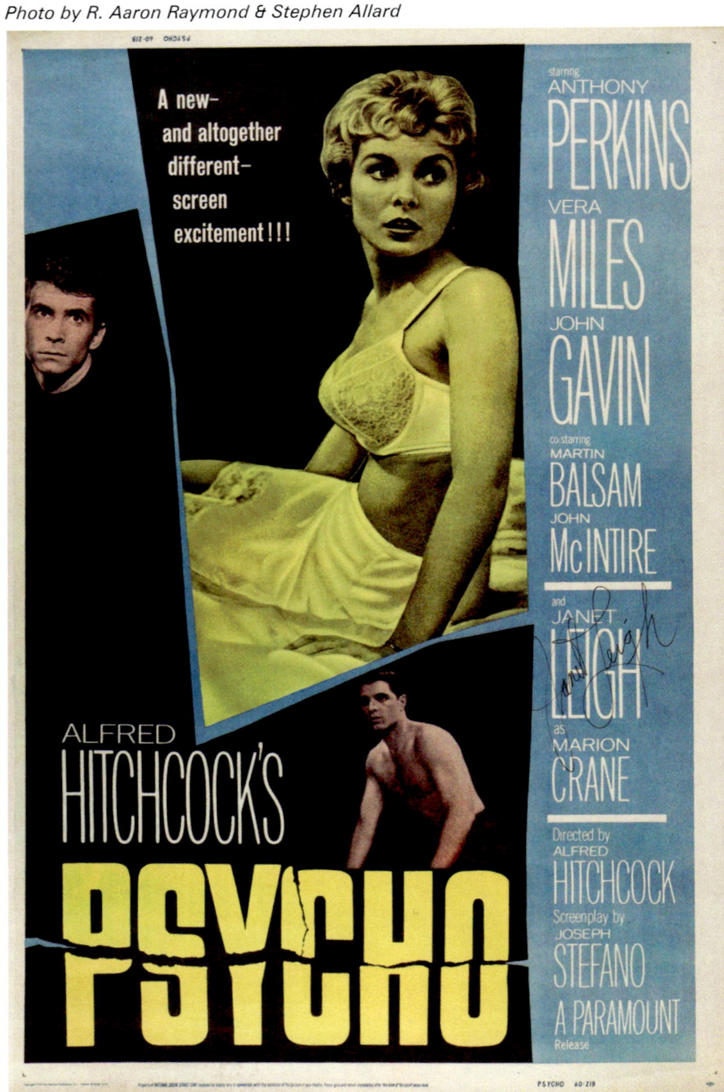

Psycho—Style Z* 1960 40x60

Private (Autographed)	$3,500	NM	04/01
Sotheby's	$750	FN	12/94

Estimate: $4,500 - $6,000

• There are 2 known to exist.
* This poster is not marked with the letter "Z," but the style "Y" is marked as such.

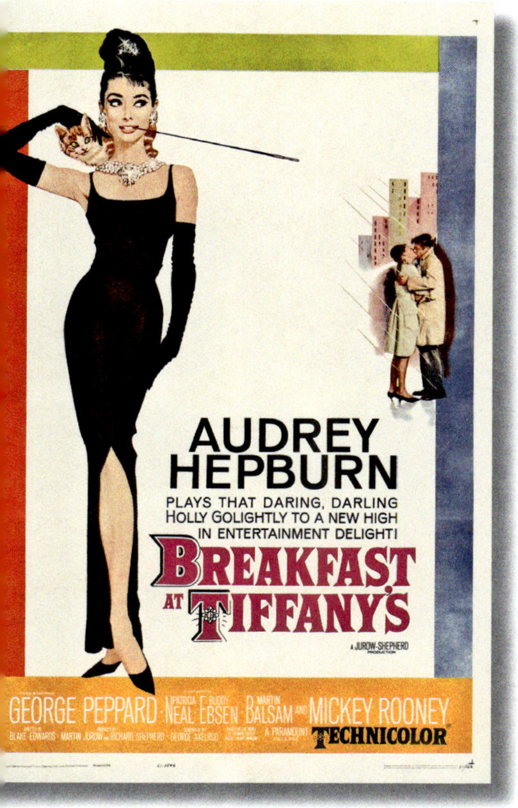

Courtesy of Heritage

Breakfast at Tiffany's	1961	27x41	
eMoviePoster	$3,300	VG/FN	12/09
Christie's	$8,260	VF-	11/09
Heritage	$3,883	VF+	07/09
eMoviePoster	$3,100	VG	07/09
Heritage	$3,107	VF+	03/09

Highest price realized:

Christie's	$10,800	M	10/00

Price in 1992:

Camden House	$275	FN	03/92

•This poster has appeared at auction 67 times since 1989.

reakfast at Tiffany's	1961	30x40	
rivate	$7,300	VF	02/09
ofiles in History	$5,500	FN	12/08
MoviePoster	$6,500	NM	11/06
ofiles in History	$5,500	VF	03/06
hristie's	$6,000	NM	06/05

ighest price realized:

PA	$8,500	VF	08/01

There are 8 known to exist.

Photo by R. Aaron Raymond & Stephen Allard

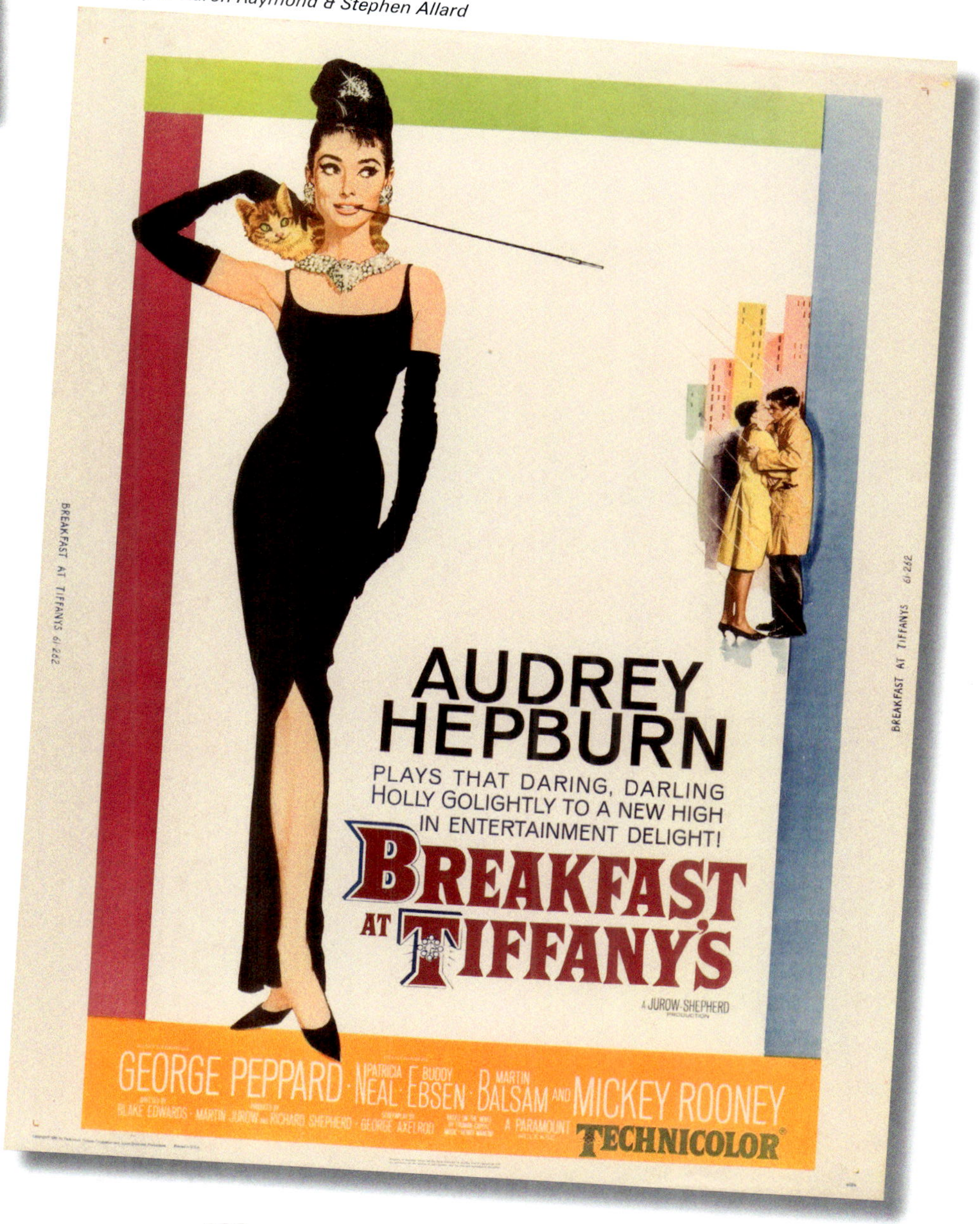

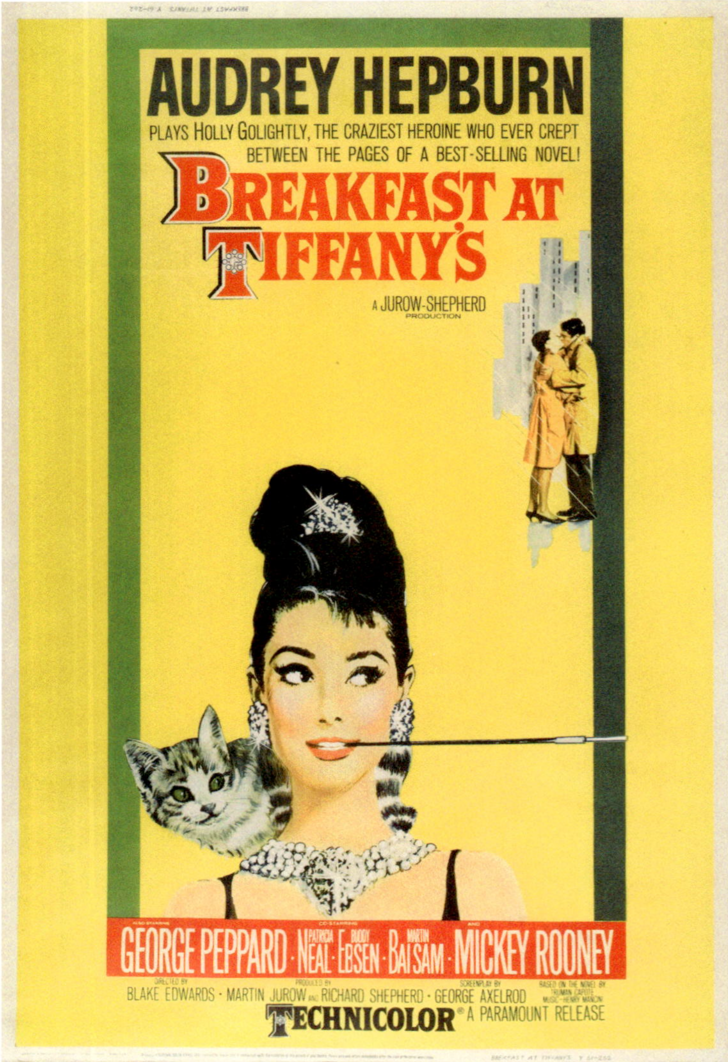

Photo by R. Aaron Raymond & Stephen Allard

Breakfast at Tiffany's—Style Y 1961 40x60

Private	$7,400	NM	07/07
Christie's	$4,800	VF-	06/05

• There are 2 known to exist.

Breakfast at Tiffany's—Style Z 1961 40x60

Christie's	$8,859	VF	03/01

• There are 3 known to exist.

Photo by R. Aaron Raymond & Stephen Allard

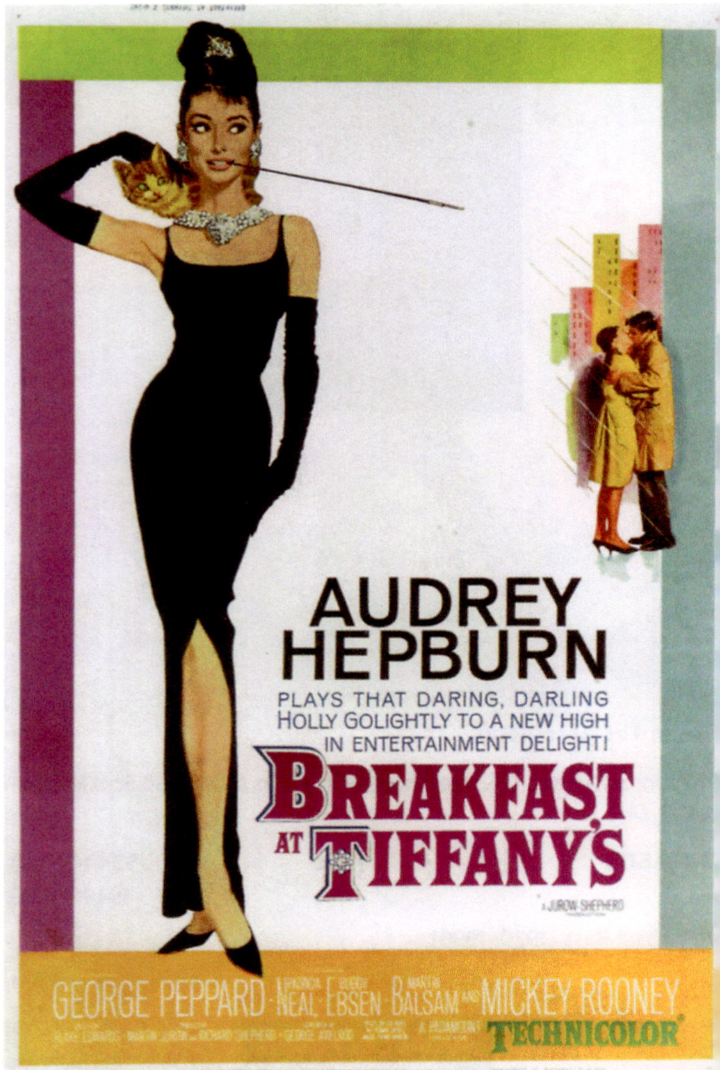

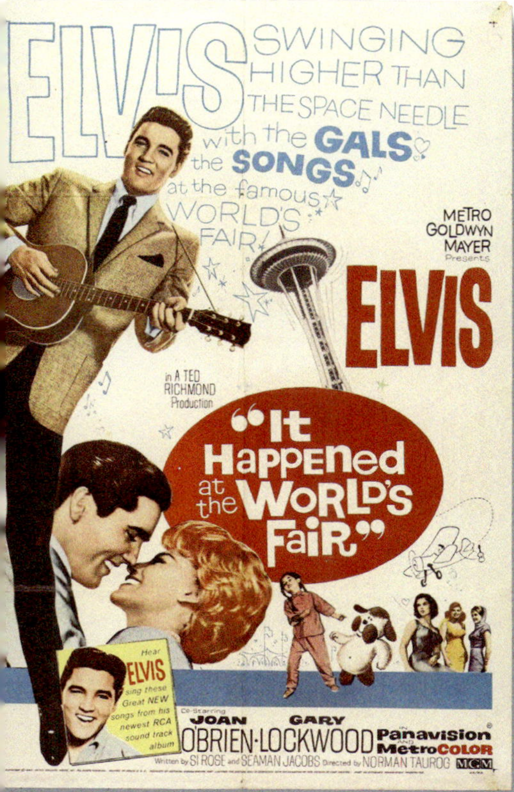

Courtesy of Heritage

It Happened at the World's Fair 1963 27x41

- This poster typically sells for $50 - $200
- This poster has appeared at auction over 75 times since 1989.

Photo by R. Aaron Raymond & Stephen Allard

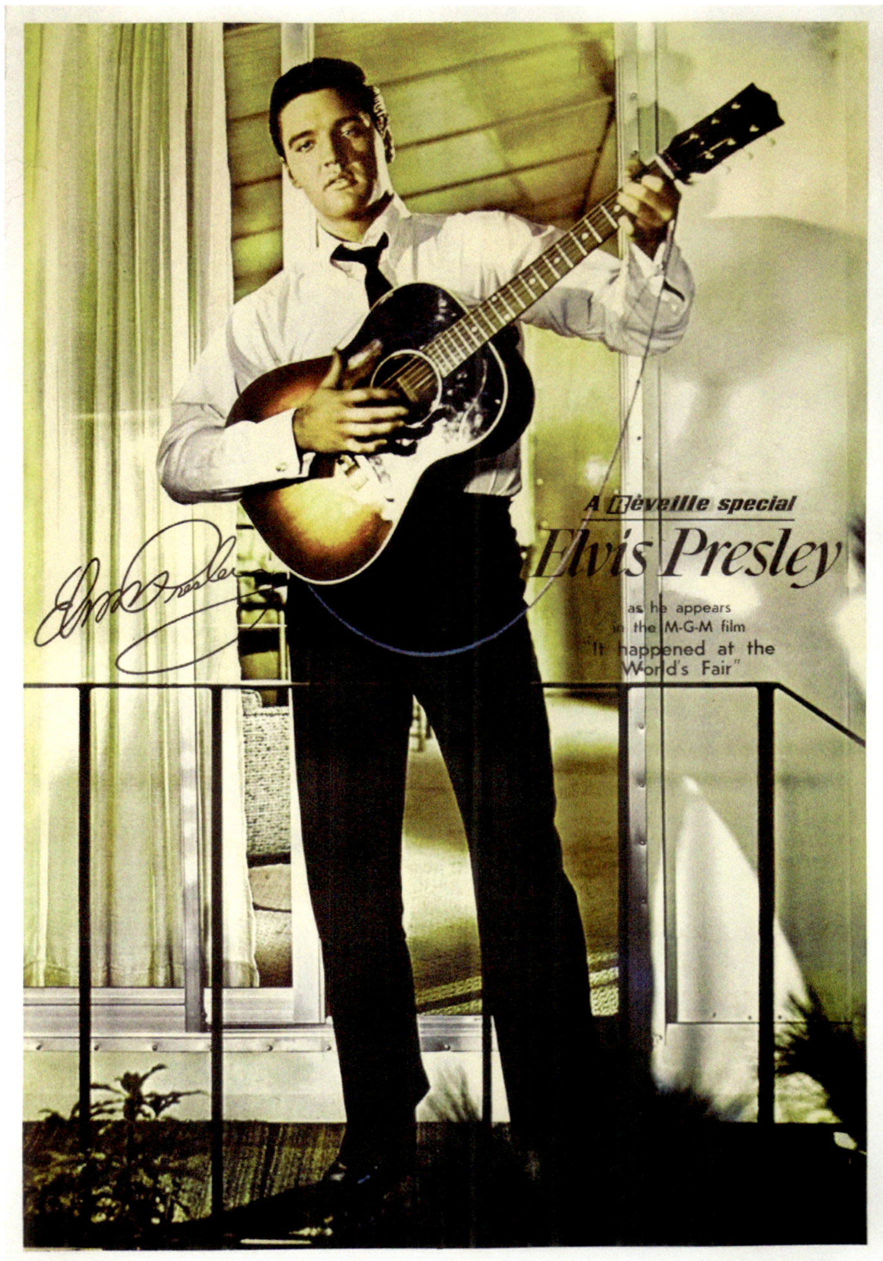

It Happened at the World's Fair 1963 40x60 *
(Special Advertisement)

Heritage	$896	VF	07/09
Heritage	$2,990	VF	03/06

- There are 5 known to exist.

* Lightweight paper, folded.

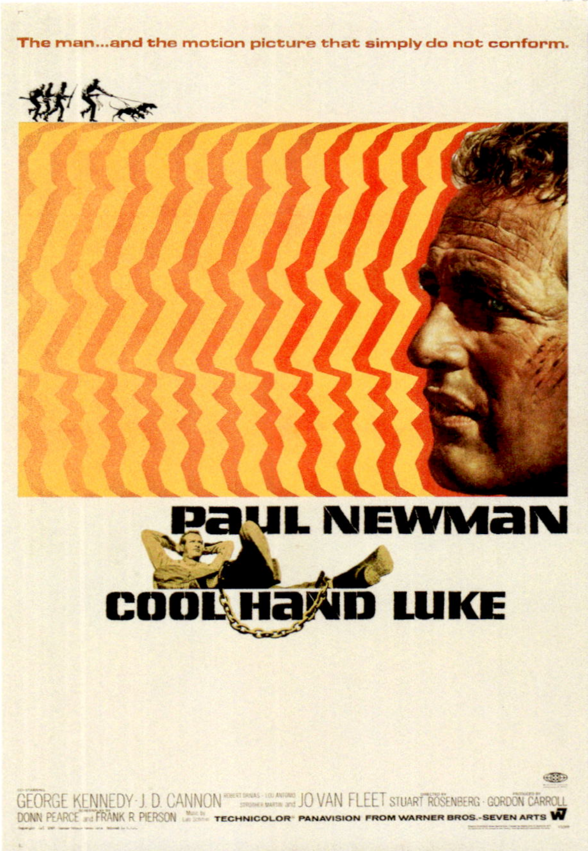

Courtesy of Heritage

Cool Hand Luke 1967 27x41

eMoviePoster	$306	GD	05/09
eMoviePoster (Autographed)	$625	VG	04/09
Heritage	$1,195	FN/VF	11/08
Heritage	$1,075	NM	03/08
Christie's	$1,600	VF	08/07

Highest price achieved:

Christie's	$1,780	VF	03/07

Price in 1996:

Christie's	$50	GD	09/96

- This poster has appeared at auction 54 times since 1989.
- There was no image available for *Cool Hand Luke* 30x40.

Photo by R. Aaron Raymond & Stephen Allard

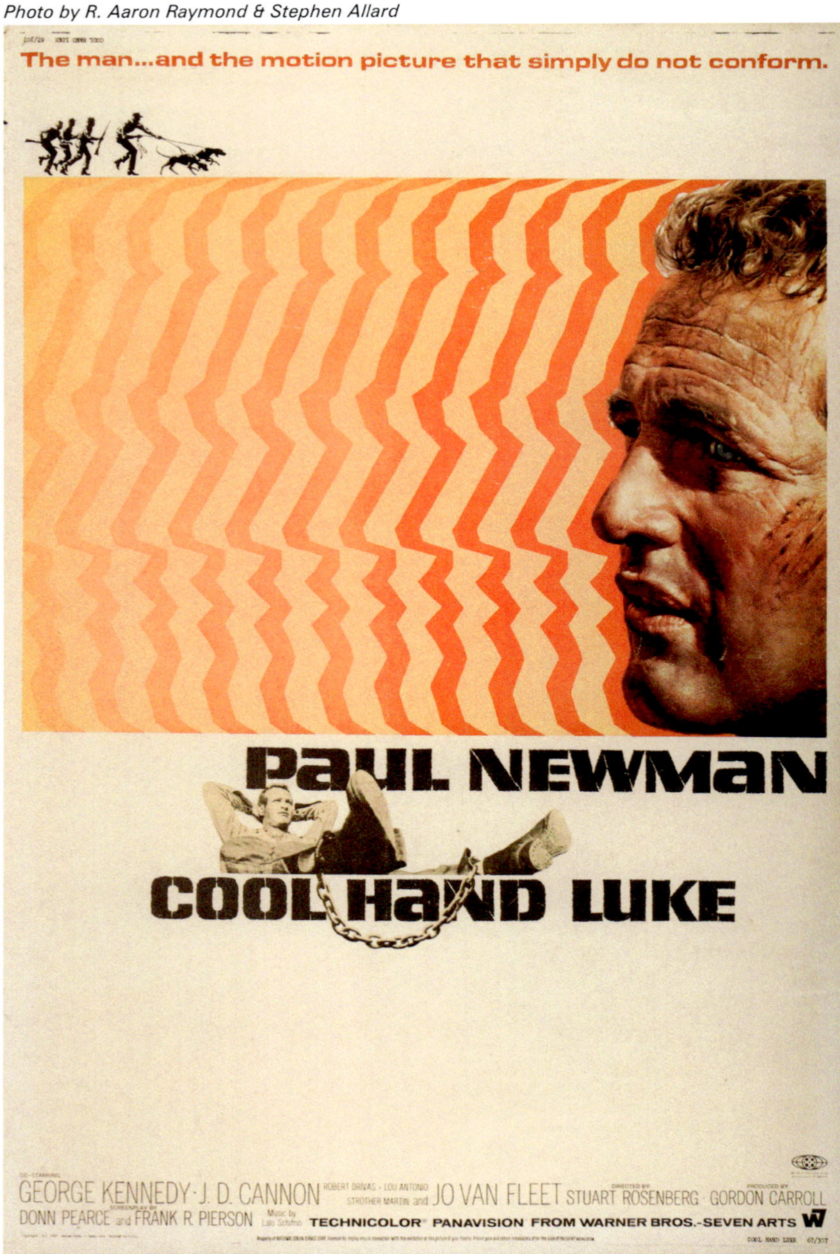

Cool Hand Luke 1967 40x60

Christie's	$1,204	VF	03/09
Private	$1,450	FN	02/07
Private	$225	FN	10/97

- There are 6 known to exist.

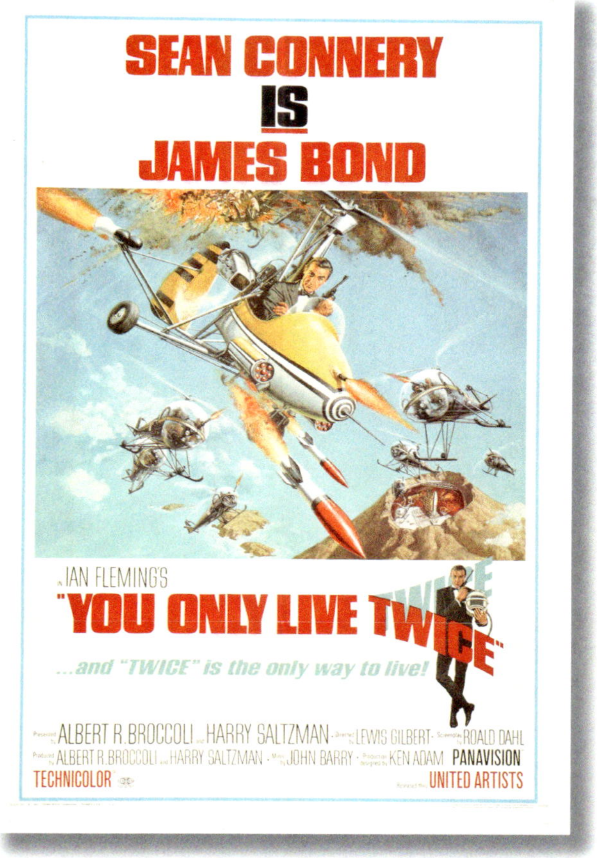

Courtesy of Heritage

You Only Live Twice—Style B	1967	27x41	
Heritage	$717	VF/NM	11/09
Heritage	$567	VF-	03/09
Heritage	$286	FN-	12/08
Heritage	$501	FN/VF	11/08
Heritage	$956	NM	07/08

Highest price realized:

Heritage	$1,015	VF	03/07

Price in 1990:

Camden House	$50*	VF	10/90

• This poster has appeared at auction 56 times since 1989.
* Sold with 6 other Bond posters totaling $350 or $50 a piece.
• There was no image available for *You Only Live Twice* 30x40.

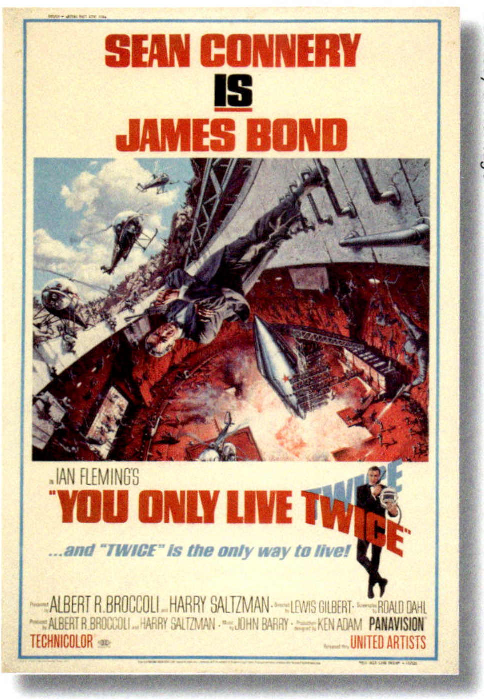

Courtesy of Heritage

You Only Live Twice	1967	40x60	
Heritage	DNS	VF/NM	11/09
Private	$550	VF	08/08
Christie's	$545	VF	03/01
Private	$616	VF	06/01
Vintage Poster	$345	FN	05/01

• There are 10 known to exist.

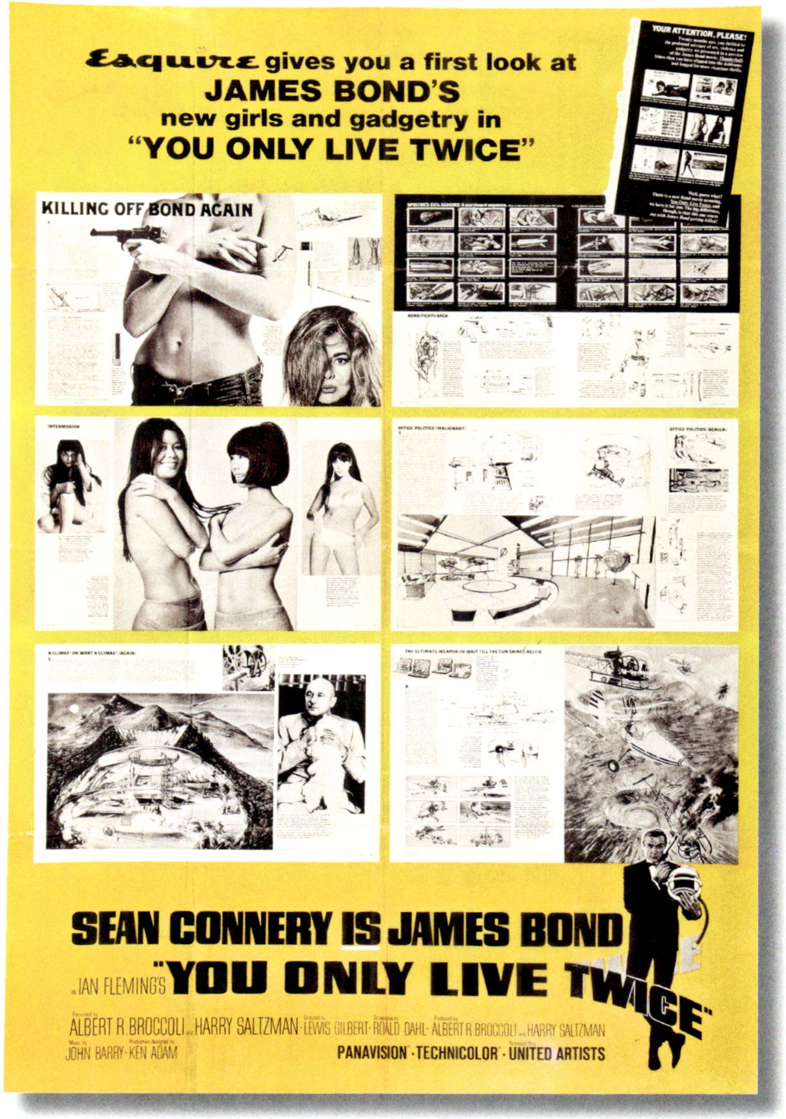

Courtesy of Heritage

You Only Live Twice Advance (Esquire *)	1967	40x60	
Heritage	$717	VF/NM	11/09
Heritage	$3,107	MN	11/07
Heritage	$920	FN-	11/05
Heritage	$420	FN/VF	07/04
Christie's	$759	VF	09/99

• There are 9 known to exist.
* Folded, lightweight paper.

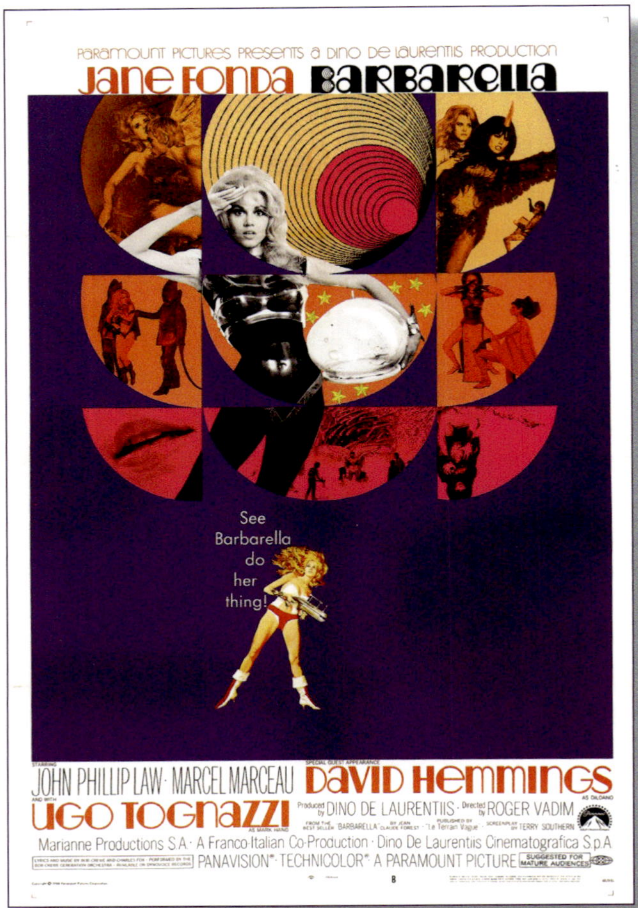

Courtesy of Heritage

Barbarella—Style B	27x41	1968	
Heritage	$567	VG/FN	11/09
Heritage	$567	VF	04/09
Heritage	$835	VF	03/09
Christie's	$722	VF-	03/09
Heritage	$1,075	VF+	03/08

Highest price realized:

Heritage	$1,075	VF+	03/08

Price in 1996:

Lowery	$95	VG	09/96

• This poster has appeared at auction 22 times since 1989.

Courtesy of Heritage

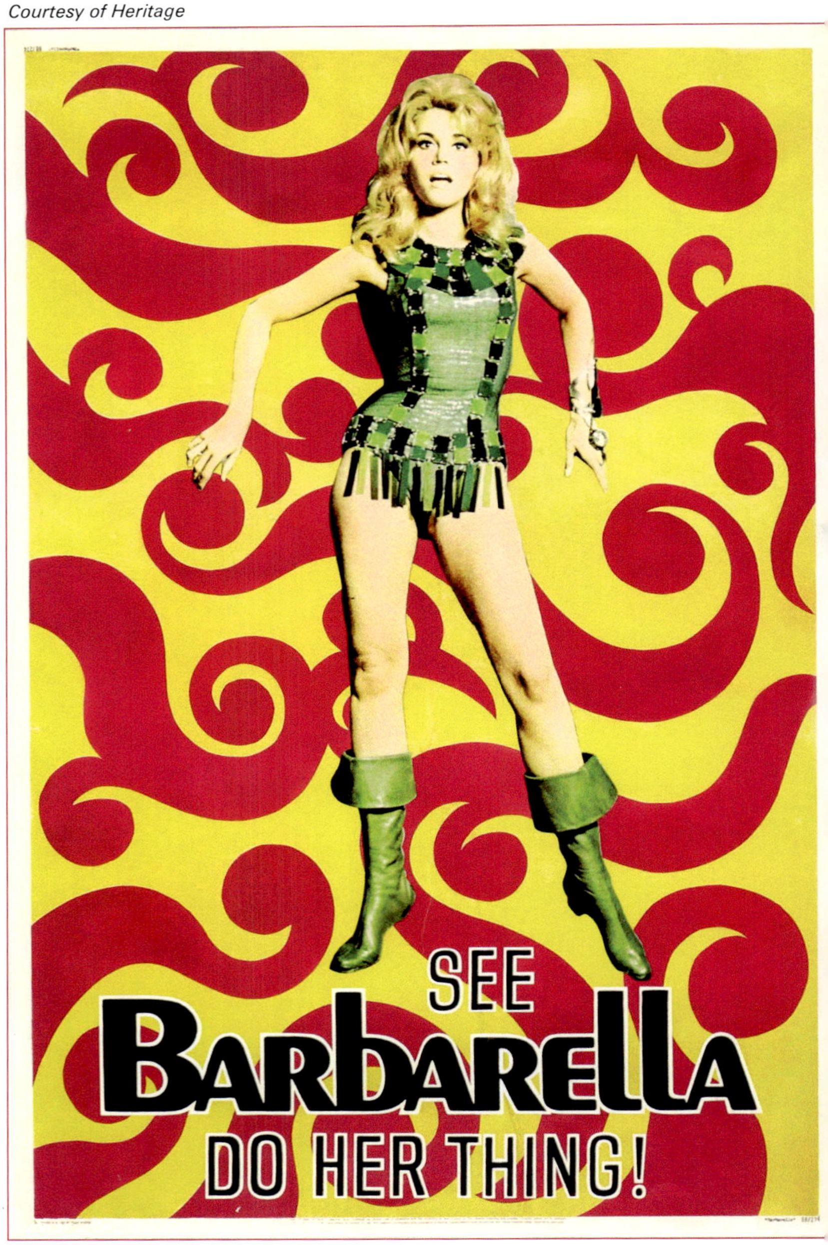

Barbarella—Advance	1968	40x60	
Heritage	$4,331	VF-	11/09
Private	$3,200	VF	03/09
Christie's	$7,831	VF	09/08
Heritage	$1,995	VG -	11/04

• There are 8 known to exist.

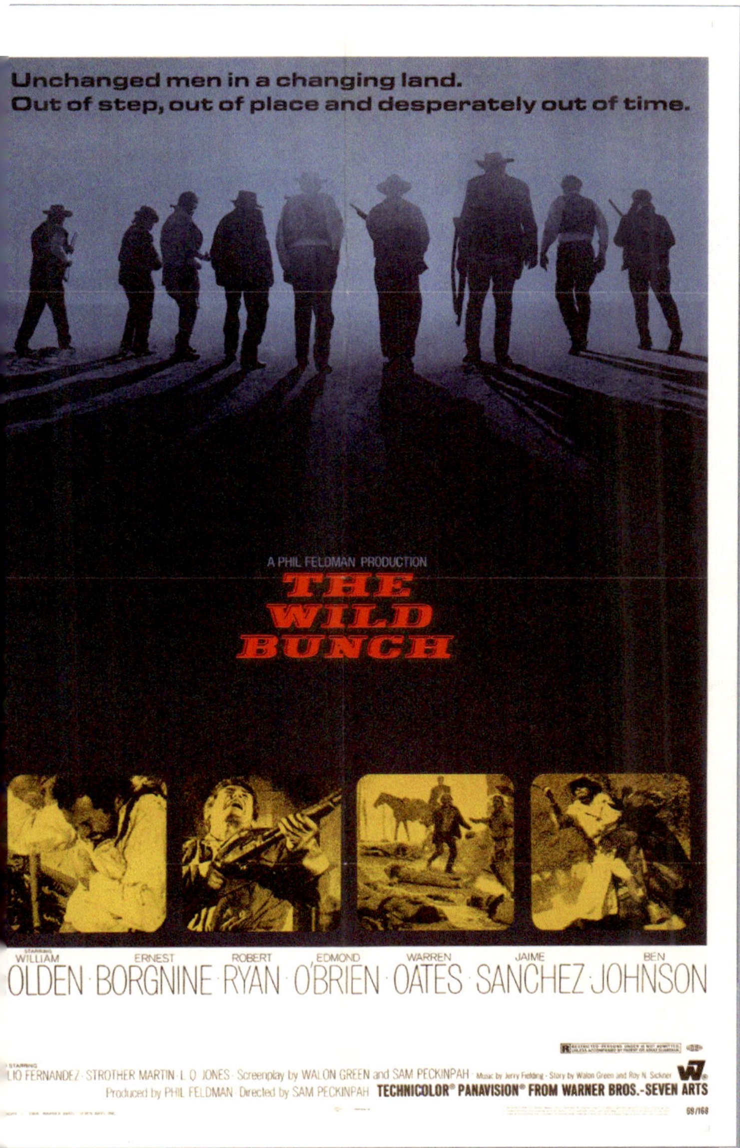

Courtesy of Heritage

Wild Bunch	1968	27x41		
Christie's		$268	VF-	11/09
eMoviePoster		$333	VG	09/09
Heritage		$250	FN/VF	07/09
eMoviePoster		$395	VG	06/09
Heritage		$262	VF	05/09

Highest price realized:

Profiles in History	$750	VF	12/08

Price in 1993:

Camden House	$200	NM	11/93

• This poster has appeared at auction 64 times since 1989.

Courtesy of Christie's

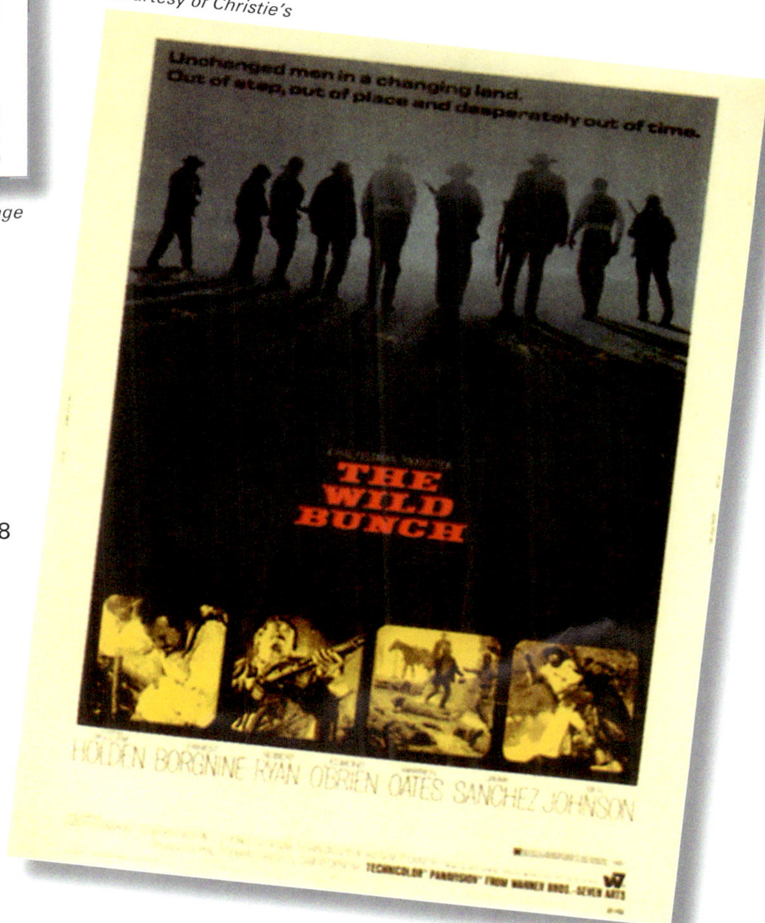

Wild Bunch	1968	30x40		
Christie's		$583	FN+	09/08

• There are 3 known to exist.

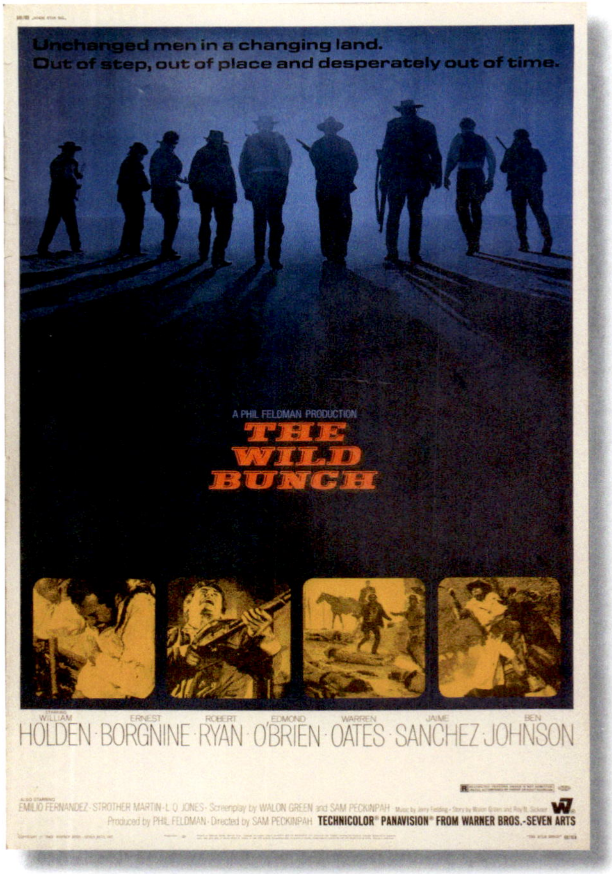

Photo by R. Aaron Raymond & Stephen Allard

Wild Bunch—Style A* 1968 40x60

Private	$650	VG	03/07
eMoviePoster	$404	VG	10/05
Private	$375	FN	10/96

* This poster is not marked with the letter "A," the style "B" is marked as such.

• There are 7 known to exist.

Photo by R. Aaron Raymond & Stephen Allard

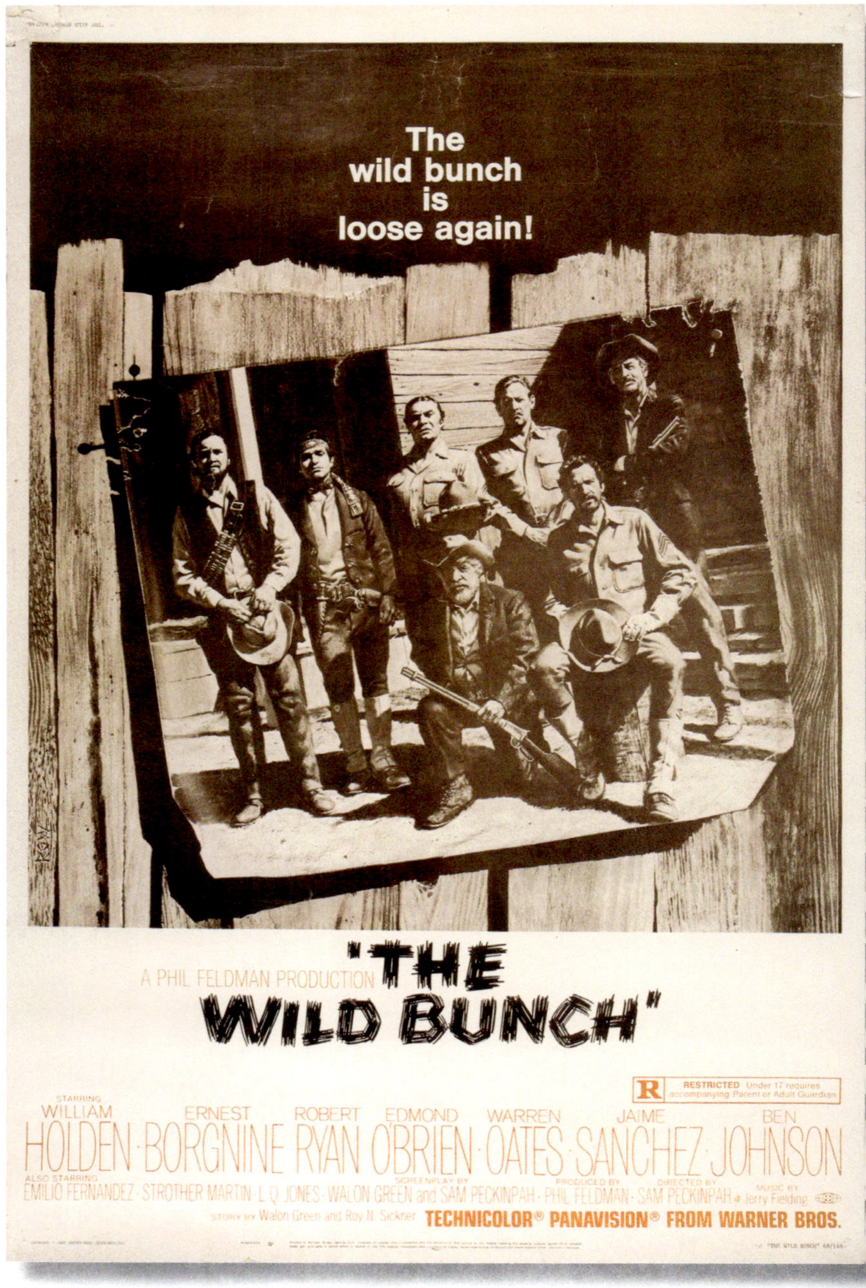

Wild Bunch—Style B 1968 40x60

Private	$1,450	FN+	06/05

Estimate: $2,500 - $3,500

• There is 1 known to exist.

MOVIE POSTERS OF THE 1970s

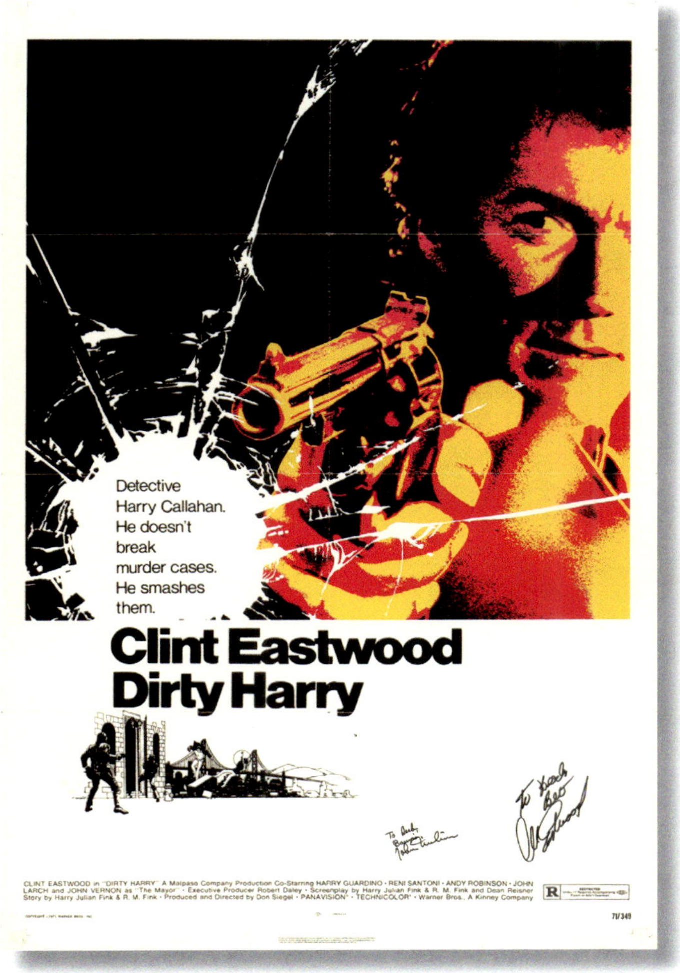

Courtesy of Heritage

Dirty Harry 1971 27x41			
eMoviePoster	$295	VF	09/09
Heritage	$143	VG/FN	06/09
Heritage	$418	VG	04/09
Heritage	$310	FN/VF	12/08
eMoviePoster	$230	FN	11/08

Highest price realized:

Heritage (Autographed)	$1,135	VF+	07/07

Price in 1994:

Christie's	$45	FN	02/94

• This poster has appeared at auction 69 times since 1989.

Dirty Harry 1971 30x40			
eMoviePoster	$156	FR/GD	11/09
CineMasterpieces	$1,295	NM	05/08
Private	$175	VF	02/97

• There are 6 known to exist.

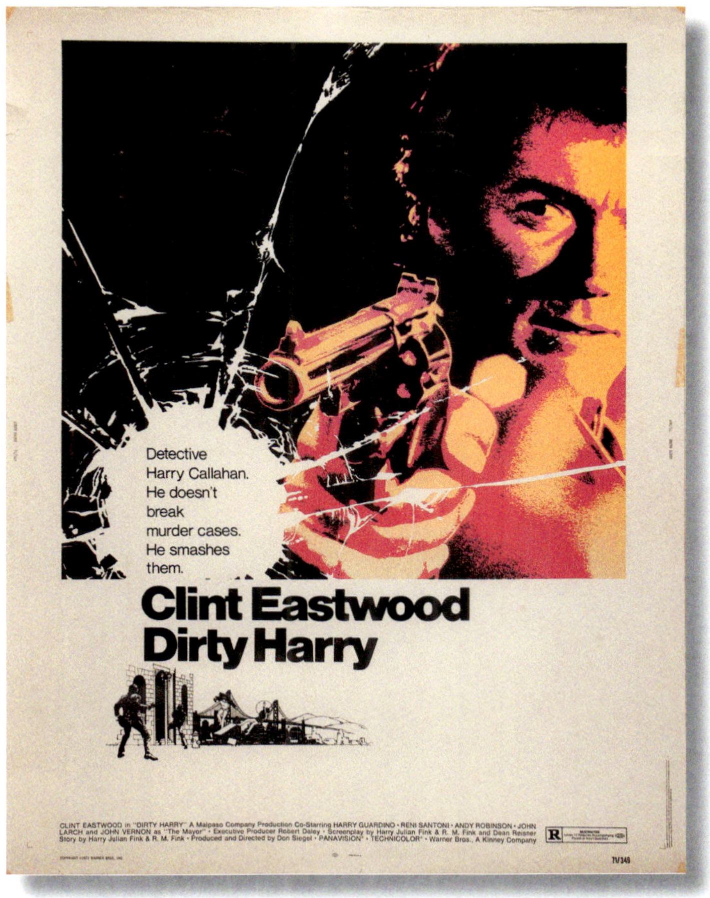

Photo by R. Aaron Raymond

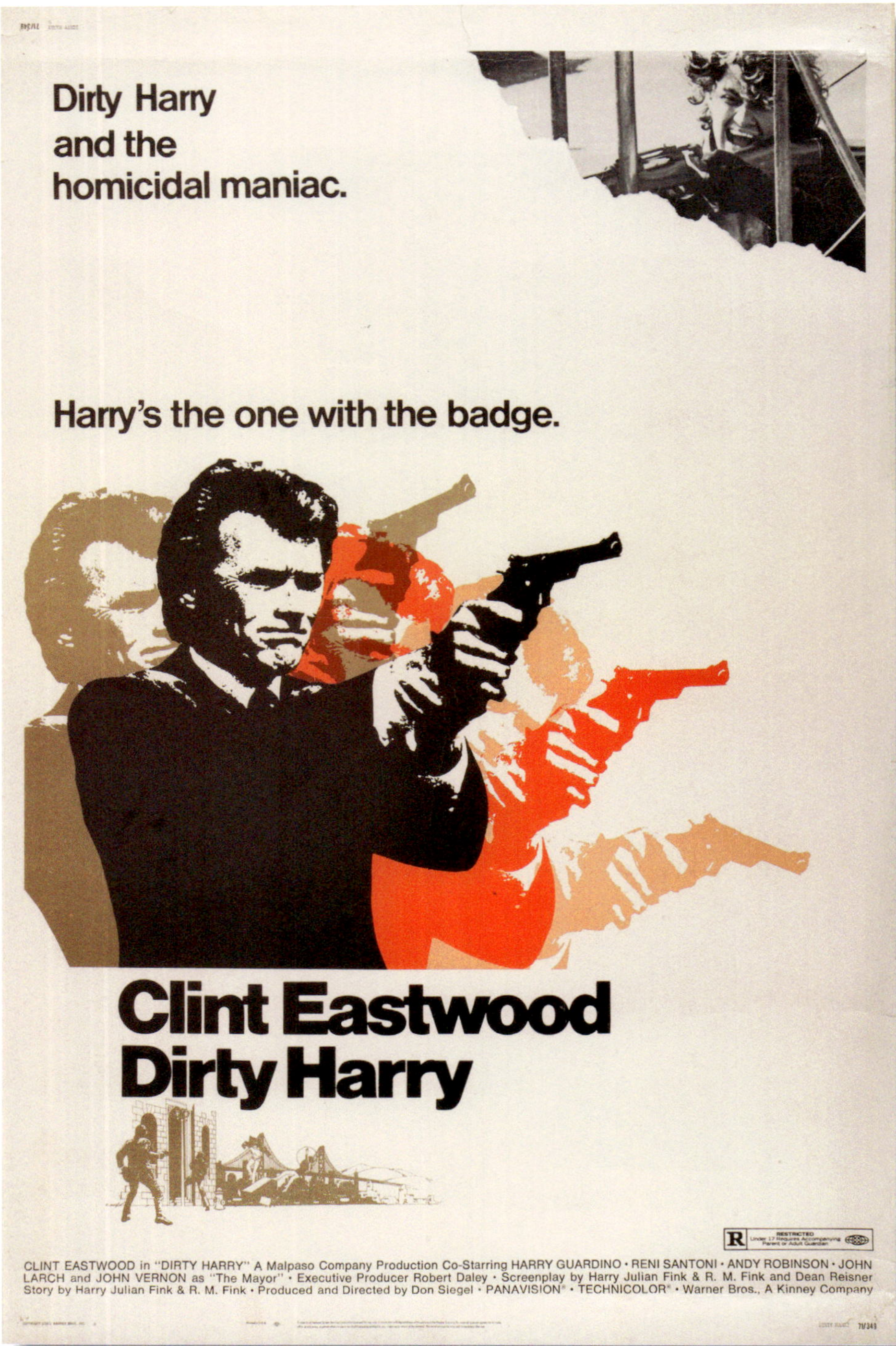

Photo by R. Aaron Raymond & Stephen Allard

Dirty Harry	1971 40x60		
Private	$4,550	VF	06/07
Heritage	$3,910	FN/VF	03/04
Christie's	$3,128	VF	03/00

- There are 5 known to exist.

Courtesy of Heritage

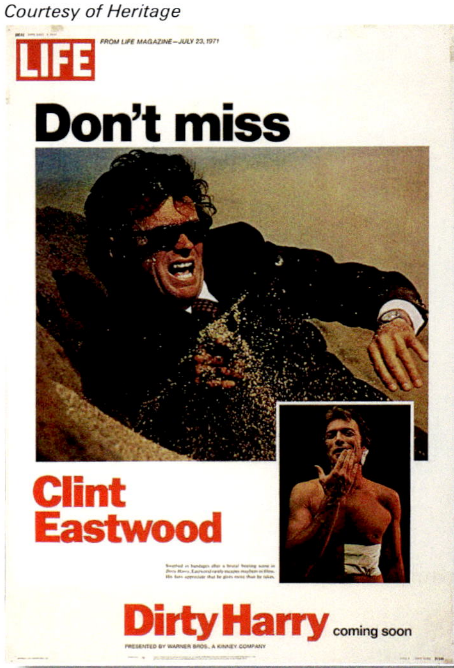

Dirty Harry— Advance (Life Magazine*)	1971 40x60		
Heritage	$2,415	FN	11/05
eMoviePoster	$2,324	GD	07/04
Christie's	$4,048	NM	03/00
Butterfield & Butterfield	$1,500	FN	11/96

- There are 6 known to exist.

* Lightweight paper, folded

Courtesy of Heritage

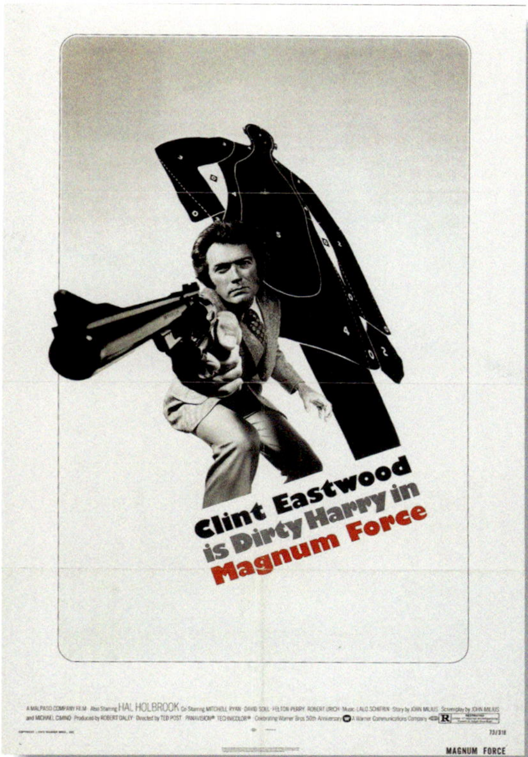

Courtesy of Hershenson/Allen archive

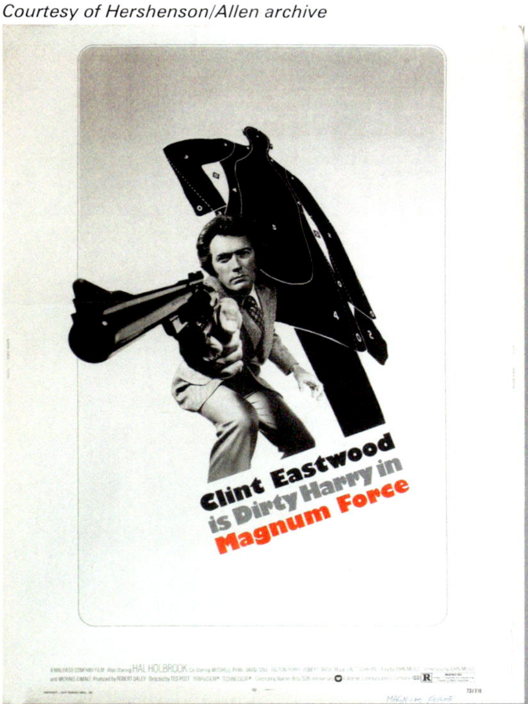

Magnum Force 1973 30x40			
eMoviePoster	$116	GD/VG	11/09
eMoviePoster	$215	GD/VG	05/09
eMoviePoster	$239	VG/FN	01/02

- There are 5 known to exist.

Magnum Force 1973 27x41

Highest price realized:

Christie's	$634	VF	09/06

- This poster typically sells for $50 - $300
- This poster has appeared at auction over 75 times since 1989.

Magnum Force 1973 40x60			
eMoviePoster	$3,900	GD	12/09
Private	$3,550	VF	07/07
Christie's	$2,303	VF	03/06
Christie's	$3,680	VF	03/00

- There are 5 known to exist.

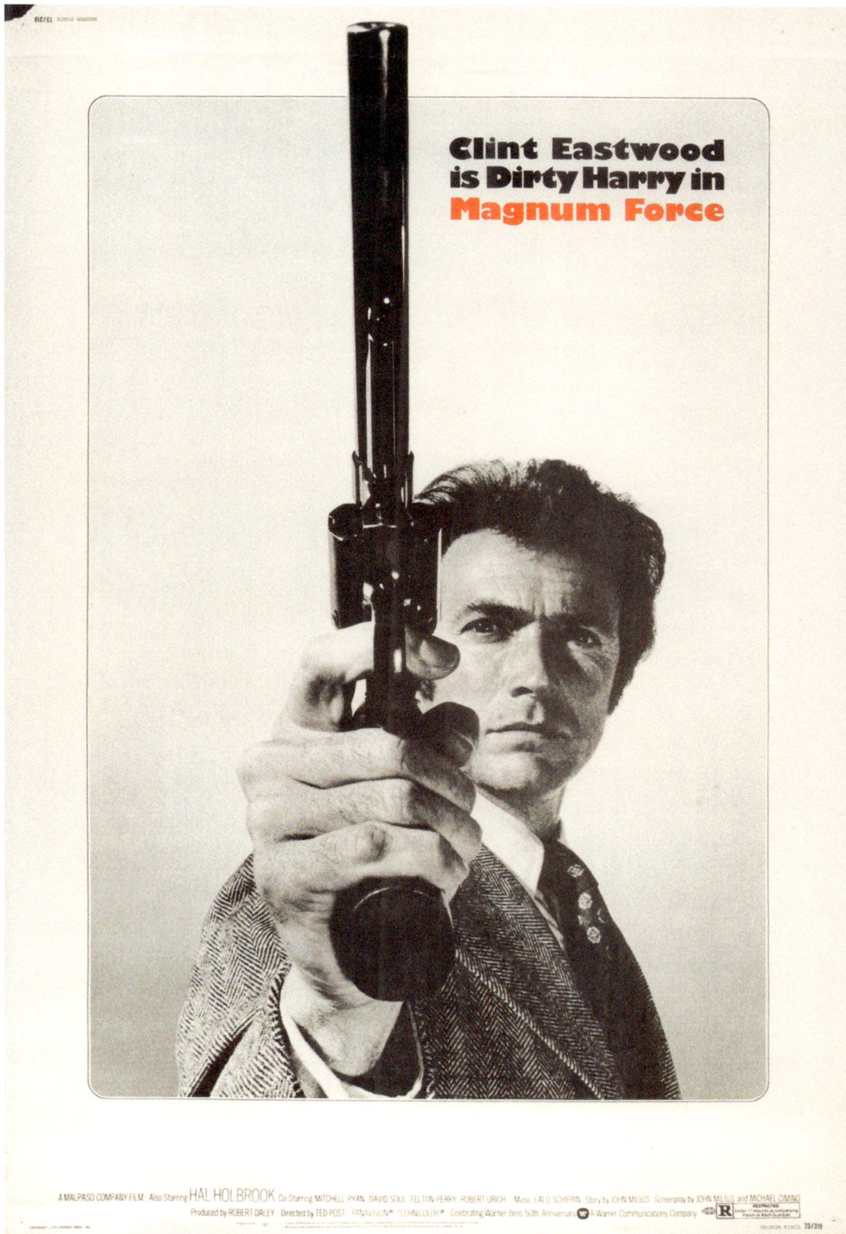

Photo by R. Aaron Raymond & Stephen Allard

The Sting 1973 27x41

- This poster sells for $50-$300
- This poster has appeared at auction over 75 times since 1989.

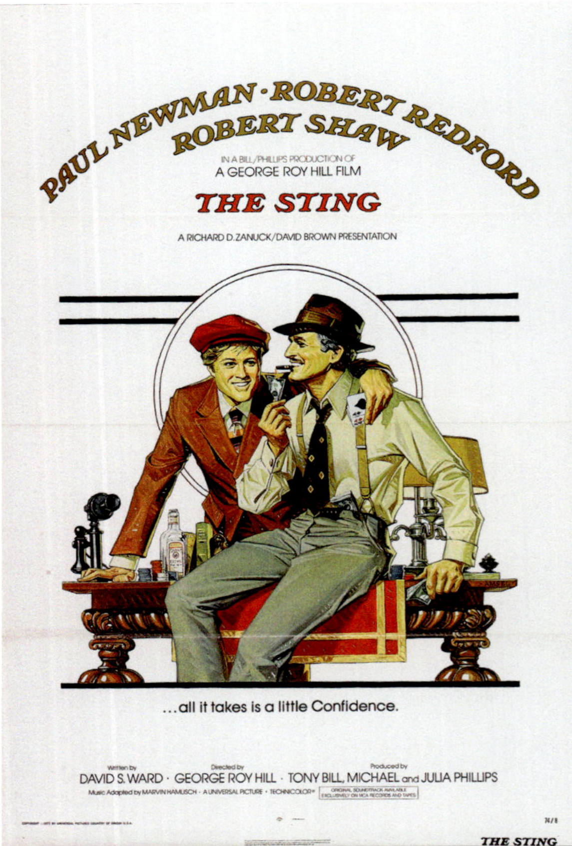

Courtesy of Heritage

The Sting 1973 40x60			
eMoviePoster	$475	VG	04/09
Heritage	$836	FN	12/08
Heritage	$1,015	VF+	07/07
Heritage	$322	GD/VG	12/05
Heritage	$546	NM	11/05

- There are 9 known to exist.

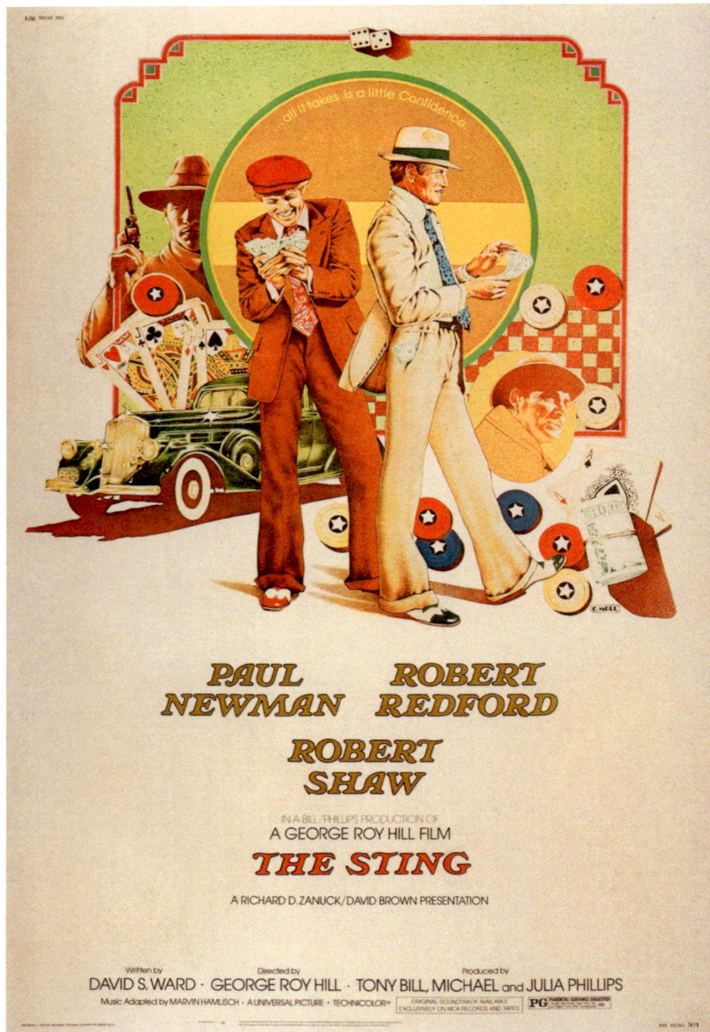

Photo by R. Aaron Raymond & Stephen Allard

The Sting 1973 30x40			
Private	$450	VF	09/09
CineMasterpieces	$1,195	NM	09/08
eMoviePoster	$82	VF	07/08

- There are 7 known to exist

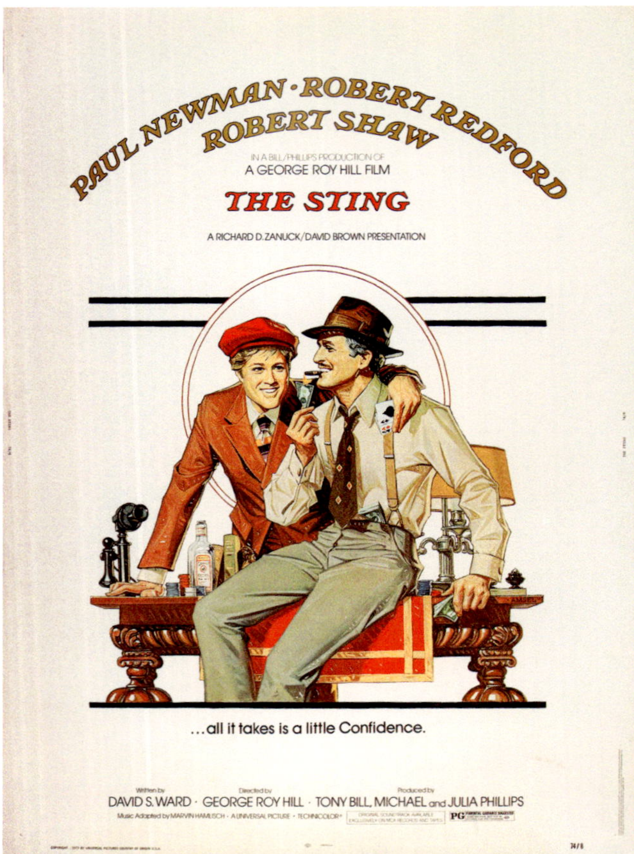

Photo by R. Aaron Raymond

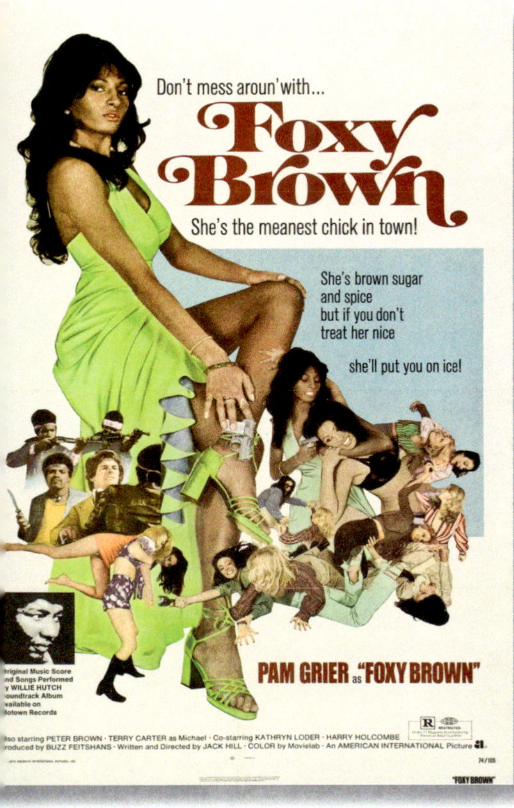

Courtesy of Heritage

Foxy Brown 1974 27x41

- This poster sells for $100 - $250
- This poster has appeared at auction over 75 times since 1989.

Courtesy of Heritage

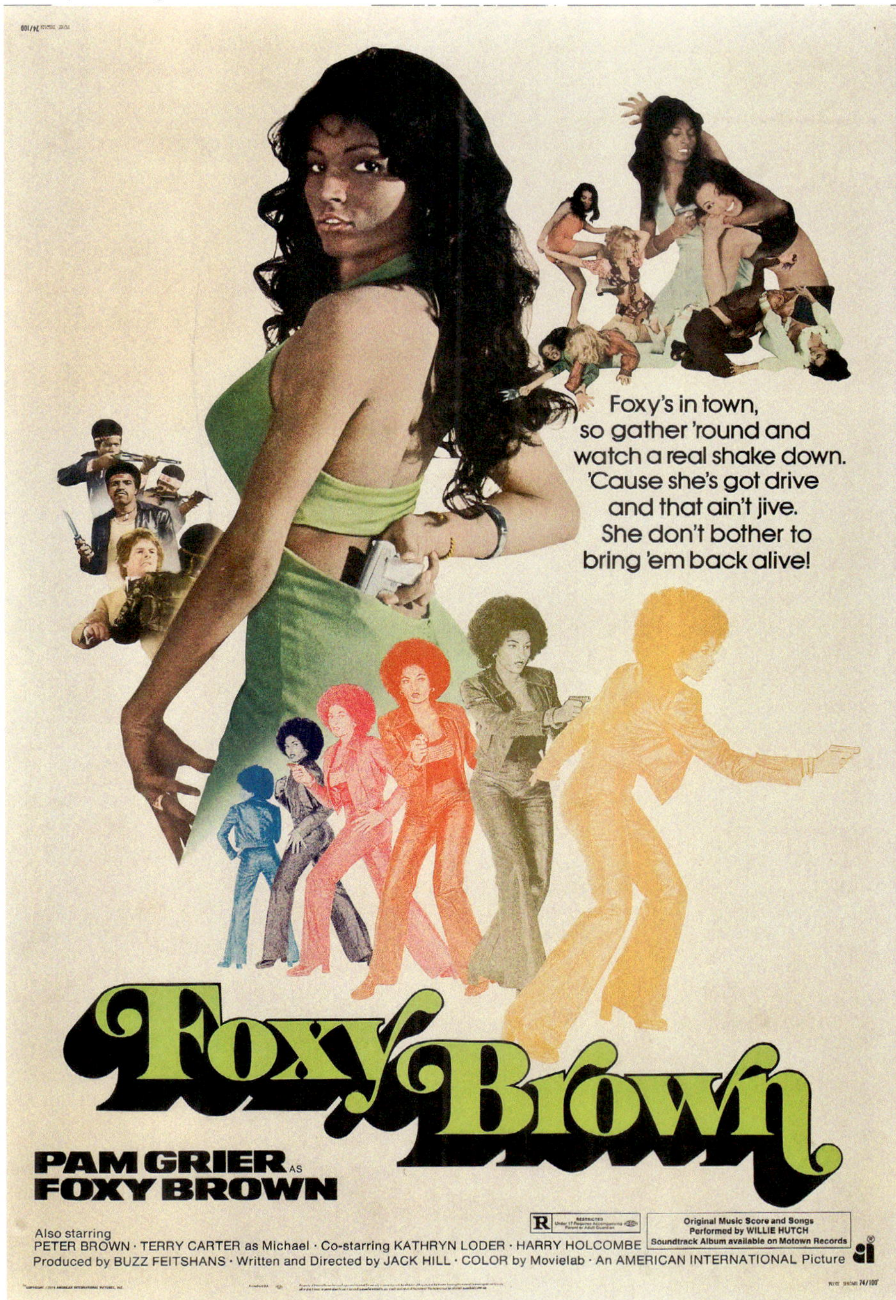

Foxy Brown 1974 40x60

Heritage	$3,107	VF	03/09
Heritage	$862	VF	03/04

- There are 6 known to exist.

RE-RELEASE OF 30x40s & 40x60s

Although re-released posters generally sell for less than the original, the following posters are extremely rare and worth noting.

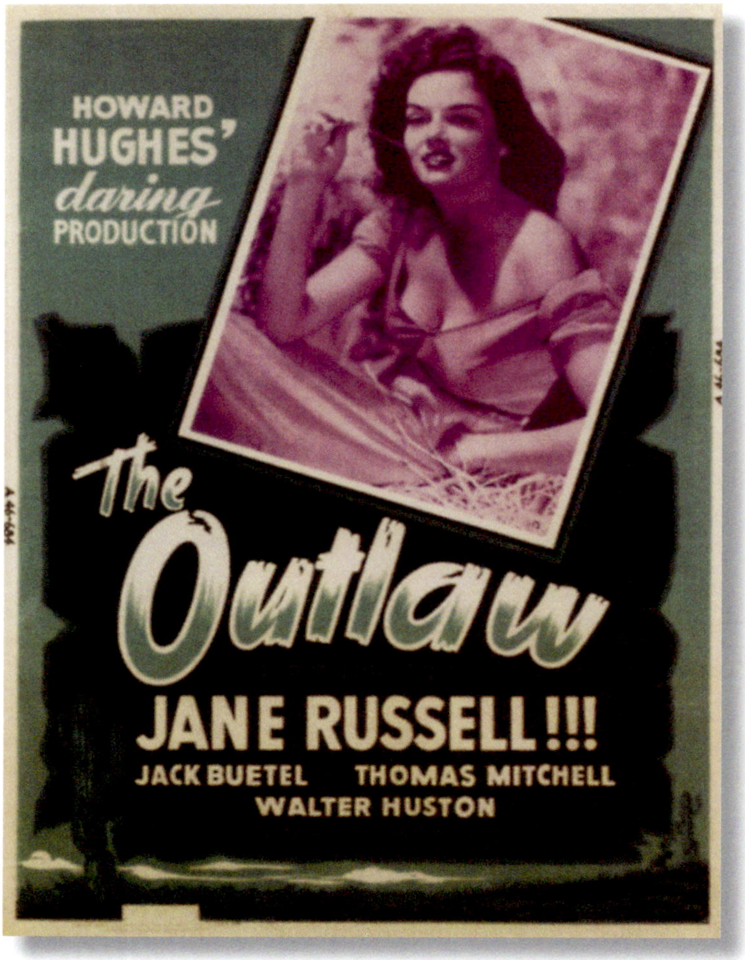

Courtesy of Christie's

Outlaw—Style A	RR 1946	30x40	
Heritage	$920	FN/VF	07/04
Christie's	$1,195	VF	12/02

• There are 2 known to exist.

Courtesy of Christie's

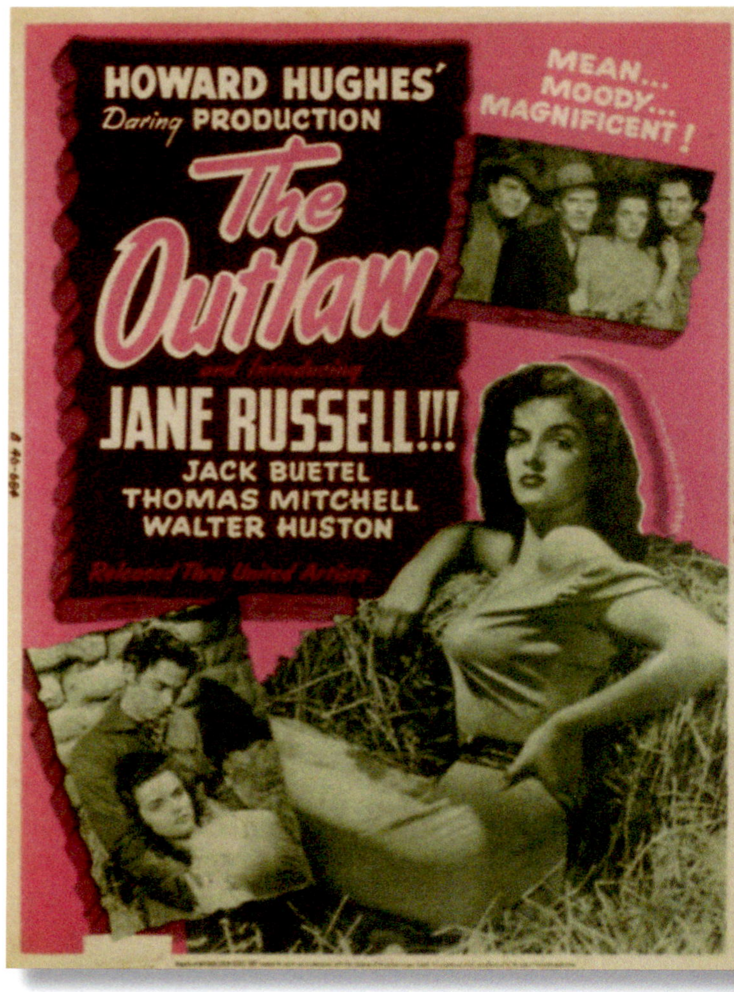

Outlaw—Style B	RR 1946	30x40	
Christie's	$1,554	VF	12/02

• There is 1 known to exist.

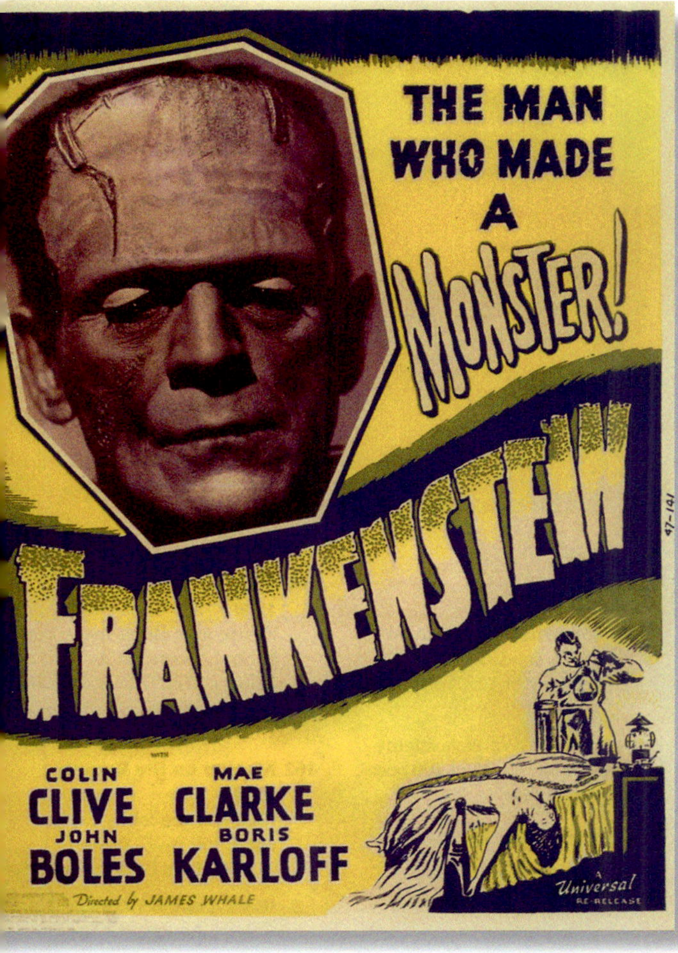

Courtesy of Sotheby's

Frankenstein RR 1947 30x40
Sotheby's $2,875 VF- 04/99

- There is 1 known to exist.

Frankenstein RR 1951 30x40
eMoviePoster $1,015 FN 04/09

- There are 3 known to exist.

Courtesy of Hershenson/ Allen archive

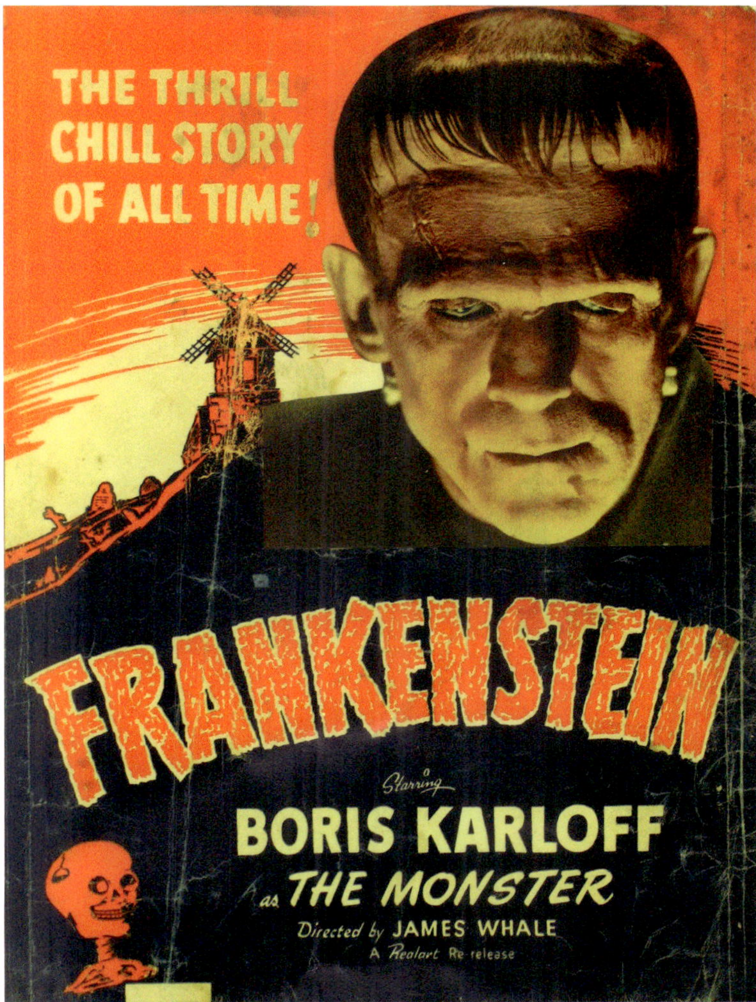

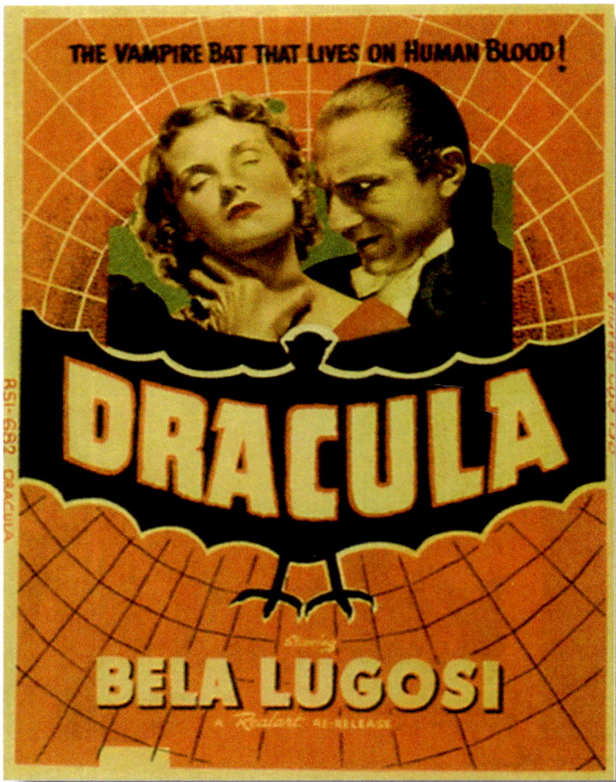

Courtesy of Sotheby's

Dracula RR 1951 30x40

Sotheby's	$1,840	VF-	04/98
Sotheby's	DNS	FN	12/94

• There are 3 known to exist

Courtesy of Heritage

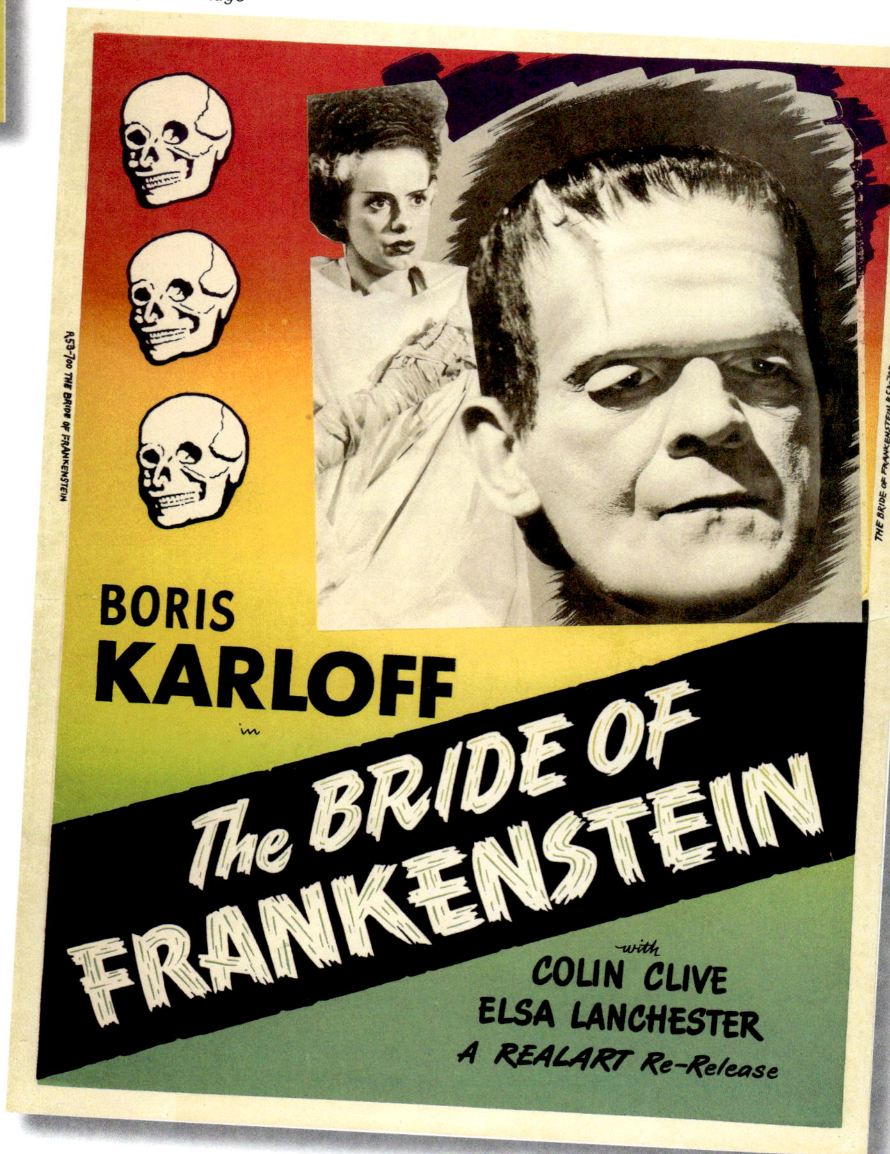

Bride of Frankenstein RR 1953 30x40

Heritage	$597	FN-	07/08*
Heritage	DNS	FN-	07/07

• There are 3 known to exist.
* This is the same poster that appeared in the 2007 Heritage Auction.

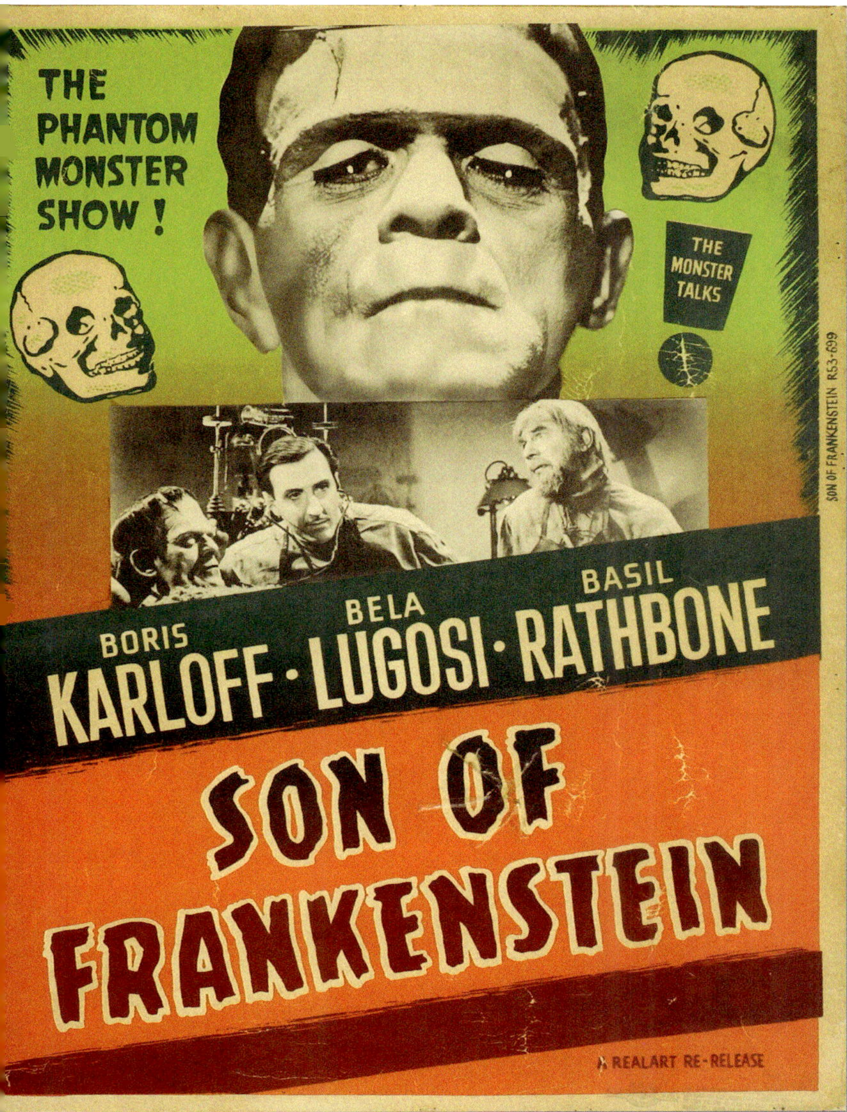

Courtesy of Heritage

Son of Frankenstein RR 1953 30x40
Heritage DNS VG/FN 03/04
Estimate: $2,000 - $3,000

- There is 1 known to exist.

Courtesy of Heritage

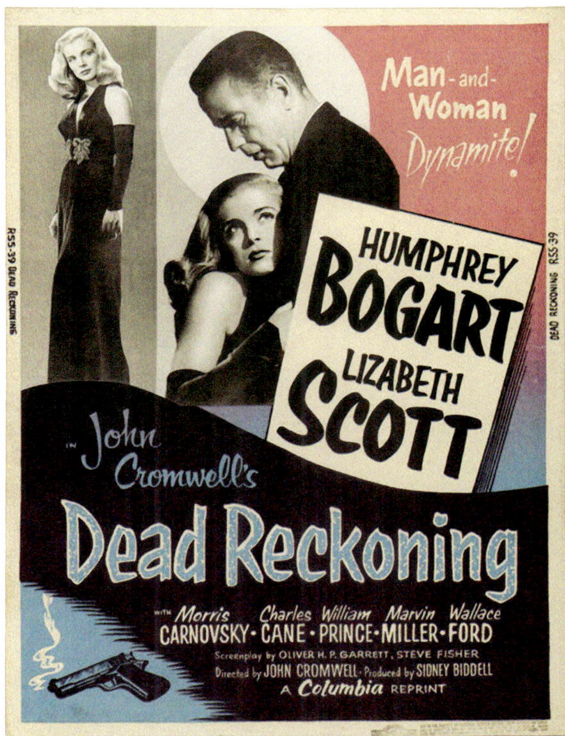

Dead Reckoning RR 1955 30x40
Heritage $1,495 FN 02/05

- There is 1 known to exist.

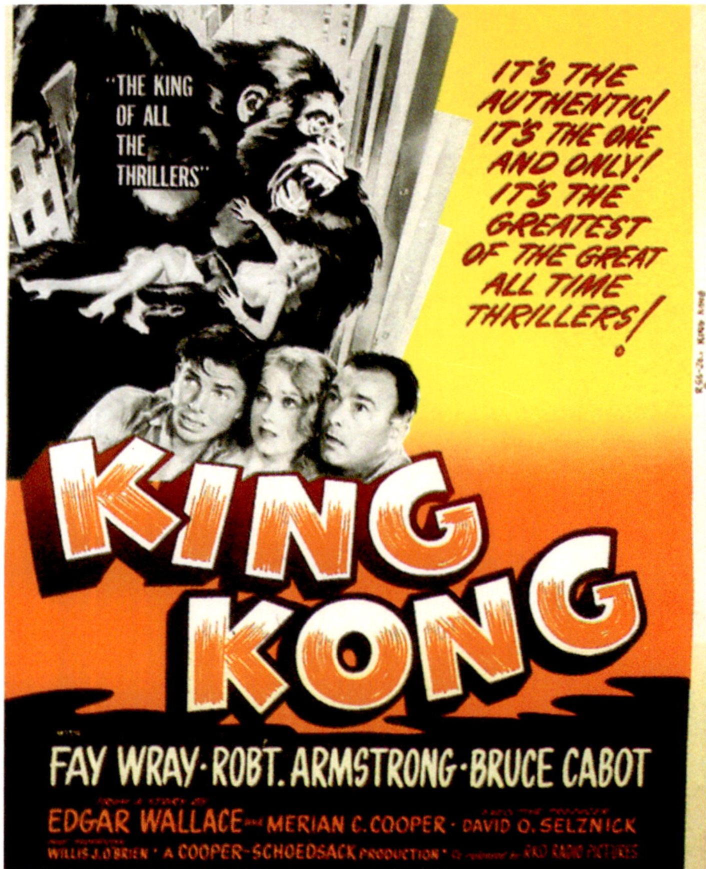

Courtesy of Camden House

King Kong RR 1956 30x40
Camden House $250 FN+ 11/94
Estimate: $1,500 - $2,500

- There is 1 known to exist.

Courtesy of Hershenson/ Allen archive

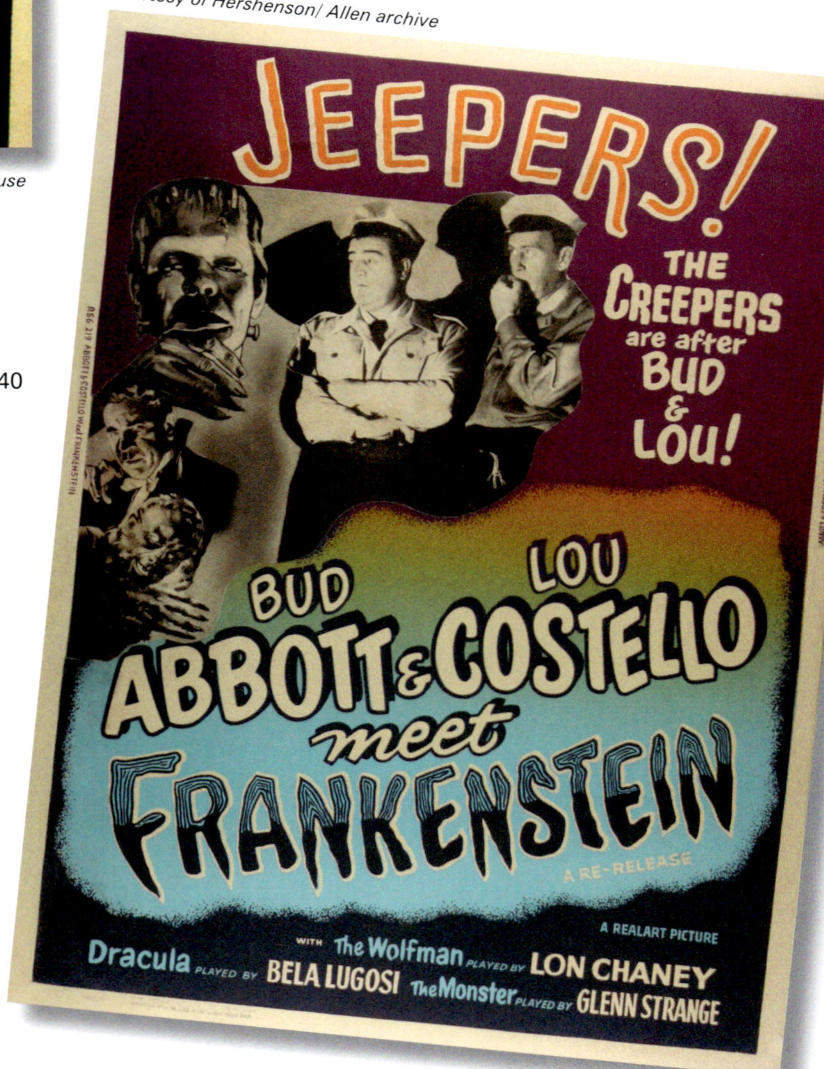

Abbott & Costello Meet Frankenstein RR 1956 30x40
eMoviePoster $1,100 GD/VG 07/09
eMoviePoster $813 GD/VG 01/03

- There are 2 known to exist.

CREDITS

Many of the photographic Images in this book were provided by:

R. Aaron Raymond Photography
1474 Allison Ave.
Los Angeles, CA 90026
323-393-5435
www.raaronraymond.com

My favorite linen and laper backing facility is "L'Imagerie Gallery" in North Hollywood, California. They also have an incredible collection of movie posters for sale.

L'Imagerie Gallery
10555 Victory Blvd.
North Hollywood, CA 91606
818-762-8488
www.limageriegallery.com

RESOURCES

CineMasterpieces
David Lieberman
15721 N. Greenway Haden Loop, Suite 105
Scottsdale, Arizona 85260
602-309-0500
www.cinemasterpieces.com

eMoviePoster
Bruce Hershenson
1 Court Square Dock
West Plains, MO 65775
417-256-9616
www.emovieposter.com

Heritage Auction Galleries
Grey Smith
3500 Maple Ave 17th Floor
Dallas, Texas 75207
800-872-6467
www.ha.com

Hollywood Movie Posters
Ron V. Borst
6727-1/2 Hollywood Blvd.
Hollywood, California 90028
323-463-1792

Movie Art
Kirby McDaniel
P.O Box 4419
Austin, Texas 78765
512-479-6680
www.movieart.net

Profile In History
26901 Agoura Rd, Suite 150
Calabasas Hills, CA 91301
310-859-7701
www.profilesinhistory.com

Reel Poster Gallery
Tony Nourmand
72 Westbourne Grove
London, W2 5SH
Tel: 020 7727 4488
www.reelposter.com

Walter Film
500 N. Harper Ave
Los Angeles, CA 90048
323-651-3313
www.walterfilm.com

Todd Feiertag
Poster City
P.O. Box 94
Orangeburg, New York 10962
1-800-272-3323
1-917-734-2290
Ebay User ID: toddfeiertag

AUCTION CATALOGS

Bonhams & Butterfields: 06/03, 11/04, 12/05, 12/06, 12/07
Butterfield & Butterfield: 10/94, 06/95, 02/96, 05/96, 09/96, 11/96, 06/97, 10/98, 02/99, 11/99, 10/00, 12/01, 06/02, 11/02
Camden House: 05/89, 03/90, 10/90, 05/91, 11/91, 03/92, 06/92, 11/92, 11/93, 06/94, 11/94, 01/95, 06/95
Christie's: 12/90, 12/91, 12/92, 06/93, 12/93, 12/94, 03/95, 06/95, 12/95, 11/96, 12/96, 09/97, 12/97, 03/98, 09/98, 03/99, 09/99, 11/99, 03/00, 05/00, 06/00, 09/00, 03/01, 09/01, 10/01, 11/01, 03/02, 09/02, 12/02, 03/02, 03/03, 09/03, 12/03, 03/04, 09/04, 12/04, 03/05, 06/05, 11/05, 03/06, 09/06, 05/07, 06/07, 03/08, 11/08, 03/09, 11/09
Executive Collectibles Gallery: 03/99
Greg Manning Auctions: 04/99, 10/00
Guernsey's Poster Auction: 4/89
Heritage Auctions: 11/01, 03/02, 06/02, 07/02, 10/02, 12/02, 03/03, 07/03, 11/03, 03/04, 04/04, 05/04, 06/04, 07/04, 11/04, 12/04, 03/05, 07/05, 11/05, 03/06, 07/06, 11/06, 03/07, 07/7, 11/07, 03/08, 07/08, 11/08, 03/09, 07/09, 11/09
Hollywood Poster Art Auction: 12/92, 06/93
Hollywood Poster Auction: #1 - #3
Odyssey Auctions: 10/93, 10/94
Poster Price Almanac: 1996, 1997, 1998, 1999, 2000, 2001, 2002
Skinner Auctions: 11/98, 05/99, 11/99
Sotheby's: 09/92, 12/93, 12/94, 12/95, 12/96, 03/97, 11/97, 03/98, 04/98, 09/98, 04/99, 05/99, 12/99, 05/00, 10/00
Vintage Hollywood Posters: 12/98, 06/99, 06/00, 06/01, 07/01, 12/02, 12/03, 07/04, 12/04, 12/05
Vintage Poster Art Auction: #1 - #17
Waddington's: 09/03

THE END

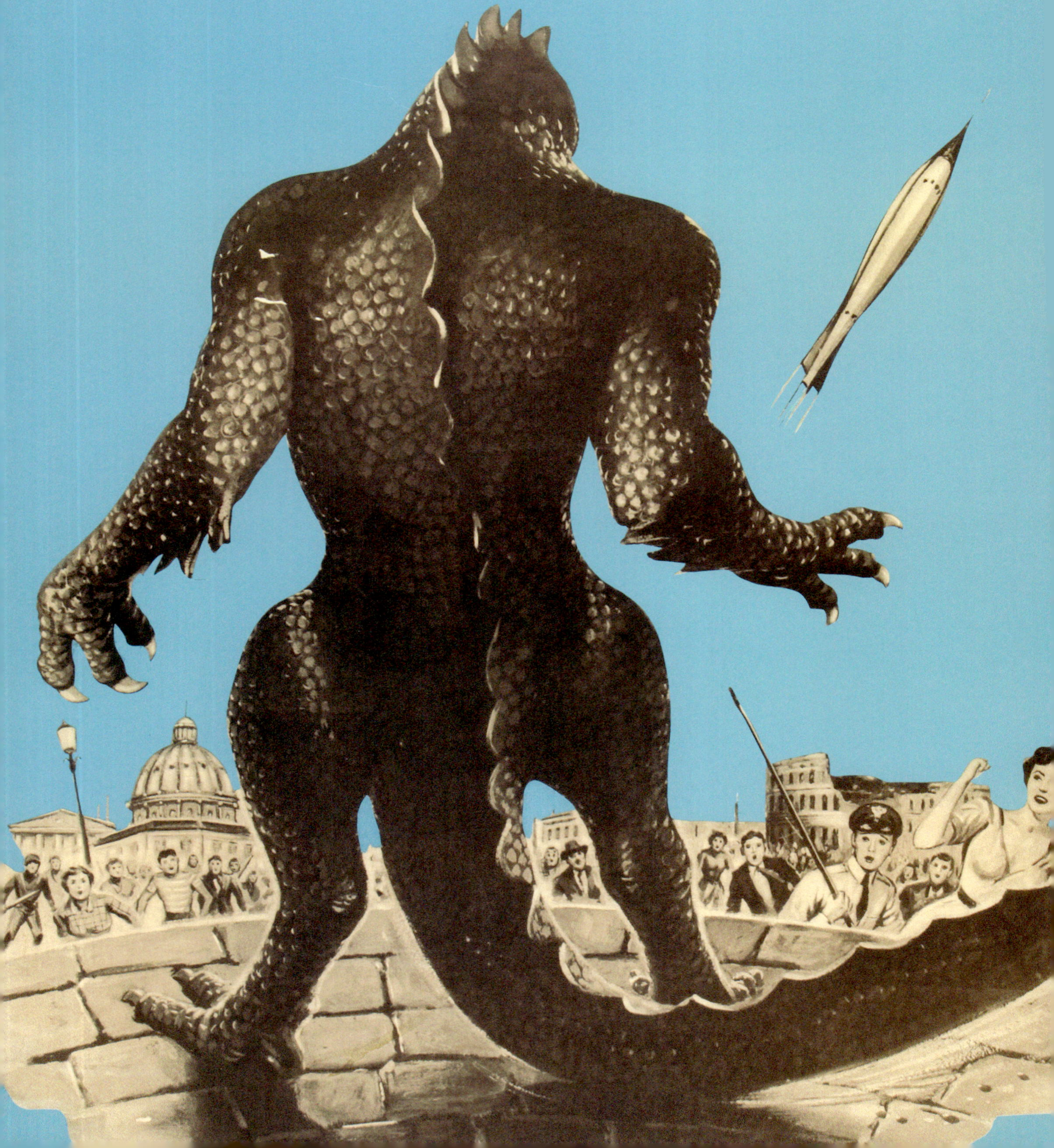